AFTER THE GREAT RECESSION

The severity of the Great Recession and the subsequent stagnation caught many economists by surprise, but a group of Keynesian scholars warned for some years that strong forces were leading the United States toward a deep, persistent downturn. This book collects essays about these events from prominent macroeconomists who developed a perspective that predicted the broad outline and many specific aspects of the crisis. From this point of view, the recovery of employment and revival of strong growth requires more than short-term monetary easing and temporary fiscal stimulus. Economists and policy makers need to explore how the process of demand formation failed after 2007, and where demand will come from going forward. Successive chapters address the sources and dynamics of demand, the distribution and growth of wages, the structure of finance, and the challenges from globalization, and provide recommendations for policies to achieve a more efficient and equitable society.

Barry Z. Cynamon is a Research Associate at the Weidenbaum Center on the Economy, Government, and Public Policy at Washington University of St. Louis. His early research on the U.S. consumer age of the past quarter century linked rising household spending and debt to group interactions and cultural norms. This work was published in 2008, just as the "risk of collapse" it identified played out to become known as the Great Recession. He has also published research on both monetary and fiscal policy. He holds an MBA from the University of Chicago.

Steven M. Fazzari is Professor of Economics and Associate Director of the Weidenbaum Center on the Economy, Government, and Public Policy at Washington University in St. Louis. He received a PhD in economics from Stanford University in 1982. The author of more than forty peer-reviewed journal articles and book chapters, Professor Fazzari's research explores two main areas: the financial determinants of investment and R&D spending by U.S. firms and the foundations of Keynesian macroeconomics. His teaching awards include the 2002 Missouri Governor's award for excellence in university teaching, the 2007 Emerson Award for teaching excellence, and Washington University's distinguished faculty award, also in 2007.

Mark Setterfield is Professor of Economics at Trinity College, Hartford (CT); Associate Member of the Cambridge Centre for Economic and Public Policy at Cambridge University (U.K.); and Senior Research Associate at the International Economic Policy Institute, Laurentian University (Canada). He is the author of *Rapid Growth and Relative Decline: Modelling Macroeconomic Dynamics with Hysteresis*, and the editor (or co-editor) of six volumes of essays, and he has published on macroeconomic dynamics and Keynesian macroeconomics in journals including the *Cambridge Journal of Economics, European Economic Review, Journal of Post Keynesian Economics,* and *The Manchester School.*

After the Great Recession

The Struggle for Economic Recovery and Growth

Edited by

BARRY Z. CYNAMON
Washington University in St. Louis

STEVEN M. FAZZARI
Washington University in St. Louis

MARK SETTERFIELD
Trinity College, CT

Foreword by **Robert Kuttner**

CAMBRIDGE
UNIVERSITY PRESS

CAMBRIDGE UNIVERSITY PRESS
Cambridge, New York, Melbourne, Madrid, Cape Town,
Singapore, São Paulo, Delhi, Mexico City

Cambridge University Press
32 Avenue of the Americas, New York, NY 10013-2473, USA

www.cambridge.org
Information on this title: www.cambridge.org/9781107015890

First published 2013

Printed in the United States of America

A catalog record for this publication is available from the British Library.

Library of Congress Cataloging in Publication data
After the great recession : the struggle for economic recovery and growth /
[edited by] Barry Z. Cynamon, Steven M. Fazzari, Mark Setterfield.
pages   cm
Includes bibliographical references and index.
ISBN 978-1-107-01589-0
1. United States – Economic policy – 2009–   2. Recessions – United States – History –
21st century.   3. Global Financial Crisis, 2008–2009.   4. Unemployment –
Effect of inflation on – United States – History – 21st century.   5. Keynesian
economics.   I. Cynamon, Barry Z., 1984– editor of compilation.   II. Fazzari,
Steven M., editor of compilation.   III. Setterfield, Mark, 1967– editor of compilation.
HC106.84.A37   2012
330.973–dc23   2012012602

ISBN 978-1-107-01589-0 Hardback

Contents

Figures

Tables

Contributors

Dean Baker, Center for Economic and Policy Research, Washington, DC

Robert A. Blecker, Department of Economics, American University, Washington, DC

James Crotty, Department of Economics, University of Massachusetts, Amherst, MA

Barry Z. Cynamon, Weidenbaum Center, Washington University, St. Louis, MO

Gerald Epstein, Department of Economics, University of Massachusetts, Amherst, MA

Steven M. Fazzari, Department of Economics, Washington University, St. Louis, MO

Jan Kregel, Jerome Levy Economics Institute, Bard College, Annandale-on-Hudson, NY

Thomas I. Palley, Economics for Democratic and Open Societies, Washington, DC

Mark Setterfield, Department of Economics, Trinity College, Hartford, CT

Pavlina R. Tcherneva, Department of Economics, Bard College, Annandale-on-Hudson, NY

L. Randall Wray, Department of Economics, University of Missouri, Kansas City, MO

Foreword

Robert Kuttner

Seldom has there been more of a disjuncture between economic reality and the national conversation about the cause and cure of our predicament. Most serious economists would agree with the core propositions put forth by the contributors to this volume. The economy is stuck in a prolonged period of deflation that is characteristic of the aftermath of a severe financial collapse. The collapse, in turn, was caused by a combination of destructive financial "innovation" and regulatory corruption. The largest banking institutions, having escaped the salutary constraints of the New Deal era, failed at their role of assessing risk and allocating credit. Instead, they behaved like hedge funds, operating at extremely high leverage ratios, creating and trading opaque securities that added nothing to economic efficiency, and hugely profiting at the expense of the real economy. All of this intensified systemic risk and inflated a series of asset bubbles. When the bubbles popped, an immense unwinding occurred, leaving the economy in a prolonged slump. The period we are in is popularly termed "The Great Recession," but it has more of the characteristics of a depression.

The divergence between productivity and wages, which began in 1973, is a big part of this story. As real wages stagnated for most working families, the economy faced a shortfall of aggregate demand. But this weakening of purchasing power coincided with a period of asset inflation created by the same financial abuses that finally resulted in the collapse of 2008. The Federal Reserve contributed by combining low real interest rates with weak regulation, inviting speculative abuses. It did so in order to bail out banks from the consequences of earlier speculative excesses. As housing prices inflated, hard-pressed workers and consumers got into the habit of borrowing against their homes. They also increased their credit card debt. Bankers were only too happy to oblige them. This also coincided with a period when student loan debt grew from almost nothing to a trillion dollars by 2012. For the three middle quintiles of the income distribution, household debt relative to household income increased from 67 percent in 1983 to 157 percent in 2007.[1] Like all bubbles, this could be sustained only as long as asset prices kept inflating.

The asset bubble and reliance on debt as a substitute for income were already well advanced when the boom in subprime mortgages after 2000 caused housing prices to inflate even more steeply. By 2007, the savings rate turned negative and aggregate demand was sustained only by asset inflation and borrowing. When it all came crashing down in 2008, these dynamics went into reverse.

Now, nearly five years later, with the federal deficit still close to 10 percent of GDP, many analysts wonder why the economy is not yet in a durable recovery. The reason, as this book so cogently explains, is that we are still in a 1930s-style debt deflation. The massive overhang of the housing collapse still drags down the recovery. Banks continue to derive the preponderance of their profits from creating and speculating in highly leveraged securities rather than pursuing the more useful, prosaic, and less remunerative business of making commercial and household loans. Wages continue to diverge from productivity growth and unemployment remains high. Consumers are prudently paying back debt. It all adds up to a classic liquidity trap, in which the economy remains stuck in an equilibrium well below its full employment potential.

In this circumstance, monetary policy by itself is powerless to ignite a recovery because banks are too traumatized to lend, consumers and businesses are too risk-averse to borrow, and aggregate demand is too weak. Even zero interest rates and unprecedented emergency bond purchases by the Federal Reserve have been sufficient only to prevent a total collapse but not to stimulate a sustainable recovery. The dynamics are very reminiscent of the middle and late 1930s, in which GDP growth turned positive but depression conditions continued.

Any competent economic historian will report that in such circumstances it takes both fiscal stimulus and the use of taxation on the well-to-do to finance public investment to compensate for the shortfall in private demand and investment. History's great example is of course World War II. The New Deal deficits of 4 percent to 6 percent of GDP were not sufficient to restore full employment. There was a lot of familiar-sounding nonsense explaining

---

[1] Edward N. Wolff, Recent Trends in Household Wealth in the United States, Levy Institute, March 2012, http://www.levyinstitute.org/pubs/wp_589.pdf.

persistent unemployment in terms of automation and what today would be called the "skills-mismatch" hypothesis.

But when war came, and government began running deficits in excess of 20 percent of GDP, unemployment melted away, a whole generation of workers got trained, a generation of industry got recapitalized, and the economy grew at the record rate of 12 percent per year for four years. The economy suddenly produced at its potential. And then, when the war ended, the economy accommodated some 12 million returning GIs as people cashed in their war bonds and the stimulus of war gave way to the stimulus of postwar recovery. In the boom that followed, wages increased slightly faster than productivity. The economy grew faster than the national debt, and the debt ratio of more than 120 percent of GDP came steadily down. There was no Bowles-Simpson commission in 1945 targeting the debt-to-GDP ratio in 1955 as a bizarre recovery strategy of confidence-building. Tight regulation of banking permitted financing of the large war debt at very low interest costs without fueling speculation.

There is almost no dispute among economists that the massive fiscal stimulus of the war, coupled with very high taxes on the affluent, produced the public spending to cure the Depression. Indeed, conservative analysts have pointed to the war in order to disparage the partial success of the New Deal.[2] But in today's very similar circumstances, the conventional wisdom is that we must somehow deflate our way to recovery. Most Democrats as well as Republicans, and prominent media commentators, are obsessed with the idea that the deficit, rather than the depressed economy, is the most urgent problem, and that recovery will somehow be stimulated by cutting public spending. There is no plausible economic theory that explains how this will occur. The extremely low interest rates on long-term bonds are evidence that there is neither "crowding out" nor investor fears of inflation. The modest financial reforms of the 2010 Dodd-Frank Act are being undermined by a rearguard lobbying action, and the same business model that caused the collapse is all too intact. There is far too little effort to alleviate the crushing overhang of the housing collapse, which functions as one more drag on recovery.

The conventional wisdom promoting an austerity cure is the result of one more imbalance in the political economy – the disproportionate political influence of finance that stems from its outsized economic influence. If we pursue this deflationary course, we will be condemned to at least a decade

---

[2] Amity Schlaes, *The Forgotten Man: A New History of the New Deal*. New York: Harper-Collins, 2008.

of a severely depressed economy. The debt-to-GDP ratio is a moving target. If we try to reduce it by rejecting expansionary policies and prematurely cutting deficits, we may eventually get to a balanced budget but a much reduced level of economic output. Or as growth and revenues both slow, we may find that debt reduction is a mirage.

Instead, the economy needs a restoration of wage income. It needs re-regulation of the financial sector so that finance can once again serve the real economy. And it needs World War II–scale public investment (without the war, thank you). But one scarcely finds this analysis in mainstream political discourse. That vacuum makes this very thoughtful volume all the more essential.

Robert Kuttner is the coeditor of *The American Prospect*, senior Fellow at Demos, and author of ten books, most recently *Debtors' Prison: The Politics of Austerity versus Possibility* (2013).

Preface

The project culminating in this book began with a conversation between Steven M. Fazzari and Thomas I. Palley about how the events of the Great Recession in 2008 and 2009 validated the economic analysis put forward by a group of Keynesian macroeconomists before the recession, in some cases well before. A group of these economists were then invited to a workshop in the summer of 2009 to discuss the remarkable economic events of the previous several years. The meeting was held at Washington University in St. Louis and organized by the Weidenbaum Center on the Economy, Government, and Public Policy. Following this interesting discussion, the Weidenbaum Center commissioned the papers that became the chapters of this book, early drafts of which were discussed in detail at a second St. Louis workshop in the summer of 2010.

The editors are grateful to the Weidenbaum Center for generous financial support throughout this project. Center Director Steven Smith offered helpful guidance as we developed the book manuscript. Center staff members Gloria Lucy, Chris Moseley, and Melinda Warren provided their typical competent and friendly help with arrangements for both of the St. Louis meetings and other administrative tasks as the book came together. Scott Parris and Kristin Purdy from the economics and finance group at Cambridge University Press provided quick responses to many queries during production of the book. The comments of three anonymous reviewers chosen by the Press significantly improved the manuscript. We thank Noah MacMillan for creative cover art. Finally, we are most grateful to the authors of the following chapters for their original and important insights, as well as the efforts they made to link their perspectives so that this book provides a coherent whole greater than the sum of its parts.

Barry Z. Cynamon, Steven M. Fazzari, and Mark Setterfield
St. Louis, Missouri
May 2012

PART ONE

INTRODUCTION AND OVERVIEW

ONE

Understanding the Great Recession

Barry Z. Cynamon, Steven M. Fazzari, and Mark Setterfield

I must say that I, back in 2007, would not have believed that the world would turn out to be as fundamentalist-Keynesian as it has turned out to be. I would have said that there are full-employment equilibrium-restoring forces in the labor market which we will see operating in a year or two to push the employment-to-population ratio back up. I would have said that the long-run funding dilemmas of the social insurance states would greatly restrict the amount of expansionary fiscal policy that could be run before crowding-out became a real issue.

I would have been wrong.

Brad DeLong blog, *Grasping Reality with Both Hands*
(from "More Results from the British Austerity Experiment,"
http://delong.typepad.com/sdj/2011/04/, April 27, 2011)

In December of 2007, the U.S. economy entered a recession. As economic statistics in the first part of 2008 confirmed an emerging downturn, the policy establishment acknowledged the weakness, but seemed to expect nothing more than a mild recession followed by a quick recovery. For example:

The U.S. economy will tip into a mild recession in 2008 as the result of mutually reinforcing cycles in the housing and financial markets, before starting a modest recovery in 2009 as balance sheet problems in financial institutions are slowly resolved. (IMF World Economic Outlook, April, 2008).

Our estimates are that we are slightly growing at the moment [April, 2008], but we think that there's a chance that for the first half [of 2008] as a whole, there might be a slight contraction.... Much necessary economic and financial adjustment has already taken place, and monetary and fiscal policies are in train that should support a return to growth in the second half of this year and next year. (Ben Bernanke, Testimony to the Joint Economic Committee, April 10, 2008)

We now know that these forecasts badly missed the mark. Job losses and financial instability accelerated through the summer of 2008. After the dramatic events in the wake of the collapse of Lehman Brothers (September 15, 2008) the U.S. economy went into a free fall that eerily tracked the first months of the Great Depression. Job losses in the United States and abroad were the worst in generations and in contrast to early predictions that recovery would come soon, the best that can be said about the U.S. economy as we approach *five years* from the official beginning of the recession is that collapse has been replaced by stagnation.

The dramatic crisis and extended stagnation seem to have caught most economists by surprise. Prior to the onset of the Great Recession in 2007, thinking had converged to the idea that since the mid-1980s, the United States (and other developed countries) had been experiencing a "Great Moderation" – a marked reduction in the volatility of the aggregate economy as compared with the 1970s and early 1980s (see, for example, Galí and Gambetti, 2009). Researchers posited a number of explanations for this favorable performance. Particularly prominent was the view that enlightened monetary policy pursued according to well-defined rules can effectively contain instability and quickly turn negative-growth hiccups back to a favorable long-run path of high employment and rising living standards.

In contrast, a group of macroeconomists, largely outside of the academic mainstream, repeatedly warned during the Great Moderation years that gradual, but very strong, forces were leading the U.S. economy toward a deep recession and persistent stagnation. These economists drew on an alternative perspective, rooted in Keynesian theory, that emphasizes the central roles played by aggregate demand, uncertainty about the future, and finance in determining the path of the aggregate economy through time. From this vantage point, the Great Moderation was not a permanent structural change that could be expected to deliver robust and low-variance growth indefinitely. Rather, the relatively good performance of the U.S. economy in the decades following the deep recession of the early 1980s arose from unique historical circumstances, most prominently a high rate of demand growth financed by unprecedented borrowing in the household sector.

The expansion of borrowing and lending was not just accommodated but, in some cases, actively encouraged by institutional changes in the financial sector. The experience of financial stability in the post–World War II era, assisted in large part by the extensive regulation imposed on the financial sector following the Great Depression, increased the confidence of financiers and their customers. Ironically, this relative financial stability that emerged in a policy-constrained environment validated the increased confidence in markets and induced the subsequent institutional changes designed to "free up" the way they work. As the system was deregulated, the degree of sophistication of financial models, credit rating systems, and trading platforms grew, and the demand stimulus from more aggressive financial practices helped reinforce optimistic perspectives about risk and returns. The economy grew, then, by gradually undermining the institutional supports responsible for generating financial stability and aggressively funding demand growth with debt. In other words, growth resulted from the steady increase of financial fragility.

This fragility remained largely contained during the superficially successful era of the Great Moderation, but since 2007 it has become dramatically manifest, with disastrous macroeconomic consequences. Moreover, now that the consumption-led and household-debt-financed engine of aggregate demand growth has ground to a halt, there is no automatic mechanism to generate the demand necessary for recovery. Insufficient demand of this nature can create a persistent problem, one not just confined to the "short run" of mainstream "New Keynesian" models. The return to economic conditions that even approximate full employment will be a difficult and protracted process. If policy is to mitigate this sluggishness, it will require much more significant intervention to create demand growth than has been pursued in the United States over recent decades. Furthermore, conventional "stimulus" policy, both monetary and fiscal, may not be sufficient to improve economic performance so that it once again appears normal by the standards set during the Great Moderation. A true recovery may be possible only with deep structural change, particularly in the distribution of income, which induces healthy demand growth without unsustainable borrowing.

This volume collects the thinking of a group of Keynesian macroeconomists whose understanding of the Great Recession (as previously summarized) is distinct from that of most academic economists, policy makers, and journalists.[1] A number of authors represented in this volume "saw it coming" and published early warnings that not only predicted a crisis of historic magnitude but also explained in broad terms how it would unfold.[2]

---

[1] As the quotation from Brad DeLong at the start of this introductory chapter suggests, a number of other economists have since come around to the more fundamentally Keynesian way of thinking that informs the contributions to this volume.

[2] The title of Palley (2002), "Economic contradictions coming home to roost? Does the US economy face a long-term aggregate demand generation problem?" says it all. Setterfield

These perspectives also implied that recovery would be sluggish (at best), both because the challenge of sustaining robust aggregate demand growth is more difficult than often appreciated and because the usual policy actions that many mainstream economists trusted during the Great Moderation period would turn out to be woefully inadequate once the household debt engine of demand growth ran out of gas.

This introductory chapter surveys the landscape of the Great Recession as it has unfolded to date, and summarizes the economic thinking that lies behind the contributions in the following chapters. A fundamental objective of this project is to explore the implications of the perspective developed here for the way forward, as the U.S. economy struggles to restore growth and fully employ its resources. Each chapter addresses this issue. In addition, the concluding chapter draws the various threads from individual authors together to discuss the challenges facing the economy over the coming years. The final chapter also addresses what the body of work presented here teaches us about what policy can – and cannot – do to enhance the prospects for recovery.

1. The Great Recession: A Brief History

The Great Recession created the most severe disruption in U.S. economic activity since the 1930s. Figure 1.1 shows the profile of employment for all U.S. recessions since 1974–75, itself a watershed event that ended the post–World War II period of relatively good macroeconomic performance. The figure indexes employment to 100 at the beginning of each recession and tracks the number of jobs through their decline and recovery until employment again reaches its pre-recession level.[3] The decline in employment at the trough of the Great Recession was roughly three times more severe than the average decline in the four other comparison events. The persistence of

(2006, p.59) warns that the U.S. "incomes policy based on fear" during the Great Moderation may be undermining the demand-generating capacity of the U.S. economy. In an op-ed in the *St. Louis Post Dispatch* (October 3, 2007, page B9) Cynamon and Fazzari warn that "the current financial instability in the mortgage markets is merely the initial rumbling of a much bigger economic storm on the horizon." Wray (2007, p.44) fears the emergence of "a huge demand gap that is unlikely to be fully restored by exploding budget deficits or by exports." Also see Godley and Izurieta (2002).

[3] The 1980–83 period is treated as a single event in this figure even though it includes two separate recessions according to National Bureau of Economic Research (NBER) dating. Employment briefly rose modestly above its pre-recession level in 1981 only to decline significantly a few months later. None of the following interpretations change if this event is treated as two separate recessions.

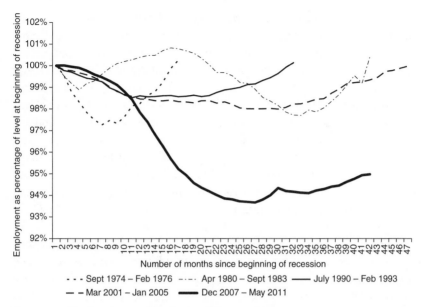

Figure 1.1. Employment profile of recent U.S. recessions.
Source: Total non-farm employees from U.S. Bureau of Labor Statistics' establishment survey. Initial employment indexed to 100 for each recession.

the job losses is also remarkable. Although modest job growth began after twenty-five months of decline, this growth only managed to recover about a quarter of the job losses in the subsequent year and a half. If this rate of growth continues, it will take about eight years from the beginning of the recession for employment to recover to its pre-recession level – a period approximately double that of the worst previous recession since the 1930s. Something fundamentally different is going on compared to more than sixty years of previous history.

The disruptions beginning in 2007 also caused the first serious drop in U.S. consumption since the early 1980s. After two decades of almost continuous increases, the ratio of consumption to disposable income tumbled about four percentage points in 2008 alone. Although this statistic fell by similar amounts during the severe 1974 and 1980 recessions, consumption bounced back quickly as robust recoveries took hold. From 2009 through mid-2011, however, the consumption-income ratio has remained about four percentage points below its 2007 levels.

Residential construction has been an unmitigated disaster. It rose substantially from 2002 to 2006 as a share of GDP, but despite common descriptions of excessive home building as a massive misallocation of resources during these years, the "boom" period was largely in line with historical fluctuations. What was unparalleled in recent history, however, was the decline in home construction beginning in 2006. By 2011, residential investment was much less than half of the value it attained at the 2005 peak, and about half of the fairly stable value for the decade prior to the pre-crisis boom.[4] A look at historical residential construction statistics shows that every U.S. recovery since (at least) 1975–76 has been driven in large part by a housing boom. In the bleak conditions for housing evident almost five years since the onset of the Great Recession, there is no prospect for anything like a return to normal, much less a boom. These declines in consumer spending and home building represent massive declines in aggregate demand, and from the Keynesian perspective, they are the proximate cause of the Great Recession.

Of course, the obvious candidate for the trigger that forced both consumption and residential construction to plummet was overextended mortgage debt and the dramatic financial crisis this debt created. Not since the early 1930s has the U.S. economy gotten close to the kind of financial collapse that followed the failure of Lehmann Brothers investment bank in the fall of 2008. The crisis largely shut down the extension of consumer credit, choking off what had become the fuel for demand expansion during the previous two decades.

Policy actions have also been dramatic during the past few years. The Federal Reserve and the U.S. Treasury pursued a wide variety of refinancing – that is, "bailout" – policies, starting in the late summer of 2007, even before the official recession began. The Fed's balance sheet expanded dramatically as it bought mortgage-backed securities and, later, long-term Treasury bonds for trillions of dollars. Fiscal stimulus took a variety of forms. The nearly $800 billion American Reinvestment and Recovery Act passed early in the Obama administration was the most prominent among "stimulus" measures. However, automatic stabilizers (rising entitlement spending and falling tax revenues) were quantitatively more important. The federal deficit rose to about 10 percent of GDP in 2010, about double the previous post–World War II record set in the early Reagan years.

Prior to the Great Recession, virtually no analyst of U.S. policy would have predicted such aggressive policy responses. Yet, the sluggish recovery and continued deep uncertainty about the economy's future several years

---

[4]   Residential construction averaged a remarkably stable 5.2% of GDP from 1993 through 2002. In 2005, it peaked at almost 6.2% of GDP, similar to its peak in the mid-1980s (earlier peaks were even higher). As of 2011, construction was about 2.5% of GDP.

after the events that triggered the Great Recession suggest, if anything, that the policy responses were too timid.

2. Mainstream Macroeconomics and the Great Recession

The essential feature of the perspective that connects the contributions to this volume is that the interplay of three central features of capitalism – aggregate demand, uncertainty, and finance – explains much of the boom of the Great Moderation period and the bust that culminated in the Great Recession.[5] Increased confidence and "animal spirits" fed into an unprecedented increase in household indebtedness that fueled the expansion of aggregate demand, until financial fragility finally cracked (initially in the subprime mortgage market), rupturing confidence and dousing animal spirits. This set up a sudden and precipitous decline in aggregate demand, as credit contraction, wealth destruction, and decreasing aggregate expenditures interacted in a vicious spiral that was only arrested by massive policy interventions.

However, this account is quite at odds with the perspective of most mainstream macroeconomics, especially as practiced prior to the dramatic events of the fall of 2008. Much mainstream theory was, and remains, committed to an avowedly supply-side view of the economy, according to which variations in aggregate demand have no direct role to play in determining "real" macroeconomic outcomes (such as unemployment), even in the short run. From this point of view, the essential cause of the Great Recession was a supply-side shock – a sudden increase in labor market frictions, or a shock to labor supply or financial intermediation, for example – causing dislocations in the economy that are most likely temporary.[6] Even if these shocks represent more persistent structural problems, the solution to them has nothing to do with replacing the aggregate demand growth that was lost with the end of the housing-debt-financed consumption boom.[7]

---

[5] Some parts of sections 2 and 3 are extensively revised from Cynamon and Fazzari (2010).
[6] For example, according to Feldstein (2010), we can look forward to a period of *faster* growth over the next ten years, as a sharp rebound from the Great Recession itself puts the United States back on the trend set by an uninterrupted natural rate of growth.
[7] For example, in mid-2010, the president of the Federal Reserve Bank of Minneapolis, Narayana Kocherlakota proposed that much of the unemployment problem is the result of mismatched skills and geographic preferences: workers are not in the places or industries where the jobs are. If this is the case, it follows that "[m]ost of the existing unemployment represents mismatch that is not readily amenable to monetary policy" (speech at Northern Michigan University, August 17, 2010).

Yet it is hard to escape the seemingly central role of finance in bringing about the Great Recession (despite the proclivity of some supply-side
accounts of recent events to do just this by focusing instead on, for example, the workings of the labor market – see Ohanian, 2010). And although
some supply-siders do see a role for finance in causing the Great Recession
(a shock to the technology of financial intermediation, for example),
their models do not, in our view, provide the best foundation for such an
account.[8] As Edmund Phelps (2010, p. 2, emphasis in original) has recently
remarked:

> [Supply-siders are] not in a position to argue that the excessive vulnerability
> of banks (and counterparties) to loans gone sour and resulting stoppage of
> loans to businesses, which has been recurrent in the past two centuries, can
> be viewed as just an unusually large value in some disturbance term in this
> school's models. After all, the precepts of this school imply that episodes of
> excessive leverage and credit stoppages *do not occur*: Markets are perfectly
> efficient to a decent approximation.... The school that laid the ground for the
> belief in "the magic of the market" cannot pretend that its models succeed in
> encompassing gross mispricing of risk and pathological values put on famil-
> iar assets.

Despite the search for an exclusively supply-side explanation for the Great
Recession among some academics, the events of the past four years have created a remarkable shift toward Keynesian thinking among many mainstream
economic analysts, including journalists and policy makers.[9] Consider first
how we understand the sources of the Great Recession. As noted earlier, the
role of finance is virtually inescapable, and so it is not surprising to find that
almost all explanations begin with problems in the U.S. mortgage market
and emphasize a channel that goes from credit to demand. The bursting of
the housing bubble created a clear and direct "demand shock." Residential
construction collapsed and the American consumer juggernaut crashed for
the first time in more than two decades. A broad swath of the economics

---

[8] This likely explains why many supply-siders were quite sanguine about the prospects for
the U.S. economy, even as it entered the teeth of the financial crisis in fall 2008. For example, in the aftermath of the failure of Lehman Brothers in the fall of 2008, University of
Chicago Professor Casey Mulligan opined that "[e]conomic research has repeatedly demonstrated that financial-sector gyrations like these are hardly connected to non-financial
sector performance ... So, if you are not employed by the financial industry (94 percent of
you are not), don't worry. The current unemployment rate of 6.1 percent is not alarming,
and we should reconsider whether it is worth it to spend $700 billion to bring it down to
5.9 percent" (Mulligan, 2008).

[9] As will become clear, this remains true despite current obsessions in the political sphere
with "excessive" public deficits and debt and the "need" for austerity measures. We return
to discussion of these themes later in this chapter.

profession and virtually all forecasters recognize the need for renewed spending, private or public, as critical for any kind of meaningful recovery. For example, Christina Romer, who had a front-row seat to the crisis in her role as chair of President Obama's Council of Economic Advisors, stated in an April 12, 2011 speech at Washington University in St. Louis, "I believe that when scholars finish analyzing both the U.S. and international evidence, the bottom line will be that fiscal stimulus is, and was in this past recession, a key tool to fight cyclical unemployment."

Macroeconomic policy has also been explicitly Keynesian, perhaps more than at any time for at least a quarter century. In the aftermath of the fall 2008 crash, fiscal stimulus packages emerged around the world with the explicit objective of boosting spending. This is a major change. Since the Reagan-Thatcher years, fiscal responses to recessions have been justified with supply-side arguments, even if it turned out that the most important effect of the resulting tax cuts was to stimulate demand rather than supply. However, discussions of recent stimulus measures in the immediate response to the most severe period of the recession largely jettisoned supply-side rationales and focused on the importance of creating spending, and doing so quickly.

Recent events have also transformed monetary policy, both its execution and how it is perceived by mainstream economists. The Bernanke Fed has cut short-term interest rates to zero for an extended period and pursued aggressive lender-of-last-resort interventions. Whereas there are clear grounds to criticize the way policy makers implemented the Troubled Asset Relief Program (TARP), the Term Asset-Backed Securities Loan Facility (TALF), bailouts of Fannie Mae, Freddie Mac, and AIG, and other such initiatives (particularly the distributional consequences of propping up massive institutions and their outrageously compensated management), the basic logic that motivates the systemic ambitions of these remarkable actions comes from Keynesian theory, broadly conceived to include Hyman Minsky's perspective on financial instability.

In addition, mainstream macroeconomic thinking may be shifting in another important but less obvious way. As economists digest the dramatic events of recent years, the relevance of the so-called new consensus approach to macroeconomics seems to be fading. These models adopt the microfoundations methods of new classical research, but price stickiness leads to short-run monetary non-neutrality. They admit short-run Keynesian features, but also posit competent monetary engineers, their tool belts equipped with Taylor rules and inflation targets, who keep the real effects of demand shocks well in check. One corollary of this thinking is that the makers of fiscal policy need not worry about Keynesian problems; they should focus instead on the classical long run, in which output converges to potential. Indeed, new consensus models are often interpreted to imply that it is best to keep fiscal policy out of macroeconomic stabilization in a slump because in the long run, government activity crowds out the private sector.

The new consensus emerged during the Great Moderation years. On the verge of the Great Recession, the new consensus models had convinced top mainstream economists such as Blanchard (2009) and Woodford (2009) that macroeconomic thinking was in good health, having survived the theoretical battles of earlier generations and arrived at a single, consistent vision of how macroeconomics should be done, what the long run looked like, and even a fairly common conception of what caused aggregate fluctuations in the short term. To be sure, some differences of opinion remained. Hence, whereas supply-siders persisted in the belief that the primary source of aggregate disturbances were technology shocks emanating from the real economy (possibly broadly defined to include labor search or financial intermediation "technologies"), "New Keynesians" emphasized monetary disturbances as a source of variations in output and employment. Nevertheless, even these differences could be boiled down to a single debate about the importance of nominal rigidities in an otherwise common methodological and theoretical framework.[10]

However, this "consensus" has suffered a bad few years. New Keynesian research had not completely ignored the uncomfortable possibility that the inability to push nominal interest rates below zero could prevent conventional monetary policy from fulfilling the stabilizing role ascribed to it in the new consensus research, with references especially to the troubles of Japan and its ever-expanding "lost decade." Yet, the full force of this modern version of the liquidity trap was not evident until recently. The nuances of the New Keynesian literature on optimal monetary policy seem of little relevance to the current crisis when the policy rate is effectively zero, banks sit on mountains of excess reserves, and there is great skepticism that two successive bouts of quantitative easing will be nearly enough to initiate a robust recovery. Indeed, despite the efforts of U.S. authorities to continue pushing on the proverbial string of monetary policy, many mainstream economists, in sharp contrast to the new consensus thinking of just a few years ago, have come to support aggressive fiscal policy, and government deficits of

---

[10]   In academic circles, this common framework is usually referred to as dynamic-stochastic general equilibrium (DSGE) theory.

a size and persistence that was unimaginable just a few years ago, as an appropriate response to a crisis of this magnitude.

3. The Case for Keynesian Insights: Outside the Mainstream

Whereas much practical economic analysis of the Great Recession and the associated discussion of policy have clear Keynesian characteristics, other important aspects of Keynesian macroeconomics have not been adequately recognized in typical accounts of recent events. The points summarized in this section, and explored in detail in the chapters to come, show how our understanding of demand, finance, and uncertainty needs to expand beyond what typically appears in mainstream analysis to account for what has happened, to offer a realistic assessment of the challenges that may stand in the way of a healthy recovery, and to provide a foundation for policy advice.

Finance and the Limits of Monetary Policy: Beyond the Zero Bound

The zero bound notwithstanding, current mainstream understanding suggests that the Great Recession is a rare event, and that enlightened monetary policy should be capable of stabilizing economic activity in normal times. Central to this perspective is the idea that substantial interest elasticities of spending are robust structural features of the economy, so that the central bank can effectively control spending by manipulating interest rates. The transmission mechanism from monetary policy to aggregate spending in most new consensus models relies on the interest sensitivity of consumption. It is difficult, however, to find empirical evidence that households do indeed raise or lower consumption by a significant amount when interest rates change. Some authors have generalized the link between interest rates and spending in new consensus models to include business investment (see Fazzari, Ferri, and Greenberg 2010 and the references provided therein), but a robust interest elasticity of investment has also been difficult to demonstrate empirically (Fazzari 1994–95). If spending is not very sensitive to the interest rate set by monetary policy, very large reductions in the interest rate are necessary to offset the effects of even modest negative-demand shocks. Thus, the zero-bound constraint may not be the once-in-a-lifetime issue suggested by much current discussion, but rather a common and persistent problem (see also Palacio-Vera 2010).

If this perspective is correct, one might ask why most new consensus research largely views the zero-bound problem as exceptional. Recent history provides part of the explanation. Thirty years ago, nominal interest rates in the U.S. economy stood at record highs as the Fed aggressively fought inflation.[11] Although monetary policy was not always stimulative in the interim, the general trend of interest rates since the end of the U.S. Great Inflation in the early 1980s has been downward. Put simply, when demand lagged, central banks always had room to cut rates. This "room for maneuver" – the product of a particular historical episode of monetary policy – has now disappeared.

However, part of the explanation is theoretical. We propose that, for the past quarter century, monetary policy has worked through channels other than those emphasized in the new consensus models. Specifically, expansionary monetary policy and the consequent decline in interest rates have stimulated demand by magnifying the general financial trends identified earlier that encouraged the unprecedented accumulation of household debt. In addition, falling interest rates created refinancing opportunities, and also increased asset prices, thereby contributing (along with a variety of other factors) to major asset-price bubbles in technology stocks and real estate. These bubbles induced wealth effects and stoked optimistic animal spirits that further boosted spending.

The point is that monetary policy has stimulated aggregate demand in recent decades, but not through sustainable channels (such as shifts in consumption from the future to the present) in which finance simply "oils the wheels" of optimal long-term spending plans. Instead, falling interest rates contributed to debt accumulation and asset price inflation that was largely predicated on increasingly buoyant animal spirits. This created the appearance of robust and relatively stable macroeconomic performance (the Great Moderation) that, in turn, largely concealed (at least to most mainstream analysts) the threat of rising financial fragility. Concealed, that is, until the financial fragility was made obvious by events from 2006 to 2008 that triggered reductions in lending, confidence, and animal spirits, causing the whole house of cards to come crashing down.

We have now seen that conventional interest rate policy, and even some less conventional monetary policies such as quantitative easing, can neither prevent nor remediate a severe recession. For this reason, we argue that a full understanding of the Great Recession, and the prospects for a robust recovery going forward, must move beyond new consensus models of monetary policy.

---

[11] The federal funds rate reached a post-1955 peak of 19% in the early 1980s.

Uncertainty and Financial Instability

At least since Keynes wrote chapter 12 of the *General Theory*, Keynesian economists have emphasized the key role of uncertainty in explaining the evolution of the economy.[12] The events leading up to the Great Recession are no exception. In the aftermath of the crash of 2008 and 2009, it has become commonplace to scold both borrowers and lenders for "irresponsible" levels of debt. Although it is not difficult to find examples of irresponsible behavior, given what we now know, we argue that the more important reason that participants in all parts of the financial debacle got into trouble was reliance on heuristics and models that helped agents make decisions in the face of uncertainty, but provided no guarantee that the resulting decisions were optimal.

The financial practices that sowed the seeds of the Great Recession evolved over nearly a quarter century of relatively good economic performance. Households enjoyed higher consumption and better housing and the financial industry reaped fantastic profits. Academic work reinforced a sense that the new practices were desirable by praising the efficiency of financial markets and arguing that complex securities and other evolving financial arrangements effectively diversified risk and therefore justified more borrowing and lending relative to income or assets. The path of the economy in the years leading up to the recession appears unsustainable to many analysts, after the fact. However, people did not broadly perceive the inevitability of a collapse because, for decades, the system appeared to work quite well.

Keynes argues that when people have no objective basis on which to forecast events that arise from a complex system, they will assume that the future will look, more or less, like the recent past. The recent past for much of the period from the middle 1980s to 2007 supported the idea that rising debt and riskier financial positions could support higher standards of living and lucrative financial returns. Crotty (1994) writes about how agents following conventional forecasts create "conditional stability" in the outcome. During the Great Moderation period, people came to trust the ascendency of institutions that claimed to deliver a reasonably benign macroeconomic environment, most notably wise central banks. It was therefore neither irrational nor really irresponsible, in the context of the times, for them to engage in what (after the fact) seems clearly unsustainable. As Crotty (1994, page

---

[12] See, in particular, the extensive work along these lines by Paul Davidson, most recently Davidson (2007).

120) writes, "history demonstrates that capitalist economies move through time with a substantial degree of order and continuity that is disrupted only on occasion by bursts of disorderly and discontinuous change." For about two decades, experience appeared to confirm that household finance – and the economy as a whole – was in reasonably good shape.

There was also a tendency for evolving institutions to select ever-riskier financial behavior prior to the recession. As the debt-financed boom generated strong growth and validated risky behavior, those who warned of looming financial excesses lost credibility. Consider this statement attributed to Boykin Curry, managing director of the financial firm Eagle Capital (quoted by Fareed Zakaria "There is a Silver Lining," *Newsweek*, October 12, 2008):

> For 20 years, the DNA of nearly every financial institution had morphed dangerously. Each time someone at the table pressed for more leverage and more risk, the next few years proved them "right." These people were emboldened, they were promoted and they gained control of ever more capital. Meanwhile, anyone in power who hesitated, who argued for caution, was proved "wrong." The cautious types were increasingly intimidated, passed over for promotion. They lost their hold on capital. This happened every day in almost every financial institution over and over, until we ended up with a very specific kind of person running things.

In retrospect, these risky behaviors look irresponsible. However, for many years the favorable conditions rewarded more aggressive financial behaviors and the systemic effects that would ultimately lead to collapse were far from obvious in the uncertain context of the times. Curry's quote refers to the control of capital in the financial sector, but similar dynamics played out among households. More risky borrowing against one's home was validated by rising housing prices. Risky mortgage terms did not typically hurt homeowners who could subsequently refinance into markets with downward-trending interest rates and ever more lenient credit standards.

It all worked well, for many years. This conditional stability encouraged ever more confidence, more aggressive financial positions, and rising financial fragility, until eventually the stress on the system was too great and it broke down.

What is the Source of Demand Growth in the Long Run?

The failure of Say's Law defines Keynesian economics: no automatic economic mechanism exists to assure demand adequate to purchase full-employment output. Most mainstream Keynesians, however, believe that problems of insufficient demand are confined to the short run. Beyond a year or two, nominal wage and price adjustment should restore demand to a level sufficient to buy whatever output the supply side can generate. From this vantage point, a perspective called the "neoclassical synthesis" by the late Paul Samuelson, Keynesian policies need focus only on the short run, to nudge along the endogenous effects of nominal adjustment. Economic growth beyond a few years should be understood as a purely supply-side phenomenon, driven by advances in technology and the availability of productive resources, with no role for aggregate demand.

Although the neoclassical synthesis is a clean, even elegant, solution to the classical-Keynesian debate, there was never much theoretical or empirical support for its assertion that declining wages and prices would endogenously boost demand, eliminate unemployment, and restore the economy to a supply-determined growth path. Keynesian economists have written for decades about how deflation (or disinflation) might actually *reduce* demand. Falling wages make it more difficult for households to pay off debts contracted in nominal terms, causing them to tighten their belts and reduce spending. In addition, because deflation raises the real value of nominal debts, it redistributes wealth from borrowers to lenders – that is, from high spenders to low spenders. This redistribution will depress demand. Finally, if deflation leads to expectations of further price declines, agents will have an incentive to defer spending. These channels imply that the price-adjustment mechanism could, perversely, *reduce* demand when output is below potential.[13]

Indeed, despite the persistent textbook interpretation of Keynesian theory as showing what happens when wages and prices are slow to adjust downward after a decline in aggregate demand, practical economists in recent years seem to have put their faith in monetary policy, rather than nominal adjustment, as the primary engine of macro stabilization. We have already discussed how the Great Recession has revealed the limitations of monetary policy. However, if we can rely on neither wage and price adjustment to restore demand endogenously and automatically, nor monetary policy to fine-tune demand through explicit policy action, what is the source of demand that keeps the economy growing over both short and long horizons? We propose that there is no single answer to this question and that

[13] Although this statement undermines the theoretical foundations of the neoclassical synthesis that dominated decades of macro textbooks, it is hardly a surprise. Keynes made these arguments and they have been explored widely in post-Keynesian research. For further references, see Fazzari, Ferri, and Greenberg (1998) and Palley (2008).

Keynesian macroeconomists and economic historians need to look at the variety of different ways that economies have (or have not) succeeded in generating sources of demand growth across time.[14]

To demonstrate how demand growth sufficient to match potential output growth in the medium and long term is hardly automatic, it is instructive to sketch the somewhat idiosyncratic ways that the challenge of creating demand has been addressed in the United States over the past century. The Roaring 1920s were fueled by a debt-financed consumption boom and strong asset price growth. Of course, this particular model for demand growth ended spectacularly with the Great Depression. The original New Deal seemed to turn things around in the middle 1930s, until fiscal policy tightened in 1937, but it ultimately took massive demand from the government in World War II to get the economy back to its pre-Depression trend. The war provided not just a direct source of demand but, through its financing, it also led to unusually liquid household and corporate balance sheets. These financial conditions along with the Marshall Plan that created an international market for U.S. exports, the Cold War military-industrial complex, hot wars in Korea and Vietnam, and another wave of consumerism in the baby-boom years, generated strong demand growth through the 1960s. Consumer spending growth in the mid-twentieth century was also supported by rising real wages that allowed the middle class to spend more without borrowing – in contrast to more recent experience. High oil prices and a wage-price spiral created trouble in the 1970s as demand growth faltered and then was deliberately suppressed by policy to rein in inflation during the monetarist experiment of the early 1980s.

The massive U.S. tax cuts during the early Reagan years were sold politically as supply-side policy designed to raise saving rates, but the result was exactly the opposite. Indeed, the share of U.S. disposable income devoted to consumption rose almost without pause through 2007, along with household debt. The rise in debt and consumer spending followed the script of a self-reinforcing boom phase of a Minsky financial "cycle," but it was not a phase of a typical business cycle. Rather, it was an extended period that contained a number of shorter cycles and lasted nearly a quarter century. In the aggregate, this particular method for generating demand growth worked well, as long as it could be sustained by falling interest rates and

---

[14] Of course, historically specific sources of demand growth alone are necessary but not sufficient for long-term economic growth. Developed economies obviously could not have expanded so much without supply-side growth. However, we part company with the common assertion that supply-side forces by themselves are *sufficient* to explain growth over decade-plus horizons.

expanding household access to credit. The Fed, with support from the academic establishment, drove interest rates lower. Financial engineers exploited new technologies – electronic credit scoring, for example – and pursued financial innovation that supposedly made risk sharing more efficient. The result was unprecedented debt pumped into the household sector. The consumption boom became a major engine of U.S. GDP growth. Unemployment fell to half-century lows. The end of this period of demand generation marked the beginning of the Great Recession.

The point of this brief historical summary is to make clear that rising demand is far from automatic. The fundamental Keynesian problem of demand-deficiency has been solved at different times by different and historically specific forces. When demand growth faltered, as in the 1970s or, more dramatically, the 1930s, the economy sputtered, and not just for a year or two. Even as mainstream forecasters are anxious to declare a more robust recovery from the Great Recession to be just around the corner, the source of the aggregate demand necessary to initiate significant growth remains a mystery. Simple faith in the mainstream mechanisms of wage and price adjustment and standard monetary policy is unjustified.

4. Where Do We Go from Here?

To explore the prospects for the U.S. economy in the aftermath of the Great Recession, we return to our organizing themes of demand, finance, and uncertainty.

By the summer of 2012, the economy had supposedly been in recovery for three years. Despite this, job growth remained minimal and the gap between actual output and sensible estimates of potential output had hardly declined. The proximate problem seemed to be a lack of adequate demand growth.[15] In the United States, consumption is 70 percent of demand. If consumption stagnates, other demand components must grow at unusually

---

[15] When output or employment fall below the long-term trend for an extended period, it is typical to hear from analysts who argue that the potential output trend must have declined, or the closely related concept of the "natural" rate of unemployment must have increased. This kind of thinking is based on the idea that demand constraints *must* disappear over a reasonably short period of time, so if the economy has fallen away from its earlier trend for a long time, the supply-driven trend itself must have changed. We reject this reasoning. As discussed earlier in this chapter, demand can constrain the economy over long periods. In the context of the Great Recession, assertions that the supply-driven trend has declined seem especially problematic because of the striking *rise* in labor productivity during this period. There is no evidence that the productivity of the U.S. economy or its workers is below the trend established through 2007.

high rates for total demand to expand at typical long-term rates of roughly 3 percent per year. In principle, consumption growth could be stimulated by another round of the lend-and-spend process, perhaps supported by yet another asset bubble, but this outcome seems both unlikely and undesirable, for obvious reasons.

The mainstream approach to the challenge of finding a source of demand growth to replace the consumption boom of recent decades would be to offset the reduction of private consumption as a share of demand with an increase in private capital investment as a share of demand. However, where should this investment come from? According to the new consensus models, the interest rate is the "magic variable" that controls the consumption-investment shares in the economy, but even with remarkably low interest rates, business investment remains depressed. If a robust recovery occurs, investment will likely follow its historical pro-cyclical pattern and rise strongly, but such a process propagates demand growth *after* a strong recovery begins; it does not initiate the recovery.[16] What about higher exports and lower imports as demand stimulus? The U.S. trade deficit did decline substantially in the teeth of the recession, greatly mitigating the collapse in demand for domestic business as a large proportion of reduced consumption and investment spending came at the expense of imports (the gap between imports and exports shrank from about 6 percent of GDP to less than 3 percent). Nevertheless, the trade gap has risen again with even the anemic recovery through 2011. Further significant declines in the trade deficit over the next few years are unlikely unless imports are once again hammered by dismal economic performance – hardly a desirable outcome.[17] For these reasons, it can be expected that stagnant private demand growth will continue to constrain the U.S. economy, a situation that will likely continue to pose a significant challenge to recovery in coming years.

Can government policies help create demand? Undoubtedly, monetary and fiscal actions by the U.S. government helped meet the immediate challenge of containing the free fall in aggregate demand of late 2008 and early 2009. Whether government actions can replace debt-led consumption as

---

[16] In 2010, business investment as share of GDP bounced back from historic lows, most likely as businesses retreated from the panic of the worst days of the recession. However, in 2011, nominal business investment remained a much smaller share of nominal GDP than it had been for almost all of the past half century.

[17] Over a longer horizon, changes in the structure of global demand may help generate U.S. demand growth. There have been some indications that China is pursuing policies that encourage domestic consumption, in part because the Great Recession demonstrated the danger of relying on exports to the United States as an engine of demand. This kind of change, however, is likely to proceed slowly.

an engine of demand *growth* in coming years, however, is less clear. At the least, government intervention would have to extend beyond the typical stabilization goals of textbook macroeconomic policy. The potential for policy to contribute to robust demand growth over a longer horizon is an important theme of the chapters to follow.

No doubt, finance will play a critical role in determining economic performance in the aftermath of the Great Recession. Looking ahead, however, the part played by finance is likely to be quite different than it was during the years prior to the collapse. From the mid-1980s through 2007, expanding credit – and in particular, expanding consumer credit – energized demand growth and asset prices, but in the sluggish initial phase of recovery, consumer credit is shrinking. In addition, what progress has been made in repairing the aggregate household balance sheet has occurred largely through loan default and not because U.S. consumers have committed to paying down their debts. On the one hand, less household borrowing is welcome. As previously intimated, we have been down the path of ever-increasing household leverage, we have seen where it leads, and we do not want to simply wind up the clock springs of another unsustainable, debt-financed growth episode that serves only to leave us wondering when the next crisis will occur. On the other hand, to the extent that the U.S. economy had come to rely on rising household debt to generate demand growth, tighter limits on consumer loans or unwillingness on the part of households to borrow will constrain the recovery. In particular, recall that the recovery from every U.S. recession since (at least) 1974–75 has been led in large part by a boom in residential construction. A residential construction boom is highly unlikely to occur for some years to come.

Uncertainty looms large over any consideration of the way forward for the U.S. economy in the aftermath of the Great Recession. Although the dynamics of recessions have changed somewhat in past decades (consider, for example, the disappointment of "jobless recoveries" after the recessions of 1990–91 and 2001), the conditions that have prevailed since the National Bureau of Economic Research (NBER) declared the official end of the Great Recession in 2009 truly do seem different from anything the U.S. economy has previously experienced, at least since the Great Depression (again, refer to the employment profile in Figure 1.1). We were not supposed to have deep recessions anymore; we were in an era called the "Great Moderation!" In addition, conventional wisdom prior to the crisis implied that if the economy did face a deep recession, the recovery would be that much brisker as a result. However, there is no evidence that such a favorable outcome will occur this time. As previously discussed, monetary policy seems particularly impotent in its ability to engineer a robust recovery, even though it has been touted in mainstream thinking as the first, if not only, line of defense against the wasted resources of downturns in the business cycle. The modest effects of the Fed's experiments with various forms of "quantitative easing" and the absence of any further creative policy initiative emanating from the central bank following the "QE2" that ended on June 30, 2011 suggest a sense of helplessness in the face of adversity.

With monetary policy adrift, uncertainty about the effects of fiscal policy risks sinking the economic ship entirely. The Obama administration responded to the early stages of the Great Recession with a historically large fiscal stimulus package. However, debates rage about whether these policies made the economy better or worse. In our view, there is no doubt that the fiscal response to the onset of the Great Recession was essential to prevent a full-blown depression. As we have already noted, a still more ambitious fiscal response is likely necessary if anything is to come of the current weak recovery. The political response to the recent stagnation of the U.S. economy, however, has been distinctly anti-Keynesian, with even President Obama (the chief architect of the stimulus package) telling U.S. citizens that since they have been forced to tighten their collective belts, their government must do so as well. Fiscal contraction despite massive unemployment had begun in earnest in Europe by 2011, and much of the political momentum in the U.S. suggests that its fiscal policy will follow the European lead toward austerity.

Extending the maritime metaphor of the previous paragraph, this book is an attempt to right the ship that is the modern U.S. economy, and to put it once again on a course toward prosperity. To understand what we should do, we must first understand why the crisis occurred. The chapters that follow explore the sources of the Great Recession from a Keynesian perspective that predicted the broad outlines of what would happen years ahead of the actual emergence of recession. This perspective stands in contrast to most mainstream economic analyses, including Keynesian variants of the new consensus. Mainstream macroeconomics had been mostly lulled into the benign thinking that accompanied the Great Moderation. This approach greatly underestimated the challenge of demand generation over longer horizons, viewing demand growth as more or less automatic, aside from the need for temporary tweaks from the central bank. Mainstream thinking similarly underestimated the potential destabilizing forces of finance and largely ignored uncertainty all together. The alternative view developed here offers a deeper understanding of what has happened in the last few turbulent years. Nevertheless, understanding what went wrong is just the first step. The following chapters also apply the Keynesian perspective to consider how policy and institutional reform can reconstitute an aggregate demand-generating process to deliver recovery and growth, along with the financial activities that support it. In this sense, we hope that this volume helps illuminate the way forward for the U.S. economy from its most challenging times in more than seventy years.

5. Outline of the Chapters that Follow

The individual chapters in this book examine in greater detail the interplay between aggregate demand, uncertainty, and finance that has been sketched in this chapter. As previously mentioned, in each chapter, emphasis is placed on both the causes of the Great Recession *and* what needs to be done to put the economy on a stronger footing that will eventually yield a sustainable recovery.

Chapter 2, written by Thomas Palley, puts forward a broad vision of the Great Recession that links its genesis to the failings of the neoliberal policy program that took hold in the United States around 1980. Neoliberalism is identified as a faulty macroeconomic paradigm for two reasons: it relies on debt accumulation and asset price inflation, rather than wage growth, to drive demand; and it involves a model of U.S. engagement with the global economy that encourages spending on imports, manufacturing job losses, and off-shoring of investment. Palley argues that the neoliberal model slowly cannibalized itself by simultaneously undermining the distribution of income and accumulating debt. As this process unfolded, augmented by financial deregulation and growing debt, the economy needed ever-larger speculative bubbles in order to grow. In the final stages of this process, the flawed model of global engagement accelerated these dynamics, creating the need for a huge bubble that only housing could provide. When that bubble burst, the Great Recession began.

According to Palley, we have reached a juncture at which the old, post–World War II growth model based on rising middle-class incomes has been dismantled, while the new, neoliberal growth model has imploded. The United States therefore needs a new macroeconomic paradigm. This is the foremost challenge confronting economists and policy makers who seek to construct a sustainable path to prosperity in the aftermath of the Great Recession.

The next three chapters discuss the role of finance in the events that led up to the Great Recession, and the sort of reforms needed to reshape the

financial sector going forward. In Chapter 3 by L. Randall Wray, the Great
Recession is characterized as a systemic crisis of what Hyman Minsky called
"money manager capitalism." Following Minsky, Wray shows how the New
Deal and big government created a paternalistic capitalism after World War
II that favored high consumption, high employment, declining economic
inequality, and financial stability. However, this stability was ultimately
destabilizing. As memories of the Depression faded and confidence grew
in the robustness of the financial system, financial innovation and deregulation gradually chipped away at the very sources of this robustness. The
result has been increasing financial fragility, which generated increasingly
frequent and severe financial crises, culminating in the events of the Great
Recession.

Wray examines in detail the various specific factors that contributed to
the crisis, including the real estate boom and bust, the rise of risky financial
instruments (such as securitized debts and credit default swaps), and the
commodities market bubble. The chapter ends with reflections on the possible consequences of the failure of money manager capitalism, and policy
proposals designed to promote more robust financial structures capable of
sustaining rising standards of living.

Chapter 4, by Jan Kregel, focuses on the banking sector, but once again
draws on Minsky's financial instability hypothesis to explain the ways in
which surreptitious financial deregulation contributed to rising financial
fragility in the run-up to the Great Recession. Kregel argues that the banking sector serves "two masters": it helps finance real economic expansion;
and it provides a stable and secure payments system. According to Kregel,
deregulation upset the balance between these functions and created increasing financial instability in the decades that preceded the Great Recession.
He argues, for example, that deregulation fueled the transformation of the
traditional "lend and hold" business model for banking, that emphasized
credit assessment for loans that would remain on the lender's balance sheet,
into the "originate and distribute" model that is predicated on increasing
lending volumes with the explicit objective of selling off the loans to get
them off the original lender's balance sheet as quickly as possible. The 1999
Financial Services Modernization Act, meanwhile, pushed investment
banks further into trading for their own account in place of their traditional
roles as market-making dealers and securities underwriters. The result was
a system that was less effective at financing business investment and that
drastically increased risk.

Informed by the need for the banking sector to successfully balance its service to "two masters," Kregel discusses the limits on existing and traditional methods of regulation to provide stability to the financial system.

The focus of Chapter 5, by James Crotty, is the internal structure of modern financial services corporations and, in particular, the bonus-driven compensation schemes employed in important financial institutions such as investment banks. According to Crotty, these compensation schemes provided the incentive for key decision makers (so-called "rainmakers") to take the excessive risk and employ the excessive leverage that helped make the financial crisis and Great Recession so severe. The chapter assesses evidence on compensation practices in investment banks that show that rainmaker compensation has been rising rapidly, is very large, and induces reckless risk-taking. For example, boom-period bonuses do not have to be returned if rainmaker decisions eventually lead to losses for their firms, and large bonuses continue to be paid even when firms, in fact, suffer large losses. Crotty also shows that rainmaker bonuses are not appropriate returns to human capital – they are simply economic rents. Finally, Crotty discusses answers to the challenging questions: what is the source of rainmaker rents and how are they sustained over time? Answers to these questions are essential to debates over the appropriate future regulation of financial markets and, in particular, executive compensation.

Having examined various aspects of the contribution of the financial sector to the Great Recession, Chapters 6 and 7 turn attention to the household sector, and to debt-financed household spending as source of both growth and accumulating financial fragility. In Chapter 6, Barry Cynamon and Steven Fazzari analyze rising consumer spending and the associated explosion of household debt in the U.S. economy. They show that consumption, financed in large part by rising debt, was the engine of U.S. demand growth for an extended period of time. This "consumer age" largely coincided with the Great Moderation period from the mid-1980s through 2007, and the authors propose that strong consumption demand contributed to the relatively stable macroeconomic performance of the United States over these years. Cynamon and Fazzari also explore the underlying source of consumption and debt decisions, arguing that they are made in a social context. Psychological characteristics of individual choice and the influence of social reference groups contributed to what ultimately was revealed to be an unsustainable path for household finance. High consumption growth was accompanied by the accumulation of financial fragility, as discussed by Hyman Minsky. The eventual collapse of this process was the proximate source of the Great Recession.

The chapter then considers the prospects for American consumption and its macroeconomic effects over the next several years. Cynamon and Fazzari question the conventional wisdom that modestly improved economic indicators since the official end of the Great Recession signal the initial stages of a sustainable recovery. Without the U.S. consumers' willingness and ability to further leverage their collective balance sheets, they argue, the source of demand growth for a meaningful recovery remains a mystery.

Mark Setterfield argues in Chapter 7 that, whereas much attention has rightly been paid to developments in the financial sector as causes of the Great Recession, long-term trends in the real economy made vitally important contributions to the genesis of the crisis. Specifically, Setterfield identifies the tendency for real wages to grow slower than productivity since the 1970s. This trend has not only increased income inequality, but has also led to a structural flaw in the process that creates the demand necessary for high employment and rising living standards in the United States. Although household debt accumulation postponed the "day of reckoning" associated with this structural flaw, Setterfield predicts that the effect of sluggish real-wage growth on the incomes of working households now has the potential to create a future of secular stagnation, not just for U.S. workers, but for the country's economy as a whole. The chapter ends with a discussion of the sort of policy measures that would be required to avert this grim prognosis.

In Chapter 8, Robert Blecker explores some of the global dimensions of the crisis and, in particular, the fabled "global imbalances" – large U.S. trade deficits accompanied by the large surpluses of several key U.S. trading partners – which were the focus of much discussion prior to the Great Recession. Blecker argues that, contrary to conventional explanations that emphasize increased budget deficits under President Bush, a low private saving rate, or a persistently overvalued U.S. dollar, these imbalances are best seen as the outgrowth of different national solutions to a common problem: the sluggish growth of working- and middle-class household incomes, and the corresponding drag on aggregate demand. Basically, the surplus countries relied on exports especially to the U.S. market, while the United States relied on debt and borrowing. Blecker argues that global imbalances were an important enabling factor in the growth of debt-financed consumption spending by U.S. households and thus contributed to the origins of the crisis. Moreover, despite their recent abatement, Blecker argues that global imbalances will reemerge during the postcrisis period, their size varying directly with the strength of the recovery. To this end, he discusses various policy measures that would redress future global imbalances without undermining economic growth.

The next four chapters focus specifically on policy lessons that can be learned from the experience of the financial crisis and Great Recession. Chapter 9, written by Gerald Epstein, argues that we have reached what he terms a "Kindleberger Moment," where, as Charles Kindleberger described in his *World In Depression, 1929–1939*, the government initially fails to act with sufficient force to expand fiscal policy and restrain the power of finance. This failure leads to such severe economic deterioration and political conflict that, even when governments know how they should act, they no longer have the political power to do so. The current revival of the "austerity buzzards" in the United Kingdom, Europe, and the United States and the inability to pass significant financial reform both presage the broader social forces that cripple the political ability to act in the United States and elsewhere.

Epstein argues that ending this paralysis requires bold new policy initiatives that effect systemic reform. His particular focus is on the restructuring of the financial sector, including monetary, financial, and regulatory policy. Epstein recommends the deployment of a broader array of credit tools to direct credit to productive and transformational end uses, and greater public involvement in financial institutions designed to create "finance without financiers." He argues that the Federal Reserve should support fiscal expansion and public financial institutions should fund key investment projects. These policies are more direct than using incentives on the credit-supply side to promote investment and employment. Direct policies are likely to be more effective in the current environment, since the lack of aggregate demand and the high risks associated with borrowing would likely limit the effectiveness of more traditional incentives to expand credit.

In Chapter 10, Dean Baker changes the focus from monetary and financial policy to fiscal policy. He critically investigates the rationale for deficit reduction as a growth strategy, and discusses the reasons why deficit reduction may not be a successful mechanism for increasing investment and net exports (the "investment" components of GDP). Baker then examines the path of the deficit, investment, and net exports under the Clinton and Bush administrations. Despite the very large shift from deficits to surpluses during the Clinton years, and from surpluses back to deficits under the Bush administration, Baker shows that the federal fiscal gyrations during the 1990s and 2000s had little meaningful impact on the investment components of GDP. The chapter ends by outlining an alternative, growth-oriented fiscal policy that focuses on public investment designed to promote productivity growth. In sharp contrast to the dominant political positions on fiscal policy that emerged in 2010 and 2011, Baker argues that a substantial commitment to public investment, financed by deficits, is far more likely to succeed in promoting growth than balancing budgets or running surpluses in the vain pursuit of private investment and net export promotion.

Barry Cynamon and Steven Fazzari continue the discussion of fiscal policy in Chapter 11 and argue that expansionary fiscal policy is a critical part of the policy mix needed in the United States going forward, again in sharp contrast to views that dominate current political discussion. The chapter takes on widely shared concerns that further fiscal expansion is undesirable, even infeasible, because of the size of federal government debt and deficits. For example, worries that fiscal deficits raise interest rates and "crowd out" capital investment are shown to be misplaced when an economy has under-utilized resources. In addition, the authors assess the size of payments to bondholders, domestic and foreign, that would arise from an aggressive fiscal policy, concluding that the costs to taxpayers and the "burden of deficits on our children and grandchildren" are often fundamentally misunderstood and exaggerated in political commentary that labels the U.S. fiscal circumstances in 2011 as "unsustainable" without really defining what the term means. The chapter concludes with a discussion of how fiscal policy, through both public spending and the tax system, can contribute to a robust and sustainable economic recovery.

In Chapter 12, Pavlina Tcherneva turns the discussion away from the instruments of macroeconomic policy and toward its ultimate objectives and, in particular, the traditional Keynesian goal of full employment. Tcherneva argues that the structure of the economy often renders "pump-priming" exercises largely ineffective as a means for achieving and maintaining full employment, and that fiscal policy must instead be wedded to direct job creation that targets not only general unemployment, but also particularly distressed industries and regions. In other words, policy makers cannot rely on market forces alone to allocate a general aggregate demand stimulus; they must instead strive to design and implement large-scale, permanent public-sector projects to address both the needs of the unemployed and those of society as a whole. The chapter assesses the merits of direct job creation in relation to more conventional macroeconomic policies designed to stimulate employment, and rebuts some of the more common objections to greater public sector involvement in the allocation (as well as aggregate utilization) of labor resources.

The volume is brought to a close by Barry Cynamon, Steven Fazzari, and Mark Setterfield with Chapter 13 that summarizes and integrates the ideas collected in the volume, and develops their implications for the future course of the U.S. economy. This concluding chapter focuses in particular on policy recommendations and on the importance of "getting policy right" if we are to successfully escape the lingering grip of the Great Recession. It reflects the general awareness evident in each of the preceding contributions to the volume that although the challenges facing the U.S. economy are formidable, a Keynesian perspective on the economy rooted in the importance of demand, uncertainty, and finance can help us understand the causes of the Great Recession, where we now stand, and what needs to happen next if we are to restore the economy to a path of sustainable growth and shared prosperity.

References

Blanchard, O. (2009) "The state of macro," *Annual Review of Economics*, **1**, 209–228.

Crotty, J. R. (1994) "Are Keynesian uncertainty and macrotheory compatible? Conventional decision making, institutional structures, and conditional stability in Keynesian macromodels," in G. Dymski and R. Pollin, eds., *New Perspectives in Monetary Macroeconomics: Explorations in the Tradition of Hyman Minsky*. Ann Arbor: University of Michigan Press, 105–142.

Davidson, P. (2007) *John Maynard Keynes*, New York: Palgrave Macmillan.

Fazzari, S. M. (1994–95) "Why doubt the effectiveness of Keynesian fiscal policy?" *Journal of Post Keynesian Economics*, Winter, **17** (2), 231–248.

Fazzari, S. M., P. Ferri, and E. Greenberg. (1998) "Aggregate demand and micro behavior: a new perspective on Keynesian macroeconomics," *Journal of Post Keynesian Economics*, **20** (4), 527–558.

Fazzari, S. M., P. Ferri, and E. Greenberg. (2010) "Investment and the Taylor rule in a dynamic Keynesian model," *Journal of Economic Dynamics and Control*, **34** (10), 2010–2022.

Feldstein, M. S. (2010) "U.S. growth in the decade ahead," National Bureau of Economic Research (NBER) Working Paper 15685.

Galí, J. and L. Gambetti. (2009) "On the sources of the Great Moderation." *American Economic Journal: Macroeconomics*, **1** (1), 26–57.

Godley, W. and Izurieta, A. (2002) "The case for a severe recession," *Challenge*, **45** (March/April), 27–51.

Mulligan, C. (2008) "An economy you can bank on," *New York Times*. Available at: http://www.nytimes.com/2008/10/10/opinion/10mulligan.html.

Ohanian, L. E. (2010) "The economic crisis from a neoclassical perspective," *Journal of Economic Perspectives*, **24**, 45–66.

Palacio-Vera, A. (2010) "The 'new consensus' and the post-Keynesian approach to the analysis of liquidity traps," *Eastern Economic Journal*, **36**, 198–216.

Palley, T. I. (2002) "Economic contradictions coming home to roost? Does the US economy face a long-term aggregate demand generation problem?" *Journal of Post Keynesian Economics*, **25**, 9–32.

Palley, T. I. (2008) "Keynesian Models of Deflation and Depression Revisited," *Journal of Economic Behavior and Organization*, **68** (1), 167–77.

Phelps, E. S. (2010) "The slump, the recovery, and the 'new normal,'" *Capitalism and Society*, **5** (2), Article 2.

Setterfield, M. (2008–09) "Balancing the macroeconomic books on the backs of workers: A simple analytical political economy model of contemporary US capitalism," *International Journal of Political Economy*, **37** (4), 104.

Woodford, M. (2009) "Convergence in macroeconomics: Elements of the new synthesis," *American Economic Journal: Macroeconomics*, **1**, 267–279.

Wray, L. R. (2007) "Lessons from the subprime meltdown," Working Paper No. 522, The Levy Economics Institute.

TWO

America's Exhausted Paradigm

Macroeconomic Causes of the Financial Crisis and Great Recession

Thomas I. Palley

The Great Recession and the financial crisis that triggered it are widely recognized as being tied to the bursting of the house price bubble and the debts accumulated in financing that bubble.[1] Most commentary has therefore focused on market failure in the housing and credit markets. However, what if the house price bubble developed because the economy needed a bubble to ensure continued growth? In that case, the real cause of the crisis would be the economy's underlying macroeconomic structure. Although instability in housing finance was undoubtedly central to dynamics of the Great Recession (as discussed in detail elsewhere in this volume), a singular focus on the microeconomics of market failure in the housing and credit markets would miss other important aspects of the crisis that are critical to not only our understanding of what has happened, but also the development of an effective policy design going forward.[2]

Despite the relevance of macroeconomic factors for explaining the financial crisis, there is resistance to such an explanation. In part, this is because such factors operate indirectly and gradually, whereas microeconomic explanations that emphasize regulatory failure and flawed incentives within financial markets operate directly. Regulatory and incentive failures are specific, easy to understand, and offer a concrete "fix it" agenda that appeals to politicians who want to show they are doing something. They also tend to be associated with tales of villainy (such as Bernie Madoff's massive Ponzi scheme or the bonus scandals at AIG and Merrill Lynch) that attract media

---

[1] An earlier version of this paper was originally released in July 2009 by the New America Foundation's Economic Growth Program, whose permission to use it is gratefully acknowledged. An abbreviated version of the paper was published in *Empirica*, 38 (1), 2011.

[2] Financial instability and its role in the Great Recession are discussed extensively in other chapters in this volume. See in particular Chapters 3, 4, and 5 by Wray, Kregel, and Crotty respectively.

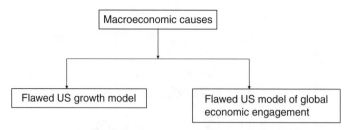

Figure 2.1. Macroeconomic causes of the economic crisis.

interest and are easily understood by the general public. Finally, and perhaps most important, a microeconomic focus does not challenge the larger structure of economic arrangements, whereas a macroeconomic focus invites controversy by placing these matters squarely on the table.

However, an economic crisis of the current magnitude does not occur without macroeconomic forces. That means the macroeconomic arrangements that have governed the U.S. economy for the past twenty-five years are critical for explaining the crisis. As illustrated in Figure 2.1, two factors in particular have been important. The first concerns the U.S. economic growth model and its impact on the pattern of income distribution and demand generation (see Setterfield's related discussion in Chapter 7 in this volume). The second concerns the U.S. model of global economic engagement and its impact on the structure of U.S. economic relations within the global economy (a theme also addressed in Chapter 8 by Blecker).

The macroeconomic forces unleashed by these twin factors have accumulated gradually and made for an increasingly fragile and unstable macroeconomic environment. The brewing instability over the past two decades has been visible in successive asset bubbles, rising indebtedness, rising trade deficits, and business cycles marked by initial weakness (so-called jobless recovery) followed by febrile booms. However, investors, policy makers, and economists chose to ignore these danger signs, and resolutely refused to examine the flawed macroeconomic arrangements that led to the cliff's edge. The challenge now, which is discussed briefly at the end of this chapter, is to design a new macroeconomic architecture that delivers shared prosperity without financial instability.

1. The Flawed U.S. Growth Model

Economic crises should be understood as a combination of proximate and ultimate factors. The proximate factors represent the triggering events, whereas the ultimate factors represent the deep causes. The meltdown of the subprime mortgage market in August 2007 triggered the current crisis, which was amplified by policy failures such as the decision to allow the collapse of Lehman Brothers. However, a crisis of the magnitude now being experienced requires a facilitating macroeconomic environment. That macroeconomic environment has been a long time in the making and can be traced back to the election of Ronald Reagan in 1980 that symbolized the inauguration of the era of neoliberal economics.

The Post–1980 Neoliberal Growth Model

The impact of the neoliberal economic growth model is apparent in the changed character of the U.S. business cycle (Palley, 2005). Before 1980, economic policy was designed to achieve full employment, and the economy was characterized by a system in which wages grew with productivity. This configuration created a virtuous circle of growth. Rising wages meant robust aggregate demand, which contributed to full employment. Full employment in turn provided an incentive to invest, which raised productivity, thereby supporting higher wages. Setterfield (Chapter 7 in this volume) explores this process in detail.

After 1980, with the advent of the new growth model, the commitment to full employment was abandoned as inflationary, with the result that the link between productivity growth and wages was severed.[3] In place of wage growth, borrowing and asset price inflation became the new engine of demand growth. Adherents of the neoliberal orthodoxy made controlling inflation their primary policy concern and set about attacking unions, the minimum wage, and other worker protections. Meanwhile, globalization brought increased foreign competition from lower-wage economies and the prospect of offshoring employment, as also discussed in Chapter 8 by Blecker.

The new neoliberal model was justified by an appeal to neoclassical economics and its claims that unfettered markets automatically generate full employment, wages are equal to labor's contribution to the value of production, and money is neutral. Yet in reality, economic growth came to rely on financial booms and cheap imports. Financial booms provided consumers and firms with collateral to support debt-financed spending.

---

[3] The change in policy is evident in changed language. After 1980 the term "full employment" gradually disappeared from the lexicon of economic policy and was replaced by the "natural rate of unemployment" (see Palley, 2007).

Borrowing was also sustained by financial innovation and deregulation that ensured a flow of new financial products, allowing increased leverage and widening the range of assets that could be collateralized (see Chapter 3 by Wray). Meanwhile, cheap imports ameliorated the impact of wage stagnation, thereby maintaining political support for the model. Additionally, rising wealth and income inequality make high-end consumption a larger and more important source of the demand necessary to support employment and growth, leading to the development of what Ajay Kapur, a former global strategist for Citigroup, termed a "plutonomy."

These features have been visible in every U.S. business cycle since 1980, and the business cycles under presidents Reagan, Bush *père*, Clinton, and Bush *fils* have robust commonalities that reveal their shared economic paradigm. Those features include asset price inflation (equities and housing), widening income inequality, detachment of worker wages from productivity growth, rising household and corporate leverage ratios measured respectively as debt/income and debt/equity ratios, a strong dollar, trade deficits, disinflation or low inflation, and manufacturing job loss.

The changes brought about by the post–1980 economic paradigm are especially evident in manufacturing employment (see Tables 2.1 and 2.2). Before 1980, manufacturing employment rose in expansions and fell in recessions, and each expansion tended to push manufacturing employment above its previous peak.[4] After 1980, the pattern changed abruptly. In the first two business cycles (between July 1980 and July 1990) manufacturing employment rose in the expansions but did not recover its previous peak. In the two most recent business cycles (between March 1991 and December 2007), manufacturing employment not only failed to recover its previous peak, but actually fell over the entirety of the expansions.[5]

---

[4]   The 1950s are an exception because of the Korean War (June 1950–July 1953), which ratcheted up manufacturing employment and distorted manufacturing employment patterns.

[5]   Defenders of the neoliberal paradigm argue that manufacturing has prospered and the decline in manufacturing employment reflects healthy productivity trends. As evidence, they argue that real manufacturing output has increased and remained fairly steady as a share of real GDP. This reflects the fact that manufacturing prices have fallen faster than other prices. However, this is due in part to hedonic "quality adjustment" statistical procedures that count improved information technology embodied in manufactured goods as increased manufacturing output. It is also because of increased use of cheap imported components that are not subject to the same hedonic statistical adjustments. As a result, the real cost of imported inputs is understated, with the effect of making it look as if real manufacturing output is higher. The stark reality is that the nominal value of manufacturing output has fallen dramatically as a share of nominal GDP. The United States has also become more dependent on imported manufactured goods, with imported manufactured goods making up a significantly increased share of total manufactured goods purchased.

Table 2.1. *Manufacturing employment by business cycle,*
October 1945–January 1980

Trough	Employment (Millions)	Peak	Employment (Millions)	Change (Millions)
Oct. 1945	12.5	Nov. 1948	14.3	1.8
Oct. 1949	12.9	July 1953	16.4	3.5
May 1954	15.0	Aug. 1957	15.9	0.9
Apr. 1958	14.5	Apr. 1960	15.7	1.2
Feb. 1961	14.8	Dec. 1969	18.6	3.8
Nov. 1970	17.0	Nov. 1973	18.8	1.8
Mar. 1975	16.9	Jan. 1980	19.3	2.4

Source: National Bureau of Economic Research, Bureau of Labor Statistics, and author's calculations.

Table 2.2. *Manufacturing employment by business cycle, July 1980–December 2007*

Trough	Employment (Millions)	Peak	Employment (Millions)	Change (Millions)
July 1980	18.3	July 1981	18.8	0.5
Nov. 1982	16.7	July 1990	17.7	1.0
Mar. 1991	17.1	Mar. 2001	16.9	−0.2
Nov. 2001	15.8	Dec. 2007	13.8	−2.0

Source: National Bureau of Economic Research, Bureau of Labor Statistics, and author's calculations.

This dramatic change in the pattern of real economic activity was accompanied by change in policy makers' attitudes, most clearly illustrated by the changed attitude toward the trade deficit. Under the earlier economic model, policy makers viewed trade deficits as cause for concern because they represented a leakage of aggregate demand that undermined the virtuous circle of growth. However, under the new model, trade deficits came to be viewed as semi-virtuous because they helped to control inflation by increasing supply and competition. Trade deficits also reflect the choices of consumers and businesses in the marketplace, and according to neoliberal economic theory, those choices represent the self-interest of economic

Moreover, U.S. purchases of manufactured goods have risen as a share of total U.S. demand, indicating that the failure lies in U.S. production of manufactured goods that has lost out to imports. See Bivens (2004).

Table 2.3. *Hourly wage and productivity growth,*
1967–2006 (2007 dollars)

Period	Productivity growth	Hourly wage growth	Productivity – wage gap
1967–73	2.5%	2.9%	–0.4
1973–79	1.2	–0.1	1.3
1979–89	1.4	0.4	1.0
1989–2000	1.9	0.9	1.0
2000–06	2.6	–0.1	2.7

Source: Lawrence Michel, Jared Bernstein, and Heidi Shierholz, *The State of Working America 2008/2009* (Ithaca, NY: ILR Press, 2009).

Table 2.4. *Distribution of family income by household income rank,*
1947–2006

Year	Bottom 40%	Next 40%	Next 15%	Top 5%
1947	16.9%	40.1%	25.5%	17.5%
1973	17.4	41.5	25.6	15.5
1979	17.0	41.6	26.1	15.3
1989	15.2	40.2	26.7	17.9
2000	14.1	38.1	26.6	21.1
2006	13.5	38.0	27.0	21.5

Source: Lawrence Michel, Jared Bernstein, and Heidi Shierholz, *The State of Working America 2008/2009* (Ithaca, NY: ILR Press, 2009).

agents, the pursuit of which is good for the economy. As a result, the trade deficit grew steadily from virtually zero prior to 1980 to nearly 6 percent of GDP prior to the Great Recession in 2007, hitting new peaks as a share of GDP in each business cycle after 1980.

The effect of the changed growth model is also evident in the detachment of wages from productivity growth, as shown in Table 2.3 (also see Setterfield, Chapter 7 in this volume). It is also evident in rising income inequality, as shown in Table 2.4. Between 1979 and 2006, the income share of the bottom 40 percent of U.S. households decreased significantly, whereas the income share of the top 20 percent increased dramatically. Moreover, a disproportionate part of that increase went to the 5 percent of families at the very top of income distribution rankings, and the top 1 percent gained even more.

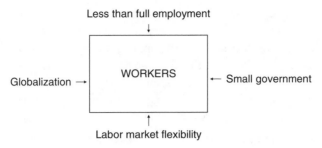

Figure 2.2. The neoliberal policy box.

The Role of Economic Policy

Economic policy played a critical role in generating and shaping the new neoliberal growth model, and the effects of that policy boxed in workers.[6] The new model can be described in terms of a neoliberal policy box (see Figure 2.2), the four sides of which are globalization, small government, labor market flexibility, and retreat from full employment. Workers are pressured on all four sides, and these pressures lead to the severing of the wage/productivity growth link.[7]

Globalization, in part spurred by policies encouraging free trade and capital mobility, means that U.S. workers are increasingly competing with lower-paid foreign workers. That pressure is further increased by the fact that foreign workers are themselves under pressure owing to the so-called Washington Consensus development policy, sponsored by the International Monetary Fund (IMF) and the World Bank, which forces them into the same neoliberal box as American workers. Thus, not only do neoliberal policies undermine demand in advanced countries, they also put pressure on demand in developing countries by promoting policies that squeeze workers there, too. This is clearly evident in China, which has been marked by rising income inequality and a sharp decline in the consumption to GDP

---

[6] Palley (1998) analyzes in detail how economic policy has impacted income distribution, unemployment, and growth. The metaphor of a box is attributable to Ron Blackwell of the AFL-CIO.

[7] There is a deeper political economy behind the neoliberal box that has been termed "financialization" (Epstein, 2001; Palley, 2008). The policy agenda embedded in the box is driven by financial markets and corporations that are now joined at the hip, with corporations pursuing a narrow financial agenda aimed at benefiting top management and financial elites.

ratio.[8] The net result of global implementation of neoliberal orthodoxy is the promotion of deflationary global economic conditions. That is because neoliberal globalization increases global supply but suppresses global demand. The underlying assumption is that demand generation is largely "automatic," at least over a horizon of a few years, and therefore, demand will always be sufficient to absorb supply – a problematic theoretical perspective addressed in Chapter 1 of this volume by Cynamon, Fazzari, and Setterfield.

Small Government policies undermine the legitimacy of government and push privatization, deregulation, and light-touch regulation. Although couched in terms of liberating the economy from detrimental governmental interference, "small government" policies have resulted in the erosion of popular economic rights and protections. This is exemplified by the 1996 reform of U.S. welfare rights that stripped workers of the right to a minimal level of support in the event of destitution. Moreover, the government's administrative capacity and ability to provide services have been seriously eroded, with many government functions outsourced to the private sector. This has led to the creation of what Galbraith (2008) terms the "predator state," in which corporations enrich themselves on government contracts, whereas the outsourced workers employed by these corporations confront worsened work conditions.

Labor Market Flexibility involves attacking unions, the minimum wage, unemployment benefits, employment protections, and employee rights. This is justified in the name of creating labor market flexibility, including downward wage flexibility, which – according to neoliberal economic theory – is supposed to generate full employment. Instead, it has led to wage stagnation and widening income inequality.

Abandonment of Full Employment means the Federal Reserve emphasizes the importance of keeping inflation low as opposed to maintaining full employment. This switch was promoted by economists' adoption of Friedman's (1968) notion of a natural rate of unemployment.[9] The theoretical claim is that monetary policy cannot affect long-run equilibrium employment and unemployment, so it should instead aim for a low and stable inflation rate. In recent years, that argument has been used to push the adoption of formal inflation targets. However, the key real-world effect of natural rate theory has been to provide the Federal Reserve and policy

---

[8]   International Monetary Fund (2006).
[9]   The natural rate of unemployment is also referred to as the NAIRU or non-accelerating inflation rate of unemployment.

makers with political cover for higher actual unemployment, which has undermined workers' bargaining power (Palley, 2007).

Moreover, this natural rate logic is now being invoked to explain and justify permanently higher unemployment after the Great Recession. The reasoning is the financial crisis and Great Recession constitute a structural shock that has (allegedly) raised the natural rate of unemployment, because, for example, worker skills in the previously booming home construction industry cannot be easily transferred to other activities.

The Neoliberal Bubble Economy

The implementation of neoliberal economic policies destroyed the stable virtuous circle growth model based on full employment and wages tied to productivity growth, replacing it with the current growth model based on rising indebtedness and asset price inflation. Since 1980, each U.S. business cycle has seen successively higher debt/income ratios at the end of expansions, and the economy has become increasingly dependent on asset price inflation to spur the growth of aggregate demand.

Compared to the period 1960–81, the period 1981–2007 saw enormous increases in the debt/GDP ratios of both the household and nonfinancial corporate sectors. This issue is discussed in greater detail in Chapter 6 of this volume by Cynamon and Fazzari. In addition, as shown in Table 2.5, debt service, measured by the Federal Reserve's Financial Obligations Ratio increased from 10.9 percent of disposable income in 1980 to 14.3 percent in 2007. That this ratio trended upward despite declining nominal interest rates is evidence of the massively increased reliance on debt by households.

Table 2.6 shows the pattern of house price inflation over the past twenty years.[10] This table is revealing in two ways. First, it shows the extraordinary scale of the 2001–06 house price bubble. Second, it reveals the systemic role of house price inflation in driving economic expansions. Over the last twenty years, the economy has tended to expand when house price inflation has exceeded CPI (consumer price index) inflation. This was true for the last three years of the Reagan expansion. It was true for the Clinton expansion. And it was also true for the G. W. Bush expansion. The one period of sustained house price stagnation was 1990–95, which was a period of recession and extended jobless recovery. This is indicative of the significance of asset price inflation in driving demand under the neoliberal model.

---

[10] S&P/Case-Shiller index data is only available from 1987.

Table 2.5. *Household debt service and financial obligations as percent of disposable income (DSR) by business cycle peaks, 1981–2007*

Year	1980.q3	1991.q3	2001.q4	2007.q4
DSR	10.9%	12.0%	13.4%	14.3%

Source: Federal Reserve Board.

Table 2.6. *CPI inflation and house price inflation based on the S&P/Case-Shiller National Home Price Values Index*

Period	1987.q1– 1990.q1	1990.q1– 1995.q1	1995.q1– 2001.q1	2001.q1– 2006.q1
House price inflation (%)	6.7	0.6	5.7	10.9
Average CPI inflation (%)	4.5	3.5	2.5	2.5
Excess house inflation (%)	2.2	-2.9	3.2	8.4

Along with rising debt ratios, households progressively cut back on their saving rates, as shown in Table 2.7. Figure 6.1 in this volume shows the substantial rise in consumption relative to disposable income during the neoliberal period, which is the complement of a falling saving rate. Lower saving provides another source of demand growth, but one that is ultimately unsustainable as saving rates get close to zero.

Lastly, the disinflation produced by the Federal Reserve's monetary policy created space for lower nominal interest rates and this, too, was critical for the new paradigm. That is because in recessions and financial upheavals, U.S. economic policy makers were quickly able to restore growth by lowering interest rates and opening the spigot of credit. This pattern is captured in Table 2.8, which shows three long cycles governing the Federal Reserve's federal funds interest rate over the period 1981–2010.

Beginning in 1981, the Federal Reserve had enormous latitude to lower interest rates during recessions, whereas rates were raised during recoveries (but without restoring their previous peaks). It was this asymmetric process that lay behind the so-called Great Moderation and the perceived success of monetary policy. However, the reality was that the Federal Reserve was consuming the disinflation dividend. That could not last forever and, during the Great Recession, the process of interest rate reduction has come to

Table 2.7. *Personal saving rate (PSR)*

Period	1960	1969	1973	1980	1981	1991	2001	2007
PSR (%)	7.3	7.8	10.5	10.0	10.9	7.3	1.8	0.6

Source: Economic Report of the President, table B.30 (2009).

Table 2.8. *Brief history of the federal funds interest rate, June 1981–January 2010*

	High (%)	Low (%)
June 1981	19.10	
December 1992		2.92
November 2001	6.51	
May 2004		1.00
July 2007	5.26	
January 2010		0.10

Source: Board of Governors of the Federal Reserve.

an end because the Fed's nominal policy interest rate has reached its zero lower bound.

In sum, although justified in terms of market efficiency, the reality of the neoliberal growth model is that it redirects income from lower- and middle-income households to corporate profits and upper-income households. Asset prices are bid up by a host of measures, including higher profits, savings by the super-rich (the top 1% of the income distribution) that are directed to asset purchases, borrowing to buy assets, and institutional changes such as the shift from traditional defined benefit pension plans to defined contribution pension plans. Consumption is maintained by lower household saving rates, by borrowing that is collateralized by higher asset prices, and by the introduction of new sources of consumer credit (see Cynamon and Fazzari , Chapter 6 in this volume). The reduction in saving rates is partly a response to squeezed incomes and partly rationalized on the grounds that households are wealthier because of higher asset prices (including house prices).

The problem with the model is that it is unsustainable. Maintaining the growth of consumption spending requires continued excessive borrowing and continued reduction in saving rates. Continued excessive borrowing requires ever increasing asset prices and debt/income ratios: hence, the systemic need for bubbles (which eventually burst). Meanwhile, when the saving rate hits zero, little further reduction is possible. Consequently, both drivers of demand eventually exhaust themselves.

The current financial crisis is different and deeper from earlier crises in two ways. First, the impact of earlier burst bubbles – such as the 2001 stock market and dot-com bubbles – was contained because their debt footprint was not that deep. Although financial wealth was destroyed and economic activity was temporarily restrained, the financial system remained intact. However, the housing bubble of 2001–07 was debt financed and massive in size, and its bursting pulled down the entire financial system. Moreover, since housing wealth is such a large component of household wealth, the collapse in house prices devastated household wealth in a way that the stock market and dot-com bubbles did not. That has had an enormous negative wealth effect on consumption spending that was absent in the 2001 stock market bust (Baker's Chapter 10 in this volume emphasizes similar forces).

Second, the drivers of aggregate demand are now exhausted because of the scale of debt accumulation and the way that the saving rate has been run down. In earlier crises, households still had unused borrowing capacity they could call on and room to further reduce their saving. Both of those channels are now exhausted, making recovery a much more difficult task. Indeed, if households try to rebuild their financial worth, the saving rate will rise in a sustained way for the first time since the dawn of the neoliberal era, which will weaken demand and further prolong stagnation.

The economic growth model adopted after 1980 lasted far longer than might have been expected because of our capacity to expand access to debt and increase leverage. That is the real significance of deregulation and financial innovation. However, delaying the day of reckoning also made the financial crisis more severe when it eventually arrived. When the subprime detonator tripped, the economy's financial structure – twenty-five years in the making and integrally linked to the economic logic of the neoliberal growth model – proved to be extremely fragile.

2. The Flawed Model of Global Economic Engagement

Although prone to instability (i.e., to boom and bust), the neoliberal growth model might have operated successfully for quite a while longer were it not for a U.S. economic policy that created a flawed engagement with the global economy. This flawed engagement undermined the economy in two ways. First, it accelerated the erosion of household incomes. Second, it accelerated the accumulation of unproductive debt – that is, debt that generates economic activity elsewhere rather than in the United States.

The most visible manifestation of this flawed engagement is the goods trade deficit, which hit a record 6.4 percent of GDP in 2006. This deficit was the inevitable product of the structure of global economic engagement put in place over the past two decades, with the most critical elements being implemented by the Clinton administration under the guidance of Treasury Secretaries Robert Rubin and Lawrence Summers. That eight-year period saw the implementation of the North American Free Trade Agreement (NAFTA), the adoption (after the East Asian financial crisis of 1997) of the "strong dollar" policy, and the establishment of permanent normal trade relations (PNTR) with China in 2000.

These measures cemented the model of globalization that had been lobbied for by corporations and their Washington think-tank allies. The irony is that giving corporations what they wanted undermined the neoliberal model, and with it the favorable conditions for doing business, by exposing the model's contradictions. The model would likely have eventually slumped because of its own internal dynamic, but the policy triumph of corporate globalization accelerated this process and transformed it into a financial crash.

The Triple Hemorrhage

Flawed global economic engagement created a "triple hemorrhage" within the U.S. economy. The first economic hemorrhage, long emphasized by Keynesian economists, was leakage out of the economy from spending on imports. Household income and borrowing was significantly spent on imports, creating incomes offshore rather than in the United States. Consequently, borrowing left behind a debt footprint but did not create sustainable jobs and incomes at home.

The second hemorrhage was the leakage of jobs from the U.S. economy as a result of offshore outsourcing. Such activities directly reduced the number of higher-paying manufacturing jobs, cutting into household income. Moreover, even when jobs did not move offshore, the threat of offshoring could be used to secure lower wages, thereby dampening wage growth and helping sever wages from productivity growth (Bronfenbrenner, 2000; Bronfenbrenner and Luce, 2004).

The third hemorrhage concerned new investment. Not only were corporations incentivized by low foreign wages, foreign subsidies, and undervalued exchange rates to close existing plants and shift their production offshore, they were also incentivized to shift new investment offshore. That did double damage. First, it reduced domestic investment spending, hurting the U.S. capital goods-producing sector and employment therein. Second, it stripped the U.S. economy of modern industrial capacity, disadvantaging U.S. competitiveness and reducing employment that would have been generated to operate that capacity.

A further unanticipated economic leakage from the flawed model of global engagement concerns energy prices. Offshoring of U.S. manufacturing capacity has often involved the closing of relatively energy-efficient and environmentally cleaner production and its replacement with less efficient and dirtier foreign production that then must also be shipped halfway around the globe. These developments added to energy demand and contributed to the 2005–08 increase in oil prices, which added to the U.S. trade deficit and effectively imposed a huge tax (paid to OPEC) on U.S. consumers. Additionally, 2008 saw a bubble in oil prices as speculative excess migrated from financial markets to commodity markets (Palley, 2008).

The flawed model of global economic engagement broke with the old model of international trade in two ways. First, instead of having roughly balanced trade, the United States ran persistent, large trade deficits. Second, instead of aiming to create a global marketplace in which U.S. companies could sell their products, the purpose of the new model was to create a global production zone in which U.S. companies could produce offshore and from which they obtained inputs. In other words, the main purpose of international economic engagement was not to increase U.S. exports, but rather to substitute cheaper imported inputs for U.S. domestic production and to facilitate American-owned production platforms in developing countries that could export to the United States.

As a result, at the bidding of corporate interests, the United States joined itself at the hip to the global economy, opening its borders to an inflow of goods and threatening its manufacturing base. This was done without safeguards to address the problems of exchange rate misalignment and systemic trade deficits, or the mercantilist policies of trading partners such as China.

NAFTA

The creation of the new system of global engagement took off in 1989 with the implementation of the Canada-U.S. Free Trade Agreement that established an integrated production zone between the two countries. The 1994 implementation of NAFTA (North American Free Trade Agreement) was the decisive next step. First, it fused Canada, the United States, and Mexico

Table 2.9. *U.S. goods trade balance with Mexico before and after NAFTA*
($ billions)

1991	1992	1993	1994	1995	1996	2000	2005	2007
2.1	5.4	1.7	1.3	−15.8	−17.5	−24.5	−49.7	−74.6

Source: U.S. Census Bureau.

into a unified North American production zone. Second, and more impor-tantly, it joined developed and developing economies, thereby establishing the template U.S. corporations wanted.

NAFTA also dramatically changed the significance of exchange rates. Before, exchange rates mattered for trade and the exchange of goods. Now, they mattered for the location of production. That in turn changed the attitude of large U.S. multinational corporations (MNCs) toward the dollar. When U.S. companies produced domestically and looked to export, a weaker dollar was in their commercial interest, and they lobbied against dollar overvalua-tion. However, under the new model, U.S. corporations looked to produce offshore and import into the United States. This reversed their commercial interest, making them proponents of a strong dollar. That is because a strong dollar reduces the dollar costs of foreign production, raising the profit mar-gins on foreign-produced goods sold in the United States at U.S. prices.

NAFTA soon highlighted this new dynamic because Mexico was hit by a financial crisis in January 1994, immediately after the implementation of the free trade agreement. To U.S. corporations, which had invested in Mexico and planned to invest more, the peso's collapse *vis-a-vis* the dollar was a boon, making it even more profitable to produce in Mexico and reex-port to the United States. With corporate interests driving U.S. economic policy, the peso devaluation problem went unattended – and as a result, it also created a critical precedent.

The effects of NAFTA and the peso devaluation were immediately felt in the U.S. manufacturing sector in the form of job loss, the diversion of investment, firms using the threat of relocation to suppress wages, and an explosion in the goods trade deficit with Mexico. As shown in Table 2.9, the United States was running a modest goods trade surplus with Mexico prior to the implementation of NAFTA. Immediately afterward the balance turned negative, reaching a deficit of $74.6 billion by 2007.

These events helped contribute to the jobless recovery of 1993–96, although the economy was eventually able to overcome its sluggishness with the emergence of the stock market bubble in 1996, the emergence of the Internet investment boom that morphed into the dot-com bubble, and the tentative beginnings of the house price bubble (which can be traced back to 1997). Together, these developments spurred a consumption and investment boom that masked the adverse structural effects of NAFTA.

The Response to the East Asian Financial Crisis

The next fateful step in the flawed model of global engagement came with the East Asian financial crisis of 1997, which was followed by a series of rolling financial crises in Russia (1998), Brazil (1999 and 2000), Turkey (2000), and Argentina (2001–02). In response to these crises, Treasury Secretaries Rubin and Summers adopted the same policy that was used to deal with the 1994 peso crisis, thereby creating a new global system that replicated the pattern of economic integration established with Mexico.[11] Specifically, large dollar loans were made to the countries in crisis to stabilize their economies. At the same time, the collapse of their exchange rates and the appreciation of the dollar was accepted and institutionalized in the form of a "strong dollar" policy.[12] This increased the buying power of U.S. consumers, which was critical because the U.S. consumer was now the lynchpin of the global economy, becoming the buyer of first and last resort.[13]

The new global economic architecture involved developing countries exporting their production to the United States. Developing countries embraced this export-led growth solution to their development problem and were encouraged to do so by the IMF and the World Bank. For developing countries, the new system had a number of advantages, including: the ability to run trade surpluses that allowed them to build up foreign exchange holdings to defend against capital flight; providing demand for their output, which led to job creation; and providing access to U.S. markets that

---

[11] It cannot be overemphasized that the policies adopted by Treasury Secretaries Robert Rubin and Lawrence Summers reflected the dominant economic paradigm. As such, Rubin and Summers had the support of the majority of the U.S. political establishment, the IMF, the World Bank, Washington's premier think tanks, and economists.

[12] China had already gone this route with a large exchange rate devaluation in 1994. Indeed, there is reason to believe that the Chinese devaluation contributed to the East Asian financial crisis by putting other East Asian economies under undue competitive pressures and diverting foreign investment from them to China.

[13] The strong dollar policy was also politically popular, constituting a form of exchange rate populism. Boosting the value of the dollar increased the purchasing power of U.S. consumers at a time when their wages were under downward pressure because of the neoliberal model. Households were under pressure from globalization, yet at the same time they were being given incentives to embrace it. This is why neoliberalism has been so hard to tackle politically.

Table 2.10. *U.S. goods trade balance ($ billions)*

1995	1996	1997	1998	1999	2000
−174.2	−191.0	−198.4	−248.2	−347.8	−454.7

Source: U.S. Census Bureau.

Table 2.11. *U.S. goods trade balance with Pacific Rim countries ($ billions)*

1995	1996	1997	1998	1999	2000
−108.1	−101.8	−121.6	−160.4	−186.0	−215.4

Source: U.S. Census Bureau.

encouraged multinational corporations to redirect investment spending toward them. The latter was especially important as it transferred technology, created jobs, and built up developing country manufacturing capacity.

U.S. multinationals were also highly supportive of the new arrangement as they now gained global access to low-cost export production platforms. Not only did this mean access to cheap foreign labor, but the overvalued dollar lowered their foreign production costs, thereby further increasing profit margins. Large importers, like Wal-Mart, also supported this arrangement. Furthermore, many foreign governments offered subsidies as an incentive to attract foreign direct investment (FDI).

In effect, the pattern of incentives established by the response to the East Asian financial crisis encouraged U.S. corporations to persistently downsize their U.S. capacity and shift production offshore for import back to the United States. This created a dynamic for progressively eroding U.S. national industrial capacity, whereas foreign economies were encouraged to steadily expand their capacity and export their way out of economic difficulties.

As with NAFTA, the adverse effects of this policy were visible almost immediately. As shown in Table 2.10, the goods trade deficit took a further leap forward, surging from $198.4 billion in 1997 to $248.2 billion in 1998, and rising to $454.7 billion in 2000. In particular, as shown in Table 2.11, there was a surge in imports from Pacific Rim countries; the U.S. trade deficit with the Pacific Rim deteriorating from $108 billion in 1995 to $215 billion by 2000. Part of the surge in the trade deficit was owing to the boom conditions sparked by stock market euphoria, the dot-com bubble, and house price inflation, but the scale of the trade deficit surge also reflects the flawed character of U.S. engagement with the global economy. The proof of this last claim is that manufacturing employment started falling despite boom conditions in the U.S. economy. Having finally started to grow in 1996, manufacturing employment peaked in March 1998 and started declining three full years before the economy went into recession in March 2001. That explains why manufacturing job growth was negative over the entirety of the Clinton expansion, a first in U.S. business cycle history.

As with NAFTA, these adverse effects were once again obscured by positive business cycle conditions. Consequently, the Clinton administration dismissed concerns about the long-term dangers of manufacturing job loss. Instead, the official interpretation was that the U.S. economy was experiencing – in the words of senior Clinton economic policy advisers Alan Blinder and Janet Yellen – a "fabulous decade" significantly driven by policy.[14] According to the ideology of the decade, manufacturing was in secular decline and destined for the dustbin of history. The old manufacturing economy was to be replaced by a "new economy" driven by computers, the Internet, and information technology.

China and PNTR

Although disastrous for the long-run health of the U.S. economy, NAFTA-style corporate globalization plus the strong dollar policy was extremely profitable for corporations. Additionally, the ultimate costs to households were still obscured by the ability of the U.S. economy to generate cyclical booms based on asset price inflation and debt accumulation. That provided political space for a continued deepening of the global engagement model, the final step of which was to incorporate China as a full-fledged participant.

Thus, corporations now pushed for the establishment of permanent normal trading relations with China, which Congress enacted in 2000. That legislation in turn enabled China to join the World Trade Organization, which had been established in 1996.

---

[14] Blinder and Yellen (2001). To the extent there was concern in the Clinton administration about manufacturing, it was about the hardships for workers regarding job dislocations. Additionally, there was political concern that produced some sweet talk (i.e., invitations to policy consultations) aimed at placating trade unions. However, there was no concern that these outcomes were owing to flawed international economic policy. Not only did this policy failure contribute to eventual disastrous economic outcomes, it may well have cost Vice President Al Gore the 2000 presidential election. The Clinton administration's economic advisers may have downplayed the significance of manufacturing job loss but blue-collar voters in Ohio did not.

Table 2.12. *U.S. goods trade balance with China before and after PNTR*
($ billions)

1998	1999	2000	2001	2002	2003	2004	2005	2007
−56.9	−68.7	−83.9	−83.1	−103.1	−124.1	−161.9	−201.5	−256.2

Source: U.S. Census Bureau.

The significance of PNTR was not about trade, but rather about making China a full-fledged part of global production arrangements. China had enjoyed access to the U.S. market for years and its entry into the WTO did generate some further tariff reductions. However, the real significance was that China became a fully legitimate destination for foreign direct investment. That is because production from China was now guaranteed permanent access to the U.S. market, and corporations were also given internationally recognized protections of property and investor rights.

Once again, as shown in Table 2.12, the results were predictable and similar to the pattern established by NAFTA – although the scale was far larger. Aided by a strong dollar, the trade deficit with China increased dramatically after 2001, growing at a rate of 25 percent per annum and jumping from $83.1 billion in 2001 to $201.5 billion in 2005. Moreover, there was also massive inflow of foreign direct investment into China so that it became the world's largest recipient of FDI in 2002 – a stunning achievement for a developing country (*OECD Observer*, 2003). So strong was China's attractiveness as an FDI destination that it not only displaced production and investment in the United States, but also displaced production and investment in Mexico (Greider, 2001).

According to academic and Washington policy orthodoxy, the new global system was supposed to launch a new era of popular shared prosperity. Demand was to be provided by U.S. consumers. Their spending was to be financed by the "new economy" based on information technology and the globalization of manufacturing, which would drive higher productivity and income. Additionally, consumer spending could be financed by borrowing and asset price inflation, which was sustainable because higher asset prices were justified by increased productivity.

This new orthodoxy was enshrined in what was termed the "New Bretton Woods Hypothesis," according to which the global economy had entered a new golden age of global development, reminiscent of the postwar era.[15]

---

[15] See, for example, Dooley, Folkerts-Landau, and Garber (2003 and 2004b).

The United States would import from East Asian and other developing economies, provide FDI to those economies, and run large trade deficits that would provide the demand for the new supply. In return, developing countries would accumulate financial obligations against the United States, principally in the form of Treasury securities. This would provide them with foreign exchange reserves and collateral that was supposed to make investors feel secure. China was to epitomize the new arrangement.[16]

The reality is that the structure of U.S. international engagement, with its lack of attention to the trade deficit and manufacturing, contributed to a disastrous acceleration of the contradictions inherent in the neoliberal growth model. That model always had a problem regarding sustainable generation of demand because of wage stagnation and high income inequality. Flawed international economic engagement aggravated this problem by draining consumer spending, manufacturing jobs, and investment and industrial capacity: the triple hemorrhage. This in turn compelled even deeper reliance on the unsustainable stopgaps of borrowing and asset price inflation to compensate and accelerated the process that culminated in the Great Recession.

As for developing economies, they embraced the post-1997 international economic order. However, in so doing, they tied their fate to the U.S. economy, creating a situation in which the global economy was flying on one engine that was bound to fail. Consequently, far from creating a de-coupled global economy, it created a linked economy characterized by a concertina effect: when the U.S. economy crashed, other economies were significantly impacted (Palley, 2008).

3. America's Exhausted Macroeconomic Paradigm

The twin macroeconomic factors of an unstable growth model and a flawed model of global economic engagement were put in place during the 1980s and 1990s. However, their full adverse effects took time to build up, and the chickens only truly came home to roost in the 2001–07 expansion. From that standpoint, the Bush administration is not responsible for the financial crisis. Its economic policies represented a continuation of the policy paradigm already in place. The financial crisis therefore represents the exhaustion of that paradigm rather than being the result of specific policy failures on the part of the Bush administration.

---

[16] For a critique of the New Bretton Woods hypothesis that explains why it was unsustainable, see Palley (2006).

In a nutshell, the U.S. implemented a neoliberal growth model that relied on debt accumulation and asset price inflation. As the neoliberal model slowly cannibalized itself, the economy needed larger speculative bubbles to grow, culminating in the need for a huge bubble, the likes of which only housing could provide. However, when that bubble burst, it pulled down the entire economy.

In many regards, the neoliberal paradigm was already showing its limits in the 1990s. An extended jobless recovery marked the early stages of the 1990s business cycle, and the subsequent boom was accompanied by a stock market bubble and the beginnings of significant house price inflation. The recession of 2001 saw the bursting of the stock market and dot-com bubbles. However, although investment spending was hit hard, consumer spending was largely untouched, owing to continued household borrowing and continued moderate increases in home prices. Additionally, the financial system was largely unscathed because the stock market bubble involved limited reliance on debt financing.

Yet, despite the relative shallowness of the 2001 recession and aggressive monetary and fiscal stimulus, the economy languished in a second extended bout of jobless recovery. According to the National Bureau of Economic Research, the recession ended in November 2001, when employment was 130.9 million. Two years later (November 2003) total employment was 130.1 million, a decrease of 800,000 jobs. Over this period, manufacturing lost 1.5 million jobs, and total manufacturing employment fell from 15.83 million to 14.32 million. A critical factor was the trade deficit and offshoring of jobs resulting from the model of globalization that had been decisively implemented in the 1990s.

The failure to develop a robust recovery, combined with persistent fears that the economy was about to slip back into recession, prompted the Federal Reserve to lower interest rates. Beginning in November 2000, the Fed cut the federal funds rate significantly, lowering it from 6.50 percent to 2.10 percent in November 2001. However, the weakness of the recovery drove the Fed to cut the rate still further, pushing it to 1.00 percent in July 2003, where it was held until June 2004.

Ultimately, the Federal Reserve's low-interest-rate policy succeeded in jump-starting the economy by spurring a house price boom, which in turn sparked both a construction boom and consumption boom. The house price boom became a bubble that burst in the summer of 2007. However, what is important about this history is that the economy needed an asset-price bubble to restore full employment, just as it had needed the stock market and dot-com bubbles to restore full employment in the 1990s.

Given the underlying structural weakness of the demand-generation process, which had been further aggravated by flawed globalization, a bubble was the only way back to full employment. Higher asset prices were needed to provide collateral to support borrowing that could then finance spending.

A housing bubble was particularly economically effective for two reasons. First, home ownership is widespread, so the consumption wealth effects of the bubble were also widespread. Second, higher house prices stimulated domestic construction employment by raising prices above the cost of construction.

The Federal Reserve is now being blamed by many for the bubble,[17] but the reality is that it felt compelled to lower interest rates for fear of the economy falling back into recession. Additionally, inflation – which is the signaling mechanism the Federal Reserve relies on to assess whether monetary policy is too loose – showed no indication of excess demand in the economy. Indeed, all the indications were of profound economic weakness and demand shortage. Finally, when the Federal Reserve started raising the federal funds' interest rates in mid-2004, the long-term rate that influences mortgages changed little. In part, this may have been because of recycling of foreign country trade surpluses back to the United States, but a larger factor was likely bond market expectations of weak future economic conditions that kept the lid on long-term interest rates.

This reality is confirmed by a look back at the expansion of 2001–07 compared to other expansions. By almost all measures it ranks as the weakest business cycle since World War II. Table 2.13 shows "trough to peak" and "peak to peak" measures of GDP growth, consumption growth, investment spending growth, employment growth, manufacturing employment growth, profit growth, compensation growth, wage and salary growth, change in the unemployment rate, and change in the employment/population ratio of this business cycle relative to other postwar cycles. The 2001–07 cycle ranks worst in seven of the ten measures, and second worst in two measures. If the comparison is restricted to the four cycles lasting twenty-seven quarters or more, the 2001–07 cycle is worst in nine of ten measures, and best in one measure only – profit growth. This weak performance occurred despite a house price and credit bubble of historic proportions. That is the clearest evidence possible of the structural weakness of the U.S. macroeconomic model and why a bubble was needed to sustain growth.

[17] See, for example, Taylor (2009).

Table 2.13. *Rank of last business cycle relative to cycles since World War II*
(1 = best; 10 = worst)

	Expansion only (1 = best, 10 = worst)	Full cycles (1 = best, 10 = worst)	Full cycles (1 = best, 4 = worst)
	All	All	Cycles lasting more than 27 quarters
Number of cycles	10	10	4
Rank of 2001–07 cycle			
GDP growth	10	8	4
Consumption growth	9	9	4
Investment growth	10	9	4
Employment growth	10	9	4
Manufacturing employment growth	10	10	4
Profit growth	4	2	1
Compensation growth	10	9	4
Wage & salary growth	10	9	4
Change in unemployment rate	9	5	4
Change in Emp./ population ratio	10	10	4

Source: Bivens and Irons (2008); author's calculations.

4. Conclusion: Where Next?

Recognizing the role of macroeconomic factors in the current crisis raises critical questions. Deregulation and massive unsound lending by financial markets are important parts of the crisis story, but they were not the ultimate cause of the crisis. Instead, financial deregulation and financial excess facilitated the bubble and are better understood as extending the life of the neoliberal growth model by supporting demand growth based on debt accumulation and asset price inflation. Absent that support, the model would have ground to a halt earlier.

At this stage, repairing regulatory and microeconomic incentive failures can limit future financial excess. However, it will not address the problems inherent in the neoliberal U.S. growth model and pattern of global economic engagement. Worse, focusing on regulation alone diverts attention from the bigger macroeconomic challenges by misleadingly suggesting that regulatory failure is the principal cause of the crisis.

The case for paradigm change has yet to be taken up politically. Those who built the neoliberal system remain in charge of economic policy. Among mainstream economists who have justified the neoliberal system, there has been some change in thinking when it comes to regulation, but there has been no change in thinking regarding the prevailing economic paradigm. This is starkly illustrated in the debate in the United States over globalization, where the evidence of failure is compelling. Yet, any suggestion that the United States should reshape its model of global economic engagement is brushed aside as "protectionism."

That leaves open the question of what will drive growth once the economy stabilizes. The postwar growth model based on rising middle-class incomes has been dismantled, while the neoliberal growth model has imploded. Moreover, stripping the neoliberal model of financial excess by means of regulation and leverage limits will leave it even more impaired. The U.S. economy needs a new growth model.

The outlines of that new model are easy to see. The most critical need is to restore the link between wages and productivity growth that drove the 1945–80 virtuous circle model of growth. This will require creating a new policy box that takes workers out and puts corporations in.

The outlines of such a box are easy to envisage and involve restoration of worker bargaining power in labor markets through strengthened unions, a higher minimum wage, and stronger employee protections; restoration of full employment as a macroeconomic policy objective; restoration of the legitimacy of regulation and increased government provision of public goods; a new international economic accord that addresses the triple hemorrhage problem created by the flawed model of global economic engagement; and reform of financial markets and corporate governance that ensures markets and corporations work to promote national economic well-being.

Whereas the economics are clear, the politics are difficult, which partially explains the resistance to change on the part of policy makers and economists aligned with the neoliberal model. The neoliberal growth model has benefitted the wealthy, whereas the model of global economic engagement has benefitted large multinational corporations. That gives these powerful political interests, with their money and well-funded captive think tanks and politicians, an incentive to block change.[18]

---

[18] Even domestic manufacturers who are harmed by the international economic agenda may abstain from opposing that agenda because they are net beneficiaries from the overall neoliberal model.

Judging by its top economics personnel, the Obama administration has decided to maintain the system rather than change it. The administration may yet manage to create another bubble, this time probably an interest-rate bubble in Treasury bonds that might weakly jump-start the borrowing cycle one more time. However, even if that were to happen, it will not fix the underlying structural problem. Most importantly, even if the neoliberal model is revved up one more time, it will not deliver shared prosperity because the model was never constructed to do so.

The bottom line is macroeconomic failure rooted in America's flawed economic paradigm is the ultimate cause of the financial crisis and Great Recession. Financial market failure played an important role in the making of the crisis, but its role was supportive and part of the flawed paradigm. Now, there is a grave danger that policy makers only focus on financial market reform and ignore reform of America's flawed economic paradigm. In that event, although the economy may stabilize, it will likely be unable to escape the pull of economic stagnation. That is because stagnation is the logical next stage of the existing paradigm.

References

Anand, S. and P. Segal. (2008) "What Do We Know About Global Income Inequality?" *Journal of Economic Literature*, **46**:1, 57–94.

Arrow, K. J. and, G. Debreu. (1954) "Existence of an Equilibrium for a Competitive Economy," *Econometrica*, **22**, 265–90.

Bivens, J. (2004) "Shifting Blame for Manufacturing Job Loss: Effect of Rising Trade Deficit Shouldn't Be Ignored," EPI Briefing Paper No. 149, Economic Policy Institute, Washington, DC.

Bivens, J. and J. Irons. (2008) "A Feeble Recovery: The fundamental economic weaknesses of the 2001–07 expansion," EPI Briefing Paper No. 214, Economic Policy Institute, Washington, DC.

Blinder, A. S. and J. Yellen. (2001) *The Fabulous Decade: Macroeconomic Lessons from the 1990s*, New York Century Foundation.

Bronfenbrenner, K. (2000) *Uneasy Terrain: The Impact of Capital Mobility on Workers, Wages, and Union Organizing*, Report prepared for the United States Trade Deficit Review Commission, Washington, DC, September.

Bronfenbrenner, K., and S. Luce. (2004) *The Changing Nature of Corporate Global Restructuring: The Impact of Production Shifts on Jobs in the U.S., China, and Around the Globe*, Report prepared for the U.S.–China Economic and Security Review Commission, Washington, DC, October.

Calomiris, C. W. and P. J. Wallison. (2008)"Blame Fannie Mae and Congress for the Credit Mess," *Wall Street Journal*, Tuesday, September 23, A.29.

Dooley, M. P., D. Folkerts-Landau, and P. Garber. (2003) "An Essay on the Revised Bretton Woods System," Working Paper 9971, Cambridge, MA: National Bureau of Economic Research, September.

56   *Palley*

(2004a) "Direct Investment, Rising Real Wages, and the Absorption of Excess labor in the Periphery," Working Paper 10626, Cambridge, MA: National Bureau of Economic Research, July.

(2004b) "The US Current Account Deficit and Economic Development: Collateral for a Total Return Swap," Working Paper 10727, Cambridge, MA: National Bureau of Economic Research, August.

Epstein, G. (2001) "Financialization, Rentier Interests, and Central Bank Policy," manuscript, Department of Economics, University of Massachusetts, Amherst, MA, December.

Fama, E. (1970) "Efficient Capital Markets: A Review of Theory and Empirical Work," *Journal of Finance*, **25** (May), 383–416.

Friedman, M. (2002) *Capitalism and Freedom*, Chicago: University of Chicago Press, 1962 and fortieth anniversary edition.

(1968) "The Role of Monetary Policy" *American Economic Review*, **58** (May), 1–17.

(1953) "The Case for Flexible Exchange Rates," *Essays in Positive Economics*, Chicago: Chicago University Press.

Galbraith, J. K. (2008) *The Predator State: How Conservatives Abandoned the Free Market and Why Liberals Should Too*, New York: Free Press.

Goodman, P. S. (2008) "The Reckoning: Taking a Hard Look at the Greenspan Legacy," *New York Times*, October 9.

Greider, W. (2001) "A New Giant Sucking Sound," *The Nation*, December 13.

Group of Thirty. (2009) "Financial Reform: A Framework for Financial Stability," Washington, DC, report issued January 15.

Husock, H. (2008) "The Financial Crisis and the CRA," *City Journal of The Manhattan Institute*, http://www.city-journal.org/2008/eon1030hh.html, October 30.

International Monetary Fund. (2006) "People's Republic of China: Staff Report for the 2006 Article IV Consultation," Washington, DC.

Jensen, M. J. and W. H. Meckling. (1976) "Theory of the Firm: Managerial Behavior, Agency Costs and Ownership Structure," *Journal of Financial Economics*, **3**, 305 – 360.

OECD Observer. (2003) "China Ahead in Foreign Direct Investment," No. 237, May.

Palley, T. I. (1998) *Plenty of Nothing: The Downsizing of the American Dream and the Case for Structural Keynesianism*, Princeton, NJ: Princeton University Press.

(2002) "Economic Contradictions Coming Home to Roost? Does the U.S. Face a Long Term Aggregate Demand Generation Problem?" Working Paper 332, Levy Economics Institute of Bard College, June 2001 and *Journal of Post Keynesian Economics*, **25** (Fall), 9–32.

(2005) "The Questionable Legacy of Alan Greenspan," *Challenge*, **48**-6 (November/December), 17–31.

(2006) "The Weak Recovery and Coming Deep Recession," *Mother Jones*, March 17.

(2006) "The Fallacy of the Revised Bretton Woods Hypothesis: Why Today's System Is Unsustainable and Suggestions for a Replacement," Public Policy Brief No. 85, The Levy Economics Institute of Bard College.

(2007) "Seeking Full Employment Again: Challenging the Wall Street Paradigm," *Challenge* **50** (November/December), 14–50.

(2008a) "America's Exhausted Growth Paradigm," *The Chronicle of Higher Education*, April 11.

(2008) "The Economic Concertina," *Comment Is Free*, September 7, 2008, http:/www. guardian.co.uk/commentisfree/2008/sep/07/economicgrowth.useeconomicgrowt h?gusrc=rss&feed=worldnews.

(2008b) "Financialization: What It Is and Why It Matters," in Eckhard Hein, Torsten Niechoj, Peter Spahn, and Achim Truger (eds.), *Finance-led Capitalism: Macroeconomic Effects of Changes in the Financial Sector*, Marburg, Germany: Metroplis-Verlag, 2008 and Working Paper 04/2008, IMK Macroeconomic Policy Institute, Dusseldorf, Germany.

Taylor. J. B. (2009) "How Government Created the Financial Crisis," *Wall Street Journal*, Monday, February 3, A.19.

Tobin, J. and W. Brainard, (1968) "Pitfalls in Financial Model Building," *American Economic Review*, **58** (May), 99–122.

PART TWO

EMERGENCE OF FINANCIAL INSTABILITY

THREE

Minsky's Money Manager Capitalism

Assessment and Reform

L. Randall Wray

The world's worst economic crisis since the 1930s is now well into its fifth year. Myriad explanations have been proffered for the crisis: lax regulation and oversight, greed and irrational exuberance, and excessive global liquidity – spurred by easy money policy in the United States and by U.S. current account deficits. Unfortunately, these stories do not recognize the systemic nature of the global crisis. This is why so many observers are misled into pronouncing that recovery is on the way – or even underway already.

I believe they are incorrect. We are perhaps in round three of a nine-round bout. The first round was a liquidity crisis – when major "shadow bank" institutions such as Lehman and Bear Stearns were unable to refinance positions in assets. The second round was a wave of insolvencies – with AIG and Merrill Lynch and a large number of home mortgage specialists failing or requiring resolution. In round three we have the financial institutions cooking the books, using government bail-out funds and creative accounting to show profits, boost stock prices, and pay huge bonuses to top "rainmakers" (see Crotty Chapter 5 in this volume). Round four could begin at any time with another wave of defaults that could deliver a knock-out punch to financial behemoths and trigger a full-fledged debt deflation.

Indeed, the giant financial institutions may still be irretrievably insolvent (in spite of the widespread belief that they recovered, as of April 2012, Moody's is considering a credit downgrade of the top global banks), but forbearance by the regulatory authorities allows them to ignore losses

I thank the editors for comments. Above all, I wish to recognize the substantial debt I owe to Hyman Minsky – the most original economist of the second half of the twentieth century.

on trash assets and remain open. If the knock-out comes, governments might be able to resuscitate them through more bail-out trillions – but this seems unlikely with voters in revolt. Hence, a knock-out punch might provide the necessary impetus for fundamental international financial reform. Otherwise, this crisis could drag on for many more years in the absence of radical policy intervention. Perhaps of more immediate importance, fiscal policy – the only way out of this deep recession – is constrained by deficit hysteria (see Nersisyan and Wray 2010b), which seems to have infected even President Obama. If a debt deflation begins, it will take a major revolution of thinking in Washington to allow for fiscal expansion on the necessary scale. As we know, it was only World War II that generated sufficient spending to get the economy out of depression; one can only hope for a less destructive impetus for more government spending this time around.

Hyman Minsky's work has enjoyed unprecedented interest as the crisis unfolded, with many calling this the "Minsky Moment" or "Minsky Crisis" (Cassidy 2008, Chancellor 2007, McCulley 2007, Whalen 2007). However, most of those who channel Minsky locate the beginnings of the crisis in this decade. I have long argued that we should not view this crisis as a "moment." Rather, as Minsky argued for nearly fifty years, we have seen a slow transformation of the global financial system toward what he later called "money manager capitalism," and it is this multi-decade process that set the stage for the recent collapse. Others have described these events with terms like "financialization," "casino capitalism," or even "neoliberalism" and "neoconservatism" (or "ownership society" within the United States – I particularly like James Galbraith's "predator state" label). I argue that Minsky's analysis is more comprehensive and, it correctly links postwar developments with prewar "finance capitalism" analyzed by Rudolf Hilferding, Thorstein Veblen, and John Maynard Keynes – and later by John Kenneth Galbraith.

Over the past quarter century we restored conditions similar to those that existed in the run-up to the Great Depression, with a similar outcome. To get out of this mess will require radical policy changes no less significant than those adopted with the New Deal. Most importantly, the New Deal downsized and then constrained the financial sector, which I argue is a precondition for creating a structure that would promote stable growth – although other policies will be required. This chapter will focus on financial system reform; other chapters discuss other necessary reforms such as reduction of inequality and a new approach to fiscal policy.

1. A Brief Financial History of the Postwar Period

The best accessible account of the Great Depression and the events leading up to it comes from J. K. Galbraith's *The Great Crash*.[1] Very briefly, the late-nineteenth century saw the rise of huge corporations – and robber barons. Modern industrial production required increasingly expensive, long-lived capital assets that required external finance. This was supplied by loans from financial institutions or by selling equity shares. As Keynes famously described in his *General Theory*, separation of nominal ownership (holders of shares) from management of enterprise meant that prices of equities would be influenced by whirlwinds of optimism and pessimism.

Worse, as Galbraith makes clear, stocks could be manipulated by insiders – Wall Street's financial institutions – through a variety of "pump and dump" schemes. Indeed, the 1929 crash resulted from excesses promoted by investment trust subsidiaries of Wall Street's banks. Because the famous firms like Goldman Sachs were partnerships, they did not issue stock; hence, they put together investment trusts that would purport to hold valuable equities in other firms and then sell shares in these trusts to a gullible public. Effectively, trusts were an early form of mutual fund, with the "mother" house investing a small amount of capital in their offspring, and then highly leveraging the capital using other people's money. Wall Street would then whip up a speculative fever in shares, reaping capital gains. However, trust investments amounted to little more than pyramid schemes – there was very little in the way of real production or income behind all this trading in paper. Indeed, as Galbraith shows, the real economy was already long past its peak – there were no "fundamentals" to drive the Wall Street boom. Inevitably, it collapsed and a debt deflation began as everyone tried to sell stocks. Spending on the real economy suffered and we were off to the Great Depression.

To deal with the effects, the Roosevelt administration adopted a variety of New Deal reforms, including direct job creation and an "alphabet soup" of programs such as the WPA and CCC; it created commodity buffer stock programs to stop the fall of agricultural prices; it enacted relief programs to provide income and reduce inequality (which had peaked in 1929 – part of the reason that the real economy had slowed was that most people were too poor to consume much); it supported labor unions to prevent falling wages; it created Social Security to provide income to the aged, thereby propping

---

[1] See Jan Kregel's contribution to this volume, Chapter 4, which takes an even longer perspective on the evolution of banking and regulation.

up aggregate demand; and – important for our story here – it reformed the financial system. This included a segregation of financial institutions by function – commercial banking, investment banking, savings and loans, and insurance each had their own lines of business. Commercial banks, thrifts, and insurance were tightly constrained on both sides of their balance sheets (what they could own and the types of liabilities they could issue).

Although these actions were not large enough to end the Great Depression – that had to wait for World War II spending – the New Deal programs did set the stage for the stable economy that followed the war. This was a high consumption economy (high and growing wages created demand), with countercyclical government deficits, a central bank ready to intervene as necessary, low interest rates, and a heavily regulated financial sector. The "golden age" of capitalism began – what Minsky called "paternalistic capitalism," or the "managerial-welfare state" (J. K. Galbraith's "new industrial state"). Recessions were mild, there were no financial crises until 1966, and when they began, crises were easily resolved through prompt government response.

This favorable environment changed in the mid-1970s, with a series of crises that became increasingly severe and ever more frequent: real estate investment trusts in the early 1970s; developing country debt in the early 1980s; commercial real estate, junk bonds, and the thrift crisis in the United States (with banking crises in many other nations) in the 1980s; stock market crashes in 1987 and again in 2000 with the dot-com bust; the Japanese meltdown from the late 1980s; Long Term Capital Management, the Russian default, and Asian debt crises in the late 1990s; and so on. Until the crisis that triggered the Great Recession, each of these was resolved (some more painfully than others – impacts were particularly severe in the developing world) with some combination of central bank or international institution (IMF, World Bank) intervention plus a fiscal rescue, often U.S. Treasury spending to prop up the U.S. economy, and to maintain imports that helped to generate growth abroad.

2. Money Manager Capitalism and the Great Recession Crisis

Four important developments precipitated the current crisis.[2] First, there was the rise of "managed money" – pension funds (private and public), sovereign wealth funds, insurance funds, university endowments, and other savings

---

[2] I thank Frank Veneroso for lengthy discussions that led to some of the ideas expressed in this section.

placed with professional money managers seeking maximum "total returns" (yield plus price appreciation). Each money manager competes on the basis of total return, earning fee income and getting more clients if successful. However, it is impossible for all to be above average – generating actions that are sure to increase risk (Nersisyan and Wray 2010a). Money managers take on riskier assets to gamble for higher returns. They innovate and actively market new products to attract clients. Often, these are purposely complex and opaque – the better to dupe clients and to prevent imitation by competing firms. And, probably most important of all, there is a strong incentive to overstate actual earnings – by failing to recognize losses, by overvaluing assets, and through misleading (even fraudulent) accounting.

This development is related to the rise of "shadow banks" – financial institutions that are not regulated as banks. Recall that the New Deal imposed heavier supervision of commercial banks and thrifts. As discussed by Kregel in Chapter 4 of this volume, highly regulated banks lost market share to institutions subject to fewer constraints. The huge pools of managed money offered an alternative source of funding for commercial activities. Firms would sell commercial paper or junk bonds to shadow banks and managed money rather than borrowing from banks. And, importantly, securitization took many types of loans off the books of banks and into affiliates (special investment or purpose vehicles, SIVs and SPVs) and managed money funds. This allowed banks to reduce reported capital leverage ratios, and at the same time created huge volumes of assets to flow into managed portfolios. The securities, themselves, became assets that could be "re-securitized," then re-re-securitized as they were "squared" and then even "cubed." Direct links to reality were finally thrown out altogether with the development of indexes and swaps that effectively allowed pure bets on credit downgrades of these derivatives (the gambler could win even if the mortgages were good – all that was necessary was imposition of a lower credit rating by one of the rating agencies). Banks continually innovated in an attempt to get around regulations, whereas government deregulated in a futile effort to keep banks competitive (Kregel 2010 and Chapter 4 in this volume; Wray 2008a, 2008b). In the end, government gave up and eliminated functional separation between commercial and investment banking in 1999 – and that is when banks and money managers really threw all caution to the wind.

In recent decades there was increased "outsourcing" with pension, insurance, and sovereign wealth fund managers hiring Wall Street firms to manage their money. Inevitably this led to abuse, with venerable investment houses shoveling trashy assets, like asset-backed securities (ABS) and collateralized debt obligations (CDOs) onto portfolios of clients. Firms like Goldman then carried it to the next logical step, betting that the toxic waste they sold to clients would crater. And, as we now know, investment banks would help their clients hide debt through opaque financial instruments, building debt loads far beyond what could be serviced – and then bet on the default of their clients through the use of credit default swaps (CDS). This is exactly what Goldman did to Greece. When markets discovered that Greece was hiding debt, Greek CDS prices increased; this raised Greece's finance costs and budget deficit, thereby fueling credit downgrades that raised its interest rates in a vicious death spiral. Investment banks thus benefited from the fee income they got by hiding debt and by gambling on inside information that excessive debt would eventually be impossible to service!

This brings us to the second transition: the investment banks went public. During the 1929 boom, Wall Street partners could not benefit directly from rising stock values (they could only earn fee income by placing equities and bonds, or by purchasing shares in traded firms) – hence, they created traded subsidiaries. In the "irrational exuberance" of the late 1990s, Wall Street firms again lamented that they could not directly benefit from the boom. Thus, Wall Street firms went public, issuing traded shares. In this way, top management's bonuses would include stocks and options to be sold at huge profit if share prices rose. Just as they did in 1929, management could manipulate share prices by over-reporting earnings, selectively leaking well-timed rumors, and trading on inside information. As Crotty (Chapter 5 in this volume) discusses in detail, the Wall Street "rainmakers" were richly rewarded. Related to this was the substitution of profit maximization of underlying firms by "total return to shareholders" (dividends plus share price appreciation) as the goal of a corporation. This increased the focus on stock prices, which can be easily manipulated for short-term gain, serving as both the justification for big rewards and as the means to enrichment for management holding options.

To be sure, traders like Robert Rubin had already come to dominate firms like Goldman. Traders necessarily take a short view – you are only as good as your last trade. More importantly, traders take a zero-sum view of deals: there will be a winner and a loser, with the financial firm pocketing fees for bringing the two sides together. Better yet, the firm would take one of the two sides – the winning side, of course – and pocket the gains. Note that before it went public, only 28 percent of Goldman's revenues came from trading and investing activities. Now, trading generates about 80 percent of revenue. Although many think of Goldman as a bank, it is really a huge hedge fund, albeit a very special one that now holds a bank charter that gives it access to the Fed's discount window and to FDIC insurance. As a result, it borrows at near-zero interest rates. Indeed, in 2009 it spent only a little more than $5 billion to borrow, versus $26 billion in interest expenses in 2008 – a $21 billion subsidy thanks to its bank charter. It was also widely believed to be "backstopped" by the government – under no circumstances would it be allowed to fail, nor would it be restrained or prosecuted – keeping its stock price up. (After the SEC brought charges, the support was somewhat in doubt, causing share prices to temporarily plummet – before rising again based on profits reports.)

Both the research arms of the big financial firms and the supposedly unbiased reporting of the financial media (especially television) became little more than marketing for the products and shares of Wall Street banks. All of this irreversibly changed the incentive structure of investment banking – away from placing equities and bonds of industrial corporations and toward a frenzy of trading in complex financial instruments with prices set by the seller in "over-the-counter," unregulated, and opaque markets. In the new environment, traders rose to the top of Wall Street firms (and then on to head the Treasury in the case of Robert Rubin and Henry Paulson). It is no wonder that "originate to distribute" securitization and trading replaced careful underwriting (assessment of borrower risk) and lending as the primary focus of financial institutions.

This fueled the third transition, deregulation and atrophy of supervision, which actually began in the U.S. in the late 1960s and built up steam through the 1980s and 1990s. We gradually allowed financial institutions to take riskier positions – holding riskier assets, taking illiquid positions (mismatched maturities of assets and liabilities, for example), increasing leverage (and moving assets off balance sheets where they would not count toward capital requirements), and using internal models to assess risk and asset values. This should be more properly called "self-supervision" rather than deregulation. The theory was that financial institutions could better evaluate risks than could government supervisors, and that relying on private credit raters and accounting firms would provide more flexibility. We also let managed money such as pension funds "diversify" portfolios – into new and complex financial instruments that promised higher and uncorrelated returns that would supposedly reduce systemic risk (Nersisyan and Wray 2010a). At the end of the 1990s we ended the functional separation of financial institutions, allowing a single holding company to engage in the full range of financial services – one-stop financial supermarkets, mostly free of government intervention.

The completion of this transformation occurred with the collapse of Lehman, Bear, and Merrill, when the last two remaining investment banks (Goldman and Morgan Stanley) were handed commercial banking charters so that they would have access to cheap and government-insured deposits. Now the riskiest of the financial institutions were gambling with "house money" – government-insured deposits (at a capital ratio of 12:1, government incurs losses of 92 cents of each dollar blown in bad bets; see Tymoigne and Wray 2009).

The fourth and, for our purposes, final transformation was the inevitable result of these three changes just examined: the rise of fraud as normal business procedure. In early spring 2010, a court-appointed investigator issued his report on the failure of Lehman. Lehman engaged in a variety of "actionable" practices (potentially prosecutable as crimes). Interestingly, it hid debt using practices similar to those employed by Goldman to hide Greek debt. The investigator also showed how Lehman set the prices on its assets with rather arbitrary procedures that could result in widely varying values. Most importantly, however, the top management as well as Lehman's accounting firm (Ernst &Young) signed off on what the investigator said was "materially misleading" accounting. That is a go-to-jail crime if proven. The question is why would a top accounting firm as well as Lehman's CEO, Richard Fuld, risk prison in the post-Enron era? There are two answers. First, it is possible that fraud is so widespread that no accounting firm could retain top clients without turning a blind eye. Second, fraud may have been so pervasive and enforcement and prosecution thought to be so lax that CEOs and accounting firms had no fear. I believe that both answers are correct.

In the aftermath of the 1980s savings and loan crisis in the United States, 1,000 top managers of failed institutions went to jail. Investigations found fraud in virtually every failed institution examined (Wray 1994). Interestingly, the FBI warned of an "epidemic" of fraud in mortgage lending as early as 2004. Subsequent detailed investigations of randomly selected mortgage-backed securities have found evidence of fraud in virtually every one. William Black (who worked in thrift supervision during the 1980s crisis, and blew the whistle on the worst criminal, Charles Keating – remembered for his association with five U.S. senators including John McCain) has convincingly argued that the environment fueled the worst kind of fraud – control fraud. This is where the top management – in this case, of a financial institution – turns a firm into a weapon of fraud in the interest of enriching top management.

The easiest example to understand is a pyramid or Ponzi scheme, with Bernie Madoff of recent note. Many of the failed savings and loans of the 1980s – and all of the most expensive failures – were control frauds. However, these are small potatoes compared with the failures of AIG or Lehman. If (as seems likely) many or all of the large financial institutions are hiding "actionable" practices approved by top management and external auditors, then we are in the midst of the biggest control fraud in history. In any case, there is no question that fraud worthy of incarceration is rampant. To date, however, there has been almost no investigation and no prosecution of top officials at any of the big banks.

To be clear, I am not saying that the crisis was caused by fraud. There has been a long-term transformation to create an environment in which fraud was encouraged. Incentives matter: deregulation and reliance on self-supervision were important; a long period without a great depression as well as prompt intervention by government to attenuate crises helped to reduce perceptions of risk; and globalization linked balance sheets so that a crisis in the United States would affect the entire world.

Further, there is the long-term growth of debt, especially household debt, which made the entire economy more vulnerable. That is a complex issue (see Wray 2005), but in short, it was encouraged not only by "democratization" of access to credit, but also by greater social acceptance of indebtedness (again in large part by absence of an experience like the Great Depression; also see Cynamon and Fazzari, Chapter 6), and by stagnant growth of median real income in the United States (inequality of income and wealth reached and perhaps exceeded the 1929 record, see Setterfield, Chapter 7). Unions lost power, unemployment and underemployment trended higher as workers lost high paying jobs, and support for the poor declined. All of these factors increased reliance on debt to maintain standards of living. At the same time, greater uncertainty made people behave in ways that seem to have been irrational and self-destructive but were in fact driven by desperation.

I argue that these problems were compounded by fiscal policy that was chronically too tight – budget deficits were too small; President Clinton actually ran a budget surplus (as discussed in this volume by Baker, Chapter 10 and Cynamon and Fazzari, Chapter 11). Given the U.S. trade deficit and a tight federal budget, the private sector had to run unprecedented deficits (spending more than its income) for more than a decade (Wray 2003, 2009).[3] That is what helped to promote all the household debt – fiscal restraint kept

---

[3] I agree with Robert Blecker's rejection of the twin deficits argument in Chapter 8, but would be still more critical of Ben Bernanke's "global savings glut" argument – that excess global savings drove the U.S. trade deficit – than he is.

economic growth low, causing stagnating incomes that forced households
to borrow to achieve U.S. lifestyles.

So in short, the crisis resulted from a number of related factors and
trends, and was a long time coming. The Queen of England famously asked
why economists did not see it coming. However, in some sense, one could
argue that over his entire career, Minsky was analyzing the developments
that made "it" (a debt deflation crisis) possible. He began writing about
money manager capitalism in the 1980s; and there are many publications
at the Levy Institute from the late 1990s and early 2000s that projected this
collapse and in general outline, captured many of the forces that brought it
on. In addition, there is plenty of evidence that traders on Wall Street also
(accurately) foresaw the bust. However, each trader thought he would be
able to sell out positions just in time to avoid losses. Of course, when all
traders tried to sell, they all found that liquidity disappeared. Only the Fed
and Uncle Sam would buy, or lend against, assets. It is only in the aftermath
of the bail-out that Wall Street suddenly found collective amnesia useful.

3. The End of Money Manager Capitalism?

Minsky insisted that there are two essential propositions of his "financial
instability hypothesis."[4] First, there are two financing "regimes" – one consistent with stability and the other that causes instability. Second, "stability is destabilizing" – endogenous processes tend to move a stable system
toward fragility. The Great Recession crisis is a natural outcome of these
processes – an unsustainable explosion of real estate prices, mortgage debt,
and leveraged positions in collateralized securities and derivatives in con-
junction with a similarly unsustainable explosion of commodities prices
and equities. The crash was inevitable, although the timing could not be
predicted ahead of time.

Hence, the problem is money manager capitalism – an environment with
highly leveraged funds seeking maximum total returns in markets that systematically underprice risk. Contrary to orthodox theory, markets generate
perverse incentives for excessive risk and punish the timid. Those playing along are rewarded with high returns, because highly leveraged funding drives up prices for the underlying assets – whether they are dot-com
stocks, Las Vegas homes, or corn futures. Those who refuse to participate
get below-average returns. As Keynes said, markets can remain "irrational"
longer than those who short the market can remain solvent.

[4]   See Papadimitriou and Wray 1998 for a summary of Minsky's approach.

We are now living with the aftermath of all this as positions are de-levered, driving prices of the underlying collateral (homes, commodities, factories) down. Previous financial crises were sufficiently limited so that only a portion of managed money was wiped out, with a new boom inevitably rising from the ashes. Even now we remain in the midst of a commodities and equities boom, so many are proclaiming that the crisis is over. I believe, however, that such declarations are premature, and expect another round of financial crisis. Perhaps the next one will be so severe that real reform will take place. In any case, the crisis and the scandals already revealed have discredited the money managers. Wall Street bankers are detested and Americans are furious about the bailout. And, in spite of the unprecedented efforts of Fed Chairman Bernanke and Treasury Secretary Geithner to save the money managers, I believe they will ultimately fail to restore "business as usual."

The main problem is that "finance" simply became too big. At the peak, it captured 40 percent of all corporate profits (it recovered that share by the beginning of 2010 thanks to the bailout and "creative" or even fraudulent accounting), and about a fifth of value added to GDP. Interestingly, we find the same phenomenon in 1929, when finance received 40 percent of the nation's profits. Perhaps such a high ratio represents a practical maximum and thus a turning point at which the economy collapses.

Furthermore, and similarly important, finance virtually captured government, with Wall Street alumni grabbing an unprecedented proportion of federal government positions connected with the financial sector – including the Treasury – under three consecutive presidents (from Clinton through Obama). It is not surprising that Wall Street gets deregulation when it wants and that, in spite of the scale of the current financial crisis, which has wiped out an estimated $50 trillion in global wealth, there has been no significant reform to date. Real reform might have to wait for another collapse. When that comes, it will wipe out even more wealth, and produce even more intolerable suffering – perhaps sufficient to finally end this stage of capitalism.

When the next crash comes, the losses must be accepted; it is necessary to wipe out Wall Street and the managed money. All "too big to fail" institutions should be resolved: if a bank is so big that its failure would threaten the financial system, then it is "systemically dangerous" and too big to save. If we had taken that approach in 2008, it would have been much easier to actually get the economy on the road to recovery. Collateral damage must be managed by directly targeting the "real" part of the economy (households and productive firms) rather than the financial sector. We need to protect jobs, wages, insured deposits, and retirements – but not financial institutions including banks or managed money. Time and economic growth can go a long way to restoring financial health. If incomes can grow sufficiently, it will be easier to service debt. However, we will still need debt relief for households. That should be direct (not through bailouts of financial institutions) taking the form of forced debt write-downs, cash subsidies to home-owners, or foreclosure and "rent-to-own" programs.

During the recovery, the private sector cannot be the main source of demand stimulus as it has been running up debt, spending more than its income for more than a dozen years. Although the government budget deficit is growing as the economy slows, this is a result primarily from deterioration of employment and income (which lowers taxes and increases transfers) – thus, it will not proactively create growth although it will help to constrain the depths of recession. What is needed is a massive fiscal stimulus – probably two or three times the $800 billion that President Obama obtained – and then a permanently larger fiscal presence to allow growth without relying on private sector debt. Yes, government will have to be bigger in the future (also see in this volume, Cynamon and Fazzari Chapter 11; Tcherneva, Chapter 12).

More generally, we need to "definancialize" the economy – reducing the role for Wall Street. For example, we need to replace "financialized" healthcare (run by insurance companies that have been given a huge boost by recent legislation misleadingly labeled as "reform") and private pensions controlled by money managers with universal and adequate publicly funded healthcare and retirement (Auerback and Wray 2010; Nersisyan and Wray 2010a). We need to finance higher education so that it is less reliant on managed endowments. And we should eliminate government subsidies of managed money – such as tax advantages and guarantees – to stop encouraging shenanigans.

Minsky (1986) argued that the Great Depression represented a failure of the small government, laissez-faire economic model, whereas the New Deal promoted a highly successful Big Government/Big Bank (Fed) model for financial capitalism. However, the latter was replaced by money manager capitalism that essentially reversed most of the gains and generated inequality and financial instability (Wray 2005). A big part of the problem is that the Fed's role as Big Bank improperly tried to backstop "too big to fail" institutions. In the final section of this chapter, I propose an alternative central bank policy. For macro stabilization, we probably need a bigger role for the Big Government and a smaller role for the Big Bank. That is also more democratic – Treasury must go through budgeting procedures, must operate in a transparent manner, and is subject to normal oversight of its accounting. The Fed operates mostly in secret. That must stop because it actually creates more financial instability by rewarding the most systemically dangerous firms.[5]

It is time to finally put global finance back in its proper place as a tool to achieving sustainable development. This means substantial downsizing and careful re-regulation. Government must play a bigger role, which in turn requires a new economic paradigm that recognizes the possibility of simultaneously achieving social justice, full employment, and price and currency stability through appropriate policy.[6]

4. Policy to Reform the Financial System

This final section will look at more concrete proposals for reform of the financial system. Let us first enumerate the essential functions of finance, as suggested by Minsky:

1. Safe and robust payments system;
2. Short-term loans to households and firms, and, possibly, to state and local government;
3. Safe and accessible housing finance system;
4. Range of financial services including insurance, brokerage, and retirement savings;
5. Long-term funding of positions in expensive capital assets.

Obviously, there is no reason why any single institution should provide all of these services, although as previously discussed, the long-run trend has been toward consolidation. The New Deal reforms separated institutions by function (see Kregel Chapter 4 in this volume), and state laws against branching provided geographic constraints. On the one hand, Minsky recognized that Glass-Steagall – a New Deal act that separated investment banking from regular banking, among other rules promulgated to enhance safety of the financial system – was anachronistic by the early 1990s, owing to innovations in both financial intermediation and the payments

---

[5] See also EpsteinChapter 9 in this volume, which also calls for greater central bank accountability. He also supports "finance without financiers" – more provision of finance directly by government (or GSEs) – along the same lines advocated later in this chapter. At the end of 2010, perhaps in response to Congress's demand for an audit of the Fed, detailed data on the "bail-out" was finally released.

[6] Tcherneva, Chapter 12 in this volume, discusses the employer-of-last-resort program Minsky favored – to promote full employment and economic stability.

mechanism. He believed these changes were largely market driven and not because of deregulation. On the other hand, Minsky argued that weakening Glass-Steagall and state limits on branching was trying to "fix something that is not broke," because small- to medium-sized banks are more profitable and relationship oriented. In other words, there was no reason to allow or promote the rise of hegemonic financial institutions with national (or international) markets and broad scope. As many others have long argued, the economies of scale associated with banking are achieved at the size of relatively small banks. Minsky was not swayed by the argument that banks were becoming uncompetitive because they could not branch across state lines or because certain practices were prohibited to them. He believed that repealing these constraints would simply reduce the profitability of the smaller, relation-oriented banks. However, he did recognize that the smaller banks would lose market share anyway, owing to competition from shadow banks. Hence, the solution would not be found in promoting bigger, less profitable banks that are not interested in relation-oriented banking. Rather, Minsky wanted greater scope for the activities of the small community banks – a defense against encroachment by shadow banks. We might call this "intensifying" banking – allowing each small institution to provide a greater range of services – as opposed to promoting branching and concentration of power.

In his proposal for development of the newly independent eastern European nations, he argued that the critical problem is to "create a monetary and financial system which will facilitate economic development, the emergence of democracy and the integration with the capitalist world" (Minsky 1992c, p. 28). Except for the latter goal, this statement applies equally well to promotion of the capital development of the western nations.

Minsky argued that there are two main ways in which the capital development of the economy can be "ill done": the "Smithian" and the "Keynesian." The first refers to what might be called "misallocation": the wrong investments are financed. The second refers to insufficient investment, which leads to unemployment. The 1980s suffered from both, but most importantly from inappropriate investment – especially in commercial real estate. We could say that the 2000s again suffered from "Smithian" ill-done capital development because far too much finance flowed into residential real estate. In both cases, Minsky would point his finger at securitization. In the 1980s, because the thrifts were not holding mortgages and lowered underwriting standards, their funding capacity flowed into commercial real estate; in the 2000s, the mania for risky (high return) asset-backed securities fueled subprime lending. In a prescient analysis, Minsky argued that one of the dangers of the move toward securitization is that "originators and the security underwriters did not hazard any of their wealth on the longer term viability of the underlying projects" (Minsky 1992b, pp. 22–23). The implication is rather obvious: good underwriting is promoted when the underwriter is exposed to the longer-term risks.

This brings us to Minsky's skeptical banker:

> When we go to the theater we enter into a conspiracy with the players to suspend disbelief. The financial developments of the 1980s [and 1990s and 2000s!] can be viewed as theater: promoters and portfolio managers suspended disbelief with respect to where the cash would come from that would [validate] the projects being financed. Bankers, the designated skeptic in the financial structure, placed their critical faculties on hold. As a result the capital development was not done well. Decentralization of finance may well be the way to reintroduce the necessary skepticism. (Minsky 1992a, p. 37)

Decentralization plus maintaining exposure to risk could reorient institutions back toward relationship banking. Unfortunately, most trends in recent years have favored concentration. The "too big to fail" doctrine that dates back to the problems of Continental Illinois in the early 1980s gives an obvious advantage to the biggest banks. They are able to finance positions at the lowest cost because government stands behind them. Local banks face higher costs as they try to attract local deposits by opening more offices than necessary, and because it costs them more to attract "wholesale" deposits in national markets. Even in the case of FDIC insured deposits (which have no default risk), smaller banks pay more simply because of the market perception that they are riskier because the government does not backstop them. As discussed, big banks are now allowed to operate like a hedge fund, but can obtain FDIC insured deposits and can rely on Fed and Treasury protection should risky trades go bad. It is very hard for a small bank to compete.

How can the system be reformed to favor relationship banking? First, it would be useful to reduce government protection for less desirable banking activities. There are two important kinds of protection government currently provides: liquidity and solvency. Liquidity is mostly provided by the Fed, which lends reserves at the discount window and buys assets. Refusing to provide liquidity is not the right way to discipline the financial system. Minsky always advocated extension of the discount window operations to include a wide range of financial institutions. In "normal" times, the Fed can discipline bank activities by limiting the range of assets it will discount. In a crisis, however, it must relax its standards. If the Fed had lent reserves without limit to all financial institutions when the crisis first hit, it is probable that the liquidity crisis could have been resolved more quickly.

It is the second kind – protection against default – that is more problematic. Deposit insurance guarantees there is no default risk on certain classes of deposits – now up to $250,000. This is essential for clearing at par and for maintaining a safe and secure payments system. There is no good reason to limit the insurance to $250,000, so the cap should be lifted. The more difficult question is about which types of institutions should be allowed to offer such deposits, or, which types of assets would be eligible for financing using insured deposits. Considerations include riskiness, maturity, and whether purchase of the assets fulfills the public purpose – the capital development of the economy. Risky assets put the FDIC on the hook since it must pay out dollar-for-dollar, but if it resolves a failing institution it will receive only cents on the dollar of assets. In his discussion of the Treasury's proposal for rescuing the FDIC, Minsky made it clear that "cost to the Treasury" should not be a major concern (another reason for removing the cap – it is not important to limit the Treasury's losses to the first $250,000 of a deposit).

We can probably also conclude for the same reason that whereas riskiness of assets financed through issuing insured deposits should be a concern, the problem is not potential losses for the FDIC. Further, maturity of the assets is no longer a concern if the Fed stands ready to lend reserves as needed – a bank could always meet deposit withdrawals by borrowing reserves at the discount window, so would not need to sell longer-term assets. Hence, the major argument for limiting financial institution ability to finance positions in assets by issuing insured deposits is that government has a legitimate interest in promoting the public purpose. Banks should be prevented from issuing insured deposits in a manner that causes the capital development of the country to be ill done.

Banks that receive government protection in the form of liquidity and (partial) solvency guarantees are essentially public–private partnerships. They promote the public purpose by specializing in activities that they can perform more competently than government can. One of these is underwriting – assessing creditworthiness and building relations with borrowers that enhance their willingness to repay. Over the past decade, a belief that underwriting is unnecessary flowered and then burst. Financial institutions discovered that credit rating scores cannot substitute for underwriting – in part because those scores can be manipulated, but also because eliminating relationship banking changes the behavior of borrowers and lenders. As a result, past default rates become irrelevant to assessing risk (as credit raters have discovered). If banks are not underwriting, it is difficult to see why government needs them as partners. It would be much simpler to have government directly finance activities it perceives to be in the public interest – home mortgages, student loans, state and local government infrastructure, and even small business activities (commercial real estate and working capital expenses). Where underwriting is not seen to fulfill a public purpose, then government can simply cut out the middle man. Indeed, there has been a movement in that direction, with government taking full control over student loans. In contrast, where underwriting is critical – say, commercial lending – then government needs the middle man to select those borrowers deserving of credit.

The problem banks have faced over the past three or four decades is the "cream skimming" of their business by shadow banks (or, as Minsky called it, managed money). Uninsured checkable deposits in managed funds (such as money market mutual funds) offer a higher earning but relatively convenient alternative to insured deposits, allowing much of the payments system to bypass banks.[7] As Minsky argued, credit cards have also diverted the payments system out of banking (although the larger banks capture a lot of the credit card business). At the same time, banks were squeezed on the other side of their balance sheet by the growing commercial paper market that allows firms to borrow short- term at interest rates below those on bank loans. Again, larger banks recaptured some of that business by earning fees for guaranteeing commercial paper. However, these competitive pressures caused banks to jettison expensive underwriting and relationship banking, replaced by the originate-to-distribute model. The incentives for banks to guarantee debt that is issued without careful underwriting are often badly aligned with social interests. Banks maximize revenue by maximizing throughput. Whereas the bank is on the hook if the guarantee is triggered, those getting the fees today do not necessarily fully account for that risk. Given the complex linkages, it is highly likely that guarantees will trigger at an inconvenient time for the banks – precisely when everything is going bad all at once, a situation that is difficult to foresee when things are going well. Hence, guarantees and linkages that grow in good times look horrible in bad times.

Some, including Minsky's Levy colleague Ronnie Phillips, have called for a return to the 100 percent money proposal of Irving Fisher and Milton Friedman. Deposit-issuing banks would be allowed to hold only Fed reserves and Treasury debt as assets. Minsky argued that this kind of proposal loses

> sight of the main objective: the capital development of the economy. The key role of banking is lending or, better, financing. The questions to be asked of

[7] Also see Kregel's discussion of the evolution of the U.S. payments system, in Chapter 4 of this volume.

any financial system are what do the assets of banks and other financial institutions represent, is the capital development of the economy better served if the proximate financiers are decentralized local institutions, and should the structure lean towards compartmentalized or broad jurisdiction institutions (Minsky 1992a, pp. 36–37).

To be sure, Minsky did not categorically reject the narrow bank proposal (indeed, he wrote a supportive note for the book by Phillips); he simply believed it addresses only a peripheral problem – safety and soundness of the payments and savings systems. It does not directly address promotion of the capital development of the economy.

Recall that there is the Smithian problem (banks might finance the wrong projects) and the Keynesian problem (they might not finance the right volume of projects). Opening the discount window to provide an elastic supply of reserve funding ensures that banks *can* finance positions in as many assets as they desire at the Fed's target rate. This does not ensure that we have solved the Keynesian problem, because banks might finance too much or too little activity to achieve full employment. Offering unlimited funding to them deals only with the liability side of banking, but leaves the asset side open. It is somewhat easier to resolve the "too much" part of the Keynesian problem because the Fed or other bank regulators can impose constraints on bank purchases of assets when it becomes apparent that they are financing too much activity. For example, in the past real estate boom it was obvious (except, apparently, to mainstream economists and many at the Fed) that lending should be curtailed.

The problem is that the orthodox response to too much lending is to raise the Fed's target rate. Because borrowing is not very interest sensitive, especially in a euphoric boom, rates must rise sharply to have much effect. Further, raising rates conflicts with the Fed's goal of maintaining financial stability because – as the Volcker experiment showed – interest rate hikes that are sufficiently large to kill a boom also cause severe financial disruption (something like three-quarters of all thrifts were driven to insolvency). Minsky argued that the early 1990s banking crisis was, in part, because of the aftermath of the Volcker experiment of a decade earlier. Indeed, this recognition is part of the reason that the Greenspan/Bernanke Fed turned to "gradualism" – a series of very small rate hikes that are well telegraphed. Unfortunately, this means that markets have plenty of time to prepare and to compensate for rate hikes, which means they have less impact.

For these reasons, rate hikes are not an appropriate means of controlling bank lending. Instead, the controls ought to be direct: raising down payments and collateral requirements, and even issuing cease and desist orders to prevent further financing of some activities. Some commentators believed that capital requirements could effectively regulate bank lending: higher capital requirements not only make banks safer, they also constrain lending unless the banks can raise capital. Unfortunately, neither claim was correct. Higher capital requirements were imposed in the aftermath of the S&L fiasco, and codified in the Basel agreements, but they did not constrain bank purchases of assets. Banks simply moved assets and liabilities off their balance sheets, putting them into special purpose vehicles, for example. Basel also used risk-adjusted weightings for capital requirements, to encourage banks to hold less risky assets for which they were rewarded with lower capital requirements. Unfortunately, banks gamed the system in two ways: a) since risk weightings were by class, banks would take the riskiest positions in each class, and b) banks worked with credit ratings agencies to structure assets such as mortgage-backed securities to achieve the risk weighting desired. For example, it was relatively easy to get triple-A rated tranches (as safe as sovereign government debt) out of packages of subprime and "liar loan" Alt-A mortgages – with 85–90 percent of the risky mortgages underlying investment-grade tranches.

Minsky (1986) also argued that all else equal high-capital ratios necessarily reduce return on equity (and, hence, growth of net worth), so it is not necessarily true that higher-capital ratios increase the safety of banks; it means they are less profitable. Indeed, with higher-capital ratios they need to choose a higher risk/return portfolio of assets to achieve a target return on equity (see Tymoigne and Wray 2009).

In contrast to policies that constrain lending, there is not much that can be done to encourage banks to lend when they do not want to. The old "you cannot push on a string" argument describes the situation in the aftermath of the Great Recession quite well. Nor should government policy try to get banks to make loans they do not want to make! After all, if banks are our underwriters, and if their assessment is that there are no good loans to be made, then we should trust their judgment. In that case, lending is not the way to stimulate aggregate demand to get the economy to move toward fuller employment. Instead, fiscal policy is the way to do it.

Solving the Smithian problem requires direct oversight of bank activity, mostly on the asset side of the bank balance sheet. Financial activities that further the capital development of the economy need to be encouraged; those that cause it to be ill done need to be discouraged. One of the reasons that Minsky wanted the Fed to lend reserves to all comers was because he wanted private institutions to be "in the bank" – that is, to be debtors to the

Fed. As a creditor, the Fed would be able to ask the banker the question: "how will you repay me?" The Fed would ask to see evidence of the cash flow that would enable the bank to service loans. It is common practice for a central bank to lend against collateral, using a "haircut" to favor certain kinds of assets (for example, a bank might be able to borrow 100 cents on the dollar against government debt but only 75 cents against a dollar of mortgages). Collateral requirements and haircuts can be used to discipline banks – to influence the kinds of assets they purchase.

Examination of the bank's books also allows the Fed to look for risky practices and to keep abreast of developments. It is clear that the Fed was caught with its pants down, so to speak, by the crisis that began in 2007 in part because it mostly supplied reserves in open market operations rather than at the discount window. Forcing private banks "into the bank" gives the Fed more leverage over their activities. For this reason, Minsky would have opposed the Treasury's proposal in early 2010 to strip the Fed of some of its responsibilities for regulation and oversight of institutions – to hand more responsibilities over to a "super" systemic regulator operated out of the Treasury. If anything, Minsky would have increased the Fed's role. He also believed that because "a central bank needs to have business, supervisory and examination relations with banks and markets if it is to be knowledgeable about what is happening," reducing its responsibility for examining and supervising banks would also inhibit its "ability to perform its monetary policy function. This is so because monetary policy operations are constrained by the Federal Reserve's views of the effect such operations would have upon bank activities and market stability" (Minsky 1992d, p. 10). The Fed would be better informed to the extent that it supervised and examined banks – leading, one hopes, to better policy formation.

Minsky worried that the trend toward megabanks "may well allow the weakest part of the system, the giant banks, to expand, not because they are efficient but because they can use the clout of their large asset base and cash flows to make life uncomfortable for local banks: predatory pricing and corners [of the market] cannot be ruled out in the American context" (1992d, p. 12). Further, since the size of loans depends on capital base, big banks have a natural affinity for "big deals," whereas small banks service smaller clients: "A 1 billion dollar bank may well have 80 million dollars in capital. It therefore would have an 8 to 12 million dollar maximum line of credit ... in the United States context this means the normal client for such banks is a community or smaller business: such banks are small business development corporations" (Minsky 1992d, p. 12).

For this reason, Minsky advocated a proactive government policy to create and support small community development banks (CDBs) (Minsky, Papadimitriou, Phillips, and Wray 1993). Very briefly, the argument advanced was that the capital development of the nation and of communities is fostered via the provision of a broad range of financial services. Unfortunately, many communities, lower-income consumers, and smaller and start-up firms are inadequately provisioned with these services. Many households do not even have checking accounts. Small business often finances activities using credit card debt. Hence, the proposal would have created a network of small community development banks to provide a full range of services (a sort of universal bank for underserved communities): 1) a payment system for check cashing and clearing, and credit and debit cards; 2) secure depositories for savings and transactions balances; 3) household financing for housing, consumer debts, and student loans; 4) commercial banking services for loans, payroll services, and advice; 5) investment banking services for determining the appropriate liability structure for the assets of a firm, and placing these liabilities; and 6) asset management and advice for households (Minsky et al. 1993, pp. 10–11). The institutions would be kept small, local, and profitable. They would be public–private partnerships, with a new Federal Bank for Community Development Banks created to provide equity and to charter and supervise the CDBs.

Reform of the financial system does need to address the shadow banks of money manager capitalism. Minsky believed that pension funds were largely responsible for the leveraged buyout boom (and bust) of the 1980s; similarly, there is strong evidence that pension funds drove the commodities boom and bust of the mid-2000s (Wray 2008b). This is just part of managed money, but it is a government protected and supported portion – both because it gets favorable tax treatment and because it has quasi-government backing through the Pension Benefit Guarantee Corporation (see Nersisyan and Wray 2010a). Hence, it is yet another public–private partnership that ought to serve the public purpose.

Greater regulation of pension funds – to ensure they serve the public purpose – is also required. For example, there is no justification for letting pension funds speculate in commodities, such as foods and energy products. Indeed, the consequences of a commodities price boom and bust are much more deleterious than the consequences of an equity markets boom and bust. After all, commodities are consumed, put into our auto fuel tanks, and go into the production of almost all manufactured goods. Letting pensions cause commodities prices to boom and bust means we let them alternately cause inflation then deflation, and cause global starvation and then bankruptcy of our farmers. Nor should pension funds be allowed to use credit default swaps to bet against firms, households, or governments. The argument that such activities are potentially profitable should hold no water – even if it were true (and it is not true – see Nersisyan and Wray 2010a). As protected and tax-supported funds, these should not be allowed to engage in activities that run counter to the public purpose.

Finally, Minsky argued that the banker is the "ephor" of capitalism – funding investment that forces the surplus (relying on the Kalecki equation, investment creates an equivalent amount of profit). By choosing who gets funding, the banker plays a role in deciding who will receive an allocation of that surplus. He would certainly be appalled at recent trends. First, there has been an important shift away from the wage share and toward gross capital income. I will not go into all the implications of this, but it is clear that stagnant wages played a role in promoting growth of household indebtedness over the past three decades, with rapid acceleration since the mid-1990s. As many at the Levy Institute have been arguing since 1996, the shift to a massive and persistent private sector deficit would prove to be unsustainable. The mountain of debt still crushing households is in part because of the shift of national income away from wages as households tried to maintain living standards (also see Setterfield, Chapter 7 in this volume).

Equally problematic is the allocation of profits toward the financial sector – just before the crisis, the fire insurance and real estate (FIRE) sector received 40 percent of all corporate profits, and its share has returned to that level. This contrasts with a 10–15 percent share until the 1970s, and a 20 percent share until the 1990s. Although value added by the FIRE sector also grew, from about 12 percent in the early postwar period to nearly 20 percent today, its share of profits was twice as high as its share of value added by the time of the 2000s bubble. Hence, there are three interrelated problems: the surplus forced by the financial sector is probably too large (the wage share is too small), the share of GDP coming from the financial sector is probably too large, and the share of the surplus allocated by the financial sector to itself is far too large. Downsizing finance is necessary to ensure that the capital development of the economy can be well done. With 40 percent of corporate profits going to finance, not only does this leave too little to other sectors, but it encourages entrepreneurial effort and innovations to be (wrongly, in the Smithian sense) directed to the financial sector.

I repeat that these fundamental reforms are not likely to go forward unless the system again collapses. I believe it will. The opportunity would then come for reforms along the lines proposed here. We need to continue to develop these reforms so that they will be ready when a renewed sense of crisis opens the political door for truly fundamental reform.

References

Auerback, M. and L. R. Wray. "Toward True Health Care Reform: more care, less insurance," Levy Economics Institute Public Policy Brief no.110, 2010, http://www.levyinstitute.org/pubs/ppb_110.pdf.

Black, W. K. (2005) *The Best Way to Rob a Bank is to Own One: How corporate executives and politicians looted the S&L industry*, Austin: University of Texas Press.

Cassidy, J. "The Minsky Moment," *The New Yorker*, Feb 4, 2008, www.newyorker.com.

Chancellor, E. "Ponzi Nation," *Institutional Investor*, Feb 7, 2007.

Eisinger, J. and J. Bernstein. "The Magnetar Trade: How one hedge fund helped keep the bubble going," ProPublica, Apr 13, 2010, www.propublica.org/feature/all-the-magnetar-trade-how-one-fund-helped-keep…

Galbraith, J. K. (2009) *The Great Crash 1929* New York: Houghton Mifflin Harcourt (1954).

Harper, C. "Taxpayers Help Goldman Reach Height of Profit in New Skyscraper," Bloomberg.com, Apr 17 2010, www.bloomberg.com/apps/news?pid=20670001&sid=aaLwI2SKYQJg.

Henning, P. J. and S. M. Davidoff, "Goldman Fraud Case Holds Risks for Both Sides," The Deal Professor *New York Times,* Apr 16, 2010.

Kregel, J. "No Going Back: Why we cannot restore Glass-Steagall's segregation of banking and finance," Levy Economics Institute Public Policy Brief no. 107, 2010.

"Minsky's Cushions of Safety: Systemic risk and the crisis in the U.S. subprime mortgage market," Levy Economics Institute Public Policy Brief no. 93, January 2008.

Mayer, M. "The Spectre of Banking," Levy Economics Institute, One-Pager No. 3, May 20, 2010.

McCulley, P. "The Plankton Theory Meets Minsky," Global Central Bank Focus, PIMCO Bonds, March 2007, www.pimco.com/leftnav/featured+market+commentary/FF.…

Minsky, H. P. (1986) *Stabilizing an Unstable Economy*, New Haven and London: Yale University Press.

"Reconstituting the United States' Financial Structure: Some fundamental issues," Levy Economics Institute Working Paper No. 69, January 1992a.

"The Capital Development of the Economy and the Structure of Financial Institutions," Levy Economics Institute Working Paper No. 72, January 1992b.

"The Economic Problem at the End of the Second Millennium: Creating capitalism, reforming capitalism and making capitalism work" (prospective chapter), manuscript in Minsky Archives at Levy Economics Institute, May 13, 1992c.

"Reconstituting the Financial Structure: The United States" (prospective chapter, four parts), manuscript in Minsky Archives at Levy Economics Institute, May 13, 1992d.

"The Essential Characteristics of Post-Keynesian Economics," manuscript in Minsky Archives at Levy Economics Institute, April 13, 1993a.

"Financial Structure and the Financing of the Capital Development of the Economy," The Jerome Levy Institute Presents Proposals for Reform of the Financial System, Corpus Christie, TX, April 23, 1993b.

"Uncertainty and the Institutional Structure of Capitalist Economies," Levy Economics Institute Working Paper No. 155, April 1996.

"Uncertainty and the Institutionalist Structure of Capitalist Economies: Remarks upon receiving the Veblen-Commons Award," *Journal of Economic Issues*, **XXX**, 2, June 1996, pp. 357–368.

Minsky, Hyman P. and Charles J. Whalen. "Economic Insecurity and the Institutional Prerequisites for Successful Capitalism", Levy Economics Institute Working Paper no. 165, May 1996.

Minsky, Hyman P., Dimitri B. Papdimitriou, Ronnie J. Phillips, and L. Randall Wray. "Community Development Banking: A proposal to establish a nationwide system of community development banks," Public Policy Brief No. 3, Levy Economics Institute, 1993.

Morgenson, G. and L. Story. "Banks Bundled Bad Debt, Bet against It, and Won," *New York Times*, Dec 24, 2009.

"Investor Who Made Billions is not Target of Suit," *New York Times*, 16 Apr 2010.

"S. E. C. Accuses Goldman of Fraud in Housing Deal," *New York Times*, 16 Apr 2010.

"Exotic Deals put Denver Schools Deeper in Debt," *New York Times*, 5 Aug 2010, www.nytimes.com/2010/08/06/business/06denver.html.

Nersisyan, Y. and L. R. Wray. "The Trouble with Pensions: Toward an alternative public policy to support pensions," Levy Economics Institute Public Policy Brief, no. 109, 2010a. http://www.levyinstitute.org/pubs/ppb_109.pdf.

"Deficit Hysteria Redux? Why we should stop worrying about U.S. government deficits," Levy Economics Institute Public Policy Brief, no 111, 2010b, http://www.levy-institute.org/pubs/ppb_111.pdf.

Nocera, J. "A Wall Street Invention let the Crisis Mutate," *New York Times,* 16 April 2010.

Papadimitriou, D. B. and L. R. Wray. "The Economic Contributions of Hyman Minsky: Varieties of capitalism and institutional reform," *Review of Political Economy*, **10**(2), 1998. pp. 199–225.

Story, L. "Investment Firm Agrees to Settle Kickback Inquiry," *New York Times,* April 15, 2010.

Tymoigne, E. and L. R. Wray. "It isn't Working: Time for more radical policies," Levy Economics Institute Public Policy Brief no. 105, 2009.

Whalen, C. "The U.S. Credit Crunch of 2007: A Minsky moment," Levy Economics Institute Public Policy Brief No. 92, 2007.

Wray, L. R. "Financial Markets Meltdown: What can we learn from Minsky?" Levy Economics Institute Public Policy Brief No 94, April 2008a.

"The Political Economy of the Current US Financial Crisis," *International Papers in Political Economy*, vol. **1**, no. 3, 1994.

"The Perfect Fiscal Storm," *Challenge*, January–February, vol. **46**, no. 1, 2003, pp. 55–78.

"The Ownership Society: Social Security is only the beginning …," Levy Economics Institute *Public Policy Brief* No. 82, August 2005.

"Financial Markets Meltdown: What can we learn from Minsky," Levy Economics Institute Public Policy Brief no. 94, April 2008a http://www.levy.org/vtype.aspx?doctype59.

"The Commodities Market Bubble: Money manager capitalism and the financialization of commodities," Levy Economics Institute Public Policy Brief no. 96, 2008b http://www.levy.org/vtype.aspx?.

"Return to Big Government: Policy advice for President Obama," Levy Economics Institute Public Policy Brief no. 99, 2009, http://www.levy.org/vtype.aspx?doctype59.

FOUR

Trying to Serve Two Masters

The Dilemma of Financial Regulation

Jan Kregel

Hyman Minsky pointed out that any capitalist banking and financing system is drawn between two masters: it must allocate financing for the capital development of the economy and it must provide a safe-and-secure payments mechanism. The dilemma inherent in this dual mandate is that financing capital development involves risks to lending institutions that threaten the safety and security of the economy's payments system. Thus, the problem facing regulatory and supervising authorities charged with the stability of the financial system is how to protect the payments system from the consequences of the losses that may ensue from development financing without choking off the flow of capital that supports economic growth (see Minsky, 1994, pp. 10–11). The history of banking and finance in the United States is characterized by a series of measures designed to overcome this dilemma, exacerbated by conflicts between federal authorities' emphasis on measures to protect the means of payment and state authorities seeking to increase the flow of development capital.

This chapter reviews this history to provide an explanation of how the conflict between Minsky's two "masters" set the stage for the dramatic financial crisis that triggered the Great Recession. In addition, a careful look at prior attempts to solve the two-masters dilemma suggests the need for a revamped financial regulatory structure in the aftermath of the crisis that embodies changes far more significant than those included in the 2010 Dodd-Frank reform bill.

1. A Brief History of how U.S. Banking Regulation Tried to Serve Two Masters

In the United States, the federal government has focused on serving the "second master" through prudential regulation and control of the financial institutions that provide the means of payment. Indeed, the Constitution reserves for the federal government the ability to incur debt and coin money.[1] However, the Constitution does not make provisions for a central bank, or for private business charters with limited liability. Thus, individual states cannot issue currency, but they can charter private banks that issue promises to pay specie. In fact, these state bank notes provided the country's basic means of payment until the middle of the nineteenth century.

The individual states had a clear preference for the "first master," and states often chartered banks with a view to provide cheap sources of finance for the development of the state.[2] The result was a dual system of regulation and supervision, federal and state, which further complicated the task of designing a financial system that would serve the two masters.

Early federal regulation thus concentrated on regulating the specific types of payments that circulated as substitutes for specie, rather than the financial institutions that issued them. In addition to providing financing for the Civil War, the 1864 National Bank Act was a response to the proliferation of state-chartered private and state-owned banks and their issue of bank notes subject to only minimal regulation, frequent fraud, and default. Between 1838 (when the second charter of the Bank of the United States lapsed) and 1860, the number of banks grew from 829 to 1,562 and the value of notes in circulation rose from around $100 million to $200 million, whereas deposits in savings banks increased from $85 million to more than $250 million. Indeed, the justification behind "free banking" introduced by state governments to fund their development financing was the belief that the market would provide the appropriate regulation to ensure stability by driving the unsafe note-issuing banks out of business. This market mechanism clearly provided insufficient service to the second means-of-payment master, as attested by the numerous bank failures and defaulted notes they issued.

The 1864 Act may be seen as an attempt by the Federal government to reclaim control over the currency by introducing national bank notes

---

[1] Section 10 of the Constitution forbids individual states the right to "coin money; emit Bills of Credit; make anything but gold and silver Coin a Tender in Payment of Debts." The intention of this Section was to reserve the right to issue any form of debt, including currency notes, to the federal government.

[2] State legislatures granted banking privileges to railroad and canal companies, to gas and waterworks, to turnpike and power companies, and other similar enterprises to enable them to secure the necessary funds by issuing paper money. These banks were chartered with the "usual banking powers" that implied a note issue of two or three times their capital, but "very little specie was ever paid in. Each institution simply created its capital in much the same way as it created the money it loaned to its patrons" (Madeleine, 1943, pp. 66–67, 70).

issued by federally chartered National Banking Associations and backed by U.S. government debt. To ensure the dominance of National Bank notes, the Act was amended to impose a penal tax on the issue of notes by state-chartered banks. The Office of the Comptroller of the Currency (OCC) was created as the federal regulator of the financial system to ensure service to the second master.

However, state banks responded by offering deposit accounts payable on demand or by check in place of bank notes, and before the turn of the century, the number of state banks exceeded national banks. Trust company banks, which grew rapidly toward the end of the century and remained outside the regulation of the OCC, also provided deposit services to clients. The regulation and supervision of the payments system was thus again escaping from federal control. Indeed, the 1907 banking crisis started with the failure of a New York City Trust bank. At the time, the New York Clearing House provided the equivalent of emergency liquidity by allowing its members to use Clearing House notes in lieu of specie for interbank settlement.[3] However, trust banks were not admitted as members of the New York Clearing House and their interbank clearings were serviced by a correspondent arrangement with a Clearing House member. When the correspondent banks clearing on behalf of the Knickerbocker Trust started to doubt its ability to meet its commitments, they refused to clear its claims. In the absence of any other source of liquidity, Knickerbocker was forced to suspend redemption of its deposit liabilities even though it appeared to be solvent. The bank run that resulted was stemmed by the famous intervention of JP Morgan. It was generally accepted that the crisis was owing to the lack of a central bank capable of providing emergency liquidity, similar to the Clearing House certificates, to banks facing short-term payments crises.

In response to the crisis, a Reserve Association was proposed to pool members' reserves in order to make them available to any bank facing a large and rapid deposit drain that could not be met from their existing resources. The idea evolved into a formal proposal for a central bank with a mix of federal control by a reserve board in Washington appointed by the federal government and by a series of district banks controlled by banks and local business representatives. Because membership in this new reserve system was not obligatory, it did not provide universal regulation of the

---

[3] It is interesting that in crisis, the Clearing House acted to protect the payments system from the consequences of development financing by extending the issue of Clearing House notes beyond specie and legal tender to a wide range of member bank liabilities.

payments system. Instead, it simply added another regulatory agency to the individual state bank regulators and the OCC. The issue of Federal Reserve Notes as the liabilities of the District Reserve banks may be seen as another attempt by the federal government to gain control over the payments system to satisfy the second master.

The Federal Reserve Act provided member banks facing liquidity shortages with the ability to obtain Federal Reserve Notes by discounting their commercial loans with the District Federal Reserve banks. It thus attempted to make the issue of liquidity responsive to the needs of trade through application of the "real bills" doctrine. The new arrangement thus retained the traditional emphasis on the second master: as Minsky notes, "the vision that underlay the Federal Reserve Act was not to finance the putting in place of durable capital assets ... The vision of the act restricted the role of banks to the financing of the movements of agricultural products from farm to city and abroad and of imports and manufacturing from source to market. The image of what went on in the economy that underlay the 1913 act was obsolete even as the act was being enacted" (1994, p. 19).

However, even the new elasticity in the means of payment provided by the Federal Reserve system proved unable to prevent the Great Depression and the government again responded with measures to shore up the safety of the payments system. However, instead of creating a Federal Reserve deposit account in the District Reserve banks as a complement to the Federal Reserve note, the Glass-Steagall Act sought to regulate the permissible activities of deposit-taking financial institutions. It divided the financial system into two separate sets of institutions, each dedicated to one of the two masters. Deposit-taking commercial banks were to provide means of payment, limiting their investments to safe, self-liquidating short-term business loans (a reaffirmation of the real bills tradition), whereas investment banks were to serve the first master and provide the financing for the long-term capital investment of the system. In addition, commercial banks were provided a federal deposit insurance fund to guarantee their transactions liabilities, whereas investment banks were required to provide full and complete information on the capital market securities they created in the financing of development and to trade them in transparent, self-regulated public markets overseen by the federal government. These provisions produced an additional layer of regulation in the form of the Federal Deposit Insurance Corporation (FDIC) and the Securities and Exchange Commission (SEC). The Glass-Steagall separation of banking and finance seemed to provide a solution to the problem of creating a regulatory and supervisory system capable of ensuring that the financial system would successfully serve the two masters. Indeed, the experience of the subsequent forty years was one of unprecedented financial stability in the payments system and sustained expansion.

Glass-Steagall sharply restricted the securities market activities of commercial banks, while placing few limits on the activities of investment banks aside from prohibiting their ability to offer payment services. But Regulation Q, which limited interest rates on core deposit funding and subsidized deposit insurance to ensure the safety of deposits, provided implicit compensation to commercial banks for the additional restrictions on their activities. However, competition from investment banks and new payments technology reduced the commercial banks' monopoly on the issue of the means of payments and they responded by seeking regulatory permission to extend their activities into securities markets activities to enhance their income. The result was a series of administrative and legislative decisions that progressively dismantled the original sharp separation of the activities of commercial and investment banks under Glass-Steagall.

The 1999 Gramm-Leach-Bliley Financial Services Modernization Act repealed what remained of the 1933 regulation, but failed to provide an alternative regulatory and supervisory system capable of serving two masters. Eventually, as Minsky predicted, this led to an increase in risk, manipulation, and fraud. These outcomes, which culminated in the banking crisis of 2007–2008 and the Great Recession, were, in part, because of the differential impact of the new legislation on commercial banks and investment banks.

The formation of bank holding companies by former commercial banks allowed them to use the core deposits of their banking subsidiaries to fund short-term lending to firms at concessional rates in exchange for commitments to provide underwriting services for the capital market issues through their investment banking subsidiaries. Investment banks could not compete in short-term lending because they could not issue deposits as a short-term source of funding; in addition, their traditionally low capital base meant that they could not compete by underwriting large capital market issues. This led investment banks to incorporate as public companies so that they could issue equity to enhance their capital base. Meanwhile, investment banks already using a public capital base sought to raise additional capital and increase leverage. In addition, investment banks came to rely increasingly on proprietary trading activities to supplement their reduced underwriting income. This competition encouraged bank holding companies to increase their size to provide a full range of banking and financial services and to grow into institutions that became "too big to fail."

The rest of this chapter draws on Minsky's insight into the banking system to explain the ways in which financial deregulation introduced by regulatory agency decisions and judicial interpretations ultimately led to the dismantling of the original Glass-Steagall legislation to such a degree that the passage of the 1999 Act simply codified these changes. The consequence, which emerges at the end of the chapter, was a banking and financial system primed to give rise to the crisis of 2008–2009, and that now requires fundamental reform if it is to ever successfully serve the two masters in the future.

2. Financial Legislation and the Structure of the Financial System

The New Deal legislation was meant to prevent deposit-taking banks from engaging in equity trading and other forms of speculation, either directly or indirectly through arms-length affiliates. Their investment activities were thus limited to the provision of short-term, self-liquidating loans to commercial borrowers. At the same time, it prohibited any bank that undertook securities market activity in any form from offering demand deposits. Changes in the returns on the different activities permitted to different types of institution, and difficulties in framing precise definitions of those activities, explain the slow dismantling of the Glass-Steagall regulatory system that culminated in the recent financial crisis.

The initial difficulty with this segregated structure was that commercial loans were already a small proportion of bank assets when it was introduced. This was due in large part to the ability of larger corporations to fund themselves through the issue of commercial paper. In the return-to-normal market conditions after the war, corporations also found it advantageous to hold their short-term funds in Treasury bills paying positive and rising interest rates, rather than in bank deposits that were limited to a zero interest rate under Regulation Q. In addition, commercial banks faced competition in the deposit markets from savings banks that had initially been excluded from Regulation Q. However, the real challenge to the income potential of the restricted range of activities granted to commercial banks under Glass-Steagall came from the emergence and growth of money market mutual funds (MMMF). These funds provided a substitute for bank deposits, and created a steady demand for the commercial paper that provided a substitute for corporate bank loans. The advent of asset securitization produced conduits issuing assets backed by commercial paper that could be purchased by MMMF and other investors, further increasing competition with commercial bank activities.

Despite providing services identical to those reserved to commercial banks under Glass-Steagall, MMMF, and commercial paper were both classified and regulated as securities market activities. As a result, commercial banks were forbidden from competing to offer such services and the MMMF were not subject to the same prudential regulations as commercial banks. Indeed, when Bankers Trust attempted to enter the commercial paper business in 1979, it was opposed in the courts by representatives of investment banks seeking to limit competition from commercial banks. The litigation turned on whether commercial paper should be considered as equivalent to a bank loan or a security. Despite overwhelming evidence to the contrary, and a positive ruling by an Appeals Court, the Supreme Court eventually ruled that commercial paper was not equivalent to a loan, but was a security and thus part of those activities forbidden to commercial banks under the 1933 Act. The Federal Reserve never acted to bring MMMF under regulation as the equivalent of commercial banks deposits, basically because they did not qualify for federal deposit insurance, although they were covered by a similar scheme that insured securities firms' brokerage accounts.

The basic principle behind the MMMF was elaborated to produce shadow banking and asset-backed securitization.[4] In these structures, longer-term securities are funded by selling shorter-term liabilities, thereby providing a competitive form of financing forbidden to regulated commercial banks because of the Glass-Steagall prohibition on commercial banks' dealing in private securities markets. As in the case of MMMF, the viability of these structured lending facilities required facilitating legislation and regulatory interpretation. Because a securitization involves the creation of an independent legal entity or trust structure that issues liabilities treated as securities, they should be subject to normal registration and reporting under SEC regulations because the entity should be considered an investment company under the 1940 Investment Company Act. However, application of these regulations would have drastically reduced the income from this form of financing. Their expansion was supported by a 1992 administrative ruling that excluded virtually all securitized entities from the definition of an investment company and associated regulation and control by the SEC (Siclari, 2001).

Because these new financing structures involved the creation of affiliates, the underwriting of securities, and other capital market activities that were off-limits under the 1933 Act, commercial banks were forced to seek

---

[4] An issue that Minsky considered crucial, but did not discuss in great length in his published work, see Minsky, 2008 and 1986, 12 ff.

exemptions from the Act in order to offer similarly competitive lending through securitized structures and thus remain competitive with investment banks. This required the creation of special-purpose entities by commercial banks that could engage in capital market and other underwriting activities. It was achieved with regulators' approval of an exemption to Section 20 of the Federal Reserve Act to allow banks to engage in limited securities activities through separate affiliates.

These measures to expand the permissible activities of commercial banks had a marked influence on the fragility of the financial system since it implicitly allowed commercial banks to engage in speculative securities market activities with customer deposits (i.e., "other peoples' money"). The Section 20 exemption that allowed commercial banks to form securities affiliates placed a limit on the share of gross earnings banks could obtain from activities specifically linked to securities. Thus, in order to expand securities activities and the earnings associated with them, commercial banks had to expand the gross non-securities-related income generated by their Section 20 securities affiliates. This was done by expanding treasury security repurchase business, matching purchases, and reverse repurchase agreements of the same security to earn the small, low-risk, bid-ask spread.[5] This "matched book" trading activity provided an expanding market for short-term collateralized lending that was eventually extended to all securities and provided a source of leverage for other non-member financial institutions and hedge funds.

The Federal Reserve could have taken action to halt the development of MMMF and the exemptions for asset-backed securities, but instead chose to suspend Glass-Steagall regulations to allow commercial banks to engage in an ever-increasing range of securities market activities. In this they were aided and abetted by a number of administrative and judicial decisions that supported the moves to allow banks greater powers to deal in securities markets.

The Liberalizing Power of "Incidental Powers"

The competitive innovations and the relaxation of prudential regulations on commercial banks played an important role in weakening Glass-Steagall

---

[5] On the original development of this practice of writing matched book repos, as well as the various frauds owing to lack of regulation, see Stigum (1978). On its role in the current crisis, see Gorton (2009). The early developments of this market drew Minsky's attention in Minsky (1957).

regulations. However, it was the legal and administrative interpretation of Section 16 that eventually proved to be even more detrimental in the evisceration of the 1933 Act and the protection it provided to the provision of payment services by commercial banks. Section 16 of the Act allows insured commercial banks "all such incidental powers as shall be necessary to carry on the business of banking" (Krooss, 1969: 2755). It was the generous interpretation of "incidental powers" that produced the majority of the exceptions that allowed commercial banks to expand their securities activities to meet the innovative competition from investment banks and the progressive erosion of Glass-Steagall.

The OCC was among the most active in allowing commercial banks to engage in presumedly prohibited securities activities through liberal interpretation of "incidental powers" to cover activities that were not specifically mentioned as being compatible with the "business of banking" in Section 16.[6] In interpreting the range of Section 16, the OCC originally applied the "look through" principle and permitted banks to deal in any underlying financial instrument that referred to an activity that was considered permissible under Section 16. For example, the OCC allowed banks to deal in derivatives on government securities because dealings in government securities were permitted by the 1933 Act. Subsequently, the OCC shifted to "functional equivalence" as the basis of its assessment of "incidental powers." Under this interpretation it argued that, since approval had been extended to derivative contracts written on permissible activities, this permission should also apply to activities providing functions similar to derivatives themselves. This made it possible to extend the approval of dealing in derivatives on government securities to derivatives written on virtually all assets, including commodities and equities, since the function was deemed equivalent (see Omarova, 2009).

The overall impact of these legal and administrative rulings was to completely reverse the original prohibition of commercial bank dealings in securities for their own account. In so doing, the rulings laid the basis for the creation of proprietary trading by banks, as well as banks dealing

---

[6] This language was originally introduced in Section 8 of the National Bank Act of 1863 granting National Associations "all such incidental powers as shall be necessary to carry on the business of banking ..." but made no reference at all to securities. See Krooss, 1969, p. 1386. There has been extended debate concerning whether these powers are restricted to those expressly mentioned in the law, or are subject to interpretation. In practice, the decision is left with the Office of the Comptroller of the Currency (OCC), created in the same legislation. A 1995 Supreme Court decision (NationsBank of North Carolina, N.A. v. Variable Annuity Life Insurance Co.) affirmed OCCs full power to interpret Section 8.

in derivative contracts, and the provisions of structured derivative lending that led to the rapid growth of over-the-counter derivatives.

By the 1990s, the only area that appeared to remain technically outside the purview of commercial banks' operations was insurance, which had been the regulatory preserve of state insurance regulators. However, many of the innovations that have occurred in the insurance industry, such as guaranteed investment contracts, were easily interpreted as financial rather than actuarial activities, and thus activity permitted to regulated banks.

As a consequence of these regulatory decisions, it has been suggested that by the 1990s, regulated banks had already been allowed to engage in all of the securities and insurance activities that were eventually granted by the 1999 Financial Modernization Act (see Fisher, 2001).

3. The Challenge and Response to Glass-Steagall Segregation of Banking and Finance

The Regulatory Dynamic of Innovation and Protection

The regulatory dynamic in the post-war period was thus one in which non-regulated investment banks produced innovative financing structures that relied on capital market securities. These innovations allowed them to compete with commercial banks in the creation of liquidity and lending accommodation to business borrowers, on terms that regulated commercial banks could not match because they were forbidden such capital market activities. Rather than prohibiting the competitive innovations of investment banks that encroached on the activities reserved for commercial banks, regulators made decisions that facilitated them and thus placed regulated commercial banks at an even greater competitive disadvantage. The monopoly protections on deposit-taking granted to commercial banks in the 1933 Act thus became a hindrance to their survival because it prevented them from offering liquidity and lending structures based on securities activities in competition with investment banks. This increasing competitive disadvantage and loss of income on the part of commercial banks was then used as an argument to reduce or eliminate the prudential regulations on commercial banks.

Erosion of Glass-Steagall Increased Financial Instability

These regulatory rulings and interpretations not only allowed changes in the operation of banks, but also produced the increased financial fragility that lay at the base of the recent financial crisis. Under the New Deal regulations, commercial bank loan officers would originate new loans to business borrowers by opening a new deposit account to the borrower's credit. It was then the responsibility of the reserve desk to find the customer deposits or to arrange interbank lending to provide the reserves required to support the loan at the statutory reserve ratio. If the banking system as a whole came up short, the Fed would have to provide the required reserves through open market purchases. However, individual banks would normally hold secondary reserve assets – liquidity cushions – that could be converted into reserves at short notice if there was a reserve shortfall, either because of an excessively exuberant loan officer or because of a decline in the quality of loans and an increase in reserves for nonpayment of loans. The loans that were initially funded by the creation of a bank deposit liability represented an unfunded liability that had to be hedged by the bank through the structuring of its balance sheet to ensure it held sufficient amounts of liquid assets to meet any potential withdrawal of deposits when they were used as means of payment to an account with another bank.

This describes the "normal business of banking," often called the "originate and hold" or "originate and reserve" business model, in which banks used zero-interest-rate deposits to create reserves to back their loan portfolios. According to Robert Morris Associates (1988, p. 26), "Given the fact that banks rarely achieve returns on assets greater than 1 percent, the charge-off of even a relatively small amount of assets can quickly eliminate bank earnings and eat up capital or reserves." Thus commercial banks had economic incentives to employ efficient and effective credit assessment in selecting borrowers.

The 1980s introduction of asset-risk-weighted capital requirements, along with the encroachment of MMMF and commercial paper markets on commercial banks' deposit and lending activities, had a negative impact on bank earnings. Data reported by Gerald Corrigan show that the return on assets (ROA) for regulated commercial banks started to decline after 1973 with the beginning of regulatory liberalization. The shift away from traditional commercial banking represented by net interest earnings on commercial and industrial lending may be seen in the decline of this source of income relative to fees and commissions. Between 1956 and 1981, fee income of insured commercial banks rose from 11.3 percent of operating income net of interest expense to 19.5 percent. This trend is also reflected in the rise in the return on equity that reached a peak in 1981.

In order to provide alternative sources of income and to respond to competition from nonregulated banks, commercial banks sought to increase their securities market activities. The introduction of capital controls at the end of the 1980s also led to attempts to shift lending activities off their balance sheets to reduce capital costs. Both of these objectives were met by increasing loan securitization. Initially introduced in the late 1970s by government-sponsored entities such as Fannie Mae and Freddie Mac, this process was eventually adopted by commercial banks in their issue of securitized credit card receivables and auto loans, and after the 1999 Act, spread to non-prime mortgages.

In a securitization, a legally independent trust or special-purpose entity is organized to issue its own capital market liabilities, the proceeds from which are used to purchase bundles of assets originated by the bank loan officer. The risk of loss is thus transferred from the bank to the special-purpose vehicle, usually a trust structure owned by third-party investors, eliminating the need for the bank to hold capital against the loans. Because the bank earns its fee and commission income at the time of the transfer of the assets and is, in principle, no longer exposed to recourse on the loans, it no longer has a direct interest in the credit quality of the assets. The bank's income is now maximized not by assessing the credit worthiness of the borrower, but by maximizing the volume of new assets to be securitized. Because no reserves or capital are required to be held against the loans, unlike the "normal business of banking," there is no control on the amount of loan origination that the bank can undertake. This bank business model is called "originate and distribute;" the only limits on credit creation are those imposed by the willingness of the capital market to absorb the liabilities of special-purpose trusts.

However, just as the regulatory impact of reserve and capital ratios was removed in this transition to originate and distribute, so too the function of the reserve desk officer was replaced by the financial engineer that produced the liability structure of the special-purpose entities. The normal due diligence process of the loan officer in judging the credit worthiness and quality of the borrower was also eliminated. Because the regulations that allowed the liabilities of these special-purpose structures to be sold to institutional buyers without SEC oversight required an investment-grade credit rating, the credit assessment process that had been the main concern of the commercial bank was transferred to private credit rating agencies (technically nationally recognized statistical ratings organizations [NRSROs], approved by the SEC). However, the NRSROs were paid for their ratings by the bank creating the securitization and the ratings were made before the liabilities issued by the special entity were sold. As such, the NRSROs had little incentive to carry out effective credit analysis of the underlying assets on which the value of the liabilities issued by the special-purpose entity was based. Furthermore, if a credit rating agency made a bad credit assessment (in particular, underestimating the risk of the special-purpose entity, the mistake had no impact on their income.[7] Rather, income was reduced when their ratings were too strict, since the issuer could then go to another rating agency for a better rating. This "shopping" for ratings created a fundamental conflict of interest that led to incentives for credit rating agencies to underestimate the risks involved.

Even more importantly, however, was the disappearance of the liquidity cushion of secondary reserves and access to market financing that were normal features of banking under the originate-and-hold model. The new originate-and-distribute system provided overcollateralization or credit enhancements from bond guarantee insurance companies or credit default swaps, but these cushions were not in the form of marketable assets. Instead, they were simply contingent liabilities of other financial institutions, added to provide credit enhancements that would cover any residual loss, thus providing the justification for the investment-grade credit ratings on the senior liabilities. The movement of the loans off the banks' balance sheets not only reduced the capital backing of outstanding loans, it also eliminated the reserves and secondary liquidity cushions normally held by banks.

The substitution of the originate-and-hold business model with the originate-and-distribute model of securitization, aided and abetted by the suspension of Glass-Steagall, had another consequence for the stability of the financial system. It meant that the creation of liquidity shifted from deposit creation by commercial banks subject to prudential regulation, to activities undertaken by securitized structures that were exempt from reporting and regulation (because they were considered capital market activities) and exempted by administrative decision from even SEC oversight. As noted earlier, this process of liquidity creation was one in which longer-term, higher-risk, lower-liquidity assets were funded through the issue of shorter-term, lower-risk, higher-liquidity assets by special-purpose entities. This describes what has now come to be known as the "shadow" banking system. In this shadow liquidity system, the prudential supports – legal reserves, secondary reserves, liquidity of the commercial and industrial loan book, and access to federal lender-of-last-resort support through the discount window – were all absent.

---

[7] In contrast, if a bank made a bad credit assessment under originate and reserve, its profits were reduced.

From Increased Financial Fragility in Originate and Distribute to Financial Instability in 2008

It was this underlying fragility that allowed the September 15, 2008 bankruptcy of Lehman Brothers investment bank to become a full-scale financial collapse. Lehman had financed its asset acquisition and its capital by the issue of short-term commercial paper that was held in magnitude by money market mutual funds. Default on these assets meant that the net asset value of a share in MMMF fell below the one-dollar guarantee that allowed it to substitute for bank deposits, and the majority of investors sought to exit these funds. This, in turn, threatened the oldest of the MMMF with having to declare suspension and default. To avoid this outcome, the government was forced to step in to provide a full credit guarantee. However, since FDIC-insured banks were providing only a $100,000 guarantee on their deposits, these deposits were quickly shifted to MMMF, producing a liquidity crisis for insured banks. A full-scale run on deposits resulting from Lehman's bankruptcy was only avoided by enlarging the FDIC guarantee to $250,000 and limiting the MMMF guarantee to balances on record before the Lehman default.

In addition, Lehman provided prime brokerage services to many hedge funds. This meant they provided loans, execution, depository, and record-keeping services. Lehman's bankruptcy meant that many hedge funds had their assets frozen in bankruptcy proceedings. Given the intention of the government to send the financial institutions a signal that they would no longer provide bailouts, hedge fund managers responded by attempting to move their assets out of other investment bank prime brokerage accounts, primarily Morgan Stanley and Goldman Sachs, who also faced the risk of suspension and insolvency. Because it was considered impossible to provide these institutions with guarantees similar to those promised to the MMMF, the decision was made by the Fed and the Treasury to go to Congress to get government assistance, which eventually came in the form of the Troubled Asset Relief Program.

The run on liquidity caused by Lehman's bankruptcy would have been enough to generate a full-scale financial meltdown. However, at virtually the same time, AIG – a large insurance firm that had provided a majority of the guarantees for securitized asset structures in the form of credit default swaps – announced that it could not meet the margin payments on those guarantees as it had exhausted its capital. This not only added to the severity of the liquidity crisis as institutions issued new margin calls, but meant that most of the securitized assets for which AIG had provided credit enhancement would be in default, including those rated AAA. Because many of these securities were being held by banks, it became impossible to assess the solvency of any financial institution. As a result, trading came to a halt in virtually all assets, and short-term money markets (including money market mutual funds) went dry, as no one was willing to lend in conditions of incalculable risk.

Thus, a liquidity crisis produced a collapse of security values, insolvency in securitized structures, and a collapse of short-term lending as financial institutions no longer had certainty about the worthiness of market counterparties. The safety net of deposit insurance and lender-of-last-resort support, created to respond to a run on commercial bank deposits, was totally ill-equipped to respond to a capital market liquidity crisis facing investment banks and bank holding companies. The difficulty with the response to the crisis was that regulators reacted in each instance to a particular failure of the existing system, and attempted to provide emergency support to restore the normal functioning of the particular sector in difficulty. When the problem was sub-prime mortgages, regulators introduced rules to deal with the problems created by sub-prime mortgages; when the problem was capital adequacy regulations, the Fed revised capital adequacy regulations; when the problem was insufficient liquidity, the Fed introduced more stringent liquidity requirements. However, if it is the normal functioning of the system that inevitably caused each of these problems, then simple repairs cannot produce stability.

4. Where Next?

As Minsky has emphasized since his earliest work on financial market regulation, it is impossible to design regulations that increase the stability of financial markets if you do not have a theory of financial market instability. If what is conceived as normal precludes instability except as a random event, regulation will always address ad hoc events that, once they have occurred, are unlikely to occur again. As a result, regulations will prove powerless to prevent future instability. Minsky argued that what was instead required was a theory in which financial instability was a normal occurrence in the financial system. Only on the basis of such a theory could regulation be properly designed and understood and, in the process, a financial system established that is truly capable of serving the two masters.

The regulatory scheme set out in the 2010 Dodd-Frank financial reform bill, most of which still remains to be written by regulators, does little to recognize this need. Although it seeks to ensure that taxpayers do not have to provide TARP-like support to failing banks, it does nothing to deal with the large size of bank holding companies or their multifunction operations.

The creation of a Financial Stability Oversight Council adds another layer of regulation on top of the myriad, often competing, regulatory agencies that already exist (although the bill does eliminate one of them, the Office of Thrift Supervision). The bill does not deal with the problem of state versus federal legislation, which Glass-Steagall had already recognized as one of the weak points in U.S. regulation, or the frequent preemption by federal regulators of state laws that have frequently been more effective than those at the federal level.

Furthermore, the Dodd-Frank bill fails to deal fully with one of the main weaknesses of the current financial system: banks speculating with "other peoples' money." The "Volcker rule" that is incorporated in the bill seeks to prohibit insured banks from engaging in proprietary trading, or direct ownership of hedge and private equity funds. Furthermore, the Lincoln amendment seeks to limit banks receiving government aid or insurance from acting as swap (derivatives) dealers. These measures have been seen as a partial attempt to return to the segmentation of banking and finance established in the 1933 Glass-Steagall legislation. Nevertheless, lobbying by financial institutions, using arguments similar to those that eviscerated Glass-Steagall, has resulted in the incorporation of exceptions, safe harbors, and delayed implementation deadlines into the final legislation, making it possible for banks to continue the activities the bill seeks to prohibit. For example, bank trading to provide hedging on behalf of the bank's clients is exempt from the provisions of the Dodd-Frank bill. However, every trade has a counterparty that can be conceived of as a "client": most of the proprietary trading in credit default swaps has been classified by the head of one of the largest investment banks as "market making" activity at client request. As a result, some banks have retained their proprietary trading operations by shifting them to client desks, or moving them to asset-management businesses where they trade with outside investors' capital.[8]

The bill's restrictions on ownership of hedge funds allows for bank ownership of up to 3 percent of its Tier 1 shareholders' equity capital, but leaves determination of the exact value of this capital ratio to the Basel III process, currently set at 7 percent of risk-adjusted assets but likely to be raised further. This means that an increase in Tier 1 capital in an attempt to provide

[8] According to the Baer, 2010 "Goldman moved a group of traders from its Principal Strategies trading arm to its asset management unit in 2007. This year JPMorgan Chase shifted its equity, emerging markets and structured-credit prop traders to the asset management division, where they will establish a new alternative-investments group. Citigroup is weighing up shifting its two dozen prop traders to other parts of the bank, including its client-facing desks."

greater safety would, at the same time, allow larger bank ownership stakes in what are essentially proprietary trading operations through participation in hedge funds.

There are similar exceptions to the Lincoln amendment, as well as to the regulation that all over-the-counter derivatives should be cleared in an organized clearing-house and traded on an organized exchange. The most important is that if a contract is not offered by any exchange, it need not be exchange traded. Because most structured derivatives products are one-off bespoke transactions depending on the particular needs of the client, it is unlikely that they could be foreseen and thus offered on a regulated exchange. They would thus continue to be traded on a bilateral private basis.

There is a very natural response to the two masters dilemma faced by financial regulation. As noted earlier, the Constitution gives the federal government the right to coin money and issue debt. From the time of the issue of private bank notes, the government has allowed private institutions to usurp that function. Prudential regulation of banks is only required because the government has allowed the private sector to provide substitutes for government currency. If the government were to provide a national transactions account – say, a Federal Reserve deposit account with an electronic payments card, much as food stamps are provided in many states – prudential regulation of banks would no longer be needed, because they could no longer provide payments services. The second master would then be perfectly served since unlike a bank, the government cannot default on its own liabilities. The system envisaged here could take the form of a national transfer account, of the sort that used to be provided by government postal systems in the United States and Europe until financial liberalization led to the privatization of these systems. Financial institutions would be limited to providing investment accounts and therefore tasked exclusively with the capital development of the economy. The government could also provide risk-free savings accounts, deposits that would be invested in Treasury securities (much like the existing government savings bond system). Under this scheme, the SEC would continue to provide regulation of investment banks, ensuring that they were run with full transparency and without fraud. Savers would then be offered a perfectly safe-and- secure payments system as well as a risk-free savings system. Those who were willing to secure higher potential returns at the cost of higher risk would be free to do so via the purchase of shares in private investment banks. The system would still be subject to crises, as Minsky stressed, since it is impossible to guarantee the returns on risky financial investments required to serve the first master. However, the size of financial institutions would be smaller and easier to regulate. Although it is impossible to stop the erosion of the cushion of safety that is produced by periods of sustained expansion, losses and insolvencies could be limited to the creditors of the institutions undertaking the risks, and losses could be met by the creditors of the institutions without recourse to taxpayer insured deposits or government bailouts.

References

Baer, J. (2010) Proprietary traders weigh up new options, Financial Times, U.S. edition, 25 October, p.16.

Corrigan, E. G. (1982) "Are Banks Special?" Appendix, Federal Reserve Bank of Minneapolis Annual Report.

Fisher, K. R. (2001) "Orphan of Invention: Why the Gramm-Leach-Bliley Act Was Unnecessary." *Oregon Law Review* **80**: 1301–1421.

Gorton, G. B. (2009) "Slapped in the Face by the Invisible Hand: Banking and the Panic of 2007." Accessed May 9 at SSRN: http://ssrn.com/abstract=1401882.

Krooss, H. E. (1969) *Documentary History of Banking and Currency in the United States.* New York: Chelsea House Publishers (in Association with McGraw-Hill).

Madelaine, M. G. (1943) *Monetary and Banking Theories of Jacksonian Democracy.* Philadelphia: Dolphin Press.

Minsky, H. P. (1957) "Central Banking and Money Market Changes." *Quarterly Journal of Economics* **71**(2): 171–87.

(1986) "Global Consequences of Financial Deregulation." The Marcus Wallenberg Papers on International Finance. Vol. 2, no. 1.

"Issues in Bank Regulation and Supervision." Jerome Levy Economics Institute, Annandale-on-Hudson, October 14, 1994.

(2008) "Securitization (with Preface and Afterword by L. Randall Wray)." PolicyNote 2008/2. Annandale-on-Hudson, NY: The Levy Economics Institute of Bard College.

Omarova, S. (2009) "The Quiet Metamorphosis: How Derivatives Changed the Business of Banking." *University of Miami Law Review* **63**: 1041–1110.

Robert Morris Associates. (1988) A Guide to analyzing foreign banks. Philadelphia: Robert Morris Associates.

Siclari, V. (2001) "A Tough Act to Follow: How to Deal with the Investment Company Act of 1940." Business Law Today 10(3). Available at: https://www.abanet.org/bus-law/blt/bltjan01siclari.html.

Stigum, M. (1983) The Money Market: Myth, Reality, and Practice.

FIVE

How Bonus-Driven "Rainmaker" Financial Firms Enrich Top Employees, Destroy Shareholder Value, and Create Systemic Financial Instability

James Crotty

It is now universally agreed that the United States and global economies recently experienced their worst financial crisis since the 1930s.[1] From a U.S.-centric perspective, it is clear that the evolution of financial markets since the end of the 1970s led almost inevitably to a crisis moment such as this. In the late 1970s and very early 1980s, the U.S. government began to accelerate an ongoing process of financial market deregulation. A combination of deregulation and fast-paced financial innovation led to a series of financial crises both in the United States and elsewhere. These crises were always met by government bailouts, which restored stability and vitality to financial markets, but also created an increasingly assured belief among leaders of financial institutions that the government would always intervene to limit the depth and duration of future financial crises. This reduced expected future losses associated with risk-taking in a financial boom, which increased the incentive for financial institutions to take more risk and use more leverage. This risk-taking strategy maximized the expected compensation of key decision-makers in financial firms – hereafter known as "rainmakers." The term rainmaker is usually taken to mean those who can generate high sales for the firm. *I use it here to denote all key people in financial firms who are responsible for generating high revenue and profit.* It thus includes top executives, traders, sales people, wealth managers, and mergers-and-acquisitions and initial-public-offerings team members.

[1] This paper is adapted from a much longer monograph available at: http://people.umass.edu/~crotty/RMFC%20paper%20-%20July%202010.pdf. I am grateful to Derek Jaskulski, Iren Levina, Rob Parenteau, Jennifer Taub, and especially Jerry Epstein for helpful comments, to Iren Levina for outstanding research assistance, and to the UMASS Economics Department's Sheridan Scholars program for research support.

Rainmakers understood that they could gain huge bonuses by using dangerous levels of leverage to fund excessive risk-taking in the boom that they did not have to return when their recklessness caused their firms and the entire financial system to crash. Indeed, they continued to receive exorbitant bonuses in the downturn. Of course, in an environment of fundamental uncertainty, rainmakers are not immune from infection by the general boom euphoria that arises in prolonged financial upturns. Some may believe that objectively risky policies are not really risky when market conditions seem ideal. However, as insiders, they are much more aware of the dangers involved in aggressive investment strategies than is the general public. There are numerous examples of financial institutions that continued to use high-risk strategies even when it became clear that the mortgage-related securities they relied on were in serious trouble.[2] Most important, the data demonstrates that it is rational for top financial-firm operatives to take excessive risk in the bubble *even if they understand that their decisions are likely to cause their firm to suffer large losses in the intermediate future.* The incentive to pursue risky strategies – inherent in rainmaker compensation schemes – combined with deregulation and destructive financial innovation, made it virtually impossible to avoid the outbreak of a serious financial and economic crisis. (For an analysis of the financial causes of the recent crisis, see Crotty (2009) and Chapters 4 and 5 by Wray and Kregel, respectively, in this volume.)

This chapter deals with the effects of perverse bonus-based compensation incentives in financial markets in general, but focuses special attention on giant investment banks. They were the source of most of the financial innovations – such as mortgage-backed securities, collateralized debt obligations of various kinds, and credit default swaps – that helped create the crisis. Investment banks were also at the center of the system's leverage creation process.

---

[2] For example, when CDOs began to lose value in 2007, giant investment banks such as Merrill Lynch and Goldman Sachs began lending money to supposedly "independent" CDO managers (who, in fact, were strongly influenced by the big banks) "so they could buy the banks' dodgy assets. ... Faced with increasing difficulty in selling the mortgage-backed securities that had been among their most lucrative products, the banks hit on a solution that preserved their quarterly earnings and huge bonuses: They created fake demand" (Pro Publica, 2010).However, to induce the CDO managers to take their "dodgy assets," the banks had to lend them the money used in the purchase. "If the managers couldn't pay the loans back – and most were thinly capitalized – the banks were on the hook for even more losses when the CDO business collapsed" Pro Publica, 2010. Nevertheless, bank rainmakers did not have to give back the bonuses associated with these deals, so it was in their interest to do them.

Although the primary focus here is on the effects of perverse rainmaker incentives on financial market performance, it is important to understand that these incentives also helped cause the Great Recession. Perverse incentives induced financial institutions to make mortgage loans to those who could not afford them, and to package mortgages into non-transparent, risky securities that infected the global financial system. They helped create an unsustainable bubble in housing prices. Perverse incentives led financial institutions to encourage households to borrow excessively on the bubble-induced rise in home equity. They contributed to a leverage-fed asset-price bubble that left the financial system in a disastrously fragile condition by 2007. When the inevitable crisis hit, household wealth collapsed, forcing consumption spending to contract and the construction industry to implode as a credit freeze restrained spending in the private sector.[3]

Section one of this chapter presents data on rainmaker compensation in giant investment banks that shows that rainmaker compensation is very large, and has asymmetric properties that generate strong incentives for excessive risk-taking in financial booms. Section two reviews the modest literature on compensation in financial firms in general and investment banks in particular. It demonstrates that large rainmaker premiums cannot be explained as returns to human capital – they are unearned rents.[4] Sections three and four discuss possible answers to the difficult question: what are the sources of rainmaker rents? The final section summarizes conclusions from this analysis.

---

[3]   See Chapter 6 by Cynamon and Fazzari on the influence of financial markets on consumption spending in the boom. Related themes are also explored in Chapter 2 by Palley, Chapter 3 by Wray, and Chapter 4 by Kregel.

[4]   The fact that rainmakers help create the revenues that are the source of their bonuses requires us to distinguish the definition of "rent" used in this paper from the definition typically used in economic discourse. The concept of rent normally refers to a situation in which agents use economic or political power to extract income they did not create and thus do not deserve. For example, a firm that possesses monopoly power can extract larger profits than would be available to firms operating under conditions assumed in theories of perfect competition. However, the revenues in modern financial markets that are the source of rainmaker bonuses are not independent of their activities. Were it not for excessive risk-taking by rainmakers induced by perverse incentives, and bubble-generated capital gains and fees, the revenues flowing to their firms would not be nearly as large as they were in recent years. To a substantial degree, rainmakers create the revenues from which their bonuses are derived, and thus their rents are different from the standard cases discussed in economic theory. They are still rents, however, because, as explained in this chapter, they are payments not justified by long-term value creation.

1. Rainmaker Compensation Schemes: The Primacy of Bonuses

Data on bank compensation practices in the recent boom and crisis was collected by New York State Attorney General Andrew Cuomo in 2009. He concludes that

> Bonuses and overall compensation did not vary significantly as profits diminished. An analysis of the 2008 bonuses and earnings at the original nine TARP recipients [of $125 billion in government bailouts] illustrates the point. *Two firms, Citigroup and Merrill Lynch suffered massive losses of more than $27 billion at each firm. Nevertheless, Citigroup paid out $5.33 billion in bonuses and Merrill paid $3.6 billion in bonuses. Together, they lost $54 billion, paid out nearly $9 billion in bonuses and then received TARP bailouts totaling $55 billion.* (Cuomo 2009, pp. 1–2, emphasis added).

Compensation failed to shrink in line with revenue and profits in the crash. Yet the main purpose of a bonus system is to reduce compensation as revenues fall, thereby protecting profit and shareholder value. Indeed, as earnings at key banks collapsed, compensation increased. For example, Cuomo reports that Bank of America's (BOA) compensation (including benefits) rose from $10 billion in 2003 to more than $18 billion near the peak of the boom in 2006. However, compensation remained at $18 billion in 2008 even though BOA's net income collapsed by 70 percent. Citigroup showed a similar pattern; compensation remained at record levels even as the firm faced a financial crisis.

Many commentators claimed that the large losses suffered by rainmakers in the crash provide evidence against the assertion that perverse incentives were an important cause of the crisis. However, although many rainmakers did suffer substantial losses on the shares they held in the latter part of 2008 and early 2009, their cash bonuses and cumulative realized gains from stock sales in preceding years far exceeded their losses. Bebchuk, Cohen, and Spamann (2009) demonstrate that the top five executives at Bear Stearns and Lehman Brothers received an average $250 million in net compensation in the period from 2000 through – and therefore including – their firms' demise.

Figure 5.1 compares bonuses at Wall Street firms (i.e., broker-dealers located in Manhattan, a sample dominated by giant investment banks) to the pre-tax profit of securities firms listed on the New York Stock Exchange (a larger sample) from 1985 to 2008. It shows not only that investment bank and security dealer profits experienced exceptional growth during this period, but also that the relationship between bonuses and pre-tax

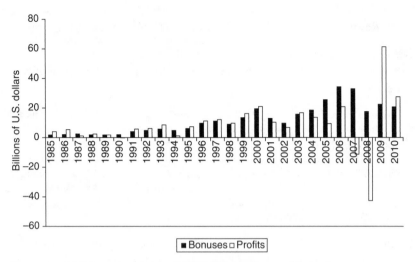

Figure 5.1. Wall Street bonuses and NYSE firms' pre-tax profits.
Note: Profits are from Securities Industry and Financial Markets Association for 1985–2007, and from New York State Comptroller's Office for 2008–2010.

profits changed substantially over time. From 2004 through 2006, the gap between bonuses and profits became very large. Bonus growth was substantially eroding profits. In 2007 these firms collectively lost $11.3 billion. To reward themselves for generating these losses, rainmakers paid themselves bonuses of $33 billion, an amount far greater than paid in any year other than 2006. Bonuses in 2007 were only $1 billion below the previous boom year. *If bonuses had declined in 2007 to their 2002 level, a year in which firms made almost $7 billion in profits, these firms would have made $26 billion in profits instead of suffering massive losses.*[5] In 2008, the full force of the meltdown caused Wall Street to lose a record-high $42.6 billion dollars. Bonuses fell substantially, but at $17.4 billion they were about equal to the 2004 bonus total when profits were $13.7 billion.

Although the financial system suffered a near-death experience in late 2008 and early 2009, a $12 trillion rescue effort by the government triggered a miraculous financial recovery. The New York State Comptroller's Office (2011) estimates that industry profits, "fueled by federal bailouts, low interest rates, and proprietary trading" exceeded $61 billion in 2009, about three times greater than the previous record high. Even 2010 profits

---

[5] Although, as noted, these series are not fully consistent, the general conclusion stated here is correct. If bonuses had been set at 2002 levels in 2007, investment banks would collectively have generated modest profits instead of suffering substantial losses.

of $27.6 billion were higher than any year except 2009. The comptroller's bonus estimates for 2009 and 2010 are $22.5 billion and $20.8 billion, higher than in any year except 2005 to 2007. However, these estimates are clearly too low. The comptroller's bonus data does not include unrealized gains on stock options and other forms of deferred bonuses. The degree of underestimation was especially pronounced in 2009 and 2010 because, under pressure from the public and some regulators, "many financial firms delayed payments and paid a greater share in stock or other forms of deferred compensation" (New York State Comptroller's Office 2010). Total compensation paid to employees at the top twenty-five Wall Street firms hit a record high in 2009, and another in 2010 (*Wall Street Journal*, "On Street, Pay Vaults to Record Level," February 2, 2011).

A standard way to measure shareholder gains over time is by calculating the "cumulative total return" (CTR) on the stock, which includes capital gains or losses over time (adjusted for stock splits) and assumes dividends are used to buy more shares. A CTR calculation requires specified dates for stock purchase and the end of the sample period. I argue in Crotty 2010 that the most relevant question for evaluating the effect of perverse incentives on shareholders is: what would have happened to shareholders if market forces had been left to determine their fate in the absence of massive government rescue efforts? It thus seems reasonable to examine shareholder and rainmaker returns along the path that their firms' market activities brought them by March 2009, prior to the rebound caused by radical government intervention in the market system.

Figure 5.2 presents inflation-adjusted CTR for the five giant investment banks that were independent prior to the crash. *If you bought stock in the big five investment banks after 1994 you would have lost wealth. Buying in 1998 would have resulted in a 67 percent loss of investment value.* Thus, over the period of the two recent financial market booms, when the new compensation system became strongly entrenched, rainmakers became phenomenally wealthy by following high-risk high-leverage strategies, whereas their stockholders were financially devastated. "All this has reinforced the idea that banking is simply a gravy train for employees" (*The Economist*, "The bonus racket," January 29, 2009).

2. Do Rainmaker Premiums Exist: If So, Are They Rent?

After observing that compensation policies that "incentivized top executives of United States financial institutions to take excessive risk" were widely believed to be a major cause of the financial crisis, Balachandran, Kogut,

110   *Crotty*

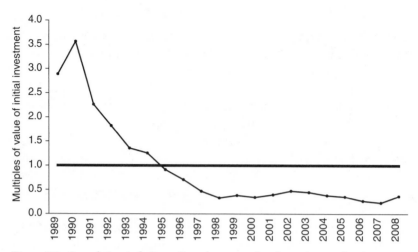

Figure 5.2. Cumulative inflation-adjusted returns for shares in top-five investment banks from date indicated on horizontal axis to March 25, 2009.
Note: Inflation adjustment with the consumer price index for all urban households.

and Harnal 2010 note: "The academic evidence that speaks to this claim of excessive risk [because of compensation schemes] is surprisingly sparse" (p. 2). However, there are a few articles that show that compensation received by financial industry rainmakers is substantially higher than the compensation of seemingly equivalent workers in nonfinancial firms. Paul Oyer 2006 uses a database that covers several thousand graduates of Stanford's MBA program. He assumes these MBAs have broadly equivalent human capital attributes. Because investment banking is an extremely popular field among Stanford MBAs, Oyer argues that the percentage of new graduates who enter investment banking is chronically constrained by job availability. That is, he sees a chronic excess supply of potential investment bank rainmakers, a finding that conflicts with the conventional justification of high rainmaker premiums discussed in this chapter – that there is a chronic excess demand for rainmakers. During stock market booms, the percentage of MBAs who can get Wall Street jobs rises. Oyer documents that, in spite of the chronic excess supply, those who get Wall Street jobs get much higher salaries than those who enter other fields. The investment banking premium is stunning.

> The [annual] premium varies from about 60% for a new MBA on Wall Street relative to one in management consulting to over 300% for investment bankers fifteen years after leaving Stanford relative to an average alumnus with the

same amount of experience in any other industry.... I estimate that a new MBA that goes to Wall Street can expect to earn between $2 million and $6 million in discounted lifetime income (in $1996) relative to what he would earn if he took a job elsewhere" (p. 2).

Oyer notes that these are underestimations of the premium. The "income premium for investment bankers ... is biased downward because so much investment banking income comes through bonuses" whereas the income measure is salaries (p. 29). Because bonuses are the main form of rainmaker compensation, often hitting 90 percent of total compensation, this underestimation must be extremely large.

Philippon and Reshef 2009 and Goldin and Katz 2008 provide persuasive evidence that these premiums are rents rather than returns to human capital. The Philippon and Reshef paper studies *average* industry wages. It thus underestimates the degree to which rainmaker incomes have risen since the 1980s because rainmaker incomes are at the very top of the distribution and have risen by much more than average incomes. The authors show that the ratio of the average wage of financial market employees relative to the average wage in other industries was high in the 1920s through the early 1930s, when it peaked at more than 1.6. It then collapsed through the early 1950s under the much stricter regulatory regime of the period, and continued to decline modestly through the late 1970s, where it approached 1.0. At this point, there was no premium. The ratio rose again through 1990 to near 1.2 as the post-Depression regulatory regime was deconstructed. It then skyrocketed through 2006, where, at 1.7, it exceeded the peak reached after the bubble of the 1920s.

Philippon and Reshef separate financial employees into three subcategories: credit intermediation (or traditional banking), insurance, and "other finance." Other finance includes commodity traders, investment funds and trusts, venture capital, hedge and private equity funds, and investment banks. It thus comes closest to the financial firms and rainmakers with which we are concerned. After 1980, the indexes for credit intermediation and insurance rise above 1.0, and eventually hit 1.5 in 2006. However, as Philippon and Reshef show in Figure 2, the relative wage for other finance remains reasonably stable at around 1.0 from 1940 through 1980. At that point, just as the secular financial market explosion begins, *the relative wage of other finance accelerates rapidly and is near 4.0 by 2006 – a ratio almost four times its 1980 value, two and one-half times higher than its early 1930s peak, and almost three times higher than compensation for credit intermediation and insurance.* The rapid rise in financial market compensation is clearly concentrated in the most speculative, risk-seeking segments of the industry. It is interesting to note that the pattern over time of other finance is quite similar to the percent of before-tax income captured by the top 0.01 percent of the income distribution (Saez 2009, figure 3).

Using Current Population Survey (CPS) data, Philippon and Reshef estimate wage regressions that include as control variables education, race, gender, marital status, urban residence, and experience. These regressions show that "individuals working in finance indeed earn more than observationally equivalent workers" in other industries (p. 24) that peaked in 2005 at 20 percent – about four times its value in the years from 1967 to 1980. Given the pronounced differences among the relative wages in credit intermediation, insurance, and other finance, it would be reasonable to assume that the other finance premium is very much larger than 20 percent. Moreover, the use of CPS data creates a very strong downward bias in these estimates because CPS incomes are top-coded – incomes above an arbitrary level are recorded as if they were equal to that level. CPS data "has a shortcoming" that makes it inappropriate for the study of very high incomes – which is the focus of interest here (Philippon and Reshef 2009 p. 10). There are thirteen times more top-coded individuals in other finance than in nonfinancial industries. The true rainmaker premium must be very large indeed.

Philippon and Reshef show that rainmaker- driven compensation growth was far greater than can be justified by the increased demand for human capital in finance. They "conclude that a large part of the excess wages … is due to rent" (p. 29). They note that large rents "explain the large flow of talent into the industry." However, Philippon and Reshef do not explain what caused or sustained the rents (p.31).

Goldin and Katz 2008 regress the annual earnings of 6,207 Harvard graduates against an impressively large set of variables. Control variables include grade point average, SAT math and verbal scores, college major, dummy variables for a number of advanced degrees, three full-time full-year work-status dummies, and nineteen different occupation dummies. They find the "the highest earnings by occupation are garnered by those in finance, for which the earnings premium relative to all other occupations is an *astounding 1.08 log points, or 195 percent*" (p. 367, emphasis added). Highly educated employees working in finance receive a huge compensation premium relative to seemingly identical employees working elsewhere. *The near 200 percent premium certainly appears to be rent.*

Bertrand, Goldin, and Katz 2009 examine the careers of University of Chicago MBAs who graduated between 1990 and 2006. After five years, mean compensation was $500,979 for investment bankers and $307,451 for all respondents – including investment bankers. Ten years or more after graduation, it was $815,914 for investment bankers and $400,715 for all respondents – *a premium in excess of 100 percent* (table 2, p. 31).

3. How Are Rainmaker Rents Created and Sustained over Time? "False Value" and Oligopoly Power

To answer the key question of how rainmaker rents can exist, be so large, and sustain themselves over time, we have to address two sub-questions. First, *why are investment bank and other financial-firm revenues per employee so large in booms?* Second, *why are rainmakers able to capture such an exceptionally large share of revenues in good times and bad?*

We preface our answer to the first question by briefly commenting on the standard answer: financial market rainmakers are paid more than others with similar backgrounds because they are smarter and more talented, and therefore more productive of long-term value than others. They are, in other words, the "best and the brightest" people in the business world. Here the case is made that there may be qualities that distinguish successful financial market rainmakers from those with similar human capital endowments as traditionally measured, but they are not qualities that lead to the generation of the above-average, long-term, risk-adjusted value creation that is typically used to justify outsized rainmaker compensation. On the contrary, they are qualities likely to generate volatile booms and busts that are value-destroying over the long run.

Both contacts on Wall Street and acquaintances who teach at elite colleges that send large portions of their graduates to Wall Street tell me that investment banks do not focus their recruiting efforts on those students with the most impressive academic credentials. Rather, they look for students at prestigious schools with acceptable grade point averages (perhaps B or better) who have demonstrated exceptional aggressiveness or competitiveness. They want dominating type-A people, not exceptionally smart or well-informed people who are not hyperaggressive. For example, they frequently recruit lacrosse, rugby, and hockey players. At the American Economic Association (AEA) annual meetings in January 2009, Nobel Laureate Joseph Stiglitz attacked the "myth that Wall Street is populated by the best and the brightest, who deserve their big paydays.... When I look at the salaries some of our B students [on Wall Street] got, it doesn't correspond to their innate ability" (*Wall Street Journal*, "Overheard," January 4, 2010, p. C8). Andrew Ross Sorkin said of the legendary investor Warren Buffet:

"he despised the trader ethos and the lucrative paydays that enriched people he thought were neither particularly intelligent or created much value" (Sorkin 2009, p. 55). Sorkin observes that investment bank trading is "like a sport, something that required skill, but not necessarily brains or creativity" (p. 24). He quotes Lehman CEO Richard Fuld using martial metaphors to describe this work: "Every day is a battle … you have to kill the enemy," (p. 28) and says that when John Mack, formerly the CEO and board chairman of Morgan Stanley was a trader, he would "stride through the trading floor and, seeing a chance to make big profits, would yell "There's blood in the water, let's go kill someone!" (p. 186–187).

Discussion of these character traits first appear after 1980, when investment banking began to change dramatically. In his 1989 best seller *Liar's Poker*, Michael Lewis described mortgage traders and other rainmakers at Salomon Brothers in the mid-1980s as hypercompetitive, risk-loving gamblers obsessed with short-term bonuses. Lewis wrote that the best rainmakers "are cutthroat, competitive, and often neurotic and paranoid," and referred to the "backstabbing and intrigue for which investment bankers are justifiably renowned" (pp. 141, 185). He argued that gambling is a consuming passion for traders: "all the boys on the trading floor loved to gamble" (p. 14). Lewis also emphasized "the insatiable hunger for more [money] felt by anyone who had succeeded at Salomon Brothers and probably at any Wall Street firm. … The most poisonous [form of greed] was the desire to have more *now*; short term greed rather than long-term greed" (1989, p. 203, emphasis in original).

In recent decades, the CEOs and other top executives of large investment banks have often been former traders who still have a trader's mentality, and top salespersons often share many of the traders' character traits. Thus, the typical investment bank rainmaker appears to be a competitive risk-loving, money-obsessed gambler with a short-term planning horizon – "I want my bonus now." It may be that it is these characteristics, rather than superior talent, that distinguish financial market rainmakers from others with similar educational credentials and experience who work elsewhere, although they do not explain where the rents come from. It is precisely people with these characteristics who, if not prevented from doing so, would be expected to maximize the amount of risk-taking in buoyant financial markets in order to simultaneously maximize their own compensation. Given the nature of modern unregulated financial markets, these were the worst, rather than the best, kind of people to put in charge.

The answer to the question of why the revenue pool that feeds the bonuses of financial market rainmakers is so high in the boom can be stated succinctly: the increase in financial-firm revenues over the past few decades have been generated primarily by speculative asset bubbles and bubble-driven fees rather than by long-term value creation, and secondarily by oligopoly pricing power.

Although other revenue and profit sources helped sustain the recent bubble, their growth would not have been possible in the absence of a strong upward trend in important security prices and the optimistic expectations generated by this trend. For example, expectations of solid returns to all mortgage-based securities in the recent boom depended on excessively optimistic expectations of future residential real estate prices. The excessive risk-taking and rising leverage in the boom create tremendous momentum for the asset-price bubbles that generate the capital gains and fees that fuel financial market profits and bonuses. However, such risk-taking always causes a financial crisis and subsequent collapse of financial asset prices, and thus of financial firms' revenue, profit, and market capitalization. Value created in the boom evaporates along with shareholder wealth, but the claims on real goods and services embodied in rainmaker bonuses survive. They thus constitute not a reward for productivity, but an unearned redistribution of wealth from the rest of society to financial rainmakers. They are rents.

Rainmakers do create market value during the bubble. They initiate, identify, exploit, and reinforce serial financial asset bubbles. However, in order for rainmaker bonuses to be considered as earned and not as rent, one must assume that the increase in the value of financial assets they help create during the boom is long term rather than transitory. History demonstrates that financial markets move through time in boom-bust cycles around some variable trend. Financial assets are grossly overvalued in the late boom, as demonstrated by the subsequent bust, and undervalued in the worst part of the crash, as demonstrated by the subsequent recovery. Thus, one way to measure the long-term value creation that should determine bonuses in speculative financial booms is to examine value after the excesses of the boom have been eliminated. However, since the government has consistently bailed out financial markets in recent downturns, even measuring value creation by rainmakers via longer-term trends grossly exaggerates their contribution to the economy. Without such interventions, modern financial markets would have been shown to be long-term value-destroying on a massive scale.

Floyd Norris showed that an investor who held the stocks in the S&P 500 stock market index and reinvested all dividends would have earned an inflation-adjusted average *annual* return over a ten-year period ending in January 2009 of *minus* 5.1 percent (Norris 2009). There was thus no financial or nonfinancial long-term value creation that could possibly justify the huge bonuses and stock options of the era.

The theory that best explains why boom-bust cycles inevitably take place in capitalist financial markets can be found in the works of Keynes, Minsky, and Marx.[6] Keynes's theory is built on the core assumption of radical or fundamental uncertainty: the future is not knowable in the present because it does not yet exist and it has not yet been determined. Agents can only guess how markets will evolve in the future and make choices based on these fallible guesses. These choices, made in ignorance, affect the system's future trajectory in an unpredictable, dynamic, path-dependent process. So-called rational expectations – or correct expectations about the future – on which modern financial economics is based, are not possible because the "fundamentals" of future economic states are undetermined at the moment of choice. It is fundamental uncertainty that creates the open-ended "decision space" within which rainmakers operate.

In a Keynesian world, expectations are formed "conventionally," normally via extrapolation from the recent past. The longer such expectations lead to decisions that generate satisfactory outcomes, as they do in booms, the greater the "confidence" that agents place in them. In Keynes's theory, confidence is defined as the subjective sense of agent certainty that their expectations are realistic. When a financial boom lasts for some time, agents begin to project its continuance. Given optimistic expectations of future prices, buying securities previously seen as risky will seem reasonable. As the boom proceeds (reinforcing optimistic expectations), buying securities with borrowed money also seems like a sensible decision. This drives the financial boom forward, raising leverage while raining capital gains on investors. The heaviest rain falls on the most aggressive investors, which lures others to mimic their strategies. Objectively risky investment strategies are eventually considered safe. Because every long-term financial boom is accompanied by the widespread belief that we have entered a "new era" in which the forces that ended all previous booms are no longer operative, the current boom eventually comes to be seen as permanent. At the peak of the boom, there is a near-universal belief that high yields previously achievable only by accepting high risk can now be gained safely. For example,

---

[6] See Crotty 1994 for a careful explanation of Keynes's theory of financial volatility. For a defense of the proposition that Marx's theory of financial market behavior has a great deal in common with the financial market theories of Keynes and Minsky, see Crotty 1985. However, there is no major role given to perverse incentives in any of these theories.

in the halcyon days just prior to the outbreak of the Great Recession, millions of people took on mortgage commitments or home equity loans whose payments could be met only if their incomes were secure, interest rates remained low, and housing prices kept rising. Financial firms relied on short-term borrowing to finance the acquisition of long-term, illiquid, risky mortgage-related securities. This helped fuel the boom, but set the stage for an inevitable crash.

The system eventually becomes, to use Minsky's famous phrase, "financially fragile." Expected future cash flows based on overly optimistic expectations are increasingly contractually committed by households and financial and nonfinancial firms to financial institutions. Increased reliance on short-term financing makes financial firms especially vulnerable when crisis conditions erupt. Financial booms end when real-sector cash flows – whose growth is constrained by resource availability, technology, and the state of aggregate demand – can no longer sustain boom-elevated security prices and dangerous leverage positions, and/or when intra-financial-sector commitments cannot be met.

The central point is that from the perspective of the most realistic theories of financial market dynamics, the value created by boom euphoria, excessive leverage and dangerous risk-taking is "false value." Because the false value that rainmakers help create is, through its direct and indirect effects, the main source of excessive rainmaker compensation, it cannot be justified as payment for contributions to increased economic efficiency and/or long-term economic growth. These payments are rents.

There has been a significant increase in the market share held by a small number of the largest firms in important financial markets in the last quarter century that has enabled these firms to use substantial market power to increase revenue, profit, and rainmaker bonuses. Crotty 2010 presents extensive evidence to support the claim that key financial segments are dominated by a handful of firms with the ability to use market power to raise mark-ups. Pricing-power based on oligopolistic financial market structures and practices has added substantially to the pool of funds created by boom-induced false values that are the main source of rainmaker compensation. One *Financial Times'* editorial argued that: "inadequate competition failed to whittle away large profits – as enormous returns on equity showed – and therefore [failed to reduce] outsize compensation, unlike in other industries" ("Public needs more bank for its bucks," October 16, 2009). Another insisted that "Banks are rent extractors – and uncompetitive ones at that. Even after paying high bonuses, the banks' return on equity is extremely high" ("Editorial Counsel of Despair," April 22, 2010).

4. How Are Rainmakers Able to Capture an Exceptionally Large Share of Revenue in Good Times and Bad?

Given that the compensation system was a serious threat to the interests of shareholders, taxpayers, the survival of the big investment banks, and the reproduction of the financial system, how were rainmakers able to maintain it? Crotty (2010) explains in detail why neither shareholders, top executives, boards of directors, capital markets, government regulators nor market competition forced a more efficient and less risky compensation system on rainmaker financial firms. Here we briefly discuss why shareholders cannot perform this task.

Mainstream financial market theory cannot explain the reproduction over a long period of time of a compensation system structured to allow rainmakers to loot shareholders and threaten the existence of the firm itself because it assumes that financial markets are efficient. Keynesian theory can help solve the puzzle represented by the sustained existence of the rainmaker financial firm because it has no paradigmatic commitment to "rational" expectations and financial market efficiency. Although the data clearly shows that existing compensation schemes induce behavior that is inconsistent with objective shareholder interests, *Keynesian theory suggests that in financial booms, shareholders are likely to believe that rainmaker compensation policies are compatible with their perceived or subjective interests.* During the boom, most shareholders, relying on conventionally-determined optimistic expectations (reinforced by the bullish business press), believe that the spectacular capital gains of the period are realistic reflections of buoyant future economic conditions. They therefore may be perfectly happy with investment bank risk-taking practices even though these practices are *objectively* counter to their longer-term interests. In the midst of boom euphoria, most people fail to understand that their banks are taking excessive risk. Thus, from a Keynesian perspective, the question of why and how rainmaker financial corporations are able to act against objective shareholder interests for years or even decades need not arise: shareholders are usually happy with their banks in the bubble. If you bought Merrill Lynch stock at $6.50 at the end of 1994, or even at its cycle-peak price of $14 at the end of 2000, you probably would have been thrilled in late 2006 when the stock reached $47 (prices are adjusted for stock splits and dividends).

However, a complete answer to the question of why shareholders did not restrain rainmaker greed must incorporate the fact that most of the equity in U.S. firms is held by financial intermediaries rather than individuals or households.[7] In the 1950s, households owned 90 percent of stocks and held their stock for about a decade. By 2007, financial institutions held two-thirds of U.S. stock. The *Wall Street Journal* reports that "18 of the top 20 share-holders at Morgan Stanley and Bank of America and 19 of the top 20 at Goldman Sachs are mutual funds " ("Critics Say Funds Should Do More to Police Corporate Pay," April 5, 2010).

The turnover rate on the New York Stock Exchange exceeded 100 per-cent in six of the seven years between 2002 and 2008, hitting 138 percent in the final year (Securities Industry and Financial Markets Association Fact Book 2009, p. 49). This implies that the time horizon of the average finan-cial intermediary is well under one year, which helps explain why insti-tutional investors are willing to buy and hold the "hottest" stocks even if they believe they are overvalued – as long as they think the bubble will last for another year or more. In recent bubbles, stocks issued by large, high-risk-taking financial corporations have been among the most buoyant of all, which, along with perverse incentives, helps explain why institutional investors held so much financial-firm stock when the crash hit.

Why do institutional investors have short-term horizons? Crotty (2008) explains that key decision makers in institutional investors such as mutual funds have perverse incentives similar to those of investment bank rain-makers that lead them to buy and hold rainmaker financial-firm stock in booms – whether their own expectations are optimistic or pessimistic. Compensation for those who run institutional investment companies rises with assets under management. This encourages firms to seek maximum growth, which in turn requires that they seek a maximum rate of return on assets. Because high returns lead to increased inflows into institutional investment firms, and this increases the size of assets under management, there are good reasons to buy high-risk, high-return assets in the boom. Money market managers "chase whatever's hot and shun whatever's not. Those who are the best at this game attract more money in rising markets and lose fewer clients in falling markets ..." (*Wall Street Journal*, "Inefficient Markets are Still Hard to Beat," July 9–10, 2009).

The positive incentives for institutional investors to support risky rain-maker policies in a boom are reinforced by competitive pressures fac-ing these firms, one form of the "destructive competition" that operates in many important markets.[8] Contracts to manage pension fund assets are awarded to firms with above-average returns on assets and may be

---

[7]   See Chapter 3 by Randall Wray in this book.
[8]   The concept of "destructive competition" is discussed in detail in Crotty (1993).

withdrawn from any firm whose returns are below average for a period as short as six to nine months. Thus, even if the top management of a mutual fund understood that holding shares of rainmaker financial corporations in the boom was likely to lead to large losses at some uncertain point in the future, it would be rational to hold these shares anyway in order to protect against the loss of large contracts and market share. Wall Street is littered with the corpses of firms that anticipated a coming crash too far ahead of the time it actually took place, and lost their customers to firms who continued to ride the bubble. A *Wall Street Journal* article discussed Citigroup CEO Charles Prince's explanation of the power of destructive competition at the peak of the boom. In his view, the forces of competition were such that Citibank could not stop taking excessive risk even as evidence mounted that a crash was coming. "Mr. Prince said Citigroup could have lost market share or key employees if it veered away from the sorts of bets that so many banks and securities firms were making at the time. ... 'It would have been impossible,' he said, 'to say to bankers, we're not going to participate ... and expect to have any people left.'" (*Wall Street Journal*, "Prince Shows Shame, Rubin Defiance Former Citigroup Officials Say They, and Regulators, Didn't See Risks," April 9, 2010). This destructive behavior is reinforced by the fact that when booming financial markets eventually crash, as they always do, and all firms lose money, no individual firm will lose contracts as long as their losses are not substantially worse than the industry average.

We conclude that, in the absence of effective government regulation, shareholders will not restrain the excesses of rainmaker compensation schemes.

Why Doesn't the Chronic Potential Excess Supply of Rainmakers Eliminate Rents?

The most widely used justification for the award of outsize bonuses to top financial firms operatives is that there is a chronic excess demand for the skills required to be a financial rainmaker; this leads to intense inter-firm competition for their talents. Philippon and Reshef 2009 show that the rainmaker pay premium has been rising since the early 1980s and the demand for financial-firm rainmakers has certainly risen rapidly over this period, so there would appear to be at least superficial evidence in support of the chronic excess demand thesis. Yet bonuses were at or near record levels in 2009 and 2010 even though there was a large excess supply of experienced rainmakers. Employment within the investment-banking and securities-dealing industry in August 2010 in New York City was down 34 percent from its June 2007 peak (*Wall Street Journal*, "Finance Jobs Fall in New York State," September 17, 2010).

The fact is that competition to get access to rainmaker jobs in the long financial boom from the early 1980s through 2007 was fierce. The Katz-Goldin study of Harvard graduates showed that the share entering banking and finance rose from less than 4 percent in the 1960s to 23 percent in recent years. The percentage of Harvard graduates who wanted to become investment bankers but were prevented from doing so by the chronic excess supply of candidates must have been substantial. Oyer's study shows the number of Stanford University MBAs who wanted to become investment bankers was always far greater than the number of jobs on offer. Kaplan and Rauh (2007) estimate there were about 10,000 rainmakers in large investment banks in 2004, yet over the years of financial-sector growth there must have been at least hundreds of thousands and perhaps millions of qualified students who aspired to be investment-bank rainmakers but could not obtain an entry position. "The new American dream was to make tens of millions of dollars on Wall Street or as a hedge fund manager in Greenwich, Connecticut" (Johnson and Kwak 2010, p. 109). Lewis 1989 states that there were sixty applicants for each of the starting positions at Salomon Brothers the year he entered the firm, that three-quarters of his graduating Princeton class applied for jobs on Wall Street, and that in 1986, 40 percent of Yale graduates applied to a single investment bank (p. 24). Yet "paychecks at Salomon Brothers spiraled higher in spite of the willingness of others who would, no doubt, do the same job for less. There was something fishy about how supply met demand in an investment bank.... The money was just there" (p. 49). Thus, the claim that there was always a chronic and substantial excess demand for people who wanted to be investment bankers lacks all credibility.

How can it possibly be that this exploding supply of job candidates with the desire and the qualifications to become future rainmakers did not eliminate or at least sharply reduce the rents associated with rainmaker positions? The most important answer is that the people who run these firms have no incentive to lower rainmaker pay even though a chronic potential excess supply would allow them to do so, because this would lower their own pay. As previously noted, under current conditions neither shareholders, top executives, boards of directors, capital markets, government regulators, nor market competition can make them do it. However, above and beyond this, there are two barriers to entry that help preserve rainmaker rents in the face of a large potential excess supply of rainmakers. I have not seen these barriers adequately addressed in the literature.[9]

First, there appears to be an "apprenticeship" process in investment banks. Investment banks hire more new employees than they need whenever their business is growing. After an initial trial period, those who do not impress their superiors are fired. Those who do well are retained by the firm and assigned to work with more experienced employees. If their progress is sufficiently impressive, they end up apprenticed to firm rainmakers. The ostensible purpose of the long apprenticeship is not only to allow newer employees to learn their trades, but also to convince current rainmakers that they can be trusted to accept important responsibilities in which they put large amounts of bank capital, and therefore rainmaker compensation, at risk. For example, apprentice traders have to demonstrate over a long period that they can be trusted to employ ever larger amounts of the firm's capital without generating large losses.[10] Aspiring mergers and acquisitions

---

[9] Huge rainmaker rents cannot be explained by the "Pavarotti effect" discussed in the "economics of super stars" or "winner take all" literature that tries to explain why a few super-talented people earn huge salaries while everyone else in the industry is poorly paid. This model does not fit the market for rainmakers because, whereas there are "stars" in U.S. investment banking who receive tens of millions of dollars in good years, tens of thousands of investment bankers receive at least a half-million dollars annually. The "insider–outsider" literature seems germane because it analyzes situations in which workers within firms resist competition with outsiders by "refusing to cooperate with or harassing outsiders who try to underbid the wages of incumbent workers" (Lindbeck and Snower [2001]). However, this theory is focused primarily on production and nonsupervisory workers, not multi-millionaire rainmakers. For example, the policies proposed by Lindbeck and Snower (2001) to alleviate this problem include "restrictions on strikes and picketing and relaxing job security and seniority legislation" to solve the problem (p. 184). Akerlof and Romer (1993) analyzed several cases in which financial-firm owners deliberately "looted" their firms into bankruptcy: "bankruptcy for profit can easily become a more attractive strategy for owners than maximizing true economic values" (p. 2). Their theory has certain elements in common with the theory of the rainmaker financial firm, but it does not attempt to explain the existence and distribution of rents, the key issue here. The analysis most relevant to the explanation of rainmaker rents may be one Oliver Williamson referred to as the "hold-up" problem (Williamson 1985). Trading and M&A teams generate a high percentage of investment banks' revenue and profit. Even though these teams were created by the firm, required the firm's capital to finance their operations, and relied heavily on the firm's reputation to build their business, the teams' leaders nevertheless have substantial bargaining power with the bank over team-members' compensation. If the team leaves the bank to work for a competitor, it can take much of the bank's profit-generating "assets" with it. The explicit or implicit threat to abscond with the bank's assets – or "hold-up" the bank – is an important reason why rainmakers get such a large percentage of the bank's rents. Godechot (2008) provides concrete examples of how this process works for trading desks.

[10] "Rogue traders" whose excessive gambling causes huge losses for their firms appear in every financial boom in modern times.

(M&A) rainmakers have to work their way into a group or team of top firm operatives, then convince the team members that they can eventually generate large volumes of M&A fees while keeping the firm's clients happy. The same process exists in sales.

Morrison and Wilhelm 2004 emphasize the importance of tacit knowledge and apprentice relations in investment banks during their partnership phase.

> Tacit human capital ... covers forms of knowledge and skills which do not easily lend themselves to codification or to arms-length exchange. Such skills include a wide range of talents such as advising clients, building relationships, reading market signals [a crucial skill for traders] and negotiating M&A deals which are essential to investment banking. The skills can only be learnt on the job.... Only a skilled agent can transfer his or her skills to a new hire, typically through a mentoring relationship (p. 2)

The key conclusion from this line of argument is that the only rainmaker candidates firms will consider fully qualified for these important jobs are those already working in financial markets at rainmaker or near-rainmaker positions – *no matter how many hundreds of thousands of potential rainmakers may be available to them.* An important financial executive stated that "for each vacant seat there are probably only five people out there who could do it" (*Financial Times*, "Banks' losses fail to damp bonus season goodwill," January 15, 2008). When markets are expanding rapidly, there will therefore be substantial competition for these five. Thus, in spite of the large chronic notional or potential excess supply of rainmakers, there may never be a substantial and effective excess supply of rainmakers available to bid away the rents.

The peculiar properties of the rainmaker firm influence the way the apprentice system works and help turn it into a means to regulate compensation pools. The firm's current rainmakers will not allow more new people through the apprenticeship process if that means their own bonuses will be reduced. New traders compete with existing traders for access to the firm's limited capital base. Strategic considerations on the part of the existing rainmakers will strongly influence the rate at which new members are accepted into and rise within their ranks.

Seasoned rainmakers can control the flow of apprentices through the firm. To slow it down, they can refuse to pass on the tricks of the trade as quickly or effectively as possible, or slow the rate at which the firm's capital is made available to apprentices. In other words, their bonuses have to be protected in order for the apprentice system to function most effectively – for them. A firm whose goal is to maximize shareholder returns would seek to build up a larger group of rainmakers working for smaller bonuses than would a rainmaker firm whose objective is to maximize bonuses per existing rainmaker. Even when markets crash, firms do not take advantage of the substantial excess supply of rainmakers created through job loss to cut bonuses aggressively. This is because these are not traditional neoclassical or Chandlerian firms seeking, respectively, long-term shareholder value or the reproduction and growth of the firm itself over the long run. These firms are run by rainmakers for rainmakers.

Second, an "old boy" informal hiring policy constitutes a significant barrier to entry. Rainmakers at top financial firms focus their recruiting on a relatively small set of prestigious private colleges and universities from which the current rainmakers graduated and to which they typically remain loyal. A friend who was a rainmaker for one of the country's largest banks told me that he was the only public university graduate among more than three hundred people with managing-director status in his division. In spite of the occasional token hire from state schools, rainmakers recruit primarily from their alma maters or schools with equivalent prestige, a practice that substantially limits the potential supply of fast-track rainmaker candidates.

5. Conclusion

Virtually all informed analysts who do not represent the interests of financial firms – and even many who do – agree that the perverse incentive schemes under which the most important employees of large financial institutions operated were a major contributor to the financial crisis and thus to the Great Recession. I have presented evidence that rainmaker bonuses were shockingly large, even after the markets crashed, and that there is good reason to believe they are unearned rents rather than a reward for genuine contributions to long-term economic growth. Not even the severe financial crisis or subsequent massive government intervention to rescue these firms (and thus preserve the jobs of most rainmakers) has affected the practice of paying gigantic bonuses to armies of rainmakers no matter how their firms perform. Because most experienced political observers see little chance that the perverse compensation schemes that helped cause the recent crisis will be banned by government changes in the rules and practices of regulation (see Chapter 9 in this volume by Epstein), we can expect such schemes to contribute to a new financial crisis in the intermediate future.

References

Akerlof, G. A. and P. M. Romer. (1993) "Looting: The Economic Underworld of Bankruptcy for Profit," *Brookings Papers on Economic Activity*, **2**, pp. 1–73.

Balachandran, S., B. Kogat, and H. Harnal (2010) "The Probability of Default, Excessive Risk, and Executive Compensation: A Study of Financial Services Firms from 1995 to 2008," Columbia University, unpublished.

Bebchuk, L. A., A. Cohen and H. Spamann (2009) "The Wages of Failure: Executive Compensation at Bear Stearns and Lehman 2000–2008," Social Science Research Network, November 24.

Bertrand, M., C. Goldin, and L. F. Katz (2009) "Dynamics of the Gender Gap for Young Professionals in the Corporate and Financial Sectors," National Bureau of Economic Research Working Paper no. 14681, July.

Crotty, J. R. (1985) "The Centrality of Money, Credit and Financial Intermediation in Marx's Crisis Theory." In S. Resnick and R. Wolff, eds., *Rethinking Marxism: Essays in Honor of Harry Magdoff and Paul Sweezy*. New York: Autonomedia, pp. 45–82.

(1993) "Rethinking Marxian Investment Theory: Keynes-Minsky Instability, Competitive Regime Shifts and Coerced Investment," *Review of Radical Political Economics*, **25**(1), March, pp. 1–26.

(1994) "Are Keynesian Uncertainty and Macrotheory Incompatible? Conventional Decision Making, Institutional Structures and Conditional Stability in Keynesian Macromodels," In G. Dymski and R. Pollin, eds., *New Perspectives in Monetary Macroeconomics: Explorations in the Tradition of Hyman Minsky*. Ann Arbor: Univ. of Michigan Press, pp. 105–142.

(2008) "If Financial Market Competition is Intense, Why are Financial Firm Profits so High? Reflections on the Current 'Golden Age' of Finance," *Competition and Change*, Vol. **12**, No. 2, June, pp. 167–183.

(2009) "Structural Causes of the Global Financial Crisis: A Critical Assessment of the 'New Financial Architecture,'" *Cambridge Journal of Economics*, July, Vol. **33**, No. 4, pp. 563–580.

(2010) "The Bonus-Driven 'Rainmaker' Financial Firm: How These Firms Enrich Top Employees, Destroy Shareholder Value and Create Systemic Financial Instability," Political Economy Research Institute, University of Massachusetts, Amherst, Working Paper No. 209, April. Available at: http://www.peri.umass.edu/fileadmin/pdf/working_papers/working_papers_201-250/WP209_revised.pdf.

Cuomo, A. (2009) "No Rhyme or Reason: The 'Heads I Win, Tails You Lose' Bank Bonus Culture," available at: http://www.oag.state.ny.us/media_center/2009/july/pdfs/Bonus%20Report%20Final%207.30.09.pdf.

Godechot, O. (2008) "Hold-up in finance: the conditions of possibility for high bonuses in the financial industry," *Revue francaise de sociologie*, Vol. **49**, Annual English Edition, pp. 95–123.

Goldin, C. and L. F. Katz. (2008) "Gender Differences in Careers, Education and Games," *American Economic Review*, Vol. **98**, No. 2, pp. 363–369, May.

Johnson, S. and J. Kwak. (2010) *13 Bankers*. New York: Pantheon Books.

Kaplan, S. N. and J. Rauh. (2007) "Wall Street and Main Street: What Contributes to the Rise in the Highest Incomes?" National Bureau of Economic Research Working Paper no. 13270, July.

Lewis, M. (1989) *Liar's Poker*. New York: W. W. Norton and Company, Inc.

Lindbeck, A. and D. J. Snower (2001) "Insiders versus Outsiders," *Journal of Economic Perspectives*, Vol. 15, No. 1, pp. 165–188, Winter.

Morrison, A. D. and W. J. Wilhelm, Jr. (2004) "The Demise of Investment Bank Partnerships: Theory and Evidence," July. Available at: http://www.finance.ox.ac.uk/file_links/finecon_papers/2004fe14.pdf.

New York State Comptroller's Office. (2010) "DiNapoli: Wall Street Bonuses Rose Sharply in 2009," Press Release, February 23.

(2011) "DiNapoli: Wall Street Bonuses Declined in 2010," Press Release, February 23.

Norris, F. (2009) "Off the Charts: A 10-Year Stretch That's Worse Than It Looks" *New York Times*, February 7.

Oyer, P. (2006) "The Making of an Investment Banker: Macroeconomic Shocks, Career Choice, and Lifetime Income," National Bureau of Economic ResearchWorking Paper no. 12059, February.

Philippon, T. and A. Reshef. (2009) "Wages and Human Capital in the US Financial Industry: 1909–2006," National Bureau of Economic Research Working Paper no. 14644, January.

Pro Publica. (2010) "Banks' Self-Dealing Super-Charged Financial Crisis," August 26. Available at: http://www.propublica.org/article/banks-self-dealing-super-charged-financial-crisis.

Saez, E. (2009) "Striking it Richer: The Evolution of Top Incomes in the United States," August 5. Available at: http://elsa.berkeley.edu/~saez/saez-UStopincomes-2007.pdf.

Securities Industry and Financial Markets Association Fact Book (SIFMA) (2009).

Sorkin, A. R. (2009) *Too Big to Fail*. London: Penguin.

Williamson, O. (1985) *The Economic Institutions of Capitalism*. New York: Free Press.

PART THREE

HOUSEHOLD SPENDING AND DEBT: SOURCES OF PAST GROWTH – SEEDS OF RECENT COLLAPSE

SIX

The End of the Consumer Age

Barry Z. Cynamon and Steven M. Fazzari

From the middle of the 1980s through 2007, the share of disposable income spent by U.S. consumers rose rapidly. Although many commentators want to slap American consumers on the hand for their profligate ways, this behavior did create strong demand and contributed much to the good U.S. economic performance relative to most other developed countries over this period. Furthermore, the absence of deep drops in the consumption rate during recessions mitigated negative demand shocks, such as the dramatic decline in capital expenditures that followed the bursting of the late 1990s high-tech bubble. Robust consumption helped create macroeconomic conditions that became known as the Great Moderation. In Cynamon and Fazzari (2008), we identified the period since the mid-1980s as the "Consumer Age."[1]

This story has a dark side, however. Although spending grew robustly across the income distribution, incomes outside of the top quintile were stagnant (see Chapters 2 and 7 in this volume by Palley and Setterfield, respectively). The result was rapid growth in debt-to-income ratios in virtually all income groups. In our 2008 article we identified a "risk of collapse" from rising financial fragility in the household sector. By mid-2010, it was clear that what had appeared as a risk several years prior had become reality. The Great Recession ended the quarter-century shopping spree by American consumers. In contrast to the recessions of 1990–91 and 2001, consumption dropped sharply in 2009 as credit markets seized up and home prices plummeted. The decline in real personal consumer spending from its peak in January 2008 to May 2009 was the largest drop since 1980.

---

[1]   This chapter is an extensive revision and update of our 2008 article "Household Debt in the Consumer Age: Source of Growth – Risk of Collapse" published in *Capitalism and Society* (BE Press, volume 3).

The cumulative loss of consumption relative to trend since 2008 now far exceeds that for any other period since World War II. Consumption and household debt dynamics were obviously central to the macroeconomic forces that led up to the Great Recession. Furthermore, an understanding of these behaviors is necessary to understand the future path of the U.S. economy and to design effective policy to combat the stagnation that continues to grip the job market as we approach four years since the beginning of the recession.

This chapter explores the source of the dramatic rise of American consumption. Whereas the conventional life-cycle theory of consumption portrays the household as an isolated agent and seeks an explanation from a familiar cast of macroeconomic variables such as wealth, taxes, and interest rates, our theory conceives of the household as a fundamentally social agent guided by norms of behavior. Thus, although conventional theory strives to explain consumer behavior considering only static preferences, prices, and budget constraints, our approach incorporates an understanding of consumers as agents embedded in a world of social cues that endogenously influence their preferences. Furthermore, conventional theory models the household as an agent that understands the true, objective probability distributions that determine future outcomes. In contrast, a central part of our explanation is the recognition that households make spending and financial choices in an environment of pervasive uncertainty.

In section one, we argue that the life-cycle model is inadequate by itself to understand modern American consumption and the evolution of the household balance sheet over the past two decades. Drawing on research from social psychology and marketing, we start from the premise that individuals make many of their choices based on their identity. That identity is formed by their experiences and the people with whom they associate, it evolves over time, and it is co-determined along with a package of social norms that dictate what one ought to do. The influence of identity is present in individuals' economic lives as well and informs their views on what they and others should and should not buy (consumption norms) and how they should handle their finances (financial norms). Contrary to conventional models, our theory starts from a premise that social interaction feeds through social norms to affect the way individuals choose to consume and the way that they finance their consumption.

Section two introduces endogenous preferences, produced in our framework by group interactions, the media, and other social influences. Households of recent decades lived in a social structure that encouraged greater spending and experienced rapid financial innovation that fundamentally transformed the way that they could finance that spending. Innovations in consumer finance combined with historically favorable circumstances such as falling interest rates greatly expanded the access to debt for American households during the Consumer Age. Through the lens of the life-cycle model, this change has potential benefits, as it enhances the ability of households to smooth consumption relative to income fluctuations. However, the heavy use of financial markets by consumers also introduces the possibility of behaviors not anticipated in models of narrow intertemporal optimizers with full information.

Behavioral patterns based on social norms, and related to those that drive consumption preferences, also contributed significantly to the household debt explosion. In a world of uncertainty, borrowing did not necessarily correspond to a careful plan for repayment consistent with forecasts of future incomes and a full understanding of how these new behaviors would affect the broader economy. Our argument is not that American consumers borrowed more simply because they could borrow more in the new institutional environment, but that changing social norms made it seem *normal* to spend more (as opposed to *desirable* to consume more – which is always the case) as well as *normal* to borrow in order to finance that spending (which was certainly not always the case). With rapidly changing technology and a proliferation of new products – both financial and electronic – past experience became a less reliable guide to sensible choices. People were encouraged to take on more debt by the fact that they observed others borrowing in new ways and it seemed to work out well for them.

Section three discusses the macroeconomic implications of these behaviors. We argue that strong consumption growth over the past two decades provided an important source of Keynesian demand stimulus that bolstered growth and mitigated the severity of recessions, especially the recession of 2001. The associated build up of household debt, however, led to the conditions that eventually brought the American consumption boom to an end and quickly pushed the economy into the Great Recession. We interpret these developments with Hyman Minsky's financial instability theory (see Chapters 3 and 4 in this volume by Wray and Kregel, respectively, for further application of Minsky's theory to this historical period). Minsky's work identifies the systematic character of aggregate debt-financed expansions that sow the seeds of their own destruction as greater leverage leads to financial fragility.

The final section of this chapter considers the forces that will shape American consumption in the aftermath of the Great Recession. The housing bust and associated financial crisis make further increases in the indebtedness of U.S. households relative to their income unlikely; indeed, many analysts argue that consumers must repair their collective balance sheets in coming years by paying down debt and raising the saving rate. Although such an outcome seems prudent in conventional terms, it raises the question of what source of demand growth can replace the debt-financed spending of the Consumer Age? Without a new process to generate demand, we fear that recovery from the Great Recession will continue to disappoint expectations.

1. Models of Household Behavior

An Overview of the Facts to Explain

Figure 6.1 documents the share of disposable income Americans spent on consumption. There are three rather distinct regimes evident in the figure. Despite month-to-month fluctuation, the trend in the consumption share was relatively stable, or even modestly declining, in the 1960s and 1970s. Starting in the mid-1980s, the consumption share trended strongly upward for more than twenty years. The share then collapsed at the beginning of the Great Recession and has remained at least four points below peak levels in the nascent recovery that began in the summer of 2009.

We argue here that the rapid rise of the consumption share, during what we call the Consumer Age period, was the primary factor that set the stage for the Great Recession.[2] To explain this remarkable change, mainstream economists would first look to the workhorse life-cycle model of consumer behavior in which rational agents use financial markets to smooth their consumption over the course of their lives. According to this model, forward-looking households form a lifetime plan to optimally allocate their current assets, their current income, and their expected future incomes to consumption. Financial behavior emerges implicitly from the optimal plan. Borrowing and saving reflect a misalignment between the optimal consumption path and the income path, as households borrow if current income falls short of optimal current consumption. In this context, debt is part of an optimal consumption plan and there is no reason to expect that debt growth should become either excessive or unsustainable (at least in

[2] We fit a piecewise linear trend (that allowed three distinct segments) to the data depicted in Figure 6.1 and used statistical procedures to find the two breakpoints in the piecewise trend to best fit the data (minimizing the sum of squared residuals between the data and the trend). This procedure chose January 1985 and April 2008 as the breakpoints, which provides a rough definition of the period of the Consumer Age.

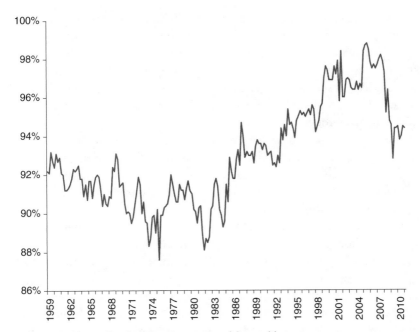

Figure 6.1. Personal outlays as a percentage of disposable income.
Source: The data plotted are 100 minus the personal saving rate (3-month moving average) computed by the Bureau of Economic Analysis.

the absence of any large, systematic, and negative shock to incomes that could not have been anticipated when the optimal consumption and borrowing plans were made.) In contrast, authors including Barba and Pivetti (2009), Brown (2004), and Cynamon and Fazzari (2008) argue that to understand the stunning rise in household debt as a percentage of disposable personal income (from about 72 percent in the middle 1980s to 134 percent on the eve of the Great Recession) requires considerations beyond the representative–agent life-cycle model. These authors all questioned how long consumption growth could be supported by debt accumulation and registered concern about what would happen if consumption ceased to grow. This concern stems in part from rising income inequality. From 1980 to 2007, the share of disposable income flowing to the top 10 percent of U.S. households increased by 10.8 percentage points (Congressional Budget Office) while middle-class incomes stagnated. If rising debt represents an attempt by a broad swath of the population to increase living standards in spite of stagnant income growth, the question of sustainability becomes obvious (also see Chapters 2 and 7 in this volume by Palley and Setterfield, respectively).

Before we turn to the macroeconomic effects of the long consumption boom and eventual bust, we will consider the circumstances that generated the 25-year trend of rising household debt. In particular, the increasing debt required two willing parties: consumers had to demand credit and lenders had to supply it. Explanations for the increasing supply of credit appear in section two; here we focus on understanding what drove consumer demand for credit.

We argue that dynamic social processes shape consumption behavior among American households and that those processes changed during this time in ways that encouraged consumers to spend a greater share of income. It is easy to identify forces that exerted upward pressure on *desired* consumption in this period; the challenge is to explain the factors that made this desire so strong that they seem to have overpowered household concerns about the impact of current borrowing on future consumption. Harking back to Veblen (1899) and Duesenberry (1949), we can see that as mean income rose along with increasing income inequality, a drive to keep up with a rising standard of living would have increased the desired level of consumption. The period in question also included the invention and proliferation of several technologies based on electronics and semiconductors. New products and advertising to drive their adoption would have increased desired consumption. With increasing access to credit and plenty of reasons for their desired level of consumption to increase, all but the highest-earning consumers would have been sorely tempted to disregard the future and fund current consumption with credit.

The Standard Model

There are at least five phenomena that could explain the rising consumption-income ratio in the context of the life-cycle model of household behavior, all of which have received some attention in mainstream discussions (see Parker 2000 for a survey). First, consumers' expectations of their future incomes could have risen over this period. As their expected total lifetime earnings increased, so did optimal consumption, with increasing current consumption (and debt) being the logical outcome. Second, if household assets appreciated in value, they could sell some assets to finance higher spending.[3] Because capital gains are not recorded as a part of income,

[3] Notice that this channel works most obviously for relatively liquid assets. If a household owns stock and it appreciates more quickly than expected, then the household can sell some shares and finance additional consumption. If a household owns a house, however, and it appreciates more quickly than expected, the household cannot simply sell part of the

this would also cause an increase in the ratio of consumption to disposable income. Third, the aggregate trend in Figure 6.1 could be driven by an underlying shift in the composition of the population toward demographic groups that spend a higher share of their income. Fourth, if households had previously wanted to borrow more, but had been unable to do so because of liquidity constraints, then it is sensible that households began borrowing more as innovations in credit markets relaxed these constraints. The fifth possibility is that consumers became less patient over this time period, in the sense that the value they placed on current consumption rose relative to their value of future consumption.

Let us consider each of these phenomena. The first and second explanations invoke the "wealth effect," which predicts that households raise spending because the value of their assets increases (Chapter 10 in this volume by Baker also considers this effect). Assets can be tangible – primarily financial assets, equity shares, and houses – or intangible – the present value of expected future earnings. Parker (2000) argues that higher tangible wealth explains, at most, 20 percent of the rise in the consumption-income ratio through the late 1990s. Moreover, the detailed timing and distribution of changes in wealth and consumption since that time do not align well. Wealth-to-income ratios did not rise between the late 1990s and the onset of the Great Recession (the Flow of Funds household net worth-to-income ratio was almost identical in 1998 and 2006) although the expenditure rate jumped by an additional two percentage points. Did expectations of future income increase rapidly and almost continuously for nearly a quarter century? It seems unlikely. In a rational setting, future income expectations would be most closely tied to rising labor productivity. Until the mid-1990s, productivity growth was disappointing, but at least half of the secular rise in the consumption-income ratio took place before "new economy" productivity gains were evident to economists, much less to typical households. Furthermore, the consumption rate continued to rise after the tech bubble burst in 2000 and the economy entered the 2001 recession, a period of stagnation, and an anemic recovery. Any explanation for a broad-based rise in consumption-income ratios that relies on wealth effects has to address the problem posed by the skewness of wealth distributions. Most wealth is held

house. To be specific, it is not as if the house has unexpectedly sprouted a new bedroom that the household can sell off to raise spending on other goods. Higher values of illiquid assets can provide collateral for new loans to finance consumption. However, pledging an illiquid asset as collateral for a new loan necessarily raises the leverage of the household, with corresponding risks that are all too apparent in the aftermath of the financial crisis of the Great Recession.

by high-income households. In 2007, the wealthiest 1 percent of families owned 33.8 percent of total family wealth, and the wealthiest 5 percent of families owned 60.4 percent (Kennickell, 2009). Yet widespread financial distress suggests that consumption rates rose unsustainably across the entire wealth distribution.

Did some kind of demographic shift cause high-spending groups to constitute a larger share of the U.S. population? We will argue that part of the explanation for the trend in the second half of Figure 6.1 is the increasing dominance of the baby-boom generation that spent more freely than their relatively thrifty parents. However, the specific structure of the life-cycle model is not helpful in understanding such a shift. Indeed, among the most prominent implications of the model is the demographic prediction that consumers borrow when they are young in anticipation of rising income, they dissave late in life when incomes tend to be low relative to lifetime averages, and they save during peak middle-age earning years. Of course, the period of rising consumption rates in Figure 6.1 corresponds to the transition of the massive baby-boom generation into their peak earning years which the model predicts should *reduce* the aggregate share of income consumed.

We are left with relaxed liquidity constraints and a shift in preferences if we are to understand consumption behavior over recent decades in terms of the life-cycle model as it is usually applied in mainstream thinking. To some extent, our approach does invoke a change in preferences. Yet the key question is *why* such changes occurred during the Consumer Age, a question that the life-cycle model does not answer. We argue in this chapter that dynamic social processes shaped consumption behavior among American households in directions that encouraged spending a greater share of income. Households also seem to have relaxed concerns about debt levels relative to income. In Minsky's terms, households let their financial "margin of safety" shrink to act on their desire to attain rising consumption. This process was made feasible by changes in the financial sector that greatly increased the ability of households to borrow which, in a broad sense, could be interpreted as relaxed liquidity constraints. However, we will argue that the typical approach to understanding the role of liquidity constraints in the context of the life-cycle model is inadequate to understand consumer behavior in recent decades.

The Consumer Problem

If the mainstream life-cycle model does not explain the rising household spending and debt that was a primary cause of the Great Recession, what does? We believe that an approach capable of making sense of consumer decision making must address the complexity of household spending and financing decisions. Earl and Potts (2004, p. 621) summarize the circumstance of consumers: "The underlying problem is of agents knowing they need to solve a problem, but not knowing how to go about it because they lack specialist knowledge of that problem domain. Our concern specifically is how they make such choices in the face of ignorance and uncertainty where the solution is bound up with acquiring, somehow, good rules for choice." They go on to discuss the complexity of the decisions facing individuals attempting to construct a lifestyle from an ensemble of durable goods and complex services. Our focus is on the source of the "rules of choice" that the agents rely on to guide their decisions in a world of uncertainty.

We follow Hodgson's (2006, p. 2) definition of institutions as "systems of established and prevalent social rules that structure social interaction," that coordinate and rationalize behavior by "imposing form and consistency on human activities" and creating "stable expectations of the behavior of others." For Hodgson, institutions include language, money, laws, and even table manners. The central defining characteristics of institutions are the rules that define them, where rules are socially transmitted normative injunctions or dispositions: in circumstance X, you should do Y. In other words, a rule is codified in discourse, is replicated through use of language within a developed social culture, and guides choice. Rules include norms of behavior and social conventions, as well as legal rules. Breaches of a rule can be identified by members of the relevant community who share tacit or explicit knowledge of the rules.

Hogg (2000) suggests that the deep motivation for people to identify with groups, and to take behavioral cues from their reference groups, may stem from a desire to reduce at least the perception of uncertainty. Uncertainty has been rampant for consumers in an environment of rapidly changing financial circumstances. Indeed, we argue that a typical assumption of the life-cycle model fails to guide our understanding to the issues of greatest importance; the assumption that there is either complete certainty or uncertainty is limited to variations in outcomes of known probability distributions. As Crotty (1994, p. 120) writes, "because they are fully human, agents have a deep psychological need to create the illusion of order and continuity even where these things may not exist." People "endeavor to fall back on the judgment of the rest of the world which is perhaps better informed," (Keynes, 1936). They look to others who appear to validate their own self-concepts and associated cognitions and behaviors.[4] Thus, the expectations and strategies that drive consumption arise from a social dynamic.[5]

To some readers, this discussion will bring to mind Akerlof and Kranton (2000, 2005), who introduce identity into economics. They link their ideas back to Pareto, Weber, and Bourdieu, pointing out among their examples the role played by norms based on social class and religion in addition to individual tastes. Our approach differs from theirs in that rather than conceiving of norms as an additional argument that determines behavior through acting on stable individual preferences, we suppose that individual preferences change over time to reflect changing norms that evolve through social processes, which are themselves appropriate objects for social science analysis.

Social References, Expectations, and Household Choices

In our framework, global rationality is beyond the capabilities of individuals who lack perfect and complete information for making choices or even for generating their "preferences." In that sense, we follow David Colander's (1998) Post-Walrasian macro by supposing that the aggregate economy achieves stability because of the existence of multi-layered institutions that structure, constrain, and enable individual behaviors and reduce the complexity of decision making for individuals. These institutions *create* both preferences and expectations through time as the household is continually buffeted by events and observes the behaviors of others. Households learn consumption patterns from their social reference groups. By analogy to the economic theory of the firm, households learn "technologies" from their reference group to "produce" utility using specific consumption goods as "inputs" (as in Becker 1965). Reference groups are an important source of information: first, they introduce an individual to new products so that choices are influenced by one's reference group; second, they provide experience and knowledge in how to appreciate, enjoy, and (consequently)

---

[4] Tajfel (1972) suggests that behavior is determined in part by group prototypes that reflect social values and act as guides for action, rather than solely by atomistic preferences. Within the marketing literature, reference groups are defined as social groups that are important to a consumer and against which he compares himself. More recent reference group research is based on conformity and social comparison theory (see Folkes and Kiesler 1991 for a review).

[5] We propose, therefore, that expectations come from an independent behavioral process. This approach contrasts with misleadingly named "rational" expectation approach of most life-cycle models. In these models, expectations are specified not by a deep analysis of how humans behave in the face of uncertainty but by the mathematical expected value of the true "fundamental"-probability distributions that determine future outcomes.

desire new products; and third, they condition expectations about future outcomes and what kinds of behavior should be considered "normal." These reference groups can be constituted by real people, such as neighbors, family, and friends, or they can be virtual, arising from behavioral models portrayed by the media.

Consider a simple example. Think of the preference for good wine less as an exogenous parameter of individual utility but rather as a learned behavior conditioned by social circumstances. An individual with a working-class reference group is unlikely to banter with friends and sommeliers about tannins, complexity, oakiness, etc. If the attributes of good wine are not typically part of a person's social reference group, it may be difficult for that person to appreciate wine qualities. Should an individual experience a large rise in income, he or she will have the means to begin dining at places, and with other people, who take their wine seriously. The association with higher-income households in the new reference group will teach, at least implicitly, the person in the new social situation about the joys of fine wine and change his or her preferences.

Individuals not only learn utility-producing technologies from their social reference groups, they also compare their consumption standards to the reference group (Frank 1997, Schor 1998). Frank, in particular, forcefully argues that people define their self-image and self-worth by what they consume and possess relative to the lifestyles of others. In addition, "habit formation" is implied from this understanding of household preferences.[6] Once an individual learns enjoyment technologies and expectations, she will not forget them, and as long as her peers persist in following these behavioral guideposts, she will be continually reminded about them. To extend the example discussed earlier, once a person learns to appreciate good wine, the individual does not forget the associated pleasures, even if her economic situation deteriorates. Thus, household preferences are path dependent and the relevant references for current decisions include both the social circumstances in which an individual is embedded at any point in time and the individual's personal history accumulated over time.

We define the *consumption norm* as the standard of consumption an individual considers normal based on his or her group identity.[7] The norm

---

[6] See Duesenberry's (1949) "relative income hypothesis." Recent references include Campbell and Cochrane(1999), Fuhrer (2000), and Morley (2007).

[7] Schor (1998) also uses the terms "social norm" and "consumption norm" in a similar context. She writes (page 9), that "the very term 'standard of living' suggests the point: the standard is the social norm." Akerlof (2007) defines norms as individuals' views about how they and others should or should not behave.

provides something like a sufficient statistic for social and habitual influences on consumer preferences and expectations that evolve through time. The norm guides choices in a world of uncertainty. To the extent that the utility function and expectation-formation process are viewed as exogenous (as is typical in most standard life-cycle models), such models abstract from the dynamic social context of choice. We argue that the consumption norm is a powerful behavioral force that cannot be ignored as we try to understand modern consumption behavior; in particular, the rising expenditure and debt accumulation previously documented.

Social references and the associated norms affect financial decisions as well as spending preferences. Indeed, in the financial sphere, uncertainty is likely to be particularly important as households must confront complex intertemporal implications of their decisions that depend on systemic conditions. Changing institutional structures interact with social norms to define which practices are responsible and sensible. For example, borrowing for a home with 20 percent down and a fixed-rate mortgage was consistent with the financial norms of the 1960s and the 1970s. Few people in that era would refinance their mortgages to get cash for a new car or a vacation. When home equity loans with tax advantages became available in the late 1980s, however, borrowing against one's home for non-housing consumption became more common. In the 1990s, innovations in the mortgage markets reduced transaction costs and cash-out refinancing became more common. Initially, these actions were simple responses to changes in available financial products. We argue, however, that what households considered normal behavior also evolved along with these changing practices.[8]

Behaviors driven to conform to evolving norms are more than just preferences in the sense in which that concept is used in mainstream modeling. Rather, they fulfill a need of individuals to participate fully in social life, something humans seem programmed by evolution to pursue vigorously. Recent magnetic resonance imaging of brain responses in the context of a social conformity experiment shows that the "opinions of others can easily affect how much we value things.... [S]ocial influence mediates very basic value signals in known reinforcement learning circuitry" (Campbell-Meiklejohn, et al. 2010). This behavior assuages the uncertainty of the complex modern environment in which Americans must make spending

---

[8] Thaler and Sunstein (2009) pointed out the consequences of changing cultural values in an op-ed. They write: "For most of the 20th century, most American homeowners had a single-minded goal: Pay off the mortgage...But in the 1990s, this principle dissolved under the pressure of temptation. With house prices rising, families started using home equity loans to finance their spending habits."

and financing choices. These choices were consistent with social conditions prevailing when they were made, but they may not anticipate the systemic effects of the aggregate financial fragility that they were creating, a theme to which we now return.

2. Evolution of Household Behavioral Norms in the Consumer Age

Social Pressures that Raise Desired Spending

To argue that individuals make consumption choices based on social institutions and norms is not itself enough to explain the rise in spending relative to income. In this section, we explore how the link between social references and household behavior raised consumption norms over the past quarter century.

First consider product innovation. Modern business has an obvious profit motive to grab consumer attention by introducing new products. Marketing helps incorporate new and better stuff into consumption norms. Some things that were "luxuries" decades ago became standard. For example, the share of Americans who considered a computer for home use a necessity rose from 4 percent in 1983 to 51 percent by 2006, whereas 49 percent considered a cell phone and 29 percent considered high-speed Internet access necessities in 2006 (Taylor and Wang, 2010). Households learn how to use new products to produce satisfaction in new ways and this learning happens through the dynamics of social interaction. Product innovation is always an objective of entrepreneurial capitalism, but there is no reason for it to proceed at the same rate over time or for it to have the same impact on social life. We believe that integration of semiconductor technology into consumer products has created a kind of innovation that transforms the nature of social interaction (social networking provides a striking recent example). Acquisition of these new products becomes necessary for individuals to fully participate in the evolving society and therefore accelerates the growth in consumption norms that encourages greater spending out of income, as well as rising debt.

In addition, the mass media shape consumption choices through time and establish expectations about what is normal. Greater media saturation encourages more consumption. We argue that this effect goes beyond simply providing information about products. The explicit objective of effective modern marketing is to change preferences by locating products in a social context, illustrated by product placement – the appearance of a product or service in a broadcast program or movie, paid for by the manufacturer to gain exposure for the product or service. Furthermore, advertising targets consumers with the means to pay for the products it hawks: potential buyers with discretionary income. However, this advertising takes place in the *mass* media, and therefore its reach extends to households with incomes lower than the target audience. The media transform at least part of the relevant social reference from actual peers and neighbors to virtual characters created for entertainment and marketing. As Schor (1998, pp. 80–81) points out, one's reference neighborhood used to consist largely of friends and family who lived in close proximity, and who likely had similar incomes and group identities and who could not overdraw their checking accounts. Media saturation, however, greatly widens the "neighborhood." The compelling lifestyle models in the media, although often portrayed as perfectly "normal," may be completely inconsistent with real-world budget constraints. They nonetheless provide social cues about what is normal consumption behavior.

If marketing is biased toward higher-income consumers with discretionary spending power, rising economic inequality also encourages increased desired spending relative to income. To illustrate this point, suppose that advertising targets households with income at the eightieth percentile. These messages influence all income groups, however. As the income gap between the marketing target group and the median-income household rises, the pressure to spend "beyond one's means" rises across the income distribution. Median households cannot afford to spend as much as those in the eightieth percentile, but they will do what they can, spending a larger share of disposable income, and, as will be discussed, borrowing more if financial institutions allow them to do so.

Undoubtedly, there are other sources of rising consumption norms in recent decades (we discuss several additional ideas in Cynamon and Fazzari, 2008). The specific examples, however, share a common underlying theme: the modern United States has become an increasingly "consumer-oriented" culture. In addition, these evolving cultural institutions have put pressure on American households to spend more by borrowing more if necessary.

Consumer Credit: Changing Attitudes – Changing Institutions

The desire for higher consumption alone is not sufficient to explain the striking upward trend in Figure 6.1 from the middle 1980s to the Great Recession presented earlier. Consumers must be able to *pay for* their spending. Figure 6.2 shows U.S. total household and mortgage debt outstanding as

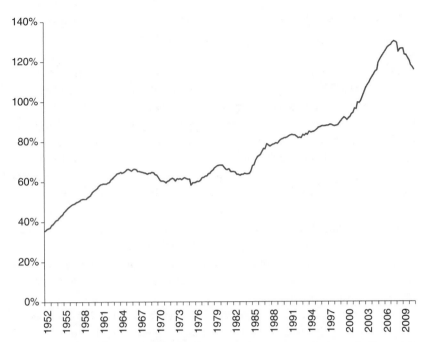

Figure 6.2. Household debt outstanding as a percentage of personal disposable income.
Source: Household credit market debt outstanding from U.S. Flow of Funds accounts, disposable personal income from Bureau of Economic Analysis NIPA accounts.

a share of disposable income. The ratio accelerates in the mid- to late-1980s, roughly the beginning of the Consumer Age. Growth in debt accelerates yet again after 2000. Something new happened to the liability side of the American household balance sheet.

Over the past thirty years, a variety of factors made it easier for American households to spend without first having cash in the bank; that is, the household budget constraint became "softer." These factors included the largely favorable macroeconomic environment of the Great Moderation, the stance of bank regulators, and the profit motive that led financial institutions to innovate in their lending policies. Until the early 1980s, the household experience with credit was largely limited to home mortgages and the finance of consumer durables, primarily cars. These loans were collateralized and required substantial down payments. However, things have changed dramatically in recent decades. Credit cards now provide a line of unsecured credit to most households, albeit with substantial interest costs. Innovations in housing finance greatly increased the ability of home owners to borrow at tax-subsidized interest rates through equity credit lines or cash-out refinancing, at least prior to the financial crisis of 2008.

One reason for these developments was new information technology that made it easier to obtain information on prospective borrowers. Standard models of credit rationing predict that lenders ration credit when they cannot distinguish the quality of borrowers, so credit became more accessible as new credit reporting technologies made it easier to identify good and bad credit risks. Unfortunately, enhanced technology for assessing individuals' credit risk based on increasingly accessible information about their past behavior did not immunize the lenders from the consequences of unanticipated changes in that behavior – particularly, changes that may have been caused in large part *by* the increased access to credit.

Tax law changes have also affected the market for household debt. In particular, the Tax Reform Act of 1986 eliminated the income tax deduction for most categories of interest expense, but retained the deductibility of home mortgage interest. Initially, home equity credit lines became a simple way to shift interest payments on traditional consumer debt (car loans, for example) from a non-deductible to a deductible expense. However, once the home equity line is in place, it becomes much easier for home owners to borrow for any purpose, including nondurable expenditures. Thus, institutional change transforms financial norms.

In addition, mortgage refinancing to exploit interest rate movements has become much more common (Hurst and Stafford 2004, Wray 2007). It is not surprising that falling interest rates would boost consumption as households refinance and their debt service payments decline. Nevertheless, the long-term trend of lower nominal interest rates since the early 1980s made refinancing "normal" and introduced new financial practices to households that in an earlier era would not likely have seemed like responsible financial behavior. Most obviously, cash-out refinancing encouraged households to exploit the benefits of a lower mortgage interest rate with a large upfront cash infusion rather than a reduction in monthly debt service payments.

Changes in attitudes, likely stimulated by increased borrowing activity, have also played a role. From the end of World War II to the 1970s, the people who made financial decisions in American households had either confronted the financial challenges of the Great Depression themselves or had parents who managed household budgets during that bleak period. These people learned an aversion to consumer debt. The Depression is two generations removed for baby boomers, however, and they have been much more willing to borrow aggressively to get what they want (see Malmendier and Nagle, 2011). Again, this phenomenon spreads through social reference groups. When the behavior of one's neighbor suggests that a home equity credit line can easily finance a vacation or home improvement, any social stigma associated with debt begins to erode. The dramatic increases in the consumption-income ratio and the debt-income ratio occurred during a time when the baby-boom generation, with its relatively relaxed attitude about debt, had become the dominant force in American consumption.

As discussed earlier, these arguments resemble a claim that household liquidity constraints have relaxed (see Carroll, 1992, for example), but there is a subtle difference between our perspective and typical liquidity constraint models. In a conventional life-cycle consumption model with liquidity constraints, households have a feasible and optimal plan that they would follow in the absence of constraints, but lack of liquidity prevents current consumption from reaching this desired level. For example, people may anticipate higher future income, some of which they would like to spend now, but they are prevented from borrowing against future income. When greater access to credit relaxes the constraint, households raise debt and consumption toward the level derived from the optimal plan. These actions can be understood by looking at a representative household in isolation, without reference to broader social forces. In our context, in contrast, we view consumption *and debt* choices as driven to an important extent by social interaction. A family, in isolation, might choose a more conservative financial path, but the influence of others, both those who have a physical presence and those whose lifestyles are piped in through the media, drives both consumption and debt higher. These behaviors may be driven less by a carefully laid optimal financial plan than by evolving social norms that guide choices, with the obvious consequence that there is no guarantee that choices will even approximate what an economist might identify as optimal.[9] This behavior may be myopic relative to the results of a standard life-cycle model with liquidity constraints.[10]

---

[9] To link these ideas to Keynesian macroeconomics, one might think of higher household debt as a reduction in liquidity preference, in a broad sense, rather than relaxed liquidity constraints. Households are willing to become less liquid by taking on higher debt relative to their income, as shown in Figure 6.2. Note, however, that although liquidity-preference theory usually addresses the relation between supply and demand for asset stocks and asset prices, the discussion here focuses on consumption and borrowing flows.

[10] Consider the case of Benjamin Franklin Baggett who filed for bankruptcy in 2003. "We came to rely on credit as part of our income.... I looked at $1,000 on my credit card as disposable income." ("Extra Credit: Lagging Behind the Wealthy, Many Use Debt to Catch Up," *Wall Street Journal*, May 17, 2005, page A1). This behavior could be "time inconsistent" as discussed in behavioral economics; for formal analysis, see Laibson (1997).

The social influences on household finance also reflect the uncertainty households face about the future. They are not really sure what kind of financial plan is feasible, but there is a perceived safety in numbers. If others borrow heavily to consume a lot now, both higher consumption and the higher debt necessary to finance it seem "normal." With rearview mirror wisdom after the dramatic financial collapses of 2008, it may have been unrealistic for households to believe that the favorable macroeconomic trends necessary for them to validate their financial positions (i.e., falling interest rates, easier lending terms, and rapidly appreciating home prices) would continue indefinitely.[11] Yet such a systemic perspective lies outside of the information that the typical household uses to make critical financial decisions. Families can observe their neighbors and media models, but they cannot be expected to appreciate the complex macroeconomics of emergent financial instability.

We invoke social norms for spending and borrowing in part because the objective is not simply to explain a rise in the ratios displayed in Figures 6.1 and 6.2. To understand the origins of the Great Recession, we argue that one must explain a rise in *financial fragility*, an environment in which further growth may depend on pushing historically risky financial positions to yet more aggressive levels, increasing the risk of collapse. Information technologies that allow lenders to better distinguish borrower quality probably reduced conventional liquidity constraints. There is no reason, however, that such innovations alone would create financial structures that sow the seeds of what became economic collapse.

Indeed, the aggregated perspective in Figure 6.2 likely understates the rise in household financial fragility because total income growth was heavily skewed toward higher earners (see the data presented elsewhere in this volume by Palley, Table 2.5 and further discussion by Setterfield, Chapter 7), whereas debt increased more heavily among lower- and middle-income groups. Figure 6.3 summarizes data from the Survey of Consumer Finance that breaks out the rise in the debt to (total) income ratio for different income groups, every third year from 1989 to 2007. Over this period, the ratio for surveyed households in the lowest quintile of the income distribution (excluding the lowest 5 percent) increased by more than 160 percent. The debt-income ratio for a broad swath of the middle class from the twentieth through the ninety-fifth percentile increased 93 percent. In the top 5 percent of surveyed earners, debt-income ratios

---

[11] Minsky (1986) uses "validate" to describe the process of meeting contractual debt service obligations. Also see Wray (2007).

rose only modestly, just 18 percent.[12] With financial innovation and greater access to debt, the year-by-year budget constraint became much softer and households responded to this greater flexibility in a way that put the system on a path toward what ultimately became unsustainable financial fragility.

Explaining lender behavior is somewhat more complicated, but is also necessary to understand the increase in financial fragility. After all, lenders' willingness to offer, even aggressively push, credit was necessary to create the conditions that led up to the Great Recession (also see Chapters 3 and 4 in this volume by Wray and Kregel, respectively). Why would they make so many loans that in retrospect seem to have been so excessively risky?

To understand this, we appeal to the concept of a *buffer*, which we define as any resource that provides a margin of safety to the agent who holds it in reserve in case of some unforeseen and unfavorable event. Buffers create redundancy in the system and their size and function are guided by prevailing institutions. For example, imposing reserve requirements on banks creates a buffer that provides a margin of safety in case of a bank run. A buffer can also be the result of an industry norm, like the 20 percent down payments on mortgages that created a margin of safety for both lenders and borrowers. These cases demonstrate the key features of buffers: first, they provide a margin of safety by leaving some potentially available resource unexploited, so there is an opportunity cost inherent in the redundancy that defines buffers; and second, that opportunity cost is an invitation to entrepreneurs to "unlock value" by eroding the institutions that enforce buffers. To wit, banks created sweep accounts to make reserve requirements a non-binding constraint (Greene, 2011), and the 20 percent down-payment requirement eroded almost completely over the course of the Consumer Age. What can be particularly damaging about buffer-erosion entrepreneurship is that it looks like a free lunch but it is not: the value that is apparently unlocked is gained in exchange for additional risk. Furthermore, if some agents probe the limits of the institution that perpetuates a buffer in good times, their behavior is likely to appear successful, inducing others

---

[12] We thank Nick Tompras for helpful discussions and Ulas Gulkirpik for research assistance that led to the information in Figure 6.3. We considered many different groupings of the data for the middle-class category, but less aggregated groups between the twentieth and ninety-fifth percentiles closely followed the middle-class trend shown in the figure. Debt to income rose even more sharply in the lowest 5 percent of the income distribution, but very low incomes in the denominator of the ratio makes this information somewhat unreliable.

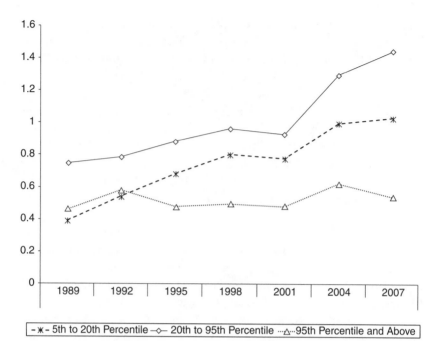

Figure 6.3. Debt to total income ratio for selected income groups.
Source: Authors' calculations from U.S. Federal Reserve Survey of Consumer Finance data, using income inclusive of capital gains of all households, including those without any debt.

to copy and extend the strategy. The connection with Minsky's dictum that "stability is destabilizing" is clear.

During the Consumer Age, the surge in credit increased the risk of individual lenders as well as systemic risk. Although warnings of systemic risk became rather common in the last few years before the Great Recession, risky loans remained highly profitable and few mainstream analysts projected anything much more severe, at worst, than a garden-variety "mild" recession and a modest decline of housing prices. For the most part, it seems that managers and investors saw the money that could be made in the short run by eroding institutional buffers, but, like the households previously discussed, they did not adequately perceive the severity of newly emerging macroeconomic risks. Furthermore, models used to measure risks by the financial sector were based on historical data and statistical relationships that no longer accurately described the new world of excessively leveraged households. As Paul Davidson has said for decades (see Davidson 2007 for a recent example), historical probability distributions can be a poor guide to those that govern current and future developments. Again, uncertainty and a socially constructed response to it plays a central role: lenders did not adequately perceive the risks they faced. They probably *could not* fully perceive the risks they faced as their aggressive lending created a new financial structure with unknown systemic characteristics. Therefore, like consumers, lenders fell back on the convention that the near future would be like the recent past. During the Consumer Age, the recent past validated the strategy of buffer erosion, further increasing confidence in the strategy as an appropriate convention, until the dramatic events of the Great Recession demonstrated that belief in such "normal" operation of the system became untenable.

3. Consumption, Debt, and U.S. Macroeconomic Performance

What are the macroeconomic implications of these developments in the modern U.S. consumer culture and the financial system that accommodated its accumulation of unprecedented debt? The basic message is simple: high consumption was a significant source of strength for the economy for more than two decades, but it also set systematic forces in motion that spawned the Great Recession and the extended period of stagnation and high unemployment that followed.

Mild Recessions and Strong Aggregate Growth during the Consumer Age

According to the Keynesian macroeconomic theory that lies at the foundation of all the analysis in this book, strong consumption creates substantial macroeconomic stimulus. One outcome was a change in the dynamics of recessions in 1990–91 and 2001 compared with recessions in 1974–75 and 1981–82. The conventional wisdom was that U.S. recessions since the early 1980s were "mild," contributing to the view that the U.S. economy had experienced a "Great Moderation," at least prior to the collapse in late 2008. Consider Figure 6.1 again. The ratio of personal outlays to disposable income obviously collapsed in both the 1974–75 and 1980–82 periods, significantly magnifying the severity of economic weakness. In contrast, during the early 1990s recession, the growth of the consumption-income ratio that started in the mid-1980s took a pause, but there was virtually no decline. In 2001, the consumption-income ratio *continued to grow* in spite of the collapse of the late 1990s bubble in technology stock prices and the fallout from the September 11, 2001 terrorist attacks.[13] Strong consumption spending greatly attenuated the declines in aggregate demand from the middle 1980s through 2007, which helped to contain recession dynamics.

Short-run macro performance in recessions does not tell the whole story, however. As we consider the way forward after the Great Recession, the dynamics of consumption during recessions may not be the most important part of the link between consumption spending and macroeconomic outcomes. In our view, the U.S. consumption boom was an important engine of demand-led growth for U.S. economy over the longer term. According to mainstream theory, high-demand growth affects macro performance at short-run frequencies relevant for business cycles, a few quarters to a couple of years. In the long run of mainstream thinking, however, supply-side forces are supposed to explain growth as wage and price adjustments, or enlightened monetary policy, offset demand factors, and the economy converges to full employment. Over a longer horizon, therefore, mainstream theory predicts that growth is governed by potential output.[14] Yet, there is little evidence that the U.S. economy faced supply constraints at the margin for most of the years since the beginning of the Consumer Age. Inflation was on a downward trend from the early 1980s. Unemployment tested multi-decade lows in the late 1990s with no adverse effects on inflation. Potential output has seemed to stay ahead of demand. That environment persisted for a relatively long period of time during which output growth was driven by demand growth, itself largely fueled by consumption spending.

Rising Household Debt and the Seeds of the Great Recession

High consumer indebtedness was critical to the forces that made the Great Recession the most severe economic downturn since the 1930s. The financial Keynesian theory of Hyman Minsky provides a framework for analyzing the dynamics of these phenomena.[15] This perspective emphasizes the two-sided character of debt-financed spending. In the growth phase of the business cycle, the creation of debt boosts demand that provides economic stimulus. However, Minsky argues that as debt continues to grow during the boom, the

---

[13] Also see Kotz (2008). The unusual nature of this phenomenon is noted by Burhouse (2003): "consumer spending and borrowing patterns during and after the 2001 recession departed significantly from historic norms. U.S. households in 2002 continue to spend and borrow at a record pace even as personal bankruptcy filings reached record levels."

[14] Furthermore, in mainstream theory, high consumption actually reduces the growth of potential output, because lower saving reduces the capital stock and labor productivity.

[15] See, in particular, Minsky (1985, pages 37–50) and also Wray, Chapter 3 in this volume.

financial system becomes more fragile. The Keynesian link between higher borrowing, rising spending, and income creation validates the decision to increase lending for a while, but that validation systematically encourages even more aggressive financial practices. Again, uncertainty is central to this process. No one knows how much financial stress the system can bear. Financial success influences conventional expectations about appropriate financial practices (financial norms) and fragility rises further. The basic logic of this process implies that the system expands until it breaks in a financial crisis, when the more aggressive financing practices can no longer generate macro results strong enough to support the increasingly fragile financial structure.

Although Minsky's theory identifies a deep family resemblance across financial cycles, the specific form of any particular cycle depends on unique historical circumstances. Minsky's writings, although they mention consumption and household debt, focus primarily on business finance and investment. We propose that innovation in consumer finance and the associated evolution of household financial norms over recent decades has shifted the locus of financial instability to the consumer sector. These themes are developed elsewhere in this volume, particularly Chapters 3 and 4 by Wray and Kregel. Here, we want to emphasize the correspondence between, first, the result from the previous subsection that strong consumption-cushioned recessions and contributed to strong secular growth in the United States over recent decades and, second, the rising financial fragility of the household sector. These are two sides of the same coin: the consumption boom sowed the seeds of its own destruction.

The consumption boom was financed by borrowing that led to Minskyan financial fragility. Indeed, since income growth was anemic over this period across most of the income distribution, debt growth was the only way to finance such a boom (see Figure 6.3, Chapter 2 by Palley and Chapter 7 by Setterfield in this volume). Wray's Chapter 3 describes the emergent financial fragility in detail as well as the particular conditions that triggered the collapse, beginning in 2007. The abrupt shift from the finance-led boom to contraction led to historic declines in both consumer spending and residential investment.

Real personal consumption expenditures peaked in January of 2008 and fell 1.9 percent to a trough in May of 2009.[16] This decline was the most severe since a 2.6 percent fall at the beginning of the 1980 recession. It is about double the decline of the worst drop during the Great Moderation

---

[16] The figures in this paragraph refer to three-month moving averages of monthly data to smooth out random volatility.

period (that occurred between September 1990 and March 1991). If one focuses on durable consumption, which clearly depends to a much greater extent on financial conditions than total expenditure, the Great Recession peak comes earlier than one might expect, in August of 2005. After a modest decline, durable spending plummets after mid-2007 to a trough also in May of 2009. The peak-to-trough decline in real durable consumption of 18.7 percent is roughly the same as the most severe drops in the postwar period (19.4 percent from April 1973 through January 1975, and 19.1 percent from June 1978 through December 1981). By mid-2011, it is also clear that the cumulative loss of consumption since 2008, relative to any reasonable estimate of trend, far exceeds the loss of any recession since World War II, and these losses are almost certain to grow larger in coming years.

In percentage terms, the decline in residential investment has been breathtaking. From the peak in the fourth quarter of 2005 to the trough in the third quarter of 2010 real construction spending on new homes fell 59 percent. The only period that comes close to the severity of this debacle in postwar U.S. history is the fourth quarter of 1978 through the third quarter of 1982 when mortgage rates exceeded 15 percent. Even in those remarkably turbulent times, residential investment declined by less from peak to trough (45 percent) than it has in recent experience. In addition, the decline from peak to trough in the late 1970s and early 1980s lasted 15 quarters and was followed by a rapid recovery, the recent collapse was 19 quarters, and there has been virtually no recovery from the trough as of this writing, more than six years after the peak.

Although the decline in percentage terms of housing investment dwarfs the fall in personal consumption, the latter is a much larger share of GDP. Together, we roughly estimate that each category is about half a trillion dollars less than what would have been predicted by the pre-recession trends. There has also been a big decline in business investment. However, in strong contrast to the 2001 recession, this decline seems to have been induced by troubles coming from the household sector. Business investment did not peak until the second quarter of 2008.

This narrative for the Great Recession is fundamentally Keynesian: the common engine of the consumption-housing boom and the subsequent collapse is demand. Nevertheless, it is misleading to think of these forces as demand "shocks." The Minsky framework illuminates the systematic dynamic character of debt-financed demand. It can be a powerful source of growth, but it leads, sooner or later, to collapse. One cannot understand the Great Recession outside of the household-finance boom of the Consumer Age that preceded it.

4. Household Finance after the Great Recession

Does the Great Recession mark the end of a Consumer Age that lasted nearly a quarter century? From the middle 1980s to 2007, economic conditions in the United States created a remarkably good environment for fast consumption growth and rising household debt. These conditions included falling energy costs, large tax cuts, a stock market boom, a historic decline in interest rates, a home-price boom turned to bubble, and financial innovation that opened new doors for consumer lending. In classic Minsky fashion, however, these favorable conditions encouraged more aggressive financial practices until they reached a breaking point. Home prices fell, mortgage lending and home building collapsed, and consumption spending declined substantially for the first time in a generation. The economy reached what the popular press has called the "Minsky Moment" when the Consumer Age boom turned into the Great Recession bust.

Where does the U.S. economy go from here? It seems impossible to expect a reprise of the debt-fueled household spending boom evident in Figures 6.1, 6.2, and 6.3. Borrowers and lenders have been decimated by the crisis. At the least, norms of lending have changed for the medium term for the banking system, if not consumption and borrowing norms for the households. Therefore, a significant source of U.S. (and global) demand growth for the past quarter century has disappeared. There seems no obvious replacement going forward. Absent a dramatic new technological development, business investment is likely to be well below the pre-recession trend for several years to come in the face of excess capacity. Government spending could be a source of demand growth, but it has been constrained by exaggerated fears of federal budget deficits.[17] The U.S. government may not act on the rhetoric of "austerity" and "fiscal responsibility" in any significant way while the economy stagnates, but the current political culture seems like it will prevent the federal government from leading demand upward as the household sector retrenches. Even defensive fiscal measures such as extensions of expiring unemployment benefits passed the U.S. Congress with great difficulty. Furthermore, state and local fiscal policy was extraordinarily weak.[18] Some U.S. policy makers spin

[17] See Chapters 10 and 11 in this volume for detailed analyses of the effect of deficits in an economy operating with persistent underutilized resources.
[18] Real state and local-government spending has declined at an annual rate of 1.5% from the fourth quarter of 2007 through the second quarter of 2011. The reductions accelerated in the first half of 2011, falling by 3.4% at an annual rate in both the first and second quarters.

fantasies about rising exports, but who will buy more U.S. goods? The U.K. and the euro zone are even more aggressive about pursuing fiscal austerity than the U.S. China and other developing countries in Asia are doing relatively well, but those countries have export-led growth models that depend on the U.S. market and are unlikely to change over the next few years (see also Chapter 8 by Blecker).

In the summer of 2009, the NBER business cycle data committee declared that the Great Recession had ended. In the following months, some households and businesses raised spending modestly as the panic of the darkest days following the collapse of Lehman Brothers receded. Yet a sustained recovery has yet to emerge more than two years after the business-cycle trough. Conventional wisdom seems to be looking just around the corner for the accelerating GDP growth that could begin to dent the tragic waste of resources and the devastating unemployment created by the recession. However, without the U.S. consumers' willingness and ability to further leverage their collective balance sheets, the source of demand growth for even a sluggish recovery remains a mystery. The way forward is likely to disappoint with extended wasted resources, further financial instability – possibly even the dreaded "double dip" recession. Even in the best case scenario, the economy will need to find an alternative source of demand growth to replace the quarter-century Consumer Age.

References

Akerlof, G. A. (2007) "The Missing Motivation in Macroeconomics," *American Economic Review*, **97**(1) March, 5–36.

Akerlof, G. A. and Rachel E. Kranton. (2000) "Economics and identity," *Quarterly Journal of Economics*, **115**(3), August, 715–53.

(2005) "Identity and the economics of organizations," *Journal of Economic Perspectives*, **19**(1), Winter, 9–32.

Barba, A., and M. Pivetti. (2009) "Rising household debt: Its causes and macroeconomic implications – a long-period analysis," *Cambridge Journal of Economics* **33**: 113–37.

Becker, G. S. (1965) "A Theory of the Allocation of Time," *The Economic Journal*, **75**(299), September, 493–517.

Brown, C. (2004) "Does Income Distribution Matter for Effective Demand? Evidence from the United States," *Review of Political Economy*, **16**(3) July, 291–307.

Burhouse, S. (2003) "Evaluating the Consumer Lending Revolution," from the FDIC electronic bulletin "FYI: An Update on Emerging Issues in Banking," September 17, http://www.fdic.gov/bank/analytical/fyi/2003/091703fyl.html.

Campbell, J. Y. and J. H. Cochrane. (1999) "By Force of Habit: A Consumption-Based Explanation of Aggregate Stock Market Behavior," *Journal of Political Economy*, **107**(2) April, 205–51.

Campbell-Meiklejohn, D. K., D. R. Bach, A. Roepstorff, R. J. Dolan, and C. D. Frith. (2010) "How the Opinion of Others Affects Our Valuation of Objects," *Current Biology*, **20**(13), 1165–70.

Carroll, C. D. (1992) "The Buffer-Stock Theory of Saving: Some Macroeconomic Evidence," *Brookings Papers on Economic Activity*, No. **2**, 61–156.

Colander, D. (1998) "Beyond New Keynesian Economics: Towards a Post Walrasian Macroeconomics," in Rod Rotheim, ed., *New Keynesian Economics/Post Keynesian Alternatives*, London: Routledge.

Congressional Budget Office. June 2010. "Average Federal Taxes by Income Group." http://www.cbo.gov/publications/collections/collections.cfm?collect=13.

Crotty, J. (1994) "Are Keynesian Uncertainty and Macrotheory Compatible? Conventional Decision Making, Institutional Structures, and Conditional Stability in Keynesian Macromodels," in Gary Dymski and Robert Pollin, eds., *New Perspectives in Monetary Macroeconomics: Explorations in the tradition of Hyman P. Minsky*, Ann Arbor: University of Michigan Press, 105–39.

Cynamon, B. Z. and S. M. Fazzari. (2008), "Household Debt in the Consumer Age: Source of Growth--Risk of Collapse," *Capitalism and Society*, **3** 2.

Davidson, P. (2007) *John Maynard Keynes*, New York: Palgrave.

Duesenberry, J. S. (1949) *Income, Saving and the Theory of Consumer Behavior*, Cambridge, MA: Harvard University Press.

Earl, P. E. and J. Potts. (2004) "The market for preferences," *Cambridge Journal of Economics* **28**(4): 619–33.

Fazzari, S. M. (2004) "A Penny Saved May Not Be a Penny Earned," working paper available at http://fazz.wustl.edu/papers.html.

Fazzari, S. M., P. Ferri, and E. Greenberg. (1998) "Aggregate Demand and Firm Behavior: A New Perspective on Keynesian Microfoundations," *Journal of Post Keynesian Economics*, **20**(4) summer, 527–58.

Festinger, Leon. (1954) "A Theory of Social Comparison Processes," *Human Relations*, **7**, 117–40.

Folkes, Valerie S. and Tina Kiesler. (1991) "Social Cognition: Consumers' Inferences About the Self and Others," in Thomas S. Robertson and Harold H. Kassarjian, eds., *Handbook of Consumer Behavior*, Englewood Cliffs, New Jersey: Prentice-Hall, 1–315.

Frank, R. H. (1989) "Frames of Reference and the Quality of Life," *American Economic Review*, **79**(2) May, 80–85.

  (1997) "The Frame of Reference as a Public Good," *Economic Journal*, **107**(445) November, 1832–47.

Fuhrer, J. C. (2000) "Habit Formation in Consumption and Its Implications for Monetary-Policy Models," *American Economic Review*, **90**(3) June, 367–90.

Goldin, C. (2005) "The U-Shaped Female Labor Force Function in Economic Development and Economic History," in T. Paul Schultz, ed., *Investment in Women's Human Capital*, Chicago: University of Chicago Press, 61–90.

Greene, C. A. (2011) "The Remarkable Long-Run Conditional Predictability of US Real M1," working paper, University of Missouri–St. Louis, January.

Greenspan, A. and J. Kennedy. (2005) "Estimates of Home Mortgage Originations, Repayments, and Debt on One-to-Four Family Residences," working paper, Federal Reserve Board Finance and Economics Discussion Series, No. 41.

Hodgson, G. M. (2006) "What Are Institutions?" *Journal of Economic Issues*, **40**(1) March, 1–25.

Hogg, M. A. (2000) "Social Identity and Social Comparison," in J. Suls & L. Wheeler, eds., *Handbook of Social Comparison: Theory and Research*, New York: Plenum, 401–21.

Hurst, E. and F. Stafford. (2004) "Home is Where the Equity Is: Mortgage Refinancing and Household Consumption," *Journal of Money, Credit, and Banking*, **36**(6) December, 985–1014.

Hyman, H. H. (1942) "The Psychology of Status," reprinted in part in H. H. Hyman and E. Singer, eds., *Readings in Reference Group Theory and Research*, New York: The Free Press.

Kennickell, A. B. (2009) "Ponds and Streams: Wealth and Income in the U.S., 1989 to 2007," working paper, Federal Reserve Board, January 7.

Keynes, J. M. (1936) *The General Theory of Employment, Interest and Money*, London: Macmillan.

Kindleberger, C. P. (1989) *Manias, Panics and Crashes: A History of Financial Crises*, second edition, London: Macmillan.

Kotz, D. M. (2008) "Contradictions of Economic Growth in the Neoliberal Era: Accumulation and Crisis in the Contemporary U.S. Economy," *Review of Radical Political Economics*, **40**(2) Spring, 174–88.

Laibson, D. (1997) "Golden Eggs and Hyperbolic Discounting," *Quarterly Journal of Economics*, **CXII**(2), 443–477.

Malmendier, U. and S. Nagel. (2011) "Depression Babies: Do Macroeconomic Experiences Affect Risk-Taking?" *Quarterly Journal of Economics*, **126**(1) February, 373–416.

McConnell, M. M. and G. Perez-Quiros. (2000) "Output Fluctuations in the United States: What Has Changed Since the Early 1980s?" *American Economic Review*, **90**(5) December, 1464–76.

Minsky, H. P. (1985) "The Financial Instability Hypothesis," in Philip Arestis and Thanos Skouras, eds., *Post Keynesian Economic Theory*, Sussex, U.K.: Wheatsheaf Books.
   (1986) *Stabilizing An Unstable Economy*, New Haven, CT: Yale University Press.

Morley, J. (2007) "The Slow Adjustment of Aggregate Consumption to Permanent Income," *Journal of Money, Credit, and Banking*, **39**(2–3) March-April, 615–38.

Neumark, D. and A. Postlewaite. (1998) "Relative Income Concerns and the Rise in Married Women's Employment," *Journal of Public Economics*, **70**(1), 157–83.

Olney, M. L. (1999) "Avoiding Default: The Role of Credit in the Consumption Collapse of 1930," *Quarterly Journal of Economics*, **114**(1) February, 319–35.

Pagano, M. and T. Jappelli. (1993) "Information Sharing in Credit Markets," *The Journal of Finance*, **48**(5) December, 1693–1718.

Palley, T. I. (2007) "Macroeconomics and Monetary Policy: Competing Theoretical Frameworks," working paper, available at www.thomaspalley.com.

Parker, J. A. (2000) "Spendthrift in America? On Two Decades of Decline in the U.S. Savings Rate," in Ben S. Bernanke and Julio J. Rotemberg, eds., *NBER Macroeconomics Annual 1999*, 317–70.

Schor, J. B. (1998) *The Overspent American*, New York: Basic Books.

Tajfel, H. (1972) "Social Categorization," English translation of "La categorisation sociale," in S. Moscovici, ed., *Introduction a la Psychologie Sociale*, Paris: Larousse, 272–302.

Taylor, P. and W. Wang. (2010) "The Fading Glory of The Television and Telephone," Pew Research Center, available at http://pewsocialtrends.org/files/2011/01/Final-TV-and-Telephone.pdf.

Thaler, R. H. and C. R. Sunstein. (2008) "Economic policy for humans," *Boston Globe*, <http://www.boston.com/bostonglobe/editorial_opinion/oped/articles/2008/04/17/economic_policy_for_humans/>

Thaler, R. H. and H. M. Shefrin. (1981) "An Economic Theory of Self-Control," *Journal of Political Economy*, **89**(2), 392–406.

Torralba, F. M. (2006) "Household Debt and Consumption Volatility," working paper, University of Chicago.

Veblen, T. (1994) [1899]. *The Theory of the Leisure Class*. Penguin twentieth-century classics. introduction by Robert Lekachman. New York, N.Y., U.S.A.: Penguin Books.

Wray, L. R. (2007) "Lessons from the Subprime Meltdown," working paper no. 522, Levy Economics Institute, December.

SEVEN

Wages, Demand, and U.S. Macroeconomic Travails

Diagnosis and Prognosis

Mark Setterfield

In recent years, the U.S. economy has faced two key sets of macroeconomic problems.[1] The first – evident to all between 2007 and 2009 –consisted of problems of an immediate or essentially short-term character. It involved emergency responses to the financial crisis designed to prevent an outright collapse of the U.S. financial sector, and putting a floor under an imploding real economy in response to the subsequent Great Recession. The second is made up of a variety of medium- to long-term problems, of which the financial crisis and Great Recession were ultimately symptoms. Among these is one particular problem that, although evident for some time, has been much less widely acknowledged and discussed than other problems of either a short-term or medium- to long-term nature (such as the need for financial reform). In a nutshell, it involves a structural flaw in the "aggregate demand-generating process" – the way in which total expenditures on goods and services are created. This structural flaw is, in turn, related most fundamentally to the stagnation of real wages for the great majority of wage earners over the last four decades, and the concomitant slow growth in the incomes of working households (and increase in household income inequality) over the same period. The focus of what follows is on this problem. From the perspective developed in this chapter, real wage stagnation has been the "soft underbelly" of the U.S. economy for many years, and now constitutes the "hard core" of the problems that the economy faces in the struggle to reconstruct growth and prosperity after the Great Recession.

[1] An earlier version of this chapter was presented at the workshop, "After the Great Recession: Keynesian Perspectives on the Way Forward" at Washington University, St. Louis in July 2010, and at Connecticut College. I would like to thank workshop and seminar participants for their comments. Any remaining errors are my own.

The argument that will be advanced is not new,[2] but it is neither sufficiently widely understood nor appreciated. Indeed, a hallmark of recent mainstream macroeconomics has been a steadfast failure (or refusal) to acknowledge the fact that weakness in the aggregate demand-generating process represents an important structural flaw in the U.S. economy. Hence, prior to the onset of the Great Recession, macroeconomics was gripped by the idea that the United States was experiencing a "Great Moderation" – a marked reduction in the volatility of the aggregate economy as compared with the 1970s and 1980s (see, for example, Davis and Kahn, 2008; Galí and Gambetti, 2009). This literature completely failed to identify an equally if not more profound tendency: the *latent fragility* that was building as a result of the way in which aggregate demand – and in particular, household-consumption expenditures – were being generated. Instead, identification and discussion of this latent fragility was confined to a small but coherent group of academic macroeconomists, largely outside of the mainstream, who drew more extensively on fundamentally Keynesian macroeconomic theory and who warned that the path of the U.S. economy was leading toward a deep and persistent recession (see, for example, Godley and Izurieta, 2002; Palley, 2002).

Even as the latent fragility of the U.S. economy became suddenly and alarmingly manifest in the wake of the financial crisis and Great Recession, mainstream macroeconomics failed to grasp the problems at hand. The mainstream view anticipates no systematic problem associated with the need to generate sufficient aggregate demand to buy up all of the output that productive forces (labor and capital) can, in principle, produce.[3] In other words, it is blind to *precisely* the problem with the aggregate demand-generating process that is (and will remain) at the core of the U.S. economy's macroeconomic travails. It is this persistent and continuing ignorance of the key medium- to long-term problem confronting the U.S. economy (rather than any particular novelty in the argument that will be advanced) that motivates the discussion that follows.

---

[2] See, for example, Chapter 2 in this volume by Palley, and Palley (2010) and the various references therein.

[3] According to Feldstein (2010), growth during the 2010s will be the same as growth during the 2000s. Feldstein reaches this conclusion on the basis of the claims that, although potential output (determined by the availability and productivity of factors of production) will grow at a slower pace over the next decade than during the 2000s, this will be offset by "the serious deepness of the hole in which the U.S. economy now finds itself," as a result of which actual output "will rise more rapidly than in the past as the labor market returns to full employment, as the labor force participation rate rises, and as capacity utilization returns to normal" (Feldstein, 2010, p.2).

The remainder of the chapter is organized as follows. Section one discusses the link between real-wage growth and the growth of aggregate expenditures necessary to maintain full (or even simply a constant rate of) employment. Section two then explores U.S. experience over the last four decades. It shows how the "golden rule" for growth consistent with a constant employment rate has been systematically violated in the U.S. economy, why it is that this did not result in persistent mass unemployment, and why, in turn, the U.S. economy thus sowed the seeds of the Great Recession even as (at least since the mid-1990s) it appeared to be performing well by historical standards.[4] Section three examines the prognosis for the U.S. economy absent major structural changes, and section four examines the policy measures that would be necessary to prevent the worst aspects of this prognosis from materializing. Section five offers some conclusions.

1. The Crux of the Problem

The central argument on which this chapter is based can be traced back to Glyn et al. (1990) who, in their analysis of the "Golden Age" of advanced capitalism (1945–73), argue that the success of the Golden Age (rapid growth and low unemployment consistent with low and stable inflation and a roughly constant distribution of income) was based, in part, on real-wage growth keeping pace with productivity growth. This simple equality results in similar rates of growth of total expenditures and potential output – or "aggregate demand and aggregate supply." In a growing economy, it therefore helps maintain balance or equilibrium in the goods market, the absence of which could, if unchecked, result in either high and rising unemployment or runaway inflation.

In simple terms, the equality of real-wage growth and labor-productivity growth can be thought of as a golden rule for sustainable growth consistent with full (or even simply a constant rate of) employment.[5] This last statement can be verified by means of some growth accounting and simple Keynesian consumption theory – which is provided, for the interested reader, in the appendix to this chapter. It can also be understood, however, by means of some straightforward intuition.

---

[4]   See, for example, Setterfield (2009).

[5]   A capitalist economy is, of course, a complex system, and the relationship between real wage and productivity growth is by no means the only relationship that matters for its performance.

As the Scottish essayist and satirist Thomas Carlyle once remarked, "teach a parrot to say 'supply and demand' and you've got an economist." At the risk of reinforcing Carlyle's impression of the "dismal science," the importance of maintaining real-wage growth consistent with productivity growth is most easily understood by appeal to aggregate supply and demand conditions in the goods market. Consider first the link between real wages and aggregate demand. Wages are, of course, a cost of production from the perspective of firms – but they are also the main source of income for the majority of families in the United States. Moreover, income is commonly understood to be the prime determinant of consumption expenditures, providing the main source of funds with which goods and services can be purchased. Profit (total income minus wages) is also a source of income, of course, but households that rely extensively or exclusively on profit as a source of income tend to spend proportionately less of their income on consumption goods. Finally, consumption is – overwhelmingly – the single largest component of total expenditures (aggregate demand) in the U.S. economy. Historically, consumption expenditures have accounted for roughly two-thirds of gross domestic product (GDP) in the United States; over the last few decades, however, the share of consumption in GDP has risen to something more like 70 percent.[6] In sum, there is an important link running from wage formation, via household income and consumption spending, to the aggregate demand for goods and services. As wages grow in real terms (i.e., in terms of what they can buy), so too does real household income, and hence real consumption, and hence real total expenditures on goods and services.

Now consider the contribution of labor productivity – output per person employed – to the potential output or "aggregate supply" of the economy. The potential output of the economy stems from both: a) the availability of factors of production (how much capital and labor is at the disposal of producers) and b) the *productivity* of these factors (how much output one unit of each factor can produce). In this way, it is always possible to think of the *potential* output of the economy – how much the economy can produce, in total, if all productive resources are fully utilized – as being equal to the size of the available labor force multiplied by output per worker (labor productivity). It follows that the *growth* of potential output must follow from either the growth of the labor force or the growth of labor productivity (or both). The growth of the labor force depends on population growth (which is very low in wealthy, industrialized countries such as the United States)

---

[6] The source of this change is one of the main themes of Chapter 6 in this volume, by Cynamon and Fazzari.

and the labor force participation rate (which cannot grow indefinitely since, ultimately, no more than 100 percent of the population can be active in the labor force). This leaves productivity growth as the main wellspring of potential output growth in the long run.

Putting the pieces together, we can now see that whereas real-wage growth fuels the largest single component of total expenditures, productivity growth plays a similarly prominent role in the expansion of potential output. This means that equality in the rates of growth of real wages and labor productivity will more or less suffice to keep total expenditures and potential output – or "aggregate demand and aggregate supply" – growing at the same rate. In other words, and as asserted earlier, the equation:

Real-wage growth = labor-productivity growth

is a good approximation for the condition necessary to maintain steady long-run growth with full employment, or even simply a constant rate of unemployment. It can therefore be regarded as a golden rule for sustainable growth consistent with full (or a constant rate of) employment.

2. Recent U.S. Experience

Diagnosis of the key medium- to long-term macroeconomic problem confronted by the U.S. economy follows directly from the analysis in the previous section. Specifically, over the past forty or so years, we have observed real wages growing at a slower pace than productivity in the U.S. economy. This inequality violates the golden rule for sustainable growth with a constant rate of employment, thus creating a structural flaw in the aggregate demand-generating process: *ceteris paribus*, aggregate demand growth cannot keep pace with the growth of potential output, or "aggregate supply."

The violation of the golden rule in the U.S. economy since the early 1970s is illustrated in Figure 7.1. This shows that the real average hourly wages of production and nonsupervisory workers roughly kept pace with increases in productivity through the early 1970s. Thereafter, however, real wages stagnated even as productivity continued to grow, resulting in an ever-widening gap between the two.

Of course, wages are not the only form of employee income funded by productivity: employer contributions to pension schemes and health insurance are also part of total compensation. Furthermore, nonwage compensation – and in particular, expenditures on health care insurance – has increased over time as a proportion of total employee compensation (Baker, 2007). Is it simply the case, then, that U.S. working households now receive

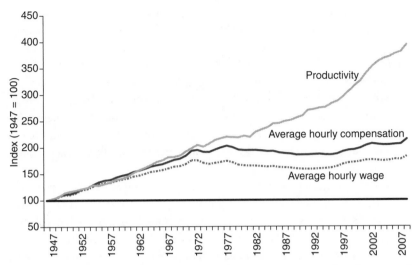

Figure 7.1. Productivity and real hourly wages and compensation of production and nonsupervisory workers, 1947–2009.
Source: Economic Policy Institute analysis of Bureau of Economic Analysis and Bureau of Labor Statistics data.

their income in a different form than they did forty years ago? Figure 7.1 reveals that this is clearly not so. The total compensation of production and nonsupervisory workers follows a pattern remarkably similar to that of hourly wages. In particular, and in tandem with average hourly wages, total compensation stagnates relative to productivity after the early 1970s.[7]

It might be argued that Figure 7.1 misrepresents the relationship between real-wage growth and productivity growth in the United States. For example, various measurement issues intrude on the calculation of real wages and productivity,[8] so that we may be comparing "apples with oranges" statistically. However, as both Baker (2007) and Fleck et al. (2011) show, even when these measurement issues are taken into account, there remains a persistent gap between real wage and productivity growth in the United States.

---

[7] Note also that it is not clear that increased expenditures on health insurance premiums are necessarily of real benefit to workers. It is possible that they are not, if higher insurance premiums represent monopoly profits earned by insurance companies. In this case, the increased proportion of employee compensation accounted for by expenditures on health insurance represents not a benign reformulation of the way in which employees are compensated, but a redistribution of real income away from working households toward insurance companies.

[8] These include the use of different price deflators to convert nominal wage and output series into real terms.

Another potential problem is that Figure 7.1 does not take into account *all* wages and salaries – including those of supervisory workers. It is certainly true that the growth of *all* wages and salaries – including those of supervisory workers – shows a less marked departure from the rate of productivity growth over the last four decades. This is because the real-wage growth of supervisory workers has fared much better than that of production and nonsupervisory workers since the 1970s, as a result of which managerial salaries now take up an increasing share of total wages and there has been a marked increase in wage inequality over the past forty years (Palley, 2002; Atkinson et al., 2011).

Even including the salaries (and nonwage income) of supervisory workers, however, employee compensation has grown at a slower pace than productivity. We know this to be true because had the golden rule for sustainable growth with a constant rate of employment been realized, the labor share of income would have remained constant over time.[9] Instead, total employee compensation as a share of national income has fallen steadily in the United States since the 1970s, from a high of 66.6 percent in 1979 to 64.2 percent in 2008.[10] Moreover, according to Mohun (2006), at least some part of the managerial "salaries" currently included in official

[9] In addition to its role in balancing the rates of growth of aggregate demand and potential output, the equality of real-wage growth (where "wages" are here understood to include all forms of employee compensation) and productivity growth is strictly necessary in order for the labor share of income to remain constant. This follows from the definition of the labor share, which can be written as:

$$\omega = \frac{WN}{Py}$$

where ω denotes the labor share of income, W is the value of the nominal wage, N is the level of employment, P is the general price level and y denotes aggregate real output (GDP). This expression can be rewritten as:

$$\omega = \frac{w}{q}$$

where $w = W/P$ is the real wage and $q = y/N$ is the level of labor productivity. It is clear from this last expression that, in order for the labor share to remain constant, any increase in q must be matched by an equal proportional increase in w. In other words, real wages must grow at the same rate as labor productivity.

[10] Author's calculations from Bureau of Economic Analysis data. See also Fleck et al. (2011). The decline in the labor share since the 1970s is evident throughout the OECD (see, for example, Korpi, 2002; Jorgenson and Timmer, 2011). In light of this, it is perhaps not surprising that Jorgenson and Timmer (2011) have recently identified a falling labor share as one of the new "stylised facts" of growth in advanced capitalist economies – in contrast to the original stylized fact of a constant labor share in the postwar growth record first identified by Kaldor (1963).

statistics measuring total employee compensation may conceptually belong in residual earnings (i.e., profits). In other words, they do not constitute wages (properly defined) at all. This view is consistent with the findings of Crotty in Chapter 5 of this volume, who argues that a substantial part of executive pay in the financial services industry is rent (rather than payment for value added in the process of production). This suggests that, by over-stating the growth of "wages," data for total employee compensation may fail to adequately represent the gap between real wage and productivity growth, and hence, the full extent of the aggregate demand-generating problem confronting the U.S. economy.[11]

In sum, Figure 7.1 does not misrepresent the fact that, for several decades, the U.S. economy has violated the golden rule for achieving balance between the growth of aggregate supply and demand, and hence, sustainable growth with a constant rate of employment. By focusing on the earnings of produc-tion and nonsupervisory workers – who make up 80 percent of the work-force – it makes clear the very real drama of real-wage stagnation relative to productivity growth (and the concomitant falling share of income) for the great majority of working Americans.[12]

All other things equal, the failure of the golden rule for sustainable growth with a constant rate of employment should have caused the U.S. economy to experience slow growth and rising unemployment over the last thirty years. Yet very clearly, it has *not*. On the contrary, growth over the past two decades – and especially during the "Roaring Nineties" – reduced U.S. unemployment to levels considered low by both contemporary international and historical standards, and well below the average levels encountered during the 1970s and 1980s.[13] This raises a very important question: what has offset the aggregate demand deficiency caused by slow real-wage growth?

The Keynesian macroeconomic theory that informs this book suggests that it is possible for some components of aggregate demand to be *stimulated*

---

[11] Note that, even if Mohun's and Crotty's arguments regarding the classification of supervi-sory workers' income are not accepted, the fact remains that higher-income supervisory workers are not inclined to spend out of additional income at the same rate as production and nonsupervisory workers, so that including their compensation in the labor share will result in an understatement of the extent to which the falling labor share has put a strain on the aggregate demand-generating process.

[12] See also Glyn (2009) and Atkinson (2009), who show how very much more dramatic is the fall of the labor share as "wage income" is disaggregated – even if no more than the top 1% of wage earners are excluded.

[13] In 1999, for example, the official U.S. unemployment rate reached 4.0% – the lowest rate since 1970.

if real wages grow slower than productivity. For example, one result of real wages growing slower than productivity is a redistribution of income toward profits. It is possible that rising profits could stimulate investment spending to an extent that more than offsets the adverse consequences for consumption of real-wage stagnation.[14] Alternatively, since wages are a cost of production, the slow growth of real wages may give domestic producers a cost advantage *vis-à-vis* foreign rivals, thus boosting exports.[15]

However, simple macroeconomic facts suggest that neither of these effects is responsible for recent U.S. macroeconomic performance. First, since the early 1970s, the United States has experienced chronic trade deficits, and it has witnessed surging investment spending only once, during the latter half of the Roaring Nineties (at the peak of the information technology boom, when even traditional businesses were seeking to establish an "online" presence).[16] Second, rather than being replaced by an alternative source of aggregate demand, the importance of consumption spending in the U.S. economy has actually *increased* even as real wages have stagnated. As noted earlier, consumption spending has traditionally accounted for about 66 percent of U.S. GDP, but in recent decades this proportion has increased to approximately 70 percent. More than ever, then, the U.S. economy is consumption-led. The question that we confront thus amounts to the following: in the absence of robust real-wage growth for the majority of the working population, what has been propelling household consumption spending?

The Overworked American?

One possibility is that even as their real wages have stagnated, the household income of production and nonsupervisory workers has been successfully shored up by increases in the number of hours worked. In principle, more and more hours worked at even the same real wage will result in rising real income, which could then fund continuing growth in household-consumption expenditures.

According to Schor (1991), U.S. employees worked 163 more hours in 1990 than they did in 1970 – that is, almost an extra month of full-time work per year. This finding suggests the reversal of a long-term trend that

[14] This possibility is discussed in detail by Bhaduri and Marglin (1990).
[15] This possibility is discussed in detail by Blecker (2002).
[16] See also Chapter 10 in this volume by Baker on the contribution of investment and net exports to GDP over the last two decades.

had previously seen working time *fall* steadily as the economy as a whole grew ever more affluent and productive. Schor's "overworked American" hypothesis is modified somewhat by Bluestone and Rose (1997), who argue that U.S. workers have become both overworked *and* underemployed, with the latter causing the former. Hence, according to Bluestone and Rose, men are caught in a "feast and famine" cycle, as a result of which they work longer hours (including overtime) when work is available in anticipation of subsequent bouts of either underemployment (part-time or temporary work) or unemployment, resulting in an overall trend *decline* in their work hours of the sort consistent with earlier trends in working time. Women, however, work unequivocally longer hours than they did forty years ago – a response in part, Bluestone and Rose hypothesize, to the male job insecurity implicit in the "feast and famine" cycle.

The upshot of all this, Bluestone and Rose contend, is that the average number of hours worked by *families* has trended upward since the early 1970s, broadly corroborating Schor's emphasis on the "overworked American." The question remains, however, as to whether or not this has had any great effect on the living standards of working families? Bluestone and Rose think not, arguing that the overall increase in household labor supply has failed to offset the stagnation of real wages to such an extent as to have mitigated the impact of the latter on working households' income. This outcome is made clear in Figure 7.2, which illustrates the stark differences in the comparative rates of growth of income in the various quintiles (and top 5 percent) of the distribution of household income in the United States, both before and after 1979 – a chronological division of the postwar period that corresponds roughly to the point at which the golden rule for sustainable growth with a constant rate of employment was first violated in the United States.

Figure 7.2 calls attention to two salient facts. First, it illustrates that *ceteris paribus*, changes in the distribution of income between wages and profits, are an important driver of rising inequality in the distribution of household income (Atkinson, 2009; Glyn, 2009). Simply put, if real-wage growth lags productivity growth for the majority of the working population, the result will be an increase in household income inequality. This is exactly what we observe in panel (b) of Figure 7.2, where the differential rates of growth of household income across quintiles imply changes in the income shares of these quintiles, with households near to the top of the income distribution gaining at the expense of those near the bottom.[17]

---

[17] On the evolution of inequality in the size distribution of income in the United States, see, for example, Piketty and Saez (2003).

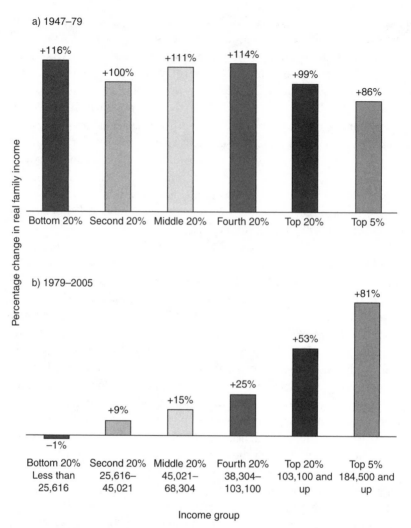

Figure 7.2. Changes in real family income by quintile (and top 5%), 1947–1979 and 1979–2005.
Source: Korty (2008, pp. 1, 2).

Second, even though other things have *not*, in fact, remained equal (since evidence suggests that the overworked American phenomenon is real), panel (b) of Figure 7.2 shows that stagnant real-wage growth for the majority of the working population has translated into no or slow growth in household real income for the majority of households. Hence, note that the average annual rates of growth of household income for households in the bottom four quintiles in panel (b) of Figure 7.2 are –0.04 percent, 0.33 percent, 0.54 percent and 0.86 percent respectively.[18] These rates of growth of household income correspond to a period (1979–2005) during which American families worked longer hours and when real disposable income in the economy as a whole grew at an average annual rate of 3.1 percent.[19]

In short, and unlike the postwar period prior to the 1970s, it would seem that growing consumption expenditures in the (increasingly consumption-led) U.S. economy have not, for the majority of working families, been funded by robust growth in real household incomes over the past thirty years. Whatever has been responsible for shoring up aggregate demand as real wages have stagnated, it has not been the increased working time of U.S. families.[20]

Household Debt Accumulation

If the real incomes of the majority of U.S. households have stagnated since the 1970s, what has grown rapidly is the level of their indebtedness – both absolutely, and as a proportion of total household income. It is this growth of indebtedness that has financed the continued growth of household-consumption expenditures that, thanks to real-wage stagnation (and despite the increase in family working hours), cannot be funded by rising real household income (see also Barba and Pivetti, 2009).[21]

Recent trends in U.S. household debt accumulation are illustrated in Figure 6.2 in the previous chapter. Figure 6.2 shows that household

[18] Author's calculations, based on Figure 7.2.
[19] Author's calculations, based on data on real disposable income from the Bureau of Economic Analysis.
[20] This result will come as no surprise to careful readers of the Appendix to this chapter, who will notice that the consequences for the goods market of real-wage growth lagging productivity growth are inescapable, regardless of changes in hours worked. This is because an increase in hours worked contributes only to n (the rate of growth of the labor force) in the analysis in the Appendix. With $\omega_c < 1$, a rise in n makes a net contribution to the growth of potential output, exacerbating the demand-deficiency problem (see equation [5]) whereas in the limit (with $\omega_c = 1$), n has no impact whatsoever on the capacity of aggregate demand to keep pace with the growth of potential output. In other words, increasing the hours worked by U.S. families cannot, in principle, offset the aggregate demand-generating problem created by $\hat{w} < q$.
[21] In other words, and referring again to the analysis in the Appendix $\hat{D} > \hat{w} + n$, and a consequent rise in $1-\omega_Y$ (the proportion of consumption expenditures financed by debt accumulation) has offset the shortfall in real-wage growth relative to productivity growth (see equation [5]).

indebtedness as a proportion of income rose more or less continuously from the early 1970s through to the onset of the Great Recession. It also draws to attention two discrete accelerations in the pace of household debt accumulation during this interval – the first occurring during the mid-1980s, and the second (and more dramatic) taking place at the turn of the millennium.

The overall trend in household debt accumulation since the 1970s is undoubtedly associated with the substantial growth of mortgage debt.[22] *Prima facie*, this might appear to suggest that, to the extent that U.S. households have been accumulating more debt, they have been doing so in order to accumulate more assets (specifically, housing), which would (in the first instance) leave household net worth unchanged.[23] However, several comments about this sanguine view of the evolution of household balance sheets are in order. First, not all new mortgage debt accumulated by households is used to acquire (or improve) houses. As Cynamon and Fazzari discuss in Chapter 6, changes over the last four decades in both household and financial sector norms regarding the accumulation of household debt have resulted in phenomena such as the "cash-out" refinancing of homes, designed to allow households to borrow against the existing value of the equity in their homes. Additional mortgage debt accumulated in this manner may or may not be used to acquire durable assets: it can just as easily be spent on new clothing or a family vacation.

Second, even if household debt is backed by home equity, housing wealth is not fungible in the same manner as, say, a bond portfolio. To put it bluntly, a family cannot sell the roof of their house in order to pay down a portion of their outstanding mortgage debt in the same way that they *could* sell part of a bond portfolio to reduce the household's liabilities.

This brings us to the final point: mortgage debt – like all debt – must be *serviced*, drawing attention to the crucial relationship between the stock of outstanding household debt on one hand, and the flow of household *income* out of which payments toward principle and/or interest charges must be made. Even if a household accumulates debt that is backed by home equity, the household may become financially distressed if the debt accumulated places too great a debt-servicing burden on current household income.

---

[22] Cynamon and Fazzari (2008, p.18) demonstrate the close association between trends in the growth of mortgage debt and total household debt in the United States since the mid-1970s.

[23] Of course, the net worth of the household may actually improve over time if the mortgage debt is amortized and/or housing prices rise. As the subprime mortgage fiasco drew to attention, however, neither of these things can be taken for granted.

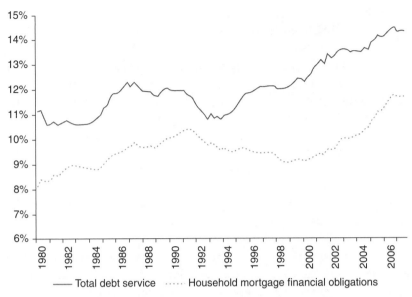

Figure 7.3. Debt service as a percentage of disposable income.
Source: Cynamon and Fazzari (2008, p. 22).

Note, then, that having begun by highlighting the use of debt as a substitute for income to finance current consumption expenditures, we now confront the possibility (once again) that weak household income growth must ultimately constrain consumption spending, this time by limiting the extent to which individual households can service debt (and therefore accumulate debt in the first place).

Figure 7.3 illustrates the growth of the debt-servicing burden faced by U.S. households prior to the onset of the Great Recession. It shows that, despite some cyclical variation, total debt service payments as a proportion of disposable income remained roughly the same through the early 1990s. Thereafter, however, the total debt service burden grew steadily. Note that even as financial obligations associated with mortgages *fell* as a proportion of disposable income from 1991 through 2000, the *total* debt service burden continued to rise. This draws attention to the fact that mortgages are not the only form of debt liabilities that U.S. households have been accumulating in recent decades. On the contrary, since the 1970s, household access to revolving debt – primarily credit card debt – has increased markedly (especially among lower-income households), as has the share of revolving debt in total consumer debt (Cynamon and Fazzari, 2008, p.15).

Finally, it is important to call attention to the fact that recent household-debt accumulation in the United States has been accompanied by marked inequality in the *distribution* of debt burdens, with lower- and middle-income households (i.e., precisely those who have suffered most from the stagnation of real wages and resulting stagnation of household real income) bearing proportionally more of the household debt burden. Figure 6.3 in Chapter 6 illustrates this point dramatically. Wealthier households accumulate more debt in absolute terms, but debt to income ratios were far higher in low- and middle-income households by 2007, and these ratios have risen dramatically for all households except those at the very top of the income distribution. It is instructive to contrast the household debt burdens depicted in Figure 6.3 with the current national debt to GDP ratios that are allegedly such cause for concern. Even by early 2011, following the dramatic reductions in tax revenues and increases in government spending triggered by the Great Recession, the net public debt to GDP ratio in the United States was below 66 percent.[24] Unlike central governments, whose main source of revenue is taxes levied on *all* productive activities (making it a very diversified income stream), the income of working households is very much more specialized, depending in the main on one or two jobs.[25] Moreover, lower- and middle-income households – those with the highest debt to income ratios – are more likely to be the ones most exposed to the increased job insecurity that has come to characterize the U.S. labor market since the early 1970s (see, for example, Setterfield, 2006; 2007). In short, they are the economic units who are least well-placed to carry the increasing debt burdens that have become a central feature of the U.S. economy.[26]

These statistics draw attention to an important stock-flow imbalance in the U.S. economy over the past four decades. Specifically, household debt grew faster than household income – especially among the lower- and middle-income households least well-placed to sustain such a financial posture – with the concomitant result that the household debt-servicing burden increased over time (again, see Figure 6.3 in Chapter 6). In the tradition of Hyman Minsky, these trends suggest that household balance sheets were deteriorating and that, as a result, the financial fragility of the household

---

[24] Net public debt excludes public debt held by government agencies, including the Social Security Administration and the Federal Reserve System.

[25] Of course, this is not the only difference between central governments and households that affects their respective capacities to carry debt. See Chapter 11 by Cynamon and Fazzari in this volume.

[26] See also Barba and Pivetti (2009, pp.129–31).

sector (and by extension, the U.S. economy as a whole) was increasing over time.[27]

From the Keynesian perspective developed in this book, these developments herald two problems. First, debt servicing involves transferring income from lower-income (and proportionally higher spending) net-debtor households to higher-income (and proportionally lower-spending) creditor households. This only serves to exacerbate the basic flaw in the aggregate demand-generating process that debt accumulation is supposed to offset. As such, it requires still more aggressive household debt accumulation if the potential shortfall of aggregate demand stemming from the real-wage stagnation experienced by the majority of working households is not to become manifest. Second, as much of the preceding discussion suggests, the entire process of household debt accumulation is rather like putting the plug in the bathtub, turning on the taps and walking away: an exercise that can only be indulged for so long before disaster strikes. In this case, the disaster precipitated by an unsustainable pattern of household debt accumulation is widespread default. Default not only has an adverse effect on the borrowing and hence spending abilities of debtor households, but also destroys the wealth (and hence reduces the willingness to spend) of creditor households, as the value of bad debts (which constitute assets from the point of view of creditors) are written down or written off. In other words, the economic equivalent of water spilling over the rim of the bathtub, onto the bathroom floor, and through the living room ceiling is a sudden, sharp reduction in aggregate demand (with the inevitable adverse consequences for output and employment), as borrowing and lending freeze up and wealth is destroyed.

In sum, over the last four decades, the trajectory of the U.S. economy has been characterized not so much by the dawning of a new era of macroeconomic tranquility (as suggested by the notion of a "Great Moderation") as by increasing latent fragility. The latter has stemmed primarily from an unsustainable pattern of debt accumulation by lower- and middle-income households, seeking to offset weak real income growth caused by the failure of real wages to keep pace with productivity growth. On the basis of this analysis, the events that transpired between 2007 and 2009 are easy

---

[27] See, for example, Papadimitriou et al. (2006), Cynamon and Fazzari (2008), and Weller and Sabatini (2008) for extensive discussion of this last point. Note that these references once again exemplify the fact that, from the Keynesian perspective central to this volume, both the event and even the nature of the macroeconomic crisis that has recently beset the U.S. economy were anticipated. The account of the financial crisis and Great Recession furnished here does not involve post hoc "wisdom after the event."

to understand: beginning in the fall of 2007, the latent fragility of the U.S. economy finally became manifest, in the form of the financial crisis and, subsequently, the Great Recession.

3. Prognosis: What Lies Ahead?

The preceding analysis suggests that the stagnation of real wages experienced by the majority of the working population lies at the very core of the problems that have recently afflicted the U.S. economy. Absent major changes in the structure of the U.S. economy designed to remedy this flaw in the aggregate demand-generating process, what will the legacy of the financial crisis and Great Recession be in the medium to longer term?

From the Keynesian perspective utilized in this volume, three possibilities present themselves. The first is predicated on the notion that the pattern of household debt accumulation that characterized the period prior to 2007 is now exhausted. This scenario will materialize if either: a) the "credit crunch" that accompanied the financial crisis signals the onset of tighter credit standards in the medium to long term – i.e., an enduring unwillingness on the part of the financial sector to continue lending to households; and/or b) if the financial crisis and Great Recession trigger a change in household borrowing norms, as a result of which households become more wary of accumulating debt in the medium to long term. What we are contemplating here is an end to the use of credit to finance increases in consumption spending that cannot be funded by real income – in other words, a permanent breakdown in the debt accumulation dynamics that had previously prevented the flaw in the aggregate demand-generating process in the United States from becoming manifest. In this scenario, then, and *ceteris paribus*, the future involves secular stagnation (slow growth accompanied by persistently high unemployment), a scenario that Cynamon and Fazzari in Chapter 6 label the "end of the consumer age."

Of course, other things may not remain equal – and this brings us to the second possible legacy of the financial crisis and Great Recession. Even if the dynamics of household debt accumulation have broken down, the importance of consumption expenditures as the "engine of growth" in the U.S. economy may diminish, as some other component of aggregate demand comes to the forefront. It seems unlikely, however, that this scenario will materialize. Having acted as the "consumer of last resort" for the world economy for several decades now, it is difficult to imagine that foreign demand (in the form of a sustained export boom) will come to the rescue of the U.S. economy. Corporate investment is also unlikely to emerge as a savior. As noted earlier, investment has taken a largely backseat role in generating aggregate demand in the United States for several decades now, even despite the ever-increasing rate of profit in the U.S. economy since the early 1980s (see Mohun, 2010). Finally, and despite the remarks made earlier about the public sector being better placed than the household sector to deficit spend, political unwillingness promulgated by those who Epstein in Chapter 9 labels "austerity buzzards," is likely to thwart any attempt to use fiscal policy as an engine of medium- to long-term growth.

The last of the three possibilities alluded to earlier rests on *both* the credit crunch *and* households' reluctance to borrow proving to be strictly transitory events. In this third scenario, the financial crisis and Great Recession represent no more than a temporary interruption to the pattern of debt-financed, consumption-led growth that has come to typify the U.S. economy. Note, however, that even if this third scenario is plausible, it represents nothing more than a return to the same unsustainable growth process to which the last few decades have borne witness. The deficiency of aggregate demand caused by the stagnation of real wages experienced by the majority of workers may, once again, be offset. As a result, growth over the course of the next business cycle (or two) may suffice to lower unemployment significantly from its Great Recession peak. However, as we surely now know, the real question posed by this scenario is: when will the next crisis occur, and how bad will it be?

In any event, then, without major changes to the structure of the U.S. economy designed to offset the flaw in the aggregate demand-generating process related to real-wage stagnation, the prospects for the U.S. economy appear bleak.

4. Policy Implications: What is to be Done?

There has already been an extensive policy response to the 2007–09 financial crisis and Great Recession. This policy response includes short-term measures designed to address the illiquidity and/or insolvency of financial institutions (such as the TARP) and the loss of output and jobs in the real economy (record-low overnight interest rates and several attempts at fiscal stimulus). However, consistent with the analysis in this chapter, any policy response to recent macroeconomic conditions that hopes to succeed in the medium to long term – that is, that hopes to provide a basis for sustainable growth consistent with full (or simply a constant rate of) employment – must address the structural flaw in the aggregate demand-generating process emanating from the real-wage stagnation experienced by the majority of U.S. workers.

As first noted in section one, and as is evident from the first twenty-five years of the data presented in Figure 7.1, the U.S. economy has not always violated the golden rule for sustainable growth with a constant rate of employment during the postwar era. Glyn et al. (1990) accredit the success of the 1945–73 Golden Age, in part, to the maintenance of a rate of growth of real wages roughly equal to that of labor productivity. This outcome can, in turn, be associated with the existence of a "value sharing" norm of distributive justice during the Golden Age, brought about by a "social bargain" (Cornwall, 1990) or "capital-labor accord" (Bowles, Gordon and Weisskopf, 1990) designed to reconcile the competing claims of the social classes on total income and control over the conditions of employment. Under the terms of this social bargain, firms retained the "right to manage" (i.e., to decide what to produce, where, and how) in return for a commitment to steady growth in real wages consistent with a stable wage share of income. Instrumental in the creation and supervision of these arrangements were strong labor unions.

Since the early 1970s, changes in labor law and corporate organization have succeeded in disempowering workers – most conspicuously through a precipitous decline in rates of unionization (Palley, 1998 and Chapter 2 of this volume; Osterman, 1999). These developments have been accompanied by the demise of the postwar social bargain and its value-sharing norm of distributive justice. The latter has been replaced by a "winner-take-all" norm based on the exercise of market power (and therefore favorable, in the current environment, to corporations and their senior executives). Not surprisingly, the institutional changes just described coincide exactly with the period during which real wages have stagnated for the majority of U.S. workers, and the U.S. economy has violated the golden rule for sustainable growth with a constant rate of employment.

According to this analysis, the creation and enforcement by a strong labor movement of a particular norm of distributive justice was instrumental in ensuring that the U.S. economy satisfied the golden rule during the first three decades of the postwar period, whereas the evisceration of organized labor (and accompanying demise of the advantageous norm of distributive justice) was instrumental in the subsequent violation of this rule.[28] This,

---

[28] One measure of the impact of de-unionization on the relationship between real wage and productivity growth is provided by Fichtenbaum (2011), who finds that the decline in union density between 1997 and 2006 explains almost a third of the accompanying decline in labor's share of income over the same period.

in turn, suggests that an important condition for a return to a situation in which the golden rule is satisfied is a reinvigoration of the labor movement. This would give workers – who already have a *vested interest* in the growth of the real wage – sufficient bargaining power to actually *achieve* an increase in the growth of their real wages, which is necessary if the golden rule is once again to be satisfied.[29]

The policy interventions necessary to successfully respond to the financial crisis and Great Recession therefore go far beyond short-run macroeconomic stimulus (through monetary and fiscal policy) and even financial re-regulation. They must also address the structure of U.S. labor relations. One important starting point is labor law, changes to which have systematically disadvantaged workers since the 1970s by making union organization more difficult and de-unionization by corporations much easier (see, for example, Block et al., 1996). This was the impetus behind the recently proposed Employee Free Choice Act which, among other things, would have made it harder for firms to intimidate workers who wanted to join unions.[30]

Disadvantageous changes in labor law, however, are not the only obstacles that organized labor has confronted since the 1970s. Another challenge has arisen from the process of globalization and, in particular, the credible threat to relocate production that globalization has bestowed on U.S.-based corporations. Bronfenbrenner (2000) documents the adverse consequences that this has had for organizing unions in the United States. However, it may be the current *structure* of globalization (rather than globalization *per se*) that is disadvantageous to workers – specifically, its encouragement of competition in labor standards, which means that territories that succeed in denuding legal protections for trade unions become the most attractive to footloose corporations. This, in turn, puts pressure on other territories to relax labor standards in the hope of retaining corporations currently located within their jurisdictions. The result is a "race to the bottom" that destroys labor standards (but that ultimately means that corporations need not move anywhere). One possible policy response

---

[29] It should be noted that a stronger labor movement is a necessary but not sufficient condition for rectifying the adverse institutional changes that have occurred since the 1970s. Hence, much of the emphasis in, for example, Cornwall (1990) is on the contribution of the industrial relations system as a whole (rather than just trade unions) to postwar macroeconomic performance.

[30] Even some mainstream economists rallied behind the Employee Free Choice Act. See, for example, Paul Krugman's open letter to then President-elect Obama, published in the January 2009 issue of *Rolling Stone* magazine.

to this situation involves greater regional (and ultimately international) coordination, designed to eliminate competition in labor standards and the resulting race to the bottom in favor of commitment to a common set of labor standards (see, for example, Palley 2002b; 2004). This would help to create a platform from which a strengthened labor movement might succeed in raising the growth of real wages toward the level required to satisfy the golden rule.

Quite apart from globalization, however, unions have also been challenged by the inexorable structural change that accompanies growth in capitalist economies – in particular, the steady shift of employment away from the manufacturing sector of the economy (where trade union organization has traditionally been strongest) toward the service sector. Where the decline of manufacturing has been brought about by competitive failure due, in turn, to factors such as an overvalued exchange rate, a case can be made for policy interventions designed to redress the loss of manufacturing jobs (as is discussed further by Palley in Chapter 2 of this volume) that would, in turn, help to offset the decline of the labor movement.

There may also be alternatives – or complements – to the policy interventions discussed so far that would help revive the aggregate demand-generating process. For example, macroeconomic policies designed to create and sustain low (approximately 4 percent) unemployment would help, given the observed impact of unemployment on the labor share and income inequality more generally in both the short and long periods (Galbraith, 1998; Baker, 2007). In Chapter 12 of this volume, Tcherneva explores a variety of policies designed to improve the economy's ability to maintain true full-employment at all times, not just in recessions. In addition, fiscal policy could aim to redistribute after-tax incomes toward working households, by first raising taxes on profits and executive salaries, and then either lowering taxes on low- and middle-income families, or directly satisfying consumption through the increased provision of public goods.

Having outlined a broad range of policy options, however, it is important to acknowledge the significant obstacles that would likely impede progress on any of these fronts. With regard to redressing the changes that have denuded the bargaining power of labor, for example, it is well known that some part of the shift toward services in growing economies is caused by common developmental patterns that no obvious policy can (or should) address (Rowthorn and Wells, 1987). Moreover, the sort of interregional cooperation necessary to reverse the race to the bottom in labor standards would prove far from easy to achieve. With respect to expansionary macroeconomic and redistributive fiscal policies, meanwhile, deep-seated political preferences for small government and "self-help" may thwart the necessary policy interventions. Indeed, in the worst case scenario, it may prove to be the case that the postwar Golden Age was no more than a fleeting moment during Hobsbawm's (1994) "short twentieth century" – a transitory confluence of remarkable events (a strong labor movement, the existence of an alternative (Soviet) system of production, and the legacy of recent suffering from two world wars and the intervening Great Depression) that altered attitudes toward government intervention, increased the bargaining power of labor, and encouraged wealth owners to adopt a strategy of "concede and rule." If so, then any of the policy remedies contemplated earlier are likely futile. It is only to be hoped that this fatalistic hypothesis is incorrect and that policy interventions – even if difficult in practice – can, in principle, so affect the U.S. economy as to redress the fundamental structural flaw that is the ultimate cause of the recent crisis.

5. Conclusions

Central to the Keynesian perspective that advises this volume are the propositions that aggregate demand drives macroeconomic outcomes, and that finance is the "yin and yang" of capitalist growth and development, providing the means by which spending can exceed income, but at the same time resulting in the accumulation of debt burdens that can be the undoing of credit-fueled economic expansions.[31] Drawing on this perspective, this chapter has advanced the claim that the central dilemma confronting the U.S. economy is a structural flaw in its aggregate demand-generating process. Specifically, real wages have grown dramatically slower than productivity for the majority of the working population, resulting in an imbalance between the growth of aggregate demand and the growth of potential output ("aggregate supply"). The resulting aggregate demand shortfall has been offset by household debt accumulation, which has financed an expansion of consumption expenditures that could not be funded by the stagnant real incomes of working households. As a result, and despite ostensibly satisfactory macroeconomic performance since the 1990s, the United States has for several decades been characterized by a latent fragility that, beginning in 2007, became dramatically manifest in the forms of the financial crisis and Great Recession.

---

[31] This last point is, of course, the central focus of Minskyan interpretations of the Great Recession – see, for example, Chapter 3 (by Wray) and Chapter 6 (by Cynamon and Fazzari) in this volume.

Resolving these problems requires far more than temporary macroeconomic stimulus or even financial reform. Ultimately, it requires restructuring the U.S. economy to re-establish the robust growth of real incomes of working households last seen during the 1950s and 1960s. It is difficult to overestimate the magnitude of this task – but it is equally difficult to overstate its importance. Absent measures to correct the flaw in the aggregate demand-generating process stemming from real wage stagnation, the United States faces a future of either boom-bust cycles characterized by periodic financial crises, or else – and perhaps more likely – secular stagnation.

Appendix: Some Keynesian Growth Accounting

Goods market equilibrium with full resource utilization requires:

$$AD = Y^P$$

where AD denotes aggregate demand in real terms and Y^P is potential output, or:

$$C + A = \frac{Y^P}{L} L \qquad [1]$$

where C and A denote real consumption and non-consumption expenditures (respectively) and L is the size of the labor force.

Denoting the growth rates of variables with "hat" notation, a growing economy with full employment therefore requires:

$$\widehat{AD} = \hat{Y}^P$$

or from [1]:

$$\omega_c \hat{C} + (1 - \omega_c) \hat{A} = q + n \qquad [2]$$

where ω_c is the share of consumption in total expenditures, q is the rate of productivity growth (that is, the growth of Y^P/L), and n is the rate of growth of the labor force.

Now suppose that:

$$C = c_w wN + c_\pi \Pi + B$$

where w is the real wage, N is total employment, Π is total profit in real terms, B is the flow of new debt-financed real-consumption spending by wage earners and c_w and c_π represent the (constant) propensities to consume of wage and profit earners, respectively. Assuming that $0 = c_\pi < c_w < 1$, this expression can be rewritten as:

$$C = c_w w \frac{N}{L} L + B$$

where N/L denotes the employment rate. (Note that we assume here that wage earners service their debts $D = \Sigma B$, out of that part of wage income that is not consumed (given by $[1 - c_w]wN$) – i.e., that debt servicing is a substitute for saving out of wage income, and therefore has no effect on consumption spending.) Assuming that N/L remains constant, it follows that:

$$\hat{C} = \omega_Y(\hat{w}+n)+(1-\omega_Y)\hat{B} \qquad [3]$$

where ω_Y denotes the share of total consumption spending that is funded by current income. Substituting [3] into [2] and rearranging yields:

$$\omega_c[\omega_Y\,\hat{w}+(1-\omega_Y)\hat{B}]+(1-\omega_c)\hat{A}=q+(1-\omega_c\omega_Y)n. \qquad [4]$$

If we now assume that B grows at the same rate as wage income – which would suffice to keep the deficit to income ratio of working households constant over time – we can write:

$$\hat{B} = \hat{w}+n$$

and substituting this expression into equation [4], we arrive at:

$$\omega_c\,\hat{w}+(1-\omega_c)\hat{A}=q+(1-\omega_c)n. \qquad [5]$$

It is now obvious by inspection that as $\omega_c \to 1$, the expression in [5] reduces to:

$$\hat{w} = q \qquad [5a]$$

(Recall that, historically in the United States, $\omega_c \approx 0.66$; currently, $\omega_c \approx 0.70$.)

In sum, the equality of real wage and productivity growth is a reasonable approximation for the condition necessary for sustainable long-run growth consistent with full employment (or even simply a constant rate of unemployment) – as per Glyn et al. (1990).

References

Atkinson, A. B. (2009) "Factor shares: The principal problem of political economy?" *Oxford Review of Economic Policy*, **25**, 3–16.

Atkinson, A. B., T. Piketty, and E. Saez. (2011) "Top incomes in the long run of history," *Journal of Economic Literature*, **49**, 3–71.

Baker, D. (2007) "Behind the gap between productivity and wage growth," CEPR Issue Brief, February.

Barba, A. and M. Pivetti. (2009) "Rising household debt: Its causes and macroeconomic implications – a long-period analysis," *Cambridge Journal of Economics*, **33**, 113–37.

Bhaduri, A. and S. Marglin. (1990) "Unemployment and the real wage: The economic basis for contesting political ideologies," *Cambridge Journal of Economics*, **14**, 375–93.

Blecker, R. (2002) "Distribution, demand and growth in neo-Kaleckian models," in M. Setterfield (ed.) *The Economics of Demand-Led Growth*, Cheltenham: Edward Elgar.

Block, R. N., J. Beck, and D. H. Kruger. (1996) *Labor Law, Industrial Relations and Employee Choice*, Kalamazoo, MI: W. E. Upjohn Institute.

Bluestone, B. and S. Rose. (1997) "Overworked and underemployed: Unraveling an economic enigma," *The American Prospect*, **31**, March-April.

Bowles, S., D. Gordon, and T. Weisskopf. (1990) *After the Waste Land*, Armonk, NY: M. E. Sharpe.

Bronfenbrenner, K. (2000) "Uneasy terrain: The impact of capital mobility on workers, wages and union organizing," Report to the U.S. Trade Deficit Review Commission.

Cornwall, J. (1990) *The Theory of Economic Breakdown*, Oxford: Basil Blackwell.

Cynamon, B. Z. and S. M. Fazzari. (2008) "Household debt in the Consumer Age: Source of growth – risk of collapse," *Capitalism and Society*, **3**, 2, Article 3.

Davis, S. J. and J. A. Kahn. (2008) "Interpreting the great moderation: Changes in the volatility of economic activity at the macro and micro levels," *Journal of Economic Perspectives*, **22**, 155–80.

Feldstein, M. S. (2010) "U.S. growth in the decade ahead," National Bureau of Economic Research (NBER) Working Paper 15685.

Fichtenbaum, U. (2011) "Unions affect labor's share of income: Evidence using panel data," *American Journal of Economics and Sociology*, 70, 784–810.

Fleck, S., J. Glaser, and S. Sprague. (2011) "The compensation-productivity gap: A visual essay," *Monthly Review*, **134**, 57–69.

Galbraith, J. (1998) *Created unequal: The crisis in American pay*, New York: Free Press.

Galí, J. and L. Gambetti. (2009) "On the sources of the Great Moderation," *American Economic Journal: Macroeconomics*, **1**, 26–57.

Glyn, A. (2009) "Functional distribution and inequality," in W. Salverda, B. Nolan, and T. M. Smeeding (eds.) *Oxford Handbook of Economic Inequality*, Oxford: Oxford University Press.

Glyn, A., A. Hughes, A. Lipietz, and A. Singh. (1990) "The rise and fall of the Golden Age," in S. A. Marglin and J. B. Schor (eds.) *op. cit.*

Godley, W. and A. Izurieta (2002) "The case for a severe recession," *Challenge*, **45**, March/April, 27–51.

Hobsbawm, E. J. (1994) *The age of extremes: The short twentieth century, 1914–1991*, London: Michael Joseph.

Jorgenson, D. W. and M. P. Timmer (2011) "Structural change in advanced nations: A new set of stylised facts," *Scandinavian Journal of Economics*, **113**, 1–29.

Kaldor, N. (1963) "Capital accumulation and economic growth," in F. A. Lutz and D. C. Hague (eds.) *Proceedings of a Conference Held by the International Economics Association*, London: Macmillan, 177–222.

Korty, D. (2008) "Comment on 'household debt in the Consumer Age: Source of growth – risk of collapse' (by Barry Z. Cynamon and Steven M. Fazzari)," *Capitalism and Society*, **3**, 3, Article 6.

Marglin, S. A. and J. B. Schor. (eds.) *The Golden Age of capitalism: Reinterpreting the post war experience*, Oxford: Oxford University Press.

Mishel, L., J. Bernstein, and S. Allegretto. (2007) *The state of working America 2006/2007*, Ithaca, NY: Cornell University Press.

Mohun, S. (2006) "Distributive shares in the US economy, 1964–2001," *Cambridge Journal of Economics*, **30**, 347–70.

(2010) "The crisis of 2008 in historical perspective," paper presented at the Fourth Analytical Political Economy Workshop, Queen Mary University of London, May 14–15.

Osterman, P. (1999) *Securing prosperity: The American labor market: How it has changed and what to do about it*, Princeton, NJ: Princeton University Press.

Palley, T. I. (1998) *Plenty of nothing: The downsizing of the American dream and the case for structural Keynesianism*, Princeton, NJ: Princeton University Press.

(2002) "Economic contradictions coming home to roost? Does the US economy face a long-term aggregate demand generation problem?" *Journal of Post Keynesian Economics*, **25**, 9–32.

(2002b) "The child labor problem and the need for international labor standards," *Journal of Economic Issues*, **XXXVI**, 601–15.

(2004) "The economic case for international labor standards," *Cambridge Journal of Economics*, **28**, 21–36.

(2007) "The Fed and America's distorted expansion," *Dollars and Sense*, November/December.

(2009) "After the bust: The outlook for macroeconomics and macroeconomic policy," The Levy Economics Institute of Bard College Public Policy Brief No. 97.

(2010) "The limits of Minsky's financial instability hypothesis as an explanation of the crisis," *Monthly Review*, **61**, 28–43.

Papadimitriou, D. B., E. Chilcote, and G. Zezza. (2006) "Are housing prices, household debt, and growth sustainable?" Levy Economics Institute of Bard College Strategic Analysis, January 2006.

Piketty, T. and E. Saez. (2003) "Income inequality in the United States, 1913–1998," *Quarterly Journal of Economics*, **118**, 1–39.

Rowthorn, R. E. and J. R. Wells (1987) *De-industrialisation and foreign trade*, Cambridge: Cambridge University Press.

Schor, J. B. (1991) *The overworked American: The unexpected decline of leisure*, New York: Basic Books.

Setterfield, M. (2006) "Balancing the macroeconomic books on the backs of workers: A simple analytical political economy model of contemporary US capitalism," *International Journal of Political Economy*, **35**, 46–63. Erratum, *International Journal of Political Economy*, 37, 4, 104 (2008–09).

(2007) "The rise, decline and rise of incomes policies in the US during the post-war era: An institutional-analytical explanation of inflation and the functional distribution of income," *Journal of Institutional Economics*, **3**, 127–46.

(2009) "An index of macroeconomic performance," *International Review of Applied Economics*, **23**, 625–49.

Weller, C. E. and K. Sabatini. (2008) "From boom to bust: Did the financial fragility of homeowners increase in an era of greater financial deregulation?" *Journal of Economic Issues*, **XLII**, 607–32.

PART FOUR

GLOBAL DIMENSIONS OF U.S. CRISIS

EIGHT

Global Imbalances and the U.S. Trade Deficit

Robert A. Blecker

As the U.S. and foreign economies slowly recover from the financial crisis and Great Recession of 2008–9, attention naturally shifts to potential sources of future instability. One longer-term problem that continues to haunt the prospects for a sustained recovery is the large U.S. trade deficit and the correspondingly large surpluses of several key U.S. trading partners, a recurrent situation that has come to be known as "global imbalances." Indeed, the rapid rise of the trade deficit during the recovery has been a major reason for the sluggish increases in U.S. employment since the recession officially ended in mid-2009.

These large international trade imbalances can be viewed to a large extent as the result of different national solutions to the same underlying problem: the fact that real-wage growth has lagged behind productivity growth, thereby suppressing incomes of working-class and middle-class households and creating a latent deficiency of aggregate demand in both the United States and many other countries (see von Arnim, 2010; Cripps et al., 2011; and Chapter 2 by Palley and Chapter 7 by Setterfield in this volume). In the boom that preceded the Great Recession, the United States solved this problem by relying on the housing price bubble and household debt accumulation to boost consumption in spite of stagnant earnings, whereas the surplus nations instead relied on export markets to augment weak domestic demand and lent the United States the funds required to finance the resulting trade imbalances. Those U.S. residents who managed to keep their jobs and didn't have to compete with imports were able to benefit from cheaper imported consumer goods, while U.S. multinational corporations profited

The author is indebted to Jörg Bibow, Menzie Chinn, Rob Scott, Rudi von Arnim, and the editors of this volume for comments on earlier versions. The author alone is responsible for the views expressed here and any remaining errors.

187

from outsourcing to lower-wage locations abroad, but these gains were obtained at the cost of chronically depressed manufacturing employment and average wages at home.[1]

The global trade imbalances were not a direct cause of the financial crisis and Great Recession, although trade linkages were an important mechanism for transmitting the impact of the recession from the United States to other countries. Nonetheless, this chapter argues that the U.S. trade deficit and foreign trade surpluses were at least a contributing factor (and in some respects a necessary enabling factor) in the run-up of unsustainable financial positions by U.S. households and financial institutions that more directly led to the crisis and recession. Furthermore, the U.S. deficit will not disappear automatically during the postcrisis period, and the more rapid is the recovery, the more likely it is to increase again unless countermeasures to rebalance the global economy are adopted.

1. The Trade Deficit Trap

No single factor explains the U.S. trade deficit or the global imbalances. As argued in Blecker (2009), the United States has been caught in a "trade deficit trap," in which the trade deficit is sustained by "a web of interconnected and self-reinforcing mechanisms," both at home and abroad, "that make it very difficult to reduce the deficit through conventional policies" (p. 2). The trade deficit trap argument encapsulates a number of factors that have been argued by some to be "the" main cause of the U.S. trade deficit, and shows how these factors – far from being mutually exclusive causes – have interacted in mutually reinforcing ways to maintain a large trade deficit (except during the worst of the recession in 2008–9).[2]

The U.S. trade deficit originated in the last three decades of the twentieth century through a loss of competitiveness of U.S. industries relative to their foreign rivals combined with periodic bouts of dollar overvaluation (Blecker, 1996, 2009). By the first decade of the twenty-first century, so

---

[1] Scott (2008) estimated that 5.6 million jobs were lost or displaced by the non-oil trade deficit as of 2007, prior to the 2008–9 crisis. Mishel et al. (2009, pp. 186–200) analyze how trade pressures (not only the deficit, but also low-wage competition and globalization generally) contributed to rising inequality and stagnant incomes for most U.S. families.

[2] Chinn (2010, p. 2) identifies five different explanations for the rise of the global trade imbalances and the U.S. deficit: "(1) trends in saving and investment balances [including the fiscal balance], (2) the intertemporal approach, (3) mercantilist behavior [by the surplus countries], (4) the global saving glut, and (5) distortions in financial markets." Chinn effectively admits that (2) has no empirical support. The four other explanations are all discussed in this chapter.

many industries had moved offshore or outsourced their inputs that, even when the dollar has depreciated, many goods (both final and intermediate) have continued to be imported and prior levels of domestic production have not been restored.[3] This is an example of what economists call "hysteresis," or long-lasting effects of a temporary cause (Baldwin, 1988).

At the same time, a complex set of financial linkages developed that sustained and further widened the trade deficit. A trade deficit must always be financed by a net sale of assets to (or net borrowing from) other countries, and other countries were eager to lend to the United States because of their own excess of saving and suppression of domestic consumption, as well as their desire to sustain domestic employment. By lending the United States the funds required to pay for its excess of imports over exports, the surplus countries effectively transferred manufacturing employment from the United States to themselves. By the same token, U.S. borrowing from abroad allowed U.S. households and businesses in the aggregate to finance expenditures beyond what national income and domestic saving would otherwise have permitted.

However, the low personal saving rate in the U.S. economy in the run-up to the Great Recession should be seen at least partly as an effect, rather than a cause, of the large trade deficit. The disappearance of good-paying industrial jobs in industries battered by imports (and the suppression of wages for those workers who kept their jobs) contributed to the stagnation of middle-class incomes, which meant that families increasingly relied on debt rather than income growth to sustain their consumption standards prior to the crisis (see Chapter 2 by Palley and Chapter 7 by Setterfield in this volume). Thus, the rise in the trade deficit and the fall in the saving rate mutually reinforced each other, and the latter was not an independent cause of the former.

In some periods (for example, 1997–2002), large financial inflows into the United States helped to boost the value of the dollar, thereby disadvantaging U.S. producers. However, even when the dollar fell (for example, from 2002 to early 2008), so many U.S. industries had moved offshore that it was difficult to replace many imported goods with domestic ones (although U.S. exports did increase significantly). Meanwhile, the private lending that had sustained the trade deficit was replaced by official lending (foreign central banks buying dollar assets) that had the same effect. The

---

[3] This phenomenon can be understood economically by noting that there are fixed costs of outsourcing. So, once temporary conditions justify incurring the fixed costs, it's much more likely that corporations continue to outsource in the future even if the temporary conditions reverse; this only requires that the average variable costs abroad are less than those at home.

official intervention was largely concentrated in China and certain other East Asian countries, with the result that their currencies did not appreciate as much as the major currencies (especially the euro, British pound, and Canadian dollar) did after 2002. This growing discrepancy in the value of the dollar *vis-à-vis* different currencies became another obstacle to trade deficit adjustment, since the lower value of the dollar relative to the major currencies gave a misleading impression of how much it had depreciated relative to the currencies of the developing countries that supply a majority of U.S. imports. We will return to the role of exchange rates and international financial flows, but first we present a global perspective on the U.S. trade deficit followed by an account of its recent behavior.

2. A Global Perspective on Trade Imbalances

The term "global imbalances" is really a misnomer, because only a handful of nations account for the lion's share of the world's current account surpluses and the United States is the only country with a truly large deficit. Figure 8.1 shows all the nations that had current account imbalances in excess of (positive or negative) $25 billion at the peak of the last global expansion in 2007. These data clearly reveal the skewed nature of the world's trade imbalances. No other nation came close to the U.S. deficit of $718 billion in that year. The three countries with the largest surpluses (all more than $200 billion) were China, Germany, and Japan. After them, the countries with the next two biggest surpluses were major exporters of natural resources, Saudi Arabia and Russia. Many of the world's largest economies, such as those of Brazil, Canada, and India, did not have imbalances that reached the $25 billion threshold for inclusion in Figure 8.1.

Several conclusions emerge immediately from the data in Figure 8.1. First, there really isn't a *global* problem of current account imbalances – rather, there is a very large U.S. deficit that is primarily matched by surpluses in just three countries. Second, one cannot generalize about current account surpluses or deficits for broad groups of countries such as the industrialized, developing, and emerging market nations.[4] Third, two

---

[4] Kregel (2008) contends that global trade surpluses are largely attributable to "catching-up by late industrializing developing countries." This characterization does apply to China and some other East Asian nations (e.g., Taiwan), but not to many other late industrializers (such as India and Brazil) who do not rely on large trade surpluses. In fact, only a few developing or emerging market nations have large trade surpluses, and many of these are major resource exporters rather than late industrializers. Japan and Germany have the second and third largest trade surpluses, but cannot be considered late industrializers today (even if they were in the past).

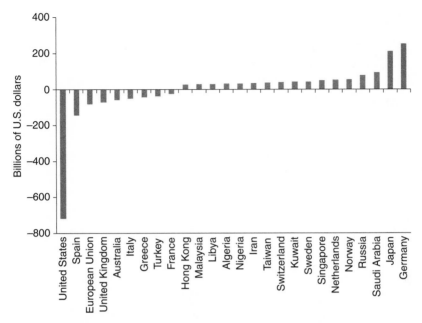

Figure 8.1. Countries with current account imbalances in excess of $25 billion, 2007. *Source:* International Monetary Fund (IMF, 2010).

regional neighbors that have large bilateral trade surpluses with the United States – Canada and Mexico – do not have large multilateral imbalances (and do not appear in Figure 8.1) because their surpluses with the United States are offset by deficits with the rest of the world. Fourth, although some individual countries in the European Union (EU) have had relatively large surpluses or deficits, these have mostly offset each other and the EU as a whole has generally had a moderate current-account deficit in recent years (except for a big spike in its deficit in 2008). Overall, the so-called global imbalances are primarily a United States-East Asian phenomenon, with secondary imbalances of smaller magnitudes both within the EU and (with some exceptions) between resource-importing and resource-exporting nations generally.

3. Trends and Cycles in the U.S. Trade Deficit

Returning to the U.S. trade deficit, Figure 8.2 shows two alternative measures: the current account balance and net exports of goods and services, both measured as percentages of gross domestic product (GDP) on

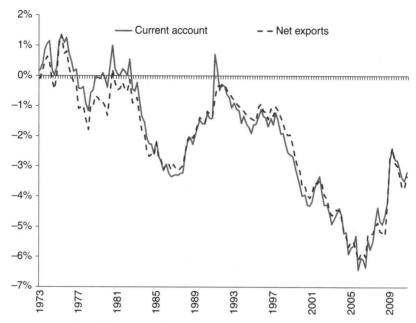

Figure 8.2. U.S. current account balance and net exports of goods and services as percentages of GDP, 1973Q1 to 2010Q4.
Source: U.S. Bureau of Economic Analysis (BEA, 2011a) and author's calculations. Net exports of goods and services and GDP are from table 1.1.5 and the current account balance is measured by "net lending" in table 5.1.

a quarterly basis from 1973 to 2010. These two measures have generally been fairly close in magnitude, so for the rest of this chapter we will use the terms "current account" and "trade balance" interchangeably except where the distinction is important.[5] By either measure, the trade deficit increased steadily during the fifteen-year period between 1992 and 2007, with only a brief pause during the recession of 2001. The trade deficit worsened notably in 2003–6, when consumer spending boomed as a result of the housing price bubble and household debt accumulation. The current account deficit peaked at $803 billion, or about 6 percent of GDP, in 2006.[6] The collapse of

[5] The current account includes net international investment income and net transfer payments in addition to net exports of goods and services. For the United States, net investment income is normally positive and net transfers are normally negative, and these two have largely offset each other except for a few periods in the late 1970s and early 1990s.

[6] In this paragraph, dollar values for the U.S. current account are from U.S. Bureau of Economic Analysis (BEA, 2011b), table 1, but the current account as a percentage of GDP

domestic consumer and investment demand during the 2008–9 recession reduced the current account deficit substantially, cutting it to $378 billion or 2.7 percent of GDP in 2009. However, even the tepid recovery of late 2009 and 2010 led to a strong rebound in the trade deficit, which rose to $496 billion for net exports of goods and services ($470 billion measured by the current account balance) in 2010 (U.S. Bureau of Economic Analysis [BEA], 2011b) in spite of sluggish GDP growth and unemployment that averaged 9.6 percent in that year.

The changes in the trade deficit diminished the magnitude of the changes in output and employment during the recession and recovery (both on the downside and in the upswing) while transmitting these shocks to other countries. For example, between 2008Q2 and 2009Q2, real GDP fell by 4.1 percent but real imports of goods fell by 21.1 percent, whereas between 2009Q3 and 2010Q3, GDP increased by 3.2 percent but goods imports rose by 18.3 percent (U.S. BEA, 2010, table 8). The much greater swings in imports were caused partly by the contraction of trade financing during the financial panic in late 2008 and early 2009,[7] but also by the strong dependency of the U.S. economy on imports of final goods and outsourced inputs alike in the most cyclically sensitive sectors, particularly manufacturing.

As a result of these large fluctuations in imports, some of the job losses during the recession were transmitted to other countries that export to the United States, but by the same logic, a large portion of rising domestic demand during the recovery was siphoned off to purchase imports and did not contribute to output or job growth in the U.S. economy.[8] Although it may be hard to believe, the recession of 2008–9 would have been even worse in the United States in the absence of the fall in the trade deficit, but the impact was correspondingly more severe in U.S. trading partners. By the same token, the rising trade deficit was a major reason why the recovery in U.S. output and employment was so sluggish in 2009–10.

Taking a longer historical view, it is clear that – in spite of these large cyclical swings – the U.S. trade balance has trended downward (i.e., the deficit has increased) as a percentage of GDP during the entire period since the abandonment of the Bretton Woods system of fixed exchange rates and capital controls in 1973. Contrary to what was predicted by early advocates

is calculated from data in U.S. BEA (2011a), where the current account is measured by "net lending or borrowing" from table 5.1 and GDP is from table 1.1.5.

[7] I am indebted to Rudi von Arnim for suggesting this point.

[8] For example, in 2010Q2, the GDP growth rate would have been 5.2% instead of 1.7%, if not for the decrease in net exports during that quarter; similarly, in 2010Q3, the growth rate would have been 4.3% instead of 2.6%. Data are from U.S. BEA (2010), table 2.

of flexible exchange rates and financial market deregulation (e.g., Friedman, 1953), floating rates and financial liberalization have led to greater, not smaller, global trade imbalances (see Eatwell and Taylor, 2000; Kregel, 2008). The next sections focus on the reasons for this long-term worsening trend.

4. The Role of the Dollar's Exchange Rate

During the first two decades after the dollar began to float in value in 1973, there was a positive correlation between the value of the dollar and the trade deficit. Figure 8.3 shows this by plotting the real trade *deficit* (i.e., net exports of goods and services with the sign reversed, so that a positive number indicates a deficit, measured as a percentage of real GDP, with both net exports and GDP expressed in chained 2005 prices) versus the Federal Reserve's broad index of the real (inflation-adjusted) value of the dollar.[9] Although the correlation is far from perfect, it is clear that, until the late 1990s, increases in the dollar's value normally led to increases in the trade deficit (and decreases in the former usually led to decreases in the latter), with time lags that averaged about one to two years. The lags are explained by the time it takes to order, produce, and ship goods in response to changes in international prices.[10] The period from 2002 to 2007 was unusual, however, because the trade deficit did not begin to decline until five years after the dollar began to fall.

An important reason for the disappointing trade benefits from the falling value of the dollar in this period was the uneven degree to which the dollar fell relative to different currencies at that time. The Federal Reserve's broad index of the real value of the dollar (the solid line in Figure 8.3) shows a decline of 25.4 percent between its peak in February 2002 and its trough in April 2008. However, this decline masks important differences between the dollar's performance in relation to different groups of currencies. During the same period, the dollar fell 32.4 percent relative to the "major" currencies (the euro, Canadian dollar, Japanese yen, British pound, Swiss franc,

---

[9] Technically speaking, "chained" measures of real imports and exports are not additive, so the real net imports shown here should be regarded as an approximation to the true "real" trade deficit. Because real imports are measured at chained 2005 prices, they are not affected by oil prices as nominal imports would be, so the data in Figure 8.3 do not reflect the impact of fluctuations in oil prices on the nominal trade deficit. On the exchange rate side, the Fed's "broad" index measures the dollars' value relative to twenty-six other currencies from countries that collectively account for more than 90% of U.S. trade (Loretan, 2005).

[10] This is the famous "J-curve" pattern, named for the tendency of the trade balance to worsen in the first year or two after a currency devaluation and then to improve subsequently.

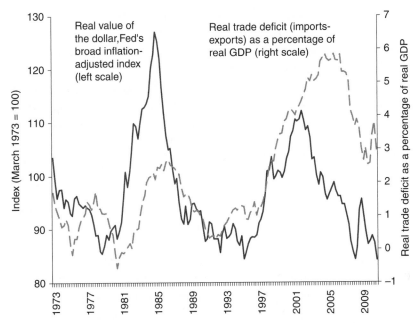

Figure 8.3. The real value of the dollar and the real trade deficit, quarterly, 1973Q1 to 2010Q4.
Source: U.S. BEA (2011a), tables 1.1.5 and 5.1; U.S. Federal Reserve Board (2011b); and author's calculations. The real trade deficit is measured by net imports of goods and services at chained 2005 prices.

Australian dollar, and Swedish krona), but only 15.6 percent relative to the currencies of what the Fed calls "other important trading partners" – the developing countries and transition economies, many of which have fixed or managed exchange rates (data from U.S. Federal Reserve, 2011b). Yet, the "other" countries (which include major exporters such as China and Mexico) account for more than half of total U.S. imports and two-thirds of the trade deficit.[11] It is very difficult for an exchange rate adjustment to eliminate a large trade deficit when most of the imports are coming from precisely those countries whose currencies are not adjusting as much.

[11] The "other important trading partners" index includes the nineteen currencies from the broad index that are not included in the major currencies index (Loretan, 2005). As of 2008, developing and emerging market countries all together (including ones not included in the exchange rate index shown here) accounted for 57.3% of U.S. goods imports and 69.5% of the goods trade deficit (calculated from data in U.S. BEA, 2011b, table 2a). See also Krugman (2008) on the changing country composition of U.S. imports and its impact on U.S. wages.

Nevertheless, the drop in the dollar *vis-à-vis* the currencies of the major industrialized countries from 2002 to early 2008 did some good at the time. Because U.S. exports of manufactures compete in global markets mainly with the products of other industrialized nations, the lower dollar relative to the euro, pound, and Canadian dollar (and, to a lesser extent, the Japanese yen) helped to stimulate U.S. exports from 2003 to 2008. Especially in 2007 and early 2008, as the housing sector collapsed and the economy was falling into a recession, exports were one of the few bright spots. This strong export growth was reversed in 2009, however, as the global recession sharply cut demand for U.S. exports.

At the end of 2008, the dollar temporarily strengthened as a perverse result of the financial crisis. Even though the crisis broke out in U.S. financial markets for securitized mortgages and derivative instruments, the global loss of confidence led to a "flight to safety" in what was still perceived as the world's safest asset, U.S. treasury bills, thus increasing the demand for dollars. A similar phenomenon occurred in mid-2010, when panic over the Greek financial crisis led currency speculators to temporarily dump euros and seek "safe haven" in the dollar and other strong currencies. In spite of these upward blips in the dollar, its overall trend remains downward, and by April 2011 (the last month for which data were available at the time of this writing) the Fed's broad index of the dollar's real value reached its lowest level since the index began in January 1973 (U.S. Federal Reserve, 2011b). Nevertheless, the future course of the dollar remains uncertain, as it continues to be driven more by global financial market conditions rather than the requisites of balancing U.S. trade. As three prominent economists have observed, "So long as the dollar exchange rate continues to be driven more by capital flows than by the correlates of the current account, and so long as the U.S. treasury market continues to be seen as a safe haven, it is hard to see how [...] the halving of the U.S. current account deficit [via dollar depreciation] can be sustained" (Chinn et al., 2010, p. 4).

5. The Trade and Budget Deficits Are Not Twins

Because dollar depreciation has not sufficed to eliminate the trade deficit, some economists and policy analysts have sought to revive the twin deficits hypothesis that was popular in the 1980s.[12] This hypothesis blames

---

[12] See Feldstein (1992) and Blecker (1996) for retrospectives, and Chinn (2005) and Chinn and Frieden (2009) for more recent restatements.

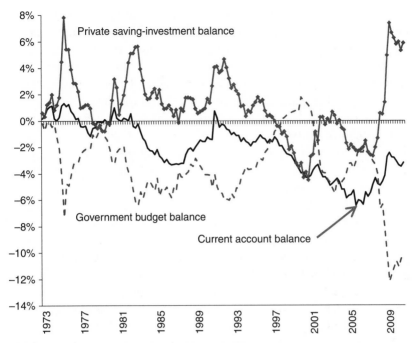

Figure 8.4. U.S. current account, government budget, and private saving-investment balances as percentages of GDP, 1973Q1 to 2010Q4.
Source: U.S. BEA (2011a) and author's calculations. GDP is from table 1.1.5, the current account balance is measured by "net lending" from table 5.1, and the government budget balance (federal, state, and local combined) is measured by "government net lending" in table 3.1.

the trade deficit primarily on the government budget deficit, and claims that the most important way of reducing the former is by lowering the latter. The main motivation behind the twin deficits argument is to absolve international trade policies and industrial competitiveness factors from any responsibility for the burgeoning U.S. external deficit, so as to weaken the case for "protectionist" responses. The fault, it is claimed, lies strictly in ourselves, in that we (the U.S. public) have been unwilling to make the "hard choices" (tax increases or spending cuts) required to reduce the budget deficit.

The raw data do not reveal much support for the twin deficit hypothesis. Figure 8.4 shows the two deficits, both measured as percentages of GDP, using quarterly data from 1973Q1 to 2010Q4. During most of the period shown, the two deficits generally moved in *opposite* directions, exactly the reverse of what the twin deficit hypothesis implies. For example, when the fiscal balance increased from a deficit of −6 percent of GDP in 1992 to a surplus of +2 percent in 2000, the current account balance did not improve, but rather worsened from about −1 percent of GDP to −4 percent during the same period. This pattern largely reflects the natural operation of the business cycle: the strong economic expansion of the late 1990s increased government tax revenue, thereby reducing the budget deficit, while it also increasing import demand, thus worsening the trade deficit. The fiscal improvement of the 1990s was aided by President Bill Clinton's tax increases of 1993 and budgetary rules that limited spending growth, but these fiscal belt-tightening measures failed to prevent the current account from worsening instead of improving.

An even more dramatic divergence between the two deficits opened up in 2008–9, when the budget deficit grew dramatically during the Great Recession to about −12 percent of GDP, but the current account deficit (as noted earlier) diminished to only about −3 percent of GDP. This opposite behavior of the two deficits was largely caused by the recession, which reduced tax revenue and prompted stimulus spending (thus increasing the government deficit) but also reduced import demand (thus moderating the current account deficit).

There were two exceptional periods when large tax cuts and increased military spending under presidents Ronald Reagan and George W. Bush helped to spark higher trade deficits in 1981–3 and 2001–3, respectively. In the more recent of these periods, the budget reversed gears and plummeted from the +2 percent of GDP surplus recorded in 2000 to a −5 percent of GDP deficit in 2003, and during this brief period the two deficits did move in the same direction. However, this temporary coincidence hardly proves the twin deficit view. After all, the trade deficit was merely continuing its long-term downward trend, and if anything, its rate of deterioration *slowed down* during 2001–3 whereas the budget balance was dropping rapidly.

Statistical studies of the relationship between the fiscal (budget) and trade (current account) balances have yielded mixed results. Empirical estimates in Blecker (2009) show no significant effects of changes in the budget balance on the U.S. trade balance, after controlling for the dollar's exchange rate and the private saving-investment balance (discussed in the next section).[13] Other studies using a variety of different methodologies have found small-to-medium-sized positive effects of the budget balance on the trade balance

---

[13] Blecker (2009) uses a vector error correction model, which controls for nonstationary but cointegrated time-series data and tries to identify the effects of "shocks" to (or "innovations" in) each variable on all the variables in the system.

(see, for example, Erceg et al., 2005; Chinn and Ito, 2007, 2008; Chinn et al., 2010). In these studies, for every one percentage point increase in the fiscal balance (usually measured as a percentage of GDP), the current account balance rises anywhere from 0.1 to 0.4 percentage points (essentially, ten to forty cents of trade improvement for every dollar of fiscal improvement). However, some of these studies include the United States in a panel data set along with many other countries, and one must be very cautious in applying results from international panel data to the United States, especially when some of those studies acknowledge that their models don't fit the U.S. data very well.[14] Generally speaking, the larger estimates of this effect come from models that control for many other determinants of the trade balance besides the fiscal balance[15] and models that use the cyclically adjusted budget balance instead of the actual balance.

Overall, these econometric estimates suggest that the relationship between the budget and trade deficits is at most partial, and if anything, is probably weaker in the United States than in many other countries. The fact that the highest coefficients are obtained in models that control for numerous other variables and that use the cyclically adjusted budget balances suggests the importance of many other causes of changes in the current account besides fiscal policy, even when the effects of the latter are found to be statistically significant. These studies also explain why a positive correlation between the two deficits is observed in the actual U.S. data only at times of relatively large fiscal policy shifts, such as when big tax cuts were enacted in 1981–3 and 2001–3.

6. Saving, Investment, and the Current Account

Although the fiscal deficit has not been strongly correlated with the trade deficit, what might be called the "private sector deficit" – the gap between

[14] The United States is an outlier in the regression models of Chinn and Ito (2007, 2008), as its current account balance is generally below a 95% confidence interval around the model's fitted values for the periods 1996–2000 and 2001–4; also their models under-predict the U.S. current account deficit in out-of-sample forecasts. Chinn et al. (2010) find that a dummy for the United States in the 2001–5 subperiod is significantly negative, suggesting that their model does not fully explain the decline in the U.S. current account balance at that time.

[15] For example, Chinn et al. (2010) include the following variables in their baseline specification: initial net foreign assets, relative income (level and squared), dependency ratio (young and old), an index of financial development, terms of trade volatility, average GDP growth, trade openness, an oil exporting dummy, and time fixed effects. Their extended model includes additional indicators of financial institutions and financial openness and interactive terms.

private investment and saving – has been more strongly correlated with the trade imbalance (see Godley, 1999; Godley, et al., 2008; Barbosa-Filho, et al., 2008; among others). To see this, consider the relationship between the two deficits and the gap between domestic (private) saving and investment that emerges from the national income accounts. This relationship, sometimes referred to as the "national income identity," can be written as follows:

Current account balance = (Saving – Investment) + Government budget
balance

This accounting identity is very important: it implies that changes in any one of the three balances (fiscal, trade, and private saving-investment) must be accompanied by offsetting changes in the other two combined.

There are two problems with the way in which this identity is often employed. First, *an accounting identity is not a causal relationship*: there is no implication that causality has to flow in any particular direction between the variables linked by it. Rather than the fiscal balance always driving the trade balance, any other direction of causality among the three balances is also possible, and it is also possible (indeed, likely) that common underlying factors (such as the business cycle) may account for coincident movements in all of these variables that together maintain the identity. Second, the identity includes the private saving-investment balance as well as the current account and government budget balances, so there is no automatic link between the latter two.

Although the fiscal balance seems to have played little role in the widening of the trade imbalance in the late 1990s and the 2003–7 period, there is more evidence that changes in the private saving-investment balance played a significant role in these episodes, at least in an accounting sense. As Figure 8.4 shows, the saving-investment balance was normally positive in the U.S. economy until the late 1990s. This meant that private, domestic saving was generally more than sufficient to finance private, domestic investment – and the private sector usually had excess funds to lend out, either to the government (if it had a budget deficit) or to foreign countries (when the United States had a current account surplus). The saving-investment balance behaved countercyclically; that is, it rose in recessions and fell in recoveries because investment is more cyclically sensitive than saving.

However, the private saving-investment balance exhibited an unprecedented drop into negative territory during the 1996–2000 period, and, after rising in the recession of 2000–1, fell back to negative levels in the subsequent recovery (especially 2004–7). During the times when the saving-investment gap was negative, the U.S. private sector was unable to finance domestic investment spending. The negative saving-investment gap had to be filled by some combination of either an increased budget surplus (which means more government net lending to the private sector) or a reduced current account balance (which implies increased borrowing from abroad). At least in an accounting sense, then, the fall in private saving relative to investment "explains" how the trade deficit could continue to worsen in the late 1990s in spite of the big improvement in the fiscal balance. Also, the budget deficit was decreasing in the years 2003–7 while the trade deficit was widening rapidly; it was again the fall in the saving-investment balance that was correlated with the worsening of the current account at that time.

During the crisis of 2008–9, the saving-investment balance recovered to the highest levels since the recession of 1975 (about +7 percent of GDP) as households were striving to restore their balance sheets and both consumption and investment spending plummeted (see Figure 8.4). This sharp rise in the saving-investment balance was virtually the mirror image of the sharp decline in the fiscal balance in those same years, and the swings in these two balances utterly swamped the relatively small increase in the current account balance. Taking the previous cycle peak year of 2007 as a base, the saving-investment balance rose by about 8 percentage points of GDP over the next two years, while the government budget balance fell by about 10 percentage points of GDP; in contrast, the current account improved by only about 2 percentage points of GDP.

Prior to the crisis, what is most striking is that the current account trended downward steadily for more than a decade (from 1993–2007) in spite of large fluctuations in the other two balances that largely offset each other (see Figure 8.4). This suggests that changes in the other two balances were mostly impacting each other, not the current account balance – an inference that is supported by the estimates from Blecker's (2009) empirical model. Furthermore, the steadiness of the downward trend in the current account balance (for about fifteen years prior to the crisis) suggests that this trend was likely to have been caused by factors that were independent of either the budget balance or private saving-investment balance taken separately, and that the sum of the latter two balances was being pulled along endogenously to match the decline in the current account (even while the division of that sum among the other two balances kept shifting).

Nevertheless, some have argued that the drop in the private saving rate during the 1997–2007 period could be an independent causal factor in explaining the rise in the current account deficit (see Chinn, 2010). Although corporate savings held steady during that period, the personal saving rate declined for reasons that are explained elsewhere in this volume (see Chapter 2 by Palley, Chapter 6 by Cynamon and Fazzari, and Chapter 7 by Setterfield). As median wages and household incomes stagnated in spite of rising productivity, households increasingly relied on debt to finance consumption expenditures, and this was aided by the boom in housing prices as well as innovative (and irresponsible) lending practices in deregulated financial markets. Thus, even if government profligacy is not to blame for the trade deficit, perhaps the consumption spending binge of the precrisis decade, which pulled the personal saving rate down to historic lows, is a culprit?

One problem with this argument is the issue of "reverse causality." As a product of the United States exporting manufacturing jobs, which contributed to the suppression of median wages and middle-class incomes at home, the trade deficit was at least partly a *cause* of the low saving rate rather than an effect. Also, what matters in the national income identity is the *difference* between saving and investment, not saving *per se*. Thus, the decline in saving alone cannot explain the rise in the trade deficit; rather, the interesting question is why private investment was able to remain relatively robust in the late 1990s and early 2000s (i.e., before the housing bubble burst in 2007–8) in spite of the decrease in private saving. To understand how this was possible, we need to examine the role of the net financial inflows from abroad that are the proverbial "other side of the coin" of the current account deficit – and which were one of the enabling factors permitting that deficit to reach new heights.

Net Financial Inflows and the "Global Saving Glut"

When the private saving-investment balance turned negative in the late 1990s and again in the early 2000s, the openness of the U.S. economy to international financial flows meant that the extra saving needed to finance domestic investment (which includes housing construction) could be borrowed from other countries. This international borrowing was a necessary enabling factor for the decline in the private saving-investment balance to occur. Without the increase in the current account deficit and the corresponding net inflow of foreign funds, it would have been impossible for the saving-investment balance to fall as far as it did up to 2006–7. To be clear, the argument is *not* that, in the absence of the increasing trade deficit, the fall in the saving rate would have raised interest rates and "crowded out" investment. Rather, the argument is that, in the absence of the trade deficit and the associated financial inflows, the saving rate could never have fallen (or consumption could not have increased) so much to begin with.

What factors drew so much foreign capital into U.S. financial markets beginning in the mid-1990s? One factor was the increases in interest rates instigated by the Federal Reserve in 1994–5, 1999–2000, and 2004–6, when it was launching preemptive strikes against possible higher inflation during periods of economic recovery or boom. Another factor was the "IT" bubble in the U.S. stock market, which attracted inflows of foreign funds in the late 1990s, followed by another stock price bubble that popped up and attracted more inflows in the mid-2000s. Yet another factor was the financial crises of the late 1990s in Asia and other developing regions, which induced risk-averse investors to park their funds in the safe haven of U.S. assets. Also, as we will discuss in more depth in the next section, an increasing portion of the net purchases of U.S. assets after the dollar began to fall in 2002 were "official" purchases by foreign central banks attempting to resist market pressures toward appreciation of their countries' currencies or seeking insurance against possible future financial crises.

One controversial explanation for the rise in net financial inflows is the hypothesis of a "global saving glut." In a series of speeches, Bernanke (2005, 2007) argued that the U.S. current account deficit has to be explained by policies and events in the surplus countries as well as in the United States, and that any explanation that rests solely on U.S. domestic causes will miss the mark. He claimed that the emerging market nations (including, but not limited to, China) developed a significant excess of domestic saving in the late 1990s and early 2000s that was invested in financial markets in the United States rather than in productive domestic investment in those nations. He expressed skepticism of orthodox economic explanations of those increased saving rates, such as a life-cycle view, because demographic factors (e.g., aging of the population) could not account for the timing and location of when and where the excess saving originated. He also rejected the twin deficit view as a leading explanation of the U.S. trade deficit.

Bernanke was right in drawing attention to economic conditions and policies in the surplus countries and in rejecting the misleading focus on the U.S. fiscal deficit. Moreover, his "saving glut" concept makes some sense if interpreted as reflecting "deficient demand" (Bibow, 2008, p. 235) in the global economy. The real issue is why consumption and investment have been systematically depressed in the surplus countries, relative to their national incomes. The core reason why consumption is repressed in most of the surplus countries is the phenomenon of wages lagging behind productivity (von Arnim, 2010; Cripps et al., 2011), a problem also found in the United States as discussed in Chapter 2 by Palley and Chapter 7 by Setterfield. Instead of encouraging households to borrow to finance additional consumption, as the United States did, these countries have instead relied on export markets to fill the resulting demand gap and maintain high employment. Their low wages (relative to productivity) and, in many cases, undervalued currencies (discussed more in the next section) contribute to their export surpluses, while their excess savings are invested in financial assets overseas (especially in the United States) thereby financing the resulting trade imbalances (and keeping the dollar overvalued).

Bernanke argued that the outflow of excess saving from the emerging market nations contributed to the high value of the dollar and to the bubbles in U.S. stock prices and housing prices that occurred at various times in the late 1990s and early 2000s. To the extent that these factors in turn facilitated the rise in U.S. consumer spending, the inflow of excess saving from abroad could be considered a contributing factor in causing the low saving rates of U.S. households during those years, and hence causation between low saving rates and the current account deficit runs both ways. This argument also implies that the rest of the world was relying on U.S. consumer borrowing and asset-price bubbles to sustain global demand, and these were not sustainable as the recent crisis has painfully illustrated.

However, other aspects of the global saving glut argument are more dubious. The exclusive focus on emerging market nations seems misplaced, since as noted earlier not all of these nations have had large surpluses whereas some of the largest surpluses have been found in industrialized countries (Germany and Japan). Also, both Bernanke and others have used the classical "loanable funds" doctrine of interest rate determination to argue that the global saving glut helps to explain low long-term interest rates in the early 2000s.[16] However, it is more credible to believe that short-term interest rates are determined by the monetary policies of central banks, whereas longer-term rates depend on both current short-term rates and expectations of future monetary policies and inflation rates. It is true that financial inflows that went toward purchasing longer-term U.S. bonds helped to keep their yields low during the middle of the decade of the 2000s, while the Fed was raising short-term rates in 2004–6, resulting in an "inverted yield curve" at that time. In addition, low interest rates on long-term debt did facilitate the expansion of U.S. consumption and investment demand during those years, as noted earlier. However, at a global level, if the excess savings of the surplus countries were simply offsetting the reduced savings of the deficit countries, it is hard to see how the total world "supply of

---

[16] See Chinn (2010) for an exposition of this argument and Bibow (2008, 2010) for critiques.

saving" was really higher as a result or how that could explain low interest rates at that time.

Bernanke (2005) suggested that "the attractiveness of the U.S. as an investment destination" and "sophistication of the country's financial markets" contributed to pulling foreign savings into U.S. financial markets; Bernanke (2007) also argued that "an underdeveloped financial sector" within the emerging market nations led to their savings being invested abroad rather than domestically. These claims have given rise to the hypothesis that "capital market imperfections" in the emerging market nations make it difficult to channel saving into investment in those countries, so that rising domestic savings result in current account surpluses rather than increased domestic investment (see Caballero et al., 2008). Empirical tests by Chinn and Ito (2008) fail to find evidence that indicators of financial market development and the strength of financial institutions are inversely related to saving rates in emerging market nations. Chinn et al. (2010) find some evidence that the interaction of capital account openness and financial market development has a negative effect on current account balances across countries, but they do not find that this is a quantitatively significant factor in explaining the U.S. deficit.

7. Policy Interventions and Structural Factors

The cumulative effect of all the borrowing to cover the trade deficits of the last generation has been to transform the United States from the world's largest creditor into the world's largest debtor nation. Although the United States switched from an overall net creditor position to net debtor status in 1986, the net debt really ballooned after 2000 when it passed the $1 trillion threshold and rapidly climbed to $3.3 trillion at the end of 2008 before dipping to $2.5 trillion at the end of 2010 (see Figure 8.5). Although the U.S. status as a net debtor has been much commented on, the degree to which it reflects the impact of foreign governments' official intervention in global currency markets has not received the same attention.[17]

Figure 8.5 shows that foreign *official* assets in the United States – essentially, U.S. currency, U.S. treasury bills, and other U.S. government-issued securities held by foreign central banks – more than account for the total

---

[17] To his credit, Bernanke (2005) recognized that a substantial part of the net financial outflows from emerging market countries were the result of intervention by central banks, rather than the autonomous operation of private capital markets. However, he underestimated how much these interventionist policies were part of mercantilist strategies of undervalued currencies for export promotion.

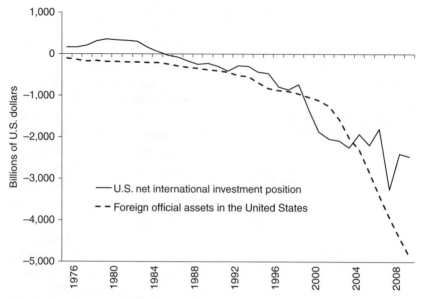

Figure 8.5. U.S. net international investment position and foreign official assets in the United States, year-end 1976 to 2010.
Source: U.S. BEA (2011c).

net international debt in every year since 2005. In fact, by the end of 2010, foreign official assets in the United States of $4.9 trillion were nearly double the overall U.S. net debtor position of $2.5 trillion. In other words, *excluding the enormous holdings of U.S. official assets by foreign central banks, the United States was still a net creditor country* to the tune of about $2.4 trillion in the rest of its international financial position (i.e., all U.S. assets abroad minus all other U.S. debts) as of year-end 2010.

Thus, the growing foreign accumulation of U.S. assets after 2000 was not primarily the result of increased confidence in the U.S. economy or U.S. assets by private-sector agents abroad, as contemplated in the models of "capital market imperfections." On the contrary, it was mainly foreign central bank intervention that financed the growing U.S. current account deficits and allowed the United States to build up this enormous foreign debt. The countries whose central banks have bought large volumes of U.S. government assets as foreign exchange reserves have done so for two main reasons. First, these countries learned the lesson from the emerging market financial crises of 1997–9 in East Asia, Russia, and Brazil that having large volumes of reserves is essential to be able to defend their currencies from speculative attacks. Second, many of these same countries have deliberately sought to prevent their currencies from appreciating as much as they would have if they had been allowed to float more freely.

The leading offender in this respect is China, which (not coincidentally) has the largest surplus globally and also the largest bilateral surplus with the United States. China did allow its currency to appreciate very slowly between 2005 and 2008, and again starting in mid-2010.[18] Notwithstanding this limited appreciation, China increased its foreign exchange reserves *more than seventeen times*, from $166 *billion* at the end of 2000 to $2.8 *trillion* at the end of 2010 (International Monetary Fund, 2011). Assuming (as seems likely) that the vast majority of its reserves are held in U.S. assets, China's reserves probably accounted for roughly half of the $4.9 trillion in total foreign official assets in the United States as of year-end 2010. Cline and Williamson (2009) estimated that the yuan would have to rise another 40 percent relative to the dollar to reduce China's current account surplus from 10 percent of its GDP in 2009 to a more sustainable 4 percent. The persistent undervaluation of the yuan helps explain not only why China is the country with which the United States has the largest bilateral deficit, but also why the U.S. deficit with China is so disproportional. In recent years, U.S. imports from China have averaged more than four *times* U.S. exports to China, a ratio far greater than with any other major trading partner.[19]

In addition to these currency market interventions, changes in global trade patterns and trade policies can have an independent impact on the trade balance. One factor that has played into rising trade deficits is the uneven impact of recent trade agreements, including the North American Free Trade Agreement (NAFTA) of 1994, the Uruguay Round agreement that created the World Trade Organization (WTO) in 1995, and – perhaps most significantly – the extension of "permanent normal trade relations" (formerly known as "most-favored nation" status) to China and China joining the WTO in 2001. Although ostensibly these trade agreements have reciprocally opened markets both in the United States and abroad – and

---

[18] From 1994 until early 2005, China kept the yuan fixed at approximately 8.28 per U.S. dollar. Starting in July 2005, China allowed the yuan to appreciate very gradually until July 2008, when the exchange rate was effectively re-pegged at around 6.83 per dollar. The gradual rise of the yuan resumed in June 2010, but the exchange rate fell to only 6.49 as of April 29, 2011. Data are from U.S. Federal Reserve (2011a).

[19] Author's calculation based on data in U.S. BEA (2011b, table 2a). This ratio declined from almost 6:1 in 2005 to just below 4:1 in 2010. Whether this is the beginning of a long-term trend reduction or merely a result of the greater cyclical slowdown in the U.S. economy remains to be seen.

foreign tariff reductions have often exceeded those of the United States – the actual impact has been a disproportionate opening of the U.S. market to imports from other countries. The main reason for this outcome is that these so-called trade agreements also include "deep integration" provisions protecting the rights of foreign investors and extending trade liberalization into services, and these provisions have largely operated to make other countries more attractive locations for production or outsourcing by U.S. corporations. Combined with the undervaluation of currencies and the suppression of wages and consumer demand in the surplus countries, the foreign market-opening provisions of the trade agreements have thus taken a back seat to their impact in encouraging importing by U.S. companies.

Finally, it is important to note that the hollowing-out of the U.S. industrial structure in the past few decades has had a lasting impact in making it more difficult for the United States to replace imports with domestic products when the dollar depreciates. Blecker (2007) estimated that the rise in the value of the dollar after 1995 had the cumulative effect of reducing the capital stock of the U.S. manufacturing sector by 17 percent by year-end 2004, compared with what it would have been if the dollar had remained at its 1995 level. These estimates also show that annual investment in manufacturing was 61 percent lower in 2004 than it would have been if the dollar had remained at its 1995 value. Not only have significant portions of manufacturing capacity been "offshored," but also the remaining manufacturing industries have become increasingly dependent on imports of intermediate goods (parts and components) that are no longer made at home. As a result, the dollar will have to go much lower and stay down much longer to make it profitable for corporations to revive their production of tradable goods in the United States.

8. Conclusions: What Kind of Global Rebalancing?

This chapter has shown that the U.S. trade deficit has been sustained by a set of self-reinforcing, mutually supportive mechanisms that are difficult to break out of, although they were temporarily suppressed during the severe economic downturn of 2008–9. No single policy lever will quickly or painlessly alter the position of the United States as the main deficit country in the global pattern of trade imbalances. Traditional remedies, such as reducing the budget deficit or depreciating the dollar, will not be sufficient, although the latter is likely to be much more helpful than the former. Moreover, the U.S. trade deficit results not only from U.S. actions and policies, but also from events and policies in other countries – especially the insufficient domestic demand and currency market interventions of the major surplus nations in East Asia and elsewhere. For the United States to be weaned off of its reliance on imports of cheap consumer goods and outsourced intermediate goods and its dependency on external borrowing, the rest of the world needs to be weaned off of its reliance on U.S. markets for export demand and U.S. assets as repositories for wealth accumulation.

This brings us to the frequently discussed idea of the need for "global rebalancing." As conventionally proposed, rebalancing involves increasing private savings and reducing budget deficits in the United States and other deficit countries, while increasing consumption and investment spending or engaging in fiscal expansion in the surplus countries. Often, rebalancing is thought to require a realignment of exchange rates in which the dollar falls further or stays low, and the currencies of the surplus countries appreciate.

One problem with this view is that all the major surplus countries have significant structural or ideological impediments to the kinds of adjustments that would be required of them (see Kregel, 2008; Chinn et al., 2010). For example, Japan has had slow growth for two decades in spite of chronically low interest rates and repeated fiscal stimuli that have led to a large government debt; no one has yet solved the puzzle of how to boost domestic consumption and investment in Japan and replace its reliance on export demand. Germany has a deeply rooted aversion to fiscal deficits, and the European Central Bank is mandated by the Maastricht Agreement to uphold the German view that monetary policy should focus strictly on price stability and not on output or employment targets. Even if Germany were to find a way to stimulate its economy, this would mainly benefit the deficit countries in Europe (United Kingdom, Ireland, Portugal, Spain, Italy, Greece, and various eastern European nations) rather than the United States.

China presents an interesting paradox. On the one hand, China currently depends on its undervalued currency and export surplus to maintain industrial employment and social peace. It has also systematically repressed household income and consumption in order to effectively subsidize manufacturing production, employment, and exports (Pettis, 2009). Chinese leaders seem aware that they need to bolster the internal market and not rely so much on export markets in the long term, but they seem fearful of taking dramatic steps in this direction in the short term (and they don't respond well to outside pressure). On the other hand, Chinese workers are becoming more restive and in recent years have won significant wage increases, which so far the government has not stepped in to prevent. Rising wages in China will have the same effect on its external competitiveness as a

currency revaluation, with the added benefit of boosting Chinese workers'
consumption. China also adopted the largest fiscal stimulus in the world,
estimated at 12.3 percent of its GDP, during the 2008–9 crisis (Kohli, 2010).
Although China did this for its own self-interest, its fiscal stimulus helped
to prevent a worse collapse in East Asia and made a much greater contribution to promoting global recovery than that of any other nation (including the United States, where Obama's modest stimulus at the federal level
was largely offset by budget cutbacks at the state and local levels). Thus,
although China may not want to be pressured into agreeing to revalue its
currency more today, it may be effectively more willing to contribute to
rebalancing efforts over the long haul than some other surplus countries,
provided that it sees its own self-interest in doing so.

On the U.S. side, it should be clear from the analysis in this chapter that
a reduction in the fiscal deficit would do little if anything to lower the trade
deficit. A strategy of budget deficit reduction would be especially inappropriate at a time when the economy still has high unemployment and
underutilized resources, and in which private demand is likely to remain
depressed because of collapsed housing prices and high debt burdens (see
von Arnim, 2010). In the long run, the federal budget deficit will not decline
significantly unless and until the economy recovers and tax revenue eventually picks up, so it makes more sense to focus on stimulating the economy
than to target deficit reduction via tax increases or spending cuts (see also
Chapter 10 by Baker and Chapter 11 by Cynamon and Fazzari, in this volume, on fiscal policy). As for inducing U.S. households to save more and
spend less, this has occurred spontaneously through the collapse of asset
values and the tightening of credit availability since the financial crisis, but
the result has been to depress aggregate demand and slow the recovery.
What does make sense, as emphasized in Chapters 2 and 7 by Palley and
Setterfield, respectively, is to restore high employment and recreate a policy
environment in which wages can grow more in step with productivity so
that household incomes can keep up with the growth of consumption and
consumers can finance their expenditures out of income rather than debt.

With regard to exchange rate realignment, it should be recalled that the
dollar's fall thus far has occurred disproportionally in relation to the major
currencies of the other industrialized nations, so its future depreciation
needs to occur more in relation to the other currencies of the emerging market and developing nations (not only China, but also all the other countries
that would gain competitive advantages if China revalues and they don't).
In other words, a currency realignment will be more effective (and possibly
more acceptable to China) if is multilateral and not just a bilateral Chinese

appreciation with the dollar. A lower dollar combined with the high prices of energy and transportation costs (both of which have rebounded since collapsing in 2009) can bring some industries back to the United States, especially producers of heavy goods such as steel and furniture. This was already starting to happen before the trend was interrupted by the financial crisis and recession (see Rubin and Tal, 2008; Mui, 2008), and the trend may resume now that the dollar is back down and transportation costs are back up – provided that the global recovery picks up steam.

Although a sustained lower dollar would eventually help to restore more balanced trade, we cannot count on global financial markets in a world of floating exchange rates to keep the dollar at an appropriately low level for rebalancing trade. The dollar is valued chiefly because of its still-preeminent role in global financial markets and as a central bank reserve asset. The dollar's exchange rate is determined mainly by the relative demand for dollar-denominated assets versus assets denominated in other currencies, not by the requisites of balancing U.S. trade. In the long term, replacing the dollar with a global currency or currency basket as the world's main reserve asset could possibly help to eliminate the dollar's recurrent episodes of overvaluation caused by financial market factors, but the political prospects for such a new global monetary system seem dim at present. More immediately, an international agreement to manage the exchange rates of the major currencies within target zones – similar to the Plaza Accord of the late 1980s – could help to moderate global trade imbalances. President Barack Obama tried to get the international community to agree on quantitative limits on current account imbalances and currency market intervention at the G20 summit in Seoul, South Korea, in November 2010, but ran into strong resistance from the surplus countries and left with only a vague commitment to continue negotiations on the subject.

In the end, the United States is stuck in somewhat of the same situation in which it found itself in the late 1960s and early 1970s under the old Bretton Woods system of adjustable pegs, as a result of being the "n^{th} country" in a world of n currencies but only $n-1$ exchange rates. Once again, this country lacks enough policy levers to reduce its own trade deficit at an acceptable domestic cost (i.e., without a permanently depressed economy), whereas the surplus countries lack incentives to cooperate. As a result, U.S. policy makers may need to think "outside the box" about unconventional remedies.

If international cooperative efforts fail, the United States should consider adopting an across-the-board tariff surcharge, as allowed for balance-of-payments purposes under Article XII of the General Agreement on Tariffs and Trade (which has been incorporated into the WTO – see Stewart and

Drake, 2009). If the tariff was across-the-board and not just targeted on China, it would not be discriminatory – and the fact that the tariff hit other countries (for example, EU members) would only encourage them to join efforts to pressure the currency manipulators to cease and desist.[20] Alternatively, there have been proposals for an import certificate program, in which the right to import goods would be auctioned or sold to companies who purchase certificates from either exporters (Buffett, 2003) or the government (Papadimitriou et al., 2008), with the quantity of certificates limited so as to achieve a target level for the trade balance. My view is that import certificate schemes would be unduly complex to administer, and a tariff is both technically simpler and (at least marginally) more politically feasible (see Blecker, 2009).

The United States would be required by the WTO to consult with other countries if it put any type of import restriction into effect, and such consultations could lead to negotiations over adjustments that could make actual implementation of the restriction unnecessary. Such a positive outcome would be more likely if the implementation of the import restriction was made contingent on the trade imbalances of the major countries being below some threshold (for example, ±2 percent of GDP at full employment). This would hopefully motivate the surplus countries to find other ways to reduce their trade surpluses with the United States, such as by letting their currencies appreciate or opening their markets more to U.S. exports.

In the absence of such efforts, it is possible that the United States will continue to muddle through with a large trade deficit, a depressed industrial sector, and a growing external debt for a long time, with at best a very slow and gradual reduction of the trade deficit if the dollar falls further and remains low. Although one does not want to "cry wolf," the recent collapse of the U.S. housing bubble and the ensuing financial crisis remind us that unsustainable situations sometimes end very abruptly and unexpectedly, with often dire consequences when they do. Having seen what a "hard landing" looks like in the housing market and on Wall Street, one would hope that both the United States and other countries would want to avoid finding out what one would look like in international currency markets and global trade relations.

---

[20] The United States might be legally obligated to exempt partner countries in free trade agreements, especially NAFTA members Mexico and Canada, from such a tariff. This would not necessarily be a bad thing, however, because regional trade in North America supports U.S. industries and employment much more than importing from other regions like East Asia that buy relatively less U.S. products (see Blecker, 2005; Blecker and Esquivel, 2010).

References

Baldwin, R. E. (1988) "Hysteresis in import prices: The beachhead effect." *American Economic Review*. Vol. **78**, no. 4, pp. 773–85.

Barbosa-Filho, N. H., C. Rada, L. Taylor, and L. Zamparelli. (2008) "Cycles and trends in U.S. net borrowing flows," *Journal of Post Keynesian Economics*. Vol. **30**, no. 4 (July), pp. 623–48.

Bernanke, B. S. (2005) "The global saving glut and the U.S. current account deficit." Sandridge Lecture, Virginia Association of Economists, Richmond, VA, March 10. www.federalreserve.gov/boarddocs/speeches/2005/200503102/.

(2007) "Global imbalances: Recent developments and prospects." Bundesbank Lecture, Berlin, Germany, September 11. www.federalreserve.gov/newsevents/speech/bernanke20070911a.htm.

Bibow, J. (2008) "The international monetary (non-) order and the 'global capital flows paradox.'" In E. Hein, T. Niechoj, P. Spahn, and A. Truger, eds. *Finance-led Capitalism? Macroeconomic Effects of Changes in the Financial Sector*. Marburg: Metropolis-Verlag, pp. 219–48.

(2010) *Bretton Woods 2 is dead, long live Bretton Woods 3?* Annandale-on-Hudson, NY: Levy Economics Institute, Working Paper No. 597 (May).

Blecker, R. A. (1996) "The trade deficit and U.S. competitiveness." In Robert A. Blecker, ed. *U.S. Trade Policy and Global Growth: New Directions in the International Economy* Economic Policy Institute Series. Armonk, NY: M. E. Sharpe, pp. 179–214.

(2005) "The North American economies after NAFTA: A critical appraisal." *International Journal of Political Economy*. Vol. 33, no. 3 (Fall 2003 issue, published 2005), pp. 5–27.

(2007) "The economic consequences of dollar appreciation for U.S. manufacturing profits and investment: A time-series analysis." *International Review of Applied Economics*. Vol. **21**, No. 4, pp. 491–517.

(2009) "The trade deficit trap: How it got so big, why it persists, and what to do about it." Working Paper No. 284. Washington, DC: Economic Policy Institute, July.

Blecker, R. A. and G. Esquivel. (2010) "NAFTA, trade, and development." *CESifo Forum*, 4/2010, pp. 17–30.

Buffett, W. (2003) "America's growing trade deficit is selling the nation out from under us. Here's a way to fix the problem – and we need to do it now." *Fortune*, November 10.

Caballero, R. J., Emmanuel Farhi, and Pierre-Olivier Gourinchas. (2008) "An equilibrium model of 'global imbalances' and low interest rates." *American Economic Review*. Vol. **98**, no. 1, pp. 358–93.

Chinn, M. D. (2005) *Getting serious about the twin deficits*. CSR No. 10. New York: Council on Foreign Relations.

(2010) "Evidence on financial globalization and crises: Global imbalances," forthcoming in *Encyclopedia of Financial Globalization*, draft of June 7.

Chinn, M. D., B. Eichengreen, and H. Ito. (2010) "Rebalancing global growth," paper prepared for the World Bank's Re-Growing Growth Project, August 16.

Chinn, M. and H. Ito. (2007) "Current account balances, financial development and institutions: Assaying the world 'savings glut,'" *Journal of International Money and Finance*. Vol. **26**, no. 4 (June): 546–69.

(2008) "Global current account imbalances: American fiscal policy versus East Asian savings," *Review of International Economics*. Vol. **16**, no. 3: 479–98.

Chinn, M. and J. Frieden. (2009) "Reflections on the causes and consequences of the debt crisis of 2008," *La Follette Policy Report*, University of Wisconsin–Madison. Vol. **19**, no. 1 (Fall), pp. 1–5.

Cline, W. R. and J. Williamson. (2009) *2009 Estimates of fundamental equilibrium exchange rates*. Washington, DC: Peterson Institute for International Economics, Policy Brief No. PB09-10.

Cripps, F., A. Izurieta, and A. Singh. (2011) "Global imbalances, under-consumption and over-borrowing: The state of the world economy and future policies," *Development and Change*. Vol. **42**, no. 1 (January), pp. 228–61.

Eatwell, J. and L. Taylor. (2000) *Global finance at risk: The case for international regulation*. New York: Policy Press.

Erceg, C., L. Guerrieri, and C. Gust. (2005) "Expansionary Fiscal Shocks and the Trade Deficit." International Finance Discussion Paper 2005-825. Washington, DC: Board of Governors of the Federal Reserve System (cited in Bernanke, 2005).

Feldstein, M. (1992) "The budget and trade deficits aren't really twins." *Challenge*. March/April, pp. 60–3.

Friedman, M. (1953) "The case for flexible exchange rates." In *Essays in Positive Economics*. Chicago: University of Chicago Press, pp. 157–203.

Godley, W. (1999) *Seven unsustainable processes: Medium-term prospects and policies for the United States and the world*. Annandale-on-Hudson, NY: Levy Institute.

Godley, W., D. B. Papadimitriou, and G. Zezza. (2008) *Prospects for the U.S. and the world: A crisis that conventional remedies cannot resolve*. Annandale-on-Hudson, NY: Levy Institute.

International Monetary Fund. (2010) *World economic outlook database, October 2010*. http://www.imf.org/external/pubs/ft/weo/2010/02/weodata/index.aspx, downloaded October 16.

(2011) *International financial statistics*. Washington, DC: IMF. www.imfstatistics.org/imf/, downloaded May 8.

Kohli, V. (2010) "The fiscal stimulus package in China," Research Brief No. 3, Mumbai, India: Project on Monitoring and Analysis of Budgets in Maharashtra State, March 28. http://www.tiss.edu/announcements/attachments/res-brief-china.pdf.

Kregel, J. (2008) "Financial flows and international imbalances: The role of catching-up by late industrialising developing countries." In E. Hein, T. Niechoj, P. Spahn, and A. Truger, eds. *Finance-led Capitalism? Macroeconomic Effects of Changes in the Financial Sector*, Marburg: Metropolis-Verlag, pp. 151–81.

Krugman, P. (2008) "Trade and wages, reconsidered." *Brookings Papers on Economic Activity*. Spring, pp. 103–54.

Loretan, M. (2005) "Indexes of the foreign exchange value of the dollar." *Federal Reserve Bulletin*. Winter, pp. 1–8.

Mishel, L., J. Bernstein, and H. Shierholz. (2009) *The state of working America, 2008/2009*. Economic Policy Institute Series. Ithaca, NY: Cornell University Press.

Mui, Y. Q. (2008) "Ikea helps a town put it together: Manufacturing jobs come back to southern Va." *Washington Post*, May 31.

Papadimitriou, D. B., G. Hannsgen, and G. Zezza. (2008) *The Buffett plan for reducing the trade deficit.* Working Paper No. 538. Annandale-on-Hudson, NY: Levy Economics Institute.

Pettis, M. (2009) *Sharing the pain: The global struggle over savings.* Washington, DC: Carnegie Endowment, Policy Brief No. 84, November.

Rubin, J. and B. Tal. (2008). "Will soaring transport costs reverse globalization?" *StrategEcon,* CIBC World Markets. May 27, pp. 4–7. <http://research.cibcwm.com/economic_public/download/smay08.pdf>.

Scott, R. E. (2008) "The burden of outsourcing: U.S. non-oil trade deficit costs more than 5 million jobs." Briefing Paper No. 222. Washington, DC: Economic Policy Institute.

Stewart, T. P. and E. J. Drake. (2009) "Addressing balance-of-payments difficulties under World Trade Organization rules." Working Paper No. 288. Washington, DC: Economic Policy Institute, December.

U.S. Bureau of Economic Analysis (BEA). (2010) "Gross domestic product: Third quarter 2010 (third estimate)," News Release, http://www.bea.gov/newsreleases/national/gdp/2010/pdf/gdp3q10_3rd.pdf, December 22.

(2011a) "National income and product account tables," Interactive Access, www.bea.gov/national/nipaweb/Index.asp, Release of March 25.

(2011b) "U.S. international transactions accounts data," www.bea.gov/international/index.htm, Interactive Tables: Detailed Estimates, Release of March 16.

(2011c) "U.S. net international investment position at yearend 2010," Table 2, http://www.bea.gov/international/xls/intinv10_t2.xls, Release of June 28.

U.S. Federal Reserve Board. (2011a) Foreign Exchange Rates – Historical Data, Release H.10. www.federalreserve.gov/releases/H10/Hist/, downloaded May 6.

(2011b) Foreign Exchange Rates – Summary Measures of the Foreign Exchange Value of the Dollar, Release H.10. www.federalreserve.gov/releases/H10/Summary/, downloaded May 6.

von Arnim, R. (2010) *Employment prospects: A global model of recovery and rebalancing.* Geneva: International Institute for Labor Studies, International Labor Organization, Discussion Paper No. 203.

PART FIVE

ECONOMIC POLICY AFTER THE GREAT
RECESSION

NINE

Confronting the Kindleberger Moment

Credit, Fiscal, and Regulatory Policy to Avoid Economic Disaster

Gerald Epstein

The term "Minsky Moment" entered the popular lexicon when, at the height of the financial crisis that led up to the Great Recession, some financial journalists, and even mainstream economists, discovered that the sensible economic theory developed decades earlier by Hyman Minsky could help us comprehend the disaster that threatened to bring down the world economy. Since that time, we briefly entered the "Keynes Moment" when politicians and economists in the United States, Europe, Asia, and even temples of neoliberalism such as the IMF, rediscovered the absolute necessity of expansionary fiscal policy to stem massive deflationary forces. For a brief period, governments pursued unprecedented Keynesian fiscal policies in an attempt to contain the downward economic spiral and, to some extent, they temporarily succeeded[1].

Now, however, ascendant forces in Europe and the United States are trying to bury Keynes and Minsky once again, and resurrect the neoliberal – now completely reactionary – policies, theory, and lexicon of a bygone age – calling for brutal austerity measures to restore the "confidence" of financial markets, which, they say, will lead the global economic recovery by bringing about lower interest rates, higher investment, and greater employment. These politicians and the economists who give them credence make such pronouncements despite the fact that it was these *same* financial markets that fueled the greatest global economic calamity since the Great Depression. Have they already forgotten that "financial confidence"

[1] This paper draws liberally on some of my previous work including *Central Banks as Agents of Economic Development, Finance without Financiers,* and joint work with James Crotty including *The Costs, Contradictions and Failure of the Lender of Last Resort Function: The Financial Crisis of 2007–2009.* Crotty is not responsible for the errors in this paper, however. I thank the editors of this Volume volume for extensive comments that markedly improved the quality of the chapter.

led primarily to speculative bubbles and fat bonuses for bankers (see Chapters 2 and 5 by Wray and Crotty) rather than productive and sustainable investment and jobs? Furthermore, both the logic and empirical evidence that lies behind the economic theory that supports the call for massive global fiscal retrenchment in deflationary economic conditions are deeply flawed (see Baker, Chapter 10, Cynamon and Fazzari, Chapter 11, and Tcherneva, Chapter 12, in this volume). Now serious financial reform regulation is threatened in the United States by strenuous bank lobbying and the increased power of the Republican Party following the 2010 midterm elections, and it is dying a slow death in Europe as a result of similar forces. If the financial system going forward will function more or less how it did in the period leading up to the crisis, why should restoring financial confidence produce outcomes any different from those we have recently experienced?

In what "moment" does the United States reside in 2012? I argue here that we have reached the dangerous and treacherous "Kindleberger Moment." In his important book, *The World In Depression, 1929–1939* the late economic historian Charles Kindleberger argued that the failure to quickly and forcefully pursue adequate expansionary fiscal policy and reverse the deflationary forces of the global economy led to fatal political forces, tearing apart political coalitions and institutions capable of bringing about real solutions to the economic crisis.[2] Kindleberger argued that this failure was due not only to lack of understanding of the importance of expansionary fiscal policy, but also to forces of financial speculation and the financial markets more generally, that made expansionary fiscal policies extremely difficult to carry out.[3] This failure of understanding and failure of will to press forward with the needed economic policies, and to push back against the forces of reaction (including finance) that were attempting to undermine them, ultimately blocked the ability to end the Great Depression through peaceful means.

We are at a "Kindleberger Moment" in another important and related sense. In his important book, *Manias, Panics and Crashes*, Kindleberger develops Minskian financial themes to show, among other things, that at

[2] *The World in Depression, 1929–1939.* Berkeley: University of California Press, 1973.
[3] Kindleberger's book is most famous for his claim that the Depression was exacerbated by a failure of global leadership. He argued that the United Kingdom was no longer capable of exerting leadership and the United States was unwilling to do so. Equally important, however, is the process by which this failure manifested itself: in the failure to conduct sufficient fiscal expansion and fight the forces of finance and speculation that ultimately led to political disintegration to the point that these policies were no longer feasible.

a time of crisis, governments and central banks throw out the so-called Bagehot rules of "lender-of-last-resort" ("lend only to solvent institutions, on good collateral and at a penalty rate of interest") and typically bail-out the masters of finance, doing whatever it takes to get the job done. As Kindleberger aptly puts it, in these situations, in practice, "the only rule is that there are no rules." So, governments and central banks in the United States and in Europe have saved the financiers, claiming, of course, that they are saving the citizens. (For example, what is most directly a bailout of European banks is marketed as a bailout of Greece.) The same powers that brought on the crisis are simply trying to hit the restart button.

However, given the severity of the crisis, as Kindleberger argued, hitting the restart button will not work. Although the initial collapse of the crisis has been contained, stagnation continued through 2010 and into early 2011 (particularly in the labor market), and instituting more austerity on the one hand and further financial bailouts on the other to restore the confidence of finance is not a real solution. It will just hasten the forces of political and economic disintegration. A look at the political paralysis in the United States and savage austerity in the United Kingdom and other parts of Europe tells the tale.

What should be done? A first and necessary antidote to this "Kindleberger Moment" is to unify political and intellectual forces that are pushing for real solutions: for Keynesian fiscal reflation and serious financial regulation, for more democratic control over central bank policy, including over the increasingly powerful European Central Bank (ECB) (whose leader is perhaps the most prominent and outspoken proponent of fiscal austerity), for more public control over credit facilities ("finance without financiers"), and for an overthrow of the now discredited economic doctrines that legitimize the misguided policies that are now once again becoming dominant in Europe and increasingly influential in the United States.

The second antidote is to provide a coherent package of specific policy proposals capable of implementing the broad solutions to the crisis previously identified. The chief purpose of this chapter is to present a range of such proposals. I will focus on the areas of monetary policy and credit policy and will also consider how these interact with fiscal policy and financial regulation. Of course, it is impossible to develop a truly comprehensive program in a single chapter. Indeed, the issues addressed here are so far-ranging as to preclude a detailed analysis. Nevertheless, the discussion that follows outlines a range of policies and initiatives that, together, are designed to help move us away from the abyss and onto a path of steady and sustainable recovery.

In short, we need an interconnected restructuring of financial markets and the banking sector to increase the flow of credit and facilitate investment in the real sector while simultaneously reducing the amount of speculative position-taking and investment in financial assets. We need to facilitate the expansion of fiscal policy to generate employment and aggregate demand, a topic addressed by Baker, Chapter 10, Cynamon and Fazzari, Chapter 11, and Tcherneva, Chapter 12, in this volume. We also need a different central bank policy that abandons failed doctrines such as inflation targeting and promotes real investment and employment (also see Chapters 3 and 4 by Wray and Kregel), and we need to increase central bank accountability. Finally, we need financial regulation that increases the likelihood that these initiatives and policies will lead to stable employment growth rather than more instability and financial speculation, a goal that will require reducing the political power of finance.

When the crisis first hit, some of these initiatives were tried, but many were not, and even those that were implemented were, for the most part, inadequate. Now it will be much more difficult, both economically and politically, to pry the economy and the political system from the grip of these destructive forces. To take but one example (discussed further in this chapter), the old financial intermediation system is broken: loose monetary policy, in the form of low interest rates and quantitative easing, does not have the desirable affect of restoring real investment. As a result, bolder financial restructuring is necessary. This is true in other areas as well, where the old macroeconomic links are weakened or broken. Although not the focus of this chapter, it is important to remember that the same bold, forceful action will be necessary in the political sphere as well.

The rest of the chapter is structured as follows. Section one discusses recent central bank policy and section two suggests how it needs to be reformed. Section three emphasizes the importance of implementing serious financial reform, directing central bank policy to supporting fiscal expansion and creating "public options" in the financial sector (finance without financiers) if we are to revive our economy and make the transitions we need to prevent disaster. Section four offers brief concluding remarks.

1. Recent Central Bank Policy and Its Shortcomings

According to Chairman Bernanke, since the start of the crisis in 2007, the Federal Reserve System's portfolio of domestic securities has increased from about $800 billion to almost $3 trillion and has shifted from consisting entirely of treasury securities to being almost two-thirds in mortgage-backed securities (primarily obligations of Freddie Mac and Fannie Mae). In addition, the average maturity of the treasury securities in the Fed's portfolio nearly doubled, from three and one-half years to almost seven years. (Bernanke, testimony to Senate Banking Committee, July 21, 2010; see also Blinder and Zandi, 2010).

These changes suggest that after the initial stabilization of the financial system through massive interventions, Federal Reserve policy has been focused on three main goals:

1) Supporting the housing market by purchasing mortgage debt, with Fannie Mae and Freddie Mac as intermediaries.
2) Improving the profitability of the major financial institutions by keeping interest rates near zero, and allowing institutions to engage in virtually any activity that will increase their profitability, including speculation and proprietary trading.
3) Keeping the cost of financing the Federal deficit relatively low to prevent an explosive increase in the deficit and debt to income ratios.

The actions that the Fed has taken to achieve these goals are, outside of the Second World War, extraordinary in historical terms. Nevertheless, they fall far short of what is needed to confront the Kindleberger moment. Through mid-2011, home foreclosures accelerated; employment was stagnant; real investment was tepid. According to one prominent interpretation, the conventional "Taylor Rule," indicates that, if it could, the Fed should set nominal short-term interest rates somewhere between *negative* 3.0 percent and negative 5.0 percent to achieve normal inflation and employment targets. Obviously, the Fed cannot do anything like that.

What is more worrisome is that even as the Federal Reserve clearly realizes that more significant expansionary policy may be needed, they are already implementing an exit strategy from the crisis policies. In Congressional testimony in 2010, with the unemployment rate still near its peak, Bernanke focused on plans to shrink the Federal Reserve's balance sheet to restore it to more "normal levels in the long-run."[4] Indeed, the Federal Reserve decided to abandon their policy of "quantitative easing II" (QEII) as of June, 2011, despite evidence that large central bank asset purchases can affect interest rates[5] and, if nothing else, support fiscal policy by keeping borrowing costs relatively low, as in war financing (Mehrling, 2011, INET www.inet.org).

---

[4] See Chairman Bernanke's Testimony to The Senate Banking Committee, July 21, 2010 http://www.federalreserve.gov/newsevents/testimony/bernanke20100721a.htm.
[5] See the references in footnote 3 of Bernanke, Monetary Report to Congress, July 13, 2011 http://www.federalreserve.gov/newsevents/testimony/bernanke20110713a.htm

The Fed is by no means the only central bank whose policies since the onset of the crisis merit criticism. In Europe, the ECB is even less committed to supporting economic growth, and is instead focused on keeping inflation low and doing whatever it can to bailout banks and fight necessary expansionary fiscal policy. In the United Kingdom, meanwhile, the Bank of England is not contemplating further expansionary policies to counteract the fiscal austerity implemented by the Conservative/Lib-Dem coalition under Prime Minister David Cameron.

These various missteps have not occurred by accident. Rather, they have occurred because of the inappropriate orientation of central bank policy. Specifically, with the support of the economics profession, the financial authorities have made four fatal mistakes in dealing with crisis: commodity inflation obsession; the surrender to fiscal policy straitjackets; ignorance of the functioning of the financial structure including the role of toxic products; and a fatal overcommitment to the prerogatives of private finance and financiers along with an associated allergy to increasing the role and power of the state. The Federal Reserve for more than a year freed itself from a number of these straitjackets, and with QEI and QEII implemented some significant monetary and credit easing. However, it was still subject to many of the other prejudices described in this chapter.

First, central bankers – persuaded by years of misleading arguments by much of the economics profession – have been obsessed with maintaining their "inflation fighting" credibility. As a result, throughout the key first year of the crisis, they engaged in lender-of-last-resort actions to help increase financial liquidity, but the specific policies were creatively designed to allow monetary policy to continue fighting a perceived threat of inflation. As a result, these early actions were insufficiently expansionary and did not slow the descent into a major recession. Second, and more importantly, the hard-fought Keynesian lesson about the need for countercyclical fiscal policy (even at the expense of running large fiscal deficits) has been, to a large extent, forgotten. In Europe especially, it is buried under the structure of the economic institutions of the European Union. In the early stages of the crisis, this led policy makers in the United States and Europe to attempt purely monetary solutions to the crisis. However, by the time these policies were implemented it was already too late because the financial crisis had destroyed many financial institutions and markets and had also become a "real" crisis, rendering standard monetary policy ineffective. Third, central bankers did not understand the key role of the housing and property bubble and bust in bringing down the banks because they did not fully understand the complex financial instruments that linked the banks to each other and financial markets generally. Nor did they understand how to deal with financial asset bubbles because of their obsession with goods (as opposed to asset) prices (i.e., inflation targeting). Neither central bankers nor the fiscal authorities developed a strategy for dealing with the crash in housing and property values. Finally, central bankers and treasury officials went to excessive lengths to preserve the prerogatives of bankers as the financial crisis deepened. This greatly limited their willingness to seize banks, reorganize them, and generally intervene in their operations to make sure they contributed to recovery in the real economy. Paul Krugman named the political system characterized by this nexus of policies: "Rule by Rentiers."[6]

The bottom line is that since 2007, whereas central bank policy has managed to temporarily save large parts of the financial sector, it has unambiguously failed to revive the real economy. A fundamentally different approach to monetary and financial policy is required if we are to escape the clutches of the current "Kindleberger moment." As I argue in what follows, the Fed must: 1) continue to support expansionary fiscal policy by continuing quantitative easing in order to help increase aggregate demand and facilitate public investment; 2) utilize new tools of credit allocation such as asset-based reserved requirements (ABRR) and help to resolve the massive mortgage debt problem that is weighing down the economy and without which there can be no recovery; 3) support the implementation and enforcement of strong financial regulation by taking a strong proactive role in enforcing the new Dodd-Frank legislation, and taking seriously its new mandate under Dodd-Frank of maintaining financial stability; and 4) facilitate more public options in banking and finance, such as state banks, infrastructure banks, coop banks and green banks.

Developing all these components in detail is well beyond the scope of one chapter, but I will outline the rationale and importance of these proposals in what follows.

2. Fixing the Broken Financial System I:
More Tools for Credit Allocation

The financial intermediation mechanism is broken. The level of excess reserves in the banking system has increased from $1.7 billion in June 2007 to $1 trillion in June 2010 and to $1.5 trillion by May, 2011(Federal Reserve Board, Statistical Release, H.3). Meanwhile, total bank credit fell in 2009 at

---

[6] Paul Krugman, "Rule By Rentiers," *New York Times*, June 10, 2011. http://www.nytimes.com/2011/06/10/opinion/10krugman.html See also Epstein and Jayadev (2009).

a rate of 6.4 percent and has continued to decline through most of 2010 and early 2011 (Federal Reserve Board of Governors, Statistical Release, H.8). Commercial and industrial loans fell at an average annual rate of more than 18 percent in 2009 and continued to decline through 2010, before picking up in 2011 and the first quarter of 2012. Meanwhile, the interest rate on industrial and commercial loans relative to the federal funds rate remains much higher than in either the early 1990s or during the 2001 recession, even though there was financial instability in those earlier periods as well. (Federal Reserve Statistical Release, h.15)

The breakdown of the intermediation mechanism is crucial for two reasons. First of all, credit, when properly allocated, plays many critical roles in the economy. Credit is crucial for small businesses, for start-up companies, for the housing sector, and for consumers. It provides the lynchpin for spending by individuals and institutions who have high demand and who can generate jobs and new capital goods that can improve productivity and raise standards of living. When the credit system is broken, the individuals and institutions that could create jobs and needed investment are not able to do so. Second, the credit mechanism is important because it is one of the main channels through which monetary policy works to expand the economy, create jobs, and stimulate productivity-enhancing investment. When it is broken, traditional expansionary monetary policy to bring the economy out of a severe recession is much less effective. So if the credit intermediation channel is broken, the central bank will have to find other means by which to revive the economy and create jobs.

It is to a discussion of these new channels that I now turn. In what follows, I argue in favor of two types of financial initiatives. First, incentive-based policy tools such as loan guarantees and asset-based reserve requirements can enhance private credit allocation. Second, in the following section, I argue that both the allocation and quantity of credit can be improved through increased public involvement in finance – that is, "finance without financiers."

Central Bank Policies after the Second World War:
Credit Allocation for Social Goals

It is useful to begin with some brief historical context that shows how credit allocation policies have been widely and successfully used in the past, especially in times of great transition and crisis.

Following the disasters of the Great Depression and the Second World War, governments in the United Kingdom, Europe, Japan, and even the

United States asserted much greater control over central banks and the banking industries. Central banks became, once again, important institutions for financing and managing government debts accumulated during the war; and after the war, central banks also became important tools for rebuilding and restructuring national economies and providing for social needs, often under governments' direction. The central banks used a variety of credit allocation techniques to accomplish these goals, and in most cases, these techniques were supported by capital and exchange controls on international capital movements (see, for example, Epstein and Schor, 1992).

The objectives of central banks, the tools they employed, and the degree of success achieved varied from country to country and over time. For example, the U.S. government created a variety of financial institutions that supported national goals. The savings and loan banks, along with other government-supported financial institutions (most obviously Fannie and Freddie) encouraged housing. Indeed, in the postwar period, Federal Reserve policy was quite sensitive to the needs of the housing market and even successfully tailored its monetary policy to avoid significantly harming it (Maisel, 1973). The U.S. government had a myriad of financial institutions, moreover, that supported national goals, notably home ownership (Dymski, 1993; Wolfson, 1993). The savings and loan banks, for example, were devoted entirely to housing. There were other specialized financial institutions, underpinned by various government agencies and guarantees that also supported housing. More relevant to this discussion, Federal Reserve policy was sensitive to these concerns with housing, and they had a significant influence on Federal Reserve Policy during this time (Maisel, 1973).

In Europe and the United Kingdom, central banks that had been independent before the war found themselves subject to state control after 1945 (Capie, et. al., 1994a, p 72). During the war, monetary policy was often implemented through direct controls while interest rates were held low and constant. Direct controls continued in the aftermath of the war with various credit allocation techniques. (Capie, 1999, p. 25.) This experience is directly relevant to our own because now, as during the war, interest rates need to be kept low for an extended period of time. Unlike the war, however, the problem confronting policy is insufficient demand, whereas during the war the issue was to ration goods in the face of excess demand (see Canova, 2006).

Credit controls are commonly defined as measures by which the authorities seek to modify the pattern and incidence of the cost and availability of credit from what markets would generate on their own (Hodgman, 1973 p. 137). Credit controls seek to influence credit allocation and interest rate structures (ibid.). In Europe, credit controls have served a number of purposes: (1) to finance government debt at lower interest rates; (2) to reduce the flow of credit to the private sector without raising domestic interest rates; (3) to influence the allocation of real resources to priority uses; (4) to block channels of financial intermediation and thus to assist restrictive general monetary policy; and (5) to strengthen popular acceptance of wage-price controls by holding down interest income (Hodgman, ibid.).

European experiences with credit controls varied from country to country. In Germany, the United Kingdom, and the Netherlands, controls were used only briefly after the Second World War or with respect to very short-run macro purposes. France, Italy, and Belgium were a different story. There, the principle of controlling credit flows and interest rates to serve the national interest was widely accepted.

France had, perhaps, among the most extensive and successful sets of controls, which were part of the government's overall approach to industrial policy. The Bank of France was nationalized in 1945 and placed under the National Credit Council, the institution in charge of implementing the financial aspects of the government plan (Hodgman, 1973, p. 147; Zysman, 1983). The broad aim of credit policy in France was to contribute to the modernization of the French economy and its ability to compete in international markets. To influence the volume and allocation of credit, the Bank of France used various methods (see Hodgman, 1973, p. 148 and Zysman, 1983 for descriptions). *Asset-based reserve requirements* were widely used. Banks were required to observe minimum reserve requirements with lower rates on privileged assets. "These asset reserve requirements had the dual purpose of adding to bank portfolio demand for the specified assets and of preventing the banks from using these eligible assets for rediscounting at the central bank" (Hodgman, 1973, p. 148.) A second technique – ceilings on credit extension – was used to reduce credit expansion without raising interest rates, and also to allocate credit: priority sectors were exempted from the ceilings. These included short-term export credits, and medium-term loans for construction. The ceilings applied to a large range of financial institutions and were accompanied, as well, by capital and exchange controls as an important concomitant (Hodgman, 1973. pp. 148–149; Zysman, 1983). A third tool was the scrutiny of individual credits made by banks. This allowed the Bank of France to approve loans for privileged purposes. The French system may be again of direct relevance here in the United States as we try to pull ourselves out of the crisis.

Zysman (1983) has emphasized the role of credit allocation techniques in helping to revive the French economy and help it adjust to structural challenges in the postwar period. This role was facilitated by a bank-based financial system in France, unlike the capital market-based systems in the United States and United Kingdom that, according to Zysman, make such credit allocation mechanisms more difficult to implement (see also Pollin, 1995 and Grabel, 1997). Italy and Belgium also used similar policies. In the case of Italy, a major goal was to help develop the southern part of the country (U.S. House of Representatives, 1972, p. 11).

Analysis by Lester Thurow and colleagues for the U.S. House Banking Committee in the early 1970s identified three main techniques for protecting or promoting priority sectors: asset-based reserve requirements; government borrowing in the capital market and re-lending to preferred sectors; and competition by government financial institutions for primary saving flows and lending captured flows to preferred sectors (for example, through the government postal savings system). In the case of Sweden, asset-based reserve requirements were used to aid the housing market (U.S. Congress, House of Representatives, 1972). In Japan, government savings institutions were used to capture personal savings flows and these were channeled by the finance ministry (of which the Bank of Japan is a part) to industries that were perceived to contribute most to economic growth (ibid., p. 13).

The general consensus of analyses of these experiences is that they are most successful when the controls apply to a broad swath of the financial sector (to prevent arbitrage and avoidance), when they are accompanied by capital and exchange controls (to curtail capital flight), and when they are part of a coherent plan of economic promotion and development (Zysman, 1987; Hodgman, 1973; U.S. Congress, House of Representatives, 1972; U.S. Congress, Joint Economic Committee, 1981).

Credit Allocation Tools to Contain the U.S. Great Recession

Credit allocation tools have been applied since the start of the financial crisis by the Federal Reserve and the U.S. Treasury. The Federal Reserve used a host of massive financial guarantees in 2008 and 2009 to prevent a total financial meltdown. These included guarantees for money market accounts, guarantees to loans and brokers, massive loans to AIG and several other institutions that allowed major banks and investment banks to unload devalued assets at full price, and massive purchases by the Federal Reserve of mortgages underwritten by Fannie Mae and Freddie Mac.

In other words, credit allocation tools were used to allocate huge amounts of credit to the financial sector itself. The key and important exception to this is the housing industry, which received significant amounts of credit from the Federal Reserve. Of course, GM and Chrysler received funds as well, but not from the Federal Reserve. In addition, the federal government has been using loan guarantees as part of the "stimulus package" including guarantees for nuclear power plants and for auto companies. A full assessment of the impact of these policies has not yet been undertaken, but some studies have suggested that they did have a substantially positive impact on jobs and incomes (Blinder and Zandi, 2010).

Extending Credit Allocation Tools to Provide Employment Generation

Thomas Palley and Robert Pollin have proposed significantly extending credit allocation tools such as loan guarantees and asset-based reserve requirements as a strategy to revive U.S. job growth in the aftermath of the Great Recession. In a recent *Nation* article, Pollin (2010) detailed a plan to mobilize bank reserves through a combination of loan guarantees and variable asset-based reserve requirements that would penalize "high stakes gambling" by banks. With asset-based reserve requirements, banks must hold reserves – and therefore cannot invest and earn interest – on a certain portion of their assets. These requirements can vary by type of asset. So, for example, if the Federal Reserve wants to discourage highly risky bets, then it can place higher reserve requirements on risky assets; if the Fed wants to encourage investments in job-creating investments, it can place lower reserve requirements on loans that generate a lot of jobs. Thomas Palley (2003a, 2003b) has also proposed using asset-based reserve requirements to regulate financial markets and help allocate resources to employment generation. His argument also relies on the property of asset-based reserve requirements that they can be raised to discourage unwanted behavior, (such as excessively risky investments) or lowered to encourage desirable behavior (such as more job creation).

A common caveat with these policies is that care has to be taken to make sure they do not lead to corruption – especially by bankers and corporations colluding to evade the monitoring of assets and targets. A strong monitoring system is necessary to successfully implement such policies. Another limitation, which Pollin recognizes, is that even though these policies might enhance the potential supply of credit, the U.S. economy in the aftermath of the Great Recession may be too depressed to generate the aggregate demand necessary to justify borrowing, even on good terms, to expand employment and production. Furthermore, because of the very limited scope of the Dodd-Frank and related European financial reform legislation, the very long phase-in periods of those aspects of it that might significantly reduce speculation, and the consequent continuing profitability of speculation, proprietary trading, and other forms of financial investing (rather than investing in employment-creating assets), loan guarantees and asset-based reserve requirements might not be sufficient to generate much investment.

In this environment, some combination of the following policies is necessary:

1. Strong financial reform must ensure that policies intended to promote investment do not simply lead to more proprietary trading and speculation.
2. Expansionary fiscal policy must create aggregate demand and investment in infrastructure employment. Here, the most important role the Federal Reserve can play in a depressed environment is the equivalent of "war finance": that is, keeping interest rates low and credit policy accommodative (Epstein and Schor, 1995).
3. More direct mobilization of credit by public institutions must provide access to finance for important investments. Targets for the amount of credit to be so provisioned should recognize the historical commitment in the United States to support housing (as discussed in this chapter) and include substantial and direct debt relief for home owners who are buried under a mound of debt that will continue to weigh down the economy for years to come.

Turning Monetary Policy into Fiscal Policy: Keep Quantitative Easing Going

When the financial intermediation process is largely broken, as it is now, then traditional monetary policy cannot work in the traditional way to address the key problem of deficient demand. Whereas the allocation policies previously discussed in this section will directly add to demand and employment, perhaps the biggest impact of the Federal Reserve's "quantitative easing" policies (after the initial bailouts of banks and financial markets) has been to keep the cost of financing the federal debt relatively low. This policy reduces both short-term interest rates (as is typical in weak economic times) and buying longer-term securities to keep long-term interest rates low (as was the explicit objective of the Fed's "QE2" policy that ended on June 30, 2011). These policies keep the costs of government borrowing low to enable expansionary fiscal policy that adds directly to demand. By mid-2011, it is precisely this policy that the Fed is under enormous pressure to limit or even abandon. However, I argue that the Fed should reinstitute this policy. As Keynes argued, in depression-like conditions, fiscal policy is the surest path to economic recovery and monetary policy is best used to support fiscal policy (see other chapters in this volume).

3. Fixing the Broken Financial System II: Financial Regulation and Finance without Financiers[7]

Finance without Financiers

In the initial stages of financial meltdown, governments in the United States, United Kingdom, and other parts of Europe took major ownership stakes in financial (and some nonfinancial) companies to bail them out and preserve employment and credit flows. However, these governments, notably the United States, ignored calls to exert significant authority over these financial institutions in order to press them into specific actions that might have improved the economy. Instead, the bailouts ended up being essentially bailouts of creditors and managers, and the large banks did very little to help homeowners, small businesses, or overall real investment. They did, however, restore the bonuses and compensation packages of the top management (see Chapter 5 by Crotty in this volume).

The U.S. government missed the opportunity to restructure finance to support the real economy when the banks were weak and in need of government support; it will now be much harder for the government to force the banks to undertake positive engagement with the economy. The U.S. government does still have some leverage, however. First, the Dodd-Frank Act gives the Federal Reserve and other regulatory agencies significant power to regulate, limit product lines and other behavior, and even break up the banks if they are seen to pose a significant risk to the financial stability of the United States. A Federal Reserve that was truly interested in pushing banks to lend and invest in the real economy would certainly have the power to do so with strategic use of, or even threats to use, these powers. Second, some of the largest banks in the United States and Europe are still quite weak, in the United States primarily because of the mortgage crisis and in Europe because of the sovereign debt crisis. Banks, therefore, are

[7] See Gerald Epstein, "Finance without Financiers: Prospects for Radical Change in Financial Governance," *Review of Radical Political Economy*, 2010.

likely to continue to need public support. So governments are likely to get a second chance to gain more control over financial institutions. What, then, should they do with this power?

In Epstein (2010), I discuss the role of public options in finance: finance without financiers. As our earlier historical discussion made clear, during times of reconstruction and economic transformation in Europe, Japan, elsewhere in Asia, and even in the United States, publicly-owned financial institutions have played a key role in helping to finance and direct large-scale public and public–private initiatives to re-orient the economy. Current discussions of a green bank, an infrastructure bank, and state banks (See DEMOS on state banks http://www.demos.org/publication.cfm?currentpublicationID=793AEBE8–3FF4–6C82–5AD-61998675D4EC0) are important initiatives along these lines. At a time when private banks are sitting on excess reserves and/or engaging in proprietary trading and paying large bonuses, the idea of having more publicly oriented institutions directed to public purposes is very appealing.

One danger is that these publicly oriented financial institutions can be perverted for private purposes. The scandal of Ginnie Mae and Freddie Mac (Morgenson and Rosner, 2011; Epstein, Triple Crisis Blog, June 3, 2011 http://triplecrisis.com/reckless-endangerment/) is the most recent egregious example. The main problem with these institutions is not that they were public. The problem is that they were not public enough. They were public–private partnerships where the private owners and managers got enormous profits and salaries, and the public bore the risk. This is obviously a recipe for disaster.

Although a full discussion of the merits and demerits of publicly-owned banks is beyond the scope of this chapter (see Epstein, 2010 for further discussion) it is important to emphasize one point here that is particularly relevant for getting the United States out of the current Kindleberger Moment. A public initiative, perhaps through a public financial institution, must implement a program to get the massive mortgage debts off of the balance sheets of households, to eliminate the problem of underwater mortgages, and dramatically reduce the foreclosure cloud that hangs over the economy. As such, the most important candidate for more finance without financiers is the development of a Homeowners Loan Corporation (HOLC) to buy up mortgages and reissue them so that homeowners can stay in their homes and increase their net wealth (see Kuttner [2010] for a recent discussion). A public financial institution is likely necessary to buy up mortgages at a reduced cost, make the banks take a haircut, and then hold the mortgages until they are restored in value (while simultaneously reducing homeowners' debt service payments). This kind of policy worked in the 1930s and 1940s and is likely to be necessary again today.[8]

The Importance of Strong Financial Regulation

One of the obstacles to the implementation of a strong policy of aggregate demand expansion and credit allocation to job creation is the continued financial fragility of the economy and the financial sector's tendency to generate instability and speculation. For example, one limit on the effectiveness of the Fed's QE2 policy is that in the absence of strong channels of financial intermediation and strong aggregate demand in the United States, much of the extended credit appeared to leave the United States seeking higher interest rates and higher returns abroad, sending significant amounts of financial inflows into emerging markets, and generating exchange rate and inflationary pressures elsewhere. These capital outflows occurred instead of stronger investment in the United States.

Thus, to prevent this type of spillover to high-risk and occasionally high-return financial strategies, strong financial regulation needs to help channel finance to more productive and less risky uses. For any of these schemes to work, there has to be strong financial regulation overall. First, it is difficult to implement new financial reform and solve problems associated with the Kindleberger Moment with continued financial instability and a financial system that allocates financial resources to either speculative ventures or excess reserves. Second, without strict and successful regulations, the attraction of very high short-run rates of return and extremely high salaries and bonuses in the private financial sector could pervert the public purposes of public banks by eroding the efficacy of monitoring and regulation, by pulling away expertise and management skill, by making it more difficult to attract capital during financial bubbles, and by eroding the confidence of regulators in the necessity and usefulness of the public banks.

In July of 2010 the U.S. Congress passed, and President Obama signed into law, a financial reform bill that in principle could help regulate the financial system along these lines. President Obama and Congressional leaders hailed the so-called Dodd-Frank Act as the most important financial reform legislation since the Great Depression. Critics, on the other

---

[8] Other important ideas for jumpstarting the economy, creating aggregate demand, and generating employment while helping with longer-run transitional needs are: a green jobs bank and a public investment bank (or set of banks) to fund green investments. A full discussion of these is beyond the scope of this chapter; see Pollin et al. (2008) and Baker and Pollin (2009).

hand, dismissed it as next to worthless. As usual, *Nation* columnist, William Greider, got it right: "Think of this as Round One.... Instead of congratulating Democrats for enacting timid measures, we should show them what we have in mind for Round Two." Greider tells progressives to put forward the good ideas that were developed during the reform fight but were blocked, defeated or, "Swiss cheesed to death."[9]

Round two, however, is proving to be exceedingly difficult for reformers, and the bankers and financial lobbyists planned it that way. The reason is that the Act deliberately left most of the details of the key reforms up in the air, to be decided by rule-making processes and studies during round two in more than ten different domestic agencies, and in overseas bodies like the Basel Committee on Banking Supervision. Indeed, the Act calls for 243 rulemakings and sixty-seven studies to be held over several years, with the final rules being phased-in over as many as twelve years. Even though this structure is set up so that, in principle, regulators like the Federal Reserve, SEC, and FDIC have the potential legal power to significantly strengthen and tighten oversight and regulation in practice, there is also enormous opportunity to interpret the new law so that banks can continue taking risk like it was 2006 all over again.

How all this turns out depends, then, on the balance of forces in the ongoing fight over financial reform. So far, the bankers, who have spent millions of dollars lobbying against Dodd-Frank, are winning. Nonetheless, there is still some possibility of a positive outcome. In the provisions of the Dodd-Frank Act there are some quite powerful provisions that, if implemented and monitored properly, could have a significant impact on some of the most dangerous and destructive dynamics in the financial system. In what follows, I list key problems of the financial system that led to the financial crisis and that, if left unresolved, could contribute to another crisis. For each of the problems raised, I discuss how it is addressed (or not) in the Dodd-Frank Act, and the alternatives developed during the Dodd-Frank debates that could have been implemented (and could again in the future).

1. *Asset bubbles*: In the run-up to the financial crisis and the Great Recession, Federal Reserve policy, at best, ignored the massive housing bubble (Baker, 2009). The Dodd-Frank Act gives the Federal Reserve the mandate *to preserve financial stability,* alongside the mandates to maintain high employment and stable prices. Maintaining financial stability could mean preventing dangerous asset bubbles. Specifically, the Act imposes

---

[9] July 02, 2010. http://www.alternet.org/story/147415/

trading limits for commodities in derivative markets. It also creates an Office of Financial Research housed in the Treasury to generate early warning data on destabilizing developments. Although these are steps in the right direction, there is no clear requirement to avoid asset bubbles in the definition of the Fed's goals. There is also no commitment to countercyclical capital requirements as discussed in Basel III.

2. *Dangerous financial products, including dangerous derivatives*: A lightly regulated financial system allowed dangerous and opaque financial products, including derivatives, whose values were unclear even in the best of times, to populate portfolios around the world. The Dodd-Frank Act requires the regulation of derivatives for the first time, and requires that standardized derivatives be traded on exchanges and cleared through a central clearinghouse. Nevertheless, nonstandard derivatives can still be sold "over the counter," so that banks will still be able to trade the majority of derivatives in-house. A possible solution to this problem would be to end the distinction between standard and nonstandard derivatives, and require *all* derivatives to be traded on exchanges and go through clearing. Better still, the Financial Product Safety Administration rules developed by Elizabeth Warren could be extended to cover investor financial products.

3. *Excessive leverage*: Excessive bank borrowing (leverage) created a system in which small losses could wipe out all of a firm's equity. The Dodd-Frank Act empowers the Financial Stability Oversight Council (FSOC) to identify systemically dangerous financial firms and impose heightened capital requirements on them and quantitative limits on their leverage. However, there is tremendous discretion in the setting of these requirements and limits, and authority over non-bank financial intermediaries is very limited. The obvious solution would be to create clear and binding limits on the extent to which financial institutions can become leveraged.

4. *Excessive reliance on short-run borrowing from shadow-banking system*: The financial crisis was precipitated, in part, by heavy reliance of megabanks on short-term funds borrowed from the "shadow banking system" of hedge funds and private equity funds to support long-term risky investments. When the value of opaque financial products collapsed there was a panic "run" on the banks by the shadow financial system desperate to get their money back, leading to widespread bank insolvency. The Dodd-Frank solution once again relies on discretionary imposition of higher capital requirements and quantitative limits by the Fed; it does not define "short-term borrowing" or impose any

requirement that the Fed limit it to safe levels. Higher capital requirements should automatically be imposed on banks using excessively short-term funding to pursue risky investments – and special bankruptcy treatment for repos should be rolled back.

5. *Shadow balance sheets*: The failure to put all assets and liabilities on bank balance sheets allowed financial firms to create the illusion of safety, avoid capital charges, and engage in highly risky activities (Taub, 2009). Unfortunately, the Dodd-Frank Act provides no clear solution to this problem. At a minimum, the SEC's existing authority under Sarbanes-Oxley could be used to require more disclosure. Ideally, all systemically important financial firms should be required to report all of their off-balance sheet activities.

6. *Too big to fail financial institutions*: Risky strategies were abetted by *moral hazard* – the fact that banks got so big that they thought they would be bailed out no matter what they did, leading them to use taxpayer guaranteed funds to gamble wildly whereas some, including Goldman Sachs, secretly bet against their own clients (Johnson and Kwak, 2010). The Dodd-Frank Act addresses this "immoral" hazard problem in a variety of ways, which include limits to the Fed's authority to bailout individual financial institutions, limits on banks' credit exposure to affiliates and other financial institutions, limitations on proprietary trading and hedge and private equity funded ownership by banks (known as the "Volcker Rule"), and (perhaps most importantly) enhanced FDIC resolution authority. However, without limiting bank size and leverage, the enhanced resolution authority lacks credibility. That is, the failure of huge institutions really would have unacceptable systemic consequences, so they are likely to be bailed out regardless of Dodd-Frank restrictions. This problem reinforces the need, as earlier emphasized, for stricter controls on the size of banks and their leverage.

7. *Dangerous and excessive banker compensation*: Prior to the crash, financial corporations instituted dangerous pay incentives for "rainmakers" who crashed their own banks and walked away with millions (Crotty, Chapter 5). The Dodd-Frank Act requires better reporting of executive compensation and gives shareholders a greater "say on pay." However, the shareholders' opinion is nonbinding, and is expressed only after the fact (i.e., after a firm has entered into a binding compensation contract with its executives). Rather than this half-hearted shareholder oversight, bank executive compensation – much of which is rent (again, see Crotty's Chapter 5 in this volume) – should simply be subject to higher taxation.

8. *Outsourcing of regulations to those having conflicts of interest*: Credit rating agencies are paid by the very banks whose assets they rate and, as the financial crisis demonstrated, are prone to giving rave reviews to what are subsequently revealed to be junk assets. Under Dodd-Frank, rating agencies can more easily be sued, whereas regulatory agencies are required to reduce their reliance on ratings when enforcing regulatory provisions. Nevertheless, issuers will still be paying for the ratings, which will likely still figure heavily in private (and public) financial decision-making. A surer method of addressing the credit rating agency problem would be to create a public utility responsible for assigning the task of rating a security to one or more ratings agencies (rather than allowing the issuer of the security to do this itself).

9. *Fraudulent behavior flourishes in "regulation lite" environment*: Financial regulators who could have done much more turned the other way, as fraudulent behavior by bankers reached epidemic proportions and was awarded with billions in bonuses – and revolving-door jobs for regulators (and congressional staffers) themselves. The Dodd-Frank Act enhances the regulatory and investigative powers of the SEC – including an enhanced "whistleblower" program – in an attempt to combat fraud. However, its prohibitions on conflict of interest are vague. Not only do the rules need to be better defined, but clearer and more meaningful penalties are required, along with the resources necessary for successful enforcement of the rules.

10. *Fleecing customers*: Bankers defrauded customers by engaging in front-running – designing and selling products they were betting against, and by selling mortgages designed to strip borrowers of their equity. Under Dodd-Frank, the newly created Consumer Financial Protection Bureau (CFPB) is designed to reduce consumer abuse. However, the CFPB is located within the Fed and may therefore lack independence from vested financial interests. At a minimum, it requires strong leadership if it is to overcome this structural problem. A better solution would be to pursue the original intention for the CFPB by making it independent of the Fed.

As this discussion illustrates, the Dodd-Frank Act addresses many of the causes of the financial crisis, but often in inadequate or indeterminate ways. Frequently there were stronger pieces of legislation (proposed by members of the House or Senate) that would have better addressed these concerns with the structure of the U.S. financial system. However, many of these were defeated or greatly weakened, sometimes at the last minute. Clearly, the problems confronting serious reform of the U.S. financial system are those of political will, rather than any dearth of ideas as to how we should proceed.

4. Conclusion

Having already experienced a "Minsky Moment," the U.S. economy is currently in the grip of a "Kindleberger Moment." Brought on by the failure to act decisively enough to *both* staunch the forces of depression *and* eliminate the subsequent possibility of secular stagnation, the United States is now unable to enact the policies necessary to put the economy back on a path toward sustainable prosperity. This has brought us to a dangerous juncture, when the forces of political and economic disintegration are gripping our economy and dragging it down in a vicious spiral. The clearest sign of this is the ascendancy of the austerity buzzards across the political landscape. In spite of the analysis presented here, and throughout this volume, that broader government intervention is an important part of the antidote to the poisoned economic circumstances following the Great Recession, the dominant thinking among policy makers seems to have shifted to the view that if only government would get out of the way, the recovery could proceed. This wrong-headed thinking has already pushed countries like Greece and Ireland into austerity-unemployment "death spirals." In the United States, this thinking has threatened and weakened essential safety net programs like basic unemployment insurance and Medicaid

To break this downward spiral and the policy-making paralysis at its core, political forces must mobilize around a bold program of economic expansion lead by expansionary, employment-generating fiscal policy, accommodative monetary policy, new credit allocation mechanisms to direct credit to effective uses, and strong financial regulation to reduce distorting speculative forces and end tax payer bailouts of finance. Nothing that comes short of this combination of macroeconomic and regulatory policies is likely to overcome the current Kindleberger Moment and move the U.S. economy to a robust and sustainable path.

References

Amsden, A. H. (2001) *The Rise of "The Rest;" Challenges to the West from Late-Industrializing Economies.* Oxford: Oxford University Press.
Baker, D. (2010) "The Benefits of Financial Transactions Taxes." CEPR.net

Baker, D. and R. Pollin. (2009) "Public Investment, Industrial Policy, and US Economic Recovery." PERI, http://scholarworks.umass.edu.silk.library.umass.edu/peri_workingpapers/177/.

Bernanke, B. (2009) "Community Development Financial Institutions: Challenges and Opportunities" in Community Development Investment Center, *The Economic Crisis and Community Development Finance: An Industry Assessment,* Federal Reserve Bank of San Francisco, Working Paper 2009 – 05, June. http://frbsf.org/cdinvestments pp. 2–5.

(2010) "Semiannual Monetary Policy Report to Congress," testimony, July 21. www.frb.gov

(2009) "The Federal Reserve Balance Sheet" speech, April 3. www.frb.gov

Board of Governors of the Federal Reserve. Statistical Release H.3. "Aggregate Reserves of Deposit Institutions and Monetary Base". Washington, D.C. http://www.federal-reserve.gov/releases/h3/current/default.htm

Board of Governors of the Federal Reserve, Statistical Release H.8. "Assets and Liabilities of Commercial Banks in the United States" Washington, D.C. http://www.federal-reserve.gov/releases/h8/current/default.htm

Board of Governors of the Federal Reserve, Statistical Release, H. 15 "Selected Interest Rates", http://www.federalreserve.gov/releases/h15/current/

Blinder, A. and M. Zandi. (2010) "How the Great Recession Was Brought to an End." www.economy.com/mark-zandi/documents/End-of-Great-Recession.pdf

Butkiewicz, J. (2002) "Reconstruction Finance Corporation." EH.Net Encyclopedia, ed. Robert Whaples, July 19. http://eh.net/encyclopedia Accessed, June 14, 2009.

Canova, T. (2006) "American Wartime Values in Historical Perspective: Full-Employment Mobilization or Business as Usual," *13:1 ILSA JOURNAL OF INTERNATIONAL AND COMPARATIVE LAW 1*

Capie, F. (1999) "Banking in Europe in the 19th Century: The Role of the Central Bank," in Sylla, et. al., *The State, the Financial System and Economic Modernization,* pp. 118–133.

Capie, F., C. Goodhart, S. F., and N. Schnadt. (1994a) *The Future of Central Banking; The Tercentenary Symposium of the Bank of England.* Cambridge: Cambridge University Press.

1994b. "The Development of Central Banking." In Capie, et. al., pp. 1–232.

Crotty, J. (2009) "Structural Causes of the Global Financial Crisis: A Critical Assessment of the "New Financial Architecture." PERI Working Paper, No. 180, September, *Cambridge Journal of Economics.*

(2010) "The Bonus-Drive 'Rainmaker' Financial Firm: How These Firms Enrich Top Employees, Destroy Shareholder Value, and Create Systemic Financial Instability," PERI. www.peri.umass.edu

Crotty, J. and G. Epstein. (2009a) "The Costs, Contradictions and Failure of the Lender of Last Resort Function: The Financial Crisis of 2007–2009." www.peri.umass.edu

(2009b) "Avoiding a Financial Meltdown." *Challenge Magazine,* January/February.

D'Arista, J. (1994) *The Evolution of U.S. Finance, Vol. II.* Armonk, NY: M. E. Sharpe.

2009. "Rebuilding the Framework for Financial Regulation." *EPI Briefing Paper #231,* May 1.

D'Arista, J. W. and T. Schlesinger. (1993) "The Parallel Banking System." In, Gary A. Dymski, Gerald Epstein, and Robert Pollin, eds., *Transforming The U.S. Financial System: Equity and Efficiency for the 21st Century*. Armonk, NY: M.E. Sharpe, Ch. 7.

Dumenil, G. and D. Levy. (2008) *Capital Resurgent: Roots of the Neoliberal Revolution*.

Dymski, G. A., G. Epstein, and R. Pollin, eds. (1993) *Transforming the U.S. Financial System: Equity and Efficiency for the 21st Century*. Washington: Economic Policy Institute.

Eichengreen, B. (2007) *The European Economy Since 1945*. Princeton, NJ: Princeton University Press.

Epstein, G., D. Plihon, A. Giannola, and C. Weller. (2009) "Finance without Financiers," *Papeles de Europa*, Vol. 19, September, Madrid: Universidad Complutense de Madrid (in Spanish),pp. 140–78.

Epstein, G. (1982) "Federal Reserve Politics and Monetary Instability." In Alan Stone and Edward J. Harpham, eds., *The Political Economy of Public Policy*, Beverly Hills: Sage Publications, pp. 211–39.

ed. (2005b) *Financialization and the World Economy*. Northampton, MA: Edward Elgar Press.

(2007) "Central Banks As Agents of Economic Development." In Ha- Joon Chang, ed. *Institutional Change and Economic Development*. United Nations University and Anthem Press, pp. 95–113.

(2009) "Taming High Finance: Why the Obama-Geithner Plan Won't Work." *New Labor Forum*, September.

(2010) Finance without Financiers: Prospects for Radical Change In Financial Governance, the David Gordon Lecture, *Review of Radical Political Economy*, 2010.

(2010–present) Triple Crisis Blog. http://triplecrisis.com/gerald-epstein-on-financial-reform/

Epstein, G. and A. Jayadev. (2009) "The Rise of Rentier Incomes in OECD Countries: Financialization, Central Bank Policy and Labor Solidarity." In Gerald A. Epstein, ed., *Financialization and the World Economy*. Northampton, MA: E. Elgar, pp. 46–74.

Epstein, G. and J. Schor, (1995) The Federal Reserve-Treasury Accord and the Construction of the Postwar Monetary Regime in the United States," *Social Concept*, pp. 7–48.

(1992) "Structural Determinants and Economic Effects of Capital Controls in OECD Countries." In Tariq Banuri and Juliet Schor, *Financial Openness and National Autonomy*. Oxford: Clarendon Press. pp. 136–61.

Essential Information/Consumer Education Foundation. (2009) "Sold-Out: How Wall Street and Washington Betrayed America." www.wallstreetwatch.org

Ferguson, T. and R. Johnson. (2009a) "Too Big to Bail: "The Paulson Put," Presidential Politics, and the Global Financial Meltdown; Part I: From Shadow Financial System to Shadow Bailout." *International Journal of Political Economy*, Vol. **38**, No. 1 (Spring).

(2009b) "Too Big to Bail: "The Paulson Put," Presidential Politics, and the Global Financial Meltdown; Part II: Fatal Reversal – Single Payer and Back." *International Journal of Political Economy*, Vol. **38**, No. 1 (Summer).

Gerschenkron, A. (1962) *Economic Backwardness in Historical Perspective.* Cambridge, MA: Harvard University Press, Belknap Press.

Gordon, D. M. (1996) *Fat and Mean: The Corporate Squeeze of Working Americans and the Myth of Managerial "Downsizing."* New York: The Free Press.

Grabel, I. (1997) "Savings, Investment and Functional Efficiency: A Comparative Examination of National Financial Complexes," in Robert Pollin (ed.), *The Macroeconomics of Finance, Saving, and Investment,* Ann Arbor: University of Michigan Press, pp. 251–97.

Greider, W. (1987) *The Secrets of the Temple.* New York: Simon and Schuster.

   (2010) "It's Going to Take a While to Bring Wall Street Under Heel." Alternet. http://www.alternet.org/story/147415/it%27s_going_to_take_a_while_to_ bring_wall_st._under_heel/

Hodgman, D. R. (1973) "Credit Controls in Western Europe: An Evaluative Review." In The Federal Reserve Bank of Boston, *Credit Allocation Techniques and Monetary Policy.* Boston: Federal Reserve Bank, pp. 137–61.

Johnson, S. and J. Kwak. 2010. *13 Bankers.* New York: Pantheon.

Kindleberger, C. P. (with R. Aliber) 1978; 2005. *Manias, Panics and Crashes: A History of Financial Crises.* New York: Basic Books, Inc.

The World In Depression, 1929–1939. Berkeley: University of California Press. 1973

Kotlikoff, L. (2010) *Jimmy Stewart is Dead: Ending the World's Ongoing Financial Plague with Limited Purpose Banking.* Hoboken, NJ: John Wiley & Sons.

Krugman, P. (2009) "Making Banking Boring." *New York Times,* April 9.

   2011. "Rule By Rentiers." *New York Times,* June 10.

Kuttner, R. (2009) "Financial Regulation After the Fall." Demos. http://www.demos. org/publication.cfm?currentpublicationID=B8B65B84–3FF4–6C82–5F3F–750B53E44E1B

   (2009) "Ten Radical Remedies America Needs." *The American Prospect.* http://prospect.org/cs/articles?article=ten_radical_remedies_america_needs

   (2010) *Presidency In Peril.* White River Junction, VT: Chelsea Green Publishing.

Maisel, S. (1973) *Managing the Dollar.* New York: Norton.

Mehrling, P., D. Grad, and D. Neilson. (2011) "The Evolution of Last Resort Operations in the Global Credit Crisis." www.danielneilson.com/media/pdf/grad-mehrling-neilson-latest.pdf

Morgenson, G. and J. Rosner. (2011) *Reckless Endangerment: How Outsized Ambition, Greed, and Corruption Led to Economic Armageddon.* New York: Times Books.

Moseley, F. (2009) "Time for Permanent Nationalization of the Banks: If the Banks are Too Big to Fail, They Should be Public." *Dollars and Sense Magazine,* March/April.

Palley, T. (2003a) "A Better Way To Regulate Financial Markets: Asset Based Reserve Requirements." http://www.thomaspalley.com/?p=161

   (2003b) "Asset Price Bubbles and the Case for Asset Based Reserve Requirements." *Challenge,* vol. **46**, no. 3, May/June.

   (2010) *Asset Based Reserve Requirements.* www.tompalley.com

Pollin, R. (1993) "Public Credit Allocation Through the Federal Reserve." In Gary A. Dymski, Gerald Epstein, and Robert Pollin, eds. *Transforming The U.S. Financial System: Equity and Efficiency for the 21st Century.* Armonk, NY: M. E. Sharpe, Ch. 12.

"Financial Structures and Egalitarian Economic Policy", *New Left Review, 214,* *November/December,* pp. 26–61.

(1997). editor. The Macroeconomics of Saving, Finance and Investment., Ann Arbor, MI: University of Michigan Press, pp. 309–66.

(2010) "18 Million Jobs By 2010." *The Nation Magazine,* March 8. http://www.thenation.com/article/18-million-jobs-2012

Pollin, R. and A. Zhu. (2005) "Economic Growth: A Cross-Country Nonlinear Analysis." PERI. http://www.peri.umass.edu/236/hash/ae49da3487ff44f6dffdb47f6cc2185b/publication/185/

Pollin, R., H. Garrett-Peltier, J. Heintz, and H. Scharber. (2008) "Green Recovery." Center for American Progress and PERI. http://www.peri.umass.edu/fileadmin/pdf/other_publication_types/peri_report.pdf

Schlesinger, T. (2001) "Six Ideas for Introducing the Fed to the 21st Century." *FOMC Alert,* March 20, Vol. 5, Issue 2.

(2004) "Institutional Design Issues at the Federal Reserve." *Remarks to The National Economists Club,* Washington, DC, June 24.

Seidman, E. (2009) Executive Summary in Community Development Investment Center, *The Economic Crisis and Community Development Finance: An Industry Assessment,* Federal Reserve Bank of San Francisco, Working Paper 2009 – 05, June, pp. 6–7. http://frbsf.org/cdinvestments

Taub, J. (2009) Enablers of Exuberance: Legal Acts and Omissions that Facilitated the Global Financial Crisis". PERI. http://www.peri.umass.edu/fileadmin/pdf/conference_papers/SAFER/Taub_Enablers_Exuberance.pdf

Thurow, L. (1972) "Proposals for Re-Channeling Funds to Meet Social Priorities." In "Policies for a More Competitive Financial System" Conference Proceedings of the Federal Reserve Bank of Boston.

U.S. Congress, House of Representatives, 92nd Congress, 2nd Session. (1972) *Foreign Experiences with Monetary Policies to Promote Economic and Social Priority Programs.*

U.S. Congress, Joint Economic Committee. (1981) *Monetary Policy, Selective Credit Policy and Industrial Policy in France, Britain, West Germany and Sweden.* Washington, DC: Government Printing Office.

Wolfson, M. (1993) "The Evolution of the Financial System and the Possibilities for Reform." In Gary A. Dymski, Gerald Epstein, and Robert Pollin, eds. *Transforming The U.S. Financial System: Equity and Efficiency for the 21st Century.* Armonk, NY: M. E. Sharpe, Ch. 6.

Zysman, J. (1983) *Governments, Markets and Growth: Financial Systems and the Politics of Industrialization.* Ithaca, NY: Cornell University Press.

TEN

Fiscal Policy

The Recent Record and Lessons for the Future

Dean Baker

For most of the last quarter century, a main focus of fiscal policy by the mainstream of the economics profession has been deficit reduction. This agenda dominated concerns not only during the high deficit years of the Reagan administration, but even when the government was running a budget surplus in the last years of the Clinton administration. At that time, paying off the national debt was considered an important goal of fiscal policy with the major debate being between those who preferred to set the earliest possible deadline and those who proposed a slower path toward elimination of public debt.

This chapter analyzes the logic and evidence that support the argument for deficit reduction. The first section outlines the motivation for lower deficits as put forward by the Clinton administration – increasing the investment components of GDP – and the mechanisms through which this is supposed to be accomplished. The second section describes the successful deficit reduction of the Clinton presidency and evaluates the extent to which it achieved its goal of increasing the investment components of GDP. I then examine the fiscal policy of the George W. Bush presidency and the impact that it had on the course of growth. The fourth section draws on the lessons of recent experience to propose principles for a sustainable fiscal path for fostering long-term growth. These principles offer a guide to policies designed to promote recovery from the Great Recession, as well as applying more generally.

The fiscal policies pursued in the Clinton and Bush years can be viewed as natural experiments. Under Clinton, there was a sharp movement toward smaller deficits, both as a result of considerable spending restraint, but also sizable tax increases. By contrast, fiscal policy in the Bush years moved aggressively in the opposite direction, with sizable increases in spending (primarily military) accompanied by substantial cuts in taxes. Rarely has the United States seen sharper changes in fiscal policy over such a short period. If the conventional view of the impact of deficit on growth and the economy is correct, then we should be able to see evidence of this impact in the sharp shift from a policy of deficit reduction to a period of substantial deficits.

1. The Logic of Deficit Reduction

The basic mainstream argument for deficit reduction in the context of the U.S. economy is straightforward.[1] In principle, budget deficits lead to higher interest rates. Higher interest rates discourage investment, thereby reducing the investment share of GDP. Furthermore, higher U.S. interest rates encourage both foreign and domestic investors to hold more dollar-denominated assets, to take advantage of the higher returns, raising the value of the dollar. The higher-valued dollar leads to more imports (since imports will now be less expensive in the United States) and fewer exports (since U.S. exports will be more expensive for people living in other countries). The result is lower trade surplus or a larger trade deficit.

In effect, deficits lower the two components of GDP that generate investment for the future. They directly reduce domestic investment and indirectly lower the trade surplus, which correspond to the accumulation of foreign financial and real assets. Foreign assets increase national income in future years; they allow the country to consume more than it produces because of its income from assets abroad.

The goal of deficit reduction is to reverse this course. Deficit reduction in principle implies reducing consumption components of GDP: either government consumption or the indirect reduction of private consumption as a result of tax increases that reduce disposable income. If the government cuts spending and/or raises taxes, it will borrow less in credit markets. Other things equal, fiscal hawks argue that this should lower interest rates, raise investment, reduce the value of the dollar, and increase net exports. In other words, the investment components of GDP replace the consumption components, creating a more prosperous future.

---

[1] This discussion ignores current concerns about large budget deficits leading to insolvency, which has been a significant threat to Greece and other countries tied to the euro. In the United States, the national debt is denominated in dollars, and therefore, insolvency is not a serious possibility since the government can freely print more currency in the event that it ever had difficulty selling its debt in credit markets. Although printing money could lead to inflation, this possibility is remote in an economy with massive unemployment. However, inflation could pose a greater threat if the economy moved closer to its capacity.

Although the conventional theory is fairly straightforward, there are several complicating factors. First, the effect of deficit reduction on interest rates is not as clear as the simple mainstream theory asserts.[2] The notion that interest rates respond quickly and unambiguously to deficit reduction is not well-supported by the data. The determinants of interest rates are complex and empirical studies have not firmly established that lower deficits necessarily lead to large and sustained declines in interest rates. If interest rates do not drop in response to deficit reduction, then there is no basis for believing that the investment components of GDP will increase, since both the business investment and net export channels depend on a fall in interest rates.

The extent to which interest rates decline in response to a reduction in the deficit is also dependent, in part, on the response of the central bank. If the central bank cooperates with the government and pursues an expansionary monetary policy, then it is more likely that lower deficits will be associated with lower interest rates. Future expectations of deficits and inflation can also affect interest rates. Concerns that a low deficit policy may not be sustained or that the economy will be prone to higher inflation in the near future may offset the impact of lower deficits on interest rates. In short, the link between lower deficits and lower interest rates is at best very weak and certainly cannot be assumed to hold in all circumstances.

The second complication to the mainstream theory is that the direct effect of deficit reduction always reduces demand. Cutbacks in government spending, as well as tax increases, lower the level of demand in the economy. Investment is sensitive not only to interest rates but also to the rate of growth of demand (Chirinko, 1993). If the demand effects of deficit reduction policies are not offset, then it is entirely possible that the slower growth will hurt investment more than any decline in interest rates will stimulate capital formation. In this case, deficit reduction could simply mean lower output without any upturn in investment.

This unfortunate outcome is especially likely if deficit reduction occurs in an economy operating well below its full-employment level of output. In this situation, interest rates are already likely to be quite low so that the impact of any marginal reduction in interest rates on investment would be small (the environment following the Great Recession provides a good example). Also, firms will typically have large amounts of excess capacity and therefore see little need to invest to meet demand growth in the near future.

[2]   See e.g., Barth et al. 1991.

The response of net exports to deficit reduction is even more questionable. In principle, a lower interest rate should reduce the value of the dollar, but the correlation between movements in the dollar and changes in interest rates is very weak. Many factors affect the exchange rate, with domestic interest rates not necessarily being an especially important one.[3] Needless to say, if the dollar does not drop in response to a fall in interest rates, then there is no reason to expect an improvement in the trade balance. This is important in the context of a deficit-reduction policy since the increase in net exports might well be more important in theory than any increase in investment. President Clinton's Council of Economic Advisors expected that as much as 40 percent of the demand response to lower interest rates would be in the form of higher net exports.[4]

There are also several reasons why, even in theory, deficit reduction may not have the desired effects on investment and net exports. First, lower interest rates can also induce more consumption, especially of durable goods. If the sensitivity of consumption to interest rates is large enough, then the effect of deficit reduction could be largely reflected in private consumption. In other words, private consumption may simply replace public consumption insofar as deficit reduction is brought about through reductions in public spending. This result is especially likely if the price of assets, like corporate equity and housing, rise in response to a fall in interest rates. The resulting wealth effect on consumption will amplify the direct interest rate effect.

In addition, a lower deficit may not be associated with a lower-valued dollar because the path of deficit reduction may boost investor confidence in the dollar.[5] In this case, deficit reduction could actually be associated with a higher-valued dollar, eliminating any possibility that it will lead to a rise in net exports. Given the erratic movements in currency markets over the last two decades, this is certainly a plausible outcome.

In short, although there are theoretical arguments as to why lower deficits could lead to increased investment and increased net exports, there are also theoretical reasons that suggest this link may be weak or even nonexistent. The relationship between interest rates and budget deficits is weak. Similarly, the relationship between interest rates and investment is weak and could easily be offset by declines in demand associated with deficit

[3] There are many factors that can limit the impact of changes in the interest rates on currency values; for example, inflation expectations and anticipated stock returns. Sims (1992) reviews the evidence on the link.

[4] Economic Report of the President, 1994, p 87.

[5] See Kim and Roubini, 2008.

reduction, as argued by Cynamon and Fazzari (this volume, Chapter 11). Finally, the link between interest rates and the value of the dollar is also very weak.

If deficit reduction does not boost investment or net exports, then its usefulness as a strategy to promote long-term prosperity is dubious. There are limits to which any country, including the United States, can raise its debt to GDP ratio. However, because the United States has the ability to print its own currency (unlike individual states or countries in the euro zone), it can typically service its debt through money creation, unless inflation poses a problem, an unlikely case unless the economy is near its full-employment level of output. This makes the maximum feasible debt to income ratio very high in deep recessions (such as the Great Recession), since investors have no qualms about the capacity of the government to service its debt.

Furthermore, the typical view of the debt as a burden on future generations is also misleading. Debt held by the public leads to redistribution from taxpayers in general to holders of the debt. It is not a net burden for the country as a whole, except insofar as taxes needed to pay the interest have a distortionary impact.[6] If the debt is financed by increased central bank holdings of debt, as should be the case in the high unemployment environment of the Great Recession, there should be no burden resulting from the debt at all. In fact, if the spending financed through the deficit leads to better infrastructure and/or crowds in more private investment, it will make future generations richer, not poorer.

2. Deficit Reduction in the Clinton Administration

When President Clinton took office in 1993, he had two conflicting agendas that he promised to pursue: 1) a "public investment" agenda centered on promoting investment in infrastructure, research and development, and education and training (this position was most strongly identified with Labor Secretary Robert Reich) and 2) deficit reduction – the belief that the top priority must be to reduce the deficit to a sustainable level, if not eliminate it altogether (this position was most strongly associated with Treasury Secretary Lloyd Bentsen and Robert Rubin, the head of Clinton's National Economic Council).

---

[6] There is a concern about foreign ownership of debt, but this is a function of the trade deficit. For a given trade deficit, there is no more burden created for future generations if it is financed by foreign purchases of government bonds, as opposed to foreign purchases of private assets.

Clearly it was not easy to both promote substantial increases in public investment and reduce the deficit at the same time. After the defeat of a modest stimulus package in the summer of 1993, the main focus of Clinton's economic policy through the rest of his administration was the reduction of the deficit. As the deficit fell more rapidly than had been anticipated, the goal shifted to a balanced budget and later to paying off the national debt. Throughout this process, public investment took a back seat, with most categories of public investment no higher (measured relative to the size of the economy) at the end of Clinton's administration than at the beginning. This is especially striking since there was a substantial reduction in defense spending in the Clinton years. In effect, none of this reduction was associated with a shift to nondefense investment spending.[7]

The rapid decline in the deficit was partly owing to tax increases and spending restraint, and partly because of an unexpected surge in tax revenue.[8] In fiscal 1992, the last full fiscal year before President Clinton took office, the deficit was $290.4 billion or 4.7 percent of GDP. The deficit in 1997, the last budget prepared in his first term in office, was just $22.0 billion, or 0.3 percent of GDP. In 2000, the surplus peaked at $236.4 billion, an amount equal to 2.4 percent of GDP.

Whatever the cause, President Clinton certainly could boast of solid economic growth, especially through his second term in office. For his presidency as whole, the annual real GDP growth rate averaged 3.6 percent. Employment growth averaged 2.8 million jobs per year and the median hourly real wage rose at a 0.5 percent annual rate. For the second term, annual real GDP growth averaged 3.9 percent, employment creation again averaged 2.8 million jobs per year, and the real median wage grew at a 2.0 percent annual rate, with unemployment falling to just 4.0 percent in 2000.[9] By these statistics, and most other measures, the economy's performance during Clinton's second term was the best since the late sixties.

---

[7] Federal nondefense spending on investment was equal to 1.8 percent of GDP in fiscal 2001, the same share as in 1992. Investment spending over the Clinton years averaged 1.7 percent of GDP (Office of Management and Budget, 2005, table 9.1).

[8] The tax share of GDP increased from 18.1 percent in 1994, when the Clinton tax increases were already fully in place, to 20.9 percent in 2000. The main factor appears to be a surge in capital gain income owing to the stock bubble. This showed up both in capital gains taxes and also in normal income taxes because short-term capital gains are taxed as normal income.

[9] Data on GDP growth, job growth, and unemployment are taken from the Economic Report of the President, 2004, tables B-2, B46, and B42, respectively. Data on the median wage is taken from Mishel, et al., 2002, table 2.6.

The proponents of deficit reduction have interpreted this performance as a vindication of their program. However, closer examination shows that this was not the case. According to the supporters of fiscal austerity, lower deficits were supposed to reduce public sector borrowing and lead to lower interest rates. Lower interest rates should then stimulate both investment and net exports (by lowering the value of the dollar), which would then boost the economy. The boost to investment would not only increase demand, it would also raise the capital stock and thereby boost labor productivity and potential output.

Regardless of the validity of this theoretical view of the economy, the pattern described clearly does not explain the growth spurt in the mid and late nineties. None of the pieces of the argument fits reality. Real interest rates did fall, but not by an especially large amount; there was an upturn in investment, but it was not nearly large enough to produce the sort of upturn in productivity the economy actually experienced; and the dollar and net exports went the wrong way – the dollar rose and net exports fell.[10]

Table 10.1 shows real interest rates for 10-year treasury bonds, 30-year mortgages, and high-grade corporate debt for the last three years of the major business cycles from the sixties through the nineties.[11] Although the real interest rates of the second Clinton term are somewhat lower than during the 1980s cycle, they are much higher than in either the 1960s or 1970s cycles. Even the gap with the end of the Reagan years appears less significant for private debt. When the government began running a surplus and paying down its debt, investors were willing to pay a scarcity premium to obtain U.S. government debt, increasing the spread between public and private debt. Of course, it is the interest rate on private debt that affects private investment.

Modest declines in interest rates do not produce explosions in investment, and no such explosion took place in the Clinton years. Table 10.2 shows the shares of the major components of GDP for the middle Clinton years (1995–97), the late Clinton years (1998–2000) and the late 1970s and late 1980s. Although there was an increase in investment over this period, it was dwarfed by the increase in consumption. The investment levels of the

---

[10] Remarkably, discussion of the link between the budget deficit and the trade deficit (through the mechanism of an inflated dollar pushed higher because of high interest rates) virtually disappeared from public debate in the late nineties. This link had been a staple of the conventional economic wisdom from the eighties through the mid-nineties (e.g., Dornbusch, 1985).

[11] The year-over-year change in the GDP implicit price deflator was subtracted from the nominal rate to obtain the real rate.

Table 10.1. *Real interest rates in final three years of recent business cycles*

	Treasury bond	Mortgages	Corporate bonds
	(10-year)	(30-year)	Aaa
1967	1.9	3.4	2.4
1968	1.4	2.7	1.9
1969	2.0	2.8	2.0
Average	1.8	2.9	2.1
1977	1.0	2.6	1.6
1978	1.4	2.6	1.7
1979	1.1	2.5	1.3
Average	1.2	2.6	1.6
1987	5.7	6.6	6.7
1988	5.5	5.8	6.3
1989	4.7	6.3	5.5
Average	5.3	6.2	6.2
1998	4.2	6.0	5.4
1999	4.3	5.6	5.6
2000	3.8	5.3	5.4
Average	4.1	5.6	5.5

Source: Economic Report of the President, 2004, table B-73.

Clinton years were higher than those at the end of the 1980s, but they never reached the peaks hit in the late 1970s. It is also important to note that the Clinton years look even less impressive if net investment is used as the basis for comparison, as shown in column seven of Table 10.2.[12]

Finally, it is informative to adjust the investment data for the treatment of car leasing in the national accounts. A consumer-purchased car counts as consumption. However, a leased car counts as investment. There was a substantial increase in car leasing over the course of the 1990s. This shift to car leasing was one of the factors in the upturn in measured investment. Adjusting for this shift, the net investment share of GDP at the peak of the 1990s cycle was less than a full percentage point greater than that achieved during the 1980s.

---

[12] The gross investment share is inflated owing to the fact that a large portion of investment in the period was in short-lived capital (computers and software) that depreciate quickly.

Table 10.2. *Historical perspectives on the composition of GDP and productivity growth in the Clinton years*

	Shares of GDP		Investment adjusted for car leasing	Housing	Government	Net exports	Net investment	Productivity growth
	Consumption	Investment						
1977	63.0	11.3		5.4	20.4	-1.1	4.9	1.6
1978	62.3	12.2		5.7	19.8	-1.1	5.8	1.3
1979	62.1	13.0		5.5	19.5	-0.9	6.1	-0.4
Average	62.4	12.2		5.6	19.9	-1.0	5.6	0.8
1987	65.4	11.1	11.0	4.9	21.1	-3.1	2.8	0.3
1988	65.7	11.0	10.9	4.7	20.4	-2.2	2.9	1.6
1989	65.6	11.1	11.0	4.4	20.0	-1.6	2.8	0.7
Average	65.6	11.1	11.0	4.7	20.5	-2.3	2.8	0.9
1995	67.3	10.9	10.6	4.1	18.5	-1.2	2.3	0.9
1996	67.2	11.2	10.8	4.3	18.1	-1.2	2.6	2.5
1997	66.8	11.7	11.3	4.2	17.7	-1.2	3.0	2.0
Average	67.1	11.3	10.9	4.2	18.1	-1.2	2.6	1.8
1998	67.2	12.0	11.6	4.4	17.4	-1.8	3.4	2.6
1999	67.8	12.2	11.8	4.6	17.5	-2.8	3.6	2.3
2000	68.7	12.6	12.2	4.6	17.5	-3.9	3.7	3.0
Average	67.9	12.3	11.9	4.5	17.5	-2.8	3.6	2.6

Source: Economic Report of the President, tables B1 and B49.*

* The adjustment for car leasing subtracts the amount paid out for leasing of motor vehicles, United States Department of Commerce, National Income Product Accounts, table 2.4.5U, Line 190. This amount represents the flow of services coming from leased vehicles in a given year. This should approximate the amount of investment recorded in NIPA accounts for vehicles purchased to be used as leased vehicles. This amount had been well below 0.1 percent of GDP until the 1990s when it grew to more than 0.4 percent. The net investment figure in column seven is based on the gross investment figure minus spending on leased cars, shown in column three.

In spite of the limited upturn in investment, there was undeniably a sharp upturn in productivity growth. Annual rates of productivity growth are shown in the final column of Table 10.2. As can be seen, productivity growth turned sharply upward beginning in 1996, even before there had been any substantial upturn in investment (the upturn actually began in the fourth quarter of 1995, when productivity grew at a 3.1 percent annual rate). There is no plausible story linking the surge in productivity growth that began in 1995 to the increases in investment witnessed up to that point.[13]

Rather than being attributable to investment induced by deficit reduction, the surge in productivity appears to have been an exogenous development associated with information technology. This is demonstrated most clearly by the Bureau of Labor Statistics' measure of technology-induced productivity growth (multifactor productivity growth). Technology contributed an average of just 0.4 percentage points to productivity growth over the years from 1973 to 1995. This increased by 0.7 percentage points to an annual rate of 1.1 percentage points in the years 1995 to 2000. Whether or not the Clinton-era policies made it easier to embrace these technologies is an open question, but clearly deficit reduction cannot be given the credit for the upturn.[14]

The rise of investment predicted by proponents of deficit reduction was minimal at best. However, net exports actually went the wrong way. Early in the Clinton administration, the dollar did fall against most major currencies and this outcome was trumpeted by many economists as one of the benefits of deficit reduction, with the expectation that a lower-valued dollar would lead to an increase in net exports. Events loosely followed this script in the

---

[13] In standard growth models, investment has a very modest impact on growth. For example, in a Cobb-Douglas production function, the coefficient on capital is usually 0.3. This means that a 1 percent increase in the capital stock leads to an increase of output of 0.3 percent. If the capital to output ratio is approximately 2 to 1, this means that an increase in investment equal to 2.0 percentage points of GDP would only increase output and productivity growth by 0.3 percentage points. The increase in investment witnessed by the time of the productivity upsurge was far less than 2.0 percentage points of GDP, and the increase in the annual rate of productivity growth was more than a full percentage point from the prior growth rates. The increase in investment during the Clinton years was far too small to explain the upsurge in productivity that the economy actually experienced.

[14] Some of this uptick in productivity growth is because of an increase in the depreciation share of output. Computers and software become obsolete quickly. If productivity growth comes from growth in GDP that does not translate into growth in net output, it provides no benefit to the economy or society. Also, some of the growth depends on measures of computer quality that show very rapid increases. Insofar as these increases in measured quality do not lead to increases in output, then this gain in productivity growth will also have no benefit to society (see Baker, 2007).

first half of the Clinton years – the trade deficit was 1.2 percent of GDP in 1997, compared to a peak deficit equal to 3.1 percent of GDP in 1987.

However, beginning in 1996 there was a sharp turn of events, with the dollar starting to rise. This rise was associated with Robert Rubin's appointment as Treasury Secretary. Unlike his predecessor, Rubin committed the country to a strong dollar policy. This commitment gained force with the East Asian financial crisis in 1997. The crisis, and the IMF's treatment of the victims of the crisis, led much of the developing world to focus their economic policy on accumulating enormous reserves of dollars in order to avoid being in the same situation as the East Asian countries in 1997. The flight to dollars led to a rise in the dollar of 26 percent on a trade-weighted basis.[15] The higher dollar had the positive short-term effect of making low-cost imported goods available. This reduced inflation and raised living standards for the country as a whole.[16] However, it also led to a rapid increase in the trade deficit. The movements in the dollar and trade deficit are shown in Figure 10.1. By 2000, the trade deficit had risen to a then record 3.9 percent of GDP.

As the data in Table 10.2 shows, the largest increase in GDP shares occurred in consumption, not investment. The consumption share of GDP in 2000 was 68.7 percent, more than three full percentage points higher than its share at the peak of the previous business cycle. There was a simple explanation for this consumption surge – the wealth effect associated with the stock bubble. At this point, there is a large body of literature linking stock wealth with consumption.[17] The conventional range of estimates is that an additional dollar of stock wealth leads to an additional three to four cents of consumption spending.

At the peak of the stock bubble in 2000, the total value of the equity issues held by the household sector was $11.0 trillion. This corresponded to a price to earnings ratio of 30.[18] Historically, the price to earnings ratio has

---

[15] This is the cumulative rise in the real value of the dollar from 1996 to 2001, using the Broad Index, Economic Report of the President, table B-110.

[16] It is important to note the redistributive effect of a high dollar. It reduces incomes in the traded goods sector, most importantly manufacturing, by lowering the price of competing goods. This means that individuals who are not working in sectors that directly face international competition gain from an overvalued dollar at the expense of workers who do face this competition.

[17] See Dynan and Maki, 2001, and Maki and Palumbo, 2001. Cynamon and Fazzari (this volume, Chapter 6) question the extent to which the decline in savings in the 1990s and 2000s was driven by the rise in stock and housing wealth. Although clearly other factors played a role in this decline, it is difficult to dismiss the fact that an extraordinary run-up in the ratio of wealth to GDP coincided with a sharp decline in the saving rate.

[18] The value of stock market wealth is taken from the Federal Reserve Board's Flow of Fund's data, table B.100, lines 24 and 25. The basis for the price to earnings ratio at the peak of

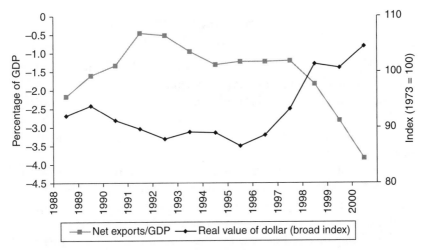

Figure 10.1. The trade deficit as a percentage of GDP and the value of the dollar. *Source:* Economic Report of the President, 2010.

averaged approximately 14.5. Measured against this ratio, at the peak of the stock bubble in 2000, households held approximately $5.0 trillion of bubble wealth in stocks, which would have led to $150 to $200 billion in additional consumption owing to the wealth effect. This would explain most of the upturn in consumption seen in this period, as the savings rate fell to what were at the time record lows, hitting 2.3 percent in 2000.[19] In short, the main prop of the Clinton-era prosperity was a consumption boom, driven by the stock bubble.

the bubble is the value of outstanding corporate equity, $17.8 trillion (Board of Governors of the Federal Reserve System, Flow of Funds data, table L.213, line 19) and the after tax profits of U.S. corporations, $552.7 billion (Economic Report of the President, 2004, table B-28).

[19] This figure likely overstates the saving rate out of disposable income. The statistical discrepancy turned negative in the late 90s as income-side GDP exceeded output-side GDP, reversing the normal pattern. The most obvious explanation for this shift is that capital gains income was being recorded as normal income. This shift was reversed when the stock bubble collapsed over the years 2000–2002. Income-side GDP again exceeded output-side GDP in the 3rd quarter of 2004 driven by the growth of the housing bubble. A regression of the statistical discrepancy on eight quarters of lags of the value of the stock market and housing market produces highly significant coefficients for both variables. For the period from the first quarter of 1990 through the third quarter of 2009, the regression gave the result:Statistical discrepancy = 0.16 -0.036 SM (lags 4–12) -0.11 HM (lags 4–12) R^2 = 0.572 (9.92) (-5.19) (-8.15) t-stats in parenthesisIf disposable income was in fact overstated as a result of capital gains being recorded as normal income, then it implies that the saving rate is lower than the data shows, since savings is defined as disposable income minus consumption.

3. The Collapse of the Stock Bubble and
Fiscal Policy in the Bush Years

The collapse of the stock bubble over the years 2000–2002 pushed the economy into a sustained downturn. Whereas the official dating puts the recession at just seven months, from March of 2001 to November of 2001, the economy continued to shed jobs all through 2002 and most of the way through 2003. It was only in September of 2003 that the economy finally began to create jobs again.

The difficulty recovering from the recession is attributable to the fact that the 2001 downturn was caused by the collapse of an asset bubble. The end of the stock bubble was a hit to both investment and consumption. The collapse of the NASDAQ put an end to the tech-sector investment that was being financed directly by stock issues. Nominal investment fell by more than $50 billion from 2000 to 2001, leading to a decline of a full percentage point in the investment share of GDP. The collapse of the bubble also crimped consumption as almost $10 trillion in stock wealth had vanished at the market lows in the summer of 2002. Prior postwar recessions were directly attributable to the Fed's decision to raise interest rates to slow the economy. Higher rates led to a falloff in home building and car purchases. To escape a traditional recession, the Fed simply lowers interest rates, which boosts home construction and car sales, an effect that is especially strong since the falloff in the recession leads to pent-up demand in these big-ticket sectors. However, declines in housing and car buying had not caused the 2001 recession, so it could not be reversed simply by a cut in interest rates.

The Bush administration did respond to the recession with the tax-cutting agenda that it put forward in the 2000 campaign as a response to the record budget surpluses that the country had been running prior to the downturn. Between the impact of the tax cuts and the recession itself, the surpluses quickly vanished. The wars in Afghanistan and Iraq also led to large increases in defense spending. Measured as a share of GDP, the surplus was nearly halved from 2000 to 2001. By 2002, the economy was again running a deficit, which rose to 3.4 percent of GDP by 2003. This figure is about three quarters the size of the peak deficits prior to the Clinton years discussed previously. Furthermore, the swing from surplus to deficit was one of the largest changes in the U.S. government fiscal position of the postwar period, measured as a share of the economy.

In spite of the Bush-era deficits, there is very little evidence for any crowding out of investment. Interest rates remained at relatively low

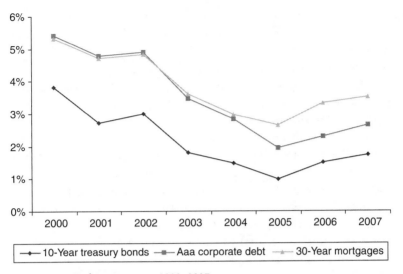

Figure 10.2. Real interest rates, 2000–2007.
Source: Economic Report of the President, 2010 and author's calculations.

levels throughout this period, undoubtedly a response to the weakness of the economy. In fact, real interest rates throughout the Bush presidency were lower than they had been at any point during the Clinton years, in spite of the shift from budget surpluses to deficits, as shown in Figure 10.2. Arguably, the low interest rates were owing to the global nature of the downturn in 2001 and the fact that interest rates were low worldwide because of a savings glut for most of the decade. However, insofar as this is true, it suggests that domestic saving is largely irrelevant for investment. Had the United States run smaller deficits or surpluses during the Bush presidency, it would have had no noticeable impact on investment.

The only factor that will have a substantial impact on the investment components of GDP would then be the value of the dollar through its impact on net exports. The course of the dollar over the last decade was not very conducive to promoting exports. The dollar rose in value at the start of the decade, undoubtedly driven in part by a flight to safety given the uncertainty surrounding the collapse of stock bubbles in the United States and elsewhere. The September 11th attack, followed by the wars in Afghanistan and later Iraq, no doubt added to this uncertainty. The decision by developing countries to accumulate large amounts of reserves as protection against financial panics also played an important role in the demand for the dollar.

In addition, there was a deliberate effort by several developing countries, most notably China, to keep their currencies low relative to the dollar as part of their development strategy.

These factors all helped to keep the dollar at levels that led to large and growing trade deficits. The trade deficit was reduced only modestly as a result of the recession, and then began to rise rapidly in the recovery. This was a predictable outcome of an overvalued currency.

It is worth noting that in this story, fiscal policy played little obvious role in the crowding out of net exports. If the United States had run lower deficits or returned to the Clinton-era surpluses, it is difficult to imagine that real interest rates would have been much lower. Furthermore, even if real interest rates had fallen, it is difficult to envision a scenario in which there would have been much impact on the value of the dollar.

Foreign investors and central banks were holding dollar assets for reasons that had little direct connection to the rate of return. Developing countries would have felt the same need to accumulate reserves, even if the interest rate on dollar assets had been considerably lower. Similarly, the pattern whereby investors grab up dollars in periods of uncertainty would not disappear if interest rates on dollar assets were lower. Nor is it likely that the developing countries pursuing an export-led growth path would have followed a different route in response to lower U.S. interest rates.

For these reasons, there is likely now very little relationship between the value of the dollar and U.S. interest rates. This means that budget deficits will have very little impact on the trade deficit, except insofar as they can increase output by bringing the economy closer to full employment. This is important because it suggests that whatever relationship there may once have been between U.S. budget deficits and the investment components of GDP no longer exists.

4. Principles for Sustainable Fiscal Policy

The prior discussion suggests that there is no simple theoretical or empirical connection between lower deficits and an increase in the investment components of GDP. The link between lower deficits and increased investment and net exports is at best weak, even in theory. The actual experience with fiscal policy over the last two decades provides little reason to believe that tight fiscal policy is an effective growth strategy. The reduction in demand associated with lower deficits in the 1990s was offset primarily by higher consumption, some of it spurred directly by lower interest rates and some of it coming as a result of the wealth effect from the stock bubble.

Although there was some decline in the value of the dollar and a resulting improvement in the trade deficit in the first years after the deficit-reduction policy was implemented, this was completely reversed in the latter part of the decade. The dollar rose sharply in value leading to what were, at the time, record trade deficits, even as the budget shifted to record surpluses.

Under the Bush administration, the dollar edged lower even as the budget shifted sharply from surplus to deficits. Although nonresidential investment was somewhat weaker during the Bush years than the Clinton years, this is much more easily explained by weak demand and the bursting of the late 1990s tech bubble than by the direct effect of the deficit. Real interest rates were actually lower in the Bush years than they had been during the Clinton years. In short, it is very hard to tie the movements in investment and net exports in the last two decades to the extraordinarily large shifts in fiscal policy.

There are a few obvious lessons from this experience. First, deficit reduction is an extremely questionable route for boosting investment. Even assuming that interest rates fall in response to a serious commitment to lower deficits, there is little reason to believe that investment will increase much. Investment is not very sensitive to interest rates. By contrast, consumption may well prove to be more responsive to interest rates than investment. This would imply that deficit reduction would simply be replacing public consumption with private consumption if done through spending cuts (assuming the cuts are in the consumption portion of government spending), or alternatively replacing public borrowing with private borrowing insofar as tax increases are the basis for the deficit reduction.

The likelihood that consumption will increase more than investment in response to deficit reduction is greater insofar as lower interest rates associated with deficit reduction lead to an increase in asset prices. In this case, the wealth effect from higher asset prices creates a second channel through which lower deficits can lead to higher consumption. In the 1990s, the rise in consumption that resulted from the stock bubble vastly exceeded the rise in investment. Despite the historic budget surpluses, at the peak of the Clinton boom, consumption reached a record share of GDP up to that point in time.

It is possible that there would have been more investment following from the Clinton deficit reduction package had the stock bubble been contained. In this case, the Fed would have allowed interest rates to stay lower longer, possibly leading to more investment. However, the record of investment in the Clinton years provides considerable grounds for skepticism about the effectiveness of deficit reduction in increasing investment.

The link between deficit reduction and net exports seems even more dubious given the experience of the Clinton years. Interest rates are simply one factor that affects the value of the dollar and not necessarily an especially important one. It certainly did not help that during Robert Rubin's tenure as Treasury Secretary, the Clinton administration had an explicit commitment to maintaining a strong dollar and sought to reinforce this commitment with its control of IMF policy. The IMF response to financial crises in the developing world led to an enormous demand for dollar reserves as a defense mechanism. This demand swamped any possible effect that lower U.S. interest rates may have had in lowering the value of the dollar. (Of course, the run-up of stock prices also helped to pull foreign money into the United States.)

If there is no reliable path from lower deficits to increased investment and net exports, then deficit reduction provides a dubious path for fostering long-term growth. However, there is an alternative of sustaining somewhat larger deficits in order to support more public investment. There is considerable literature on the productivity of public capital. Most of it shows that public capital is at least as productive on a dollar-for-dollar basis as private capital (e.g., Aschauer, 1989; Heintz, 2010; Holtz-Eakin, 1992; Munnell, 1990). However, the big advantage from the standpoint of fiscal policy is that it is possible to directly translate government spending into public capital. By contrast, the route between deficit reduction and private investment is extremely indirect, with only a small portion of any deficit reduction likely to end up as increased investment.

This perspective suggests a path of increased spending on physical infrastructure, publicly funded research and development, and education and training that can be financed by sustainable deficits.[20] The productivity-enhancing effects of this spending are likely to vastly exceed any negative effects from the loss of private investment that may be crowded out as a result of public borrowing. If the deficits are constrained so that the debt to GDP ratio remains stable over the cycle, then an ambitious public investment agenda is likely to be the best way to foster long-term growth and economic stability.[21]

---

[20] See Pollin and Baker, 2010 for a fuller agenda of public investment that can be expected to have long-lasting benefits to the economy.

[21] The relevant measure should be the ratio of net debt to GDP, which would exclude the debt held by the Federal Reserve Board. Debt held by the Fed carries no interest burden since the interest payments on this debt are refunded back to the treasury, minus the amount needed to finance the Fed's operations.

Given the weak relationship between deficit reduction and increases in investment and/or net exports, increased spending on public investment needs to meet a rather low bar in order to enhance growth. The logic is very simple. If only a fraction of a dollar in deficit reduction gets translated into an investment component of GDP (e.g., twenty to thirty cents on a dollar) then money committed to public investment rather than used for deficit reduction will be growth maximizing if its return is just 20–30 percent as high as a dollar spent on private investment. Because much of the research on the issue suggests that public investment may actually be more productive on a per-dollar basis, it is very likely that additional spending on public investment meets this test.

Of course, if the economy is typically below full-employment levels of output, as it has arguably been through most of the last three decades (the late 90s being the major exception) – and as it clearly is in the aftermath of the Great Recession – then there is no real argument against increased spending on public investment. This spending will both boost output and employment in the short-run and increase productive capacity in the long-run.

5. Conclusion

The United States had two major fiscal experiments in the last two decades. First, in the 1990s, the Clinton administration pursued a path of aggressive deficit reduction that involved (in roughly equal amounts) tax increases and cuts to spending. Second, in the 2000s, the George W. Bush administration went the opposite direction by pursuing a large tax cut at a time when it also ramped up military spending and added a large prescription drug entitlement program to Medicare.

The Clinton policy achieved substantial deficit reduction, as the federal budget went from a deficit of nearly 5.0 percent of GDP in the year before he took office to a surplus of 2.4 percent of GDP the year he left office. However, this deficit reduction was associated with a *decline* in the investment components of the economy relative to GDP. Nonresidential investment rose modestly compared with its share at the peak of the prior cycle, but net exports fell sharply. As a result, the total share of GDP going to non-residential investment and net exports was considerably lower at the peak of the 1990s cycle than at the peak of the 1980s cycle. In contrast, the share of consumption spending rose dramatically, driven by the effect of lower interest rates and a $10 trillion stock market bubble. The increase in consumption implied lowered private savings. These changes did little to set the economy on a healthy long-run growth path.

The loss of revenue from the Bush tax cuts, slow growth following the burst of the tech bubble, and increased defense spending associated with the wars in Afghanistan and Iraq led to the return of substantial deficits. However, there is little evidence of negative effects from these large deficits. Real interest rates remained at very low levels. In fact, throughout the 2000s, real interest rates were lower than at any point in the 1990s. There was a falloff in investment from the 1990s peak, but the decline was relatively modest given the size of the shift in fiscal positions.

The trade deficit did increase substantially, but this change was unlikely a result of the budget deficit. The surplus at the end of the Clinton administration diminished with the 2001 recession and turned into a deficit with the Bush tax cuts, which grew larger with the wars and uptick in defense spending following the September 11th attacks. The budget deficit then drifted lower throughout the decade until the economic crisis hit in 2008. The trade deficit grew through most of the decade in response to the high dollar and also because of the economy's growth as it recovered from the 2001 recession. It continued to rise until 2007 when it appears that the dollar had finally fallen enough to cause the trade deficit to begin to shrink. The dollar's decline was reversed at the onset of the Great Recession and the resulting flight to quality.

In both of these large fiscal policy experiments, the economy did not follow the course predicted by the simple deficit-reduction story. There is no reason to believe that the next experiment will turn out any differently than the last two. If the point is to adopt a policy that best supports long-term growth, the most reliable course would be with a strong public investment agenda that is partly deficit financed.

The lesson for the aftermath of the Great Recession is clear. In 2011, Republicans held what should have been routine policy actions, like the unavoidable increase in the federal government's debt ceiling, hostage to fiscal austerity. Mainstream Democrats resisted only mildly, seeming themselves to have caught the austerity fever that permeated the Clinton administration. The arguments here imply that these policies are misguided, especially to the extent that they curtail useful public investment at a time when, despite historically low interest rates, private investment is anemic and unemployment is rampant.

References

Aschauer, D. (1989) "Is Public Expenditure Productive?" *Journal of Monetary Economics*, V. **23**, March: 177–200.

Baker, D. (2007) "The Productivity to Paycheck Gap: What the Data Show." Washington, DC: Center for Economic and Policy Research available at http://www.cepr.net/index.php/publications/reports/the-productivity-to-paycheck-gap-what-the-data-show/.

Barth, J. R., G. Iden, F. S. Russek, and M. Wohar. (1991) "The Effects of Federal Budget Deficits on Interest Rates and the Composition of Output," in R. G. Penner, ed. *The Great Fiscal Experiment*. Washington, DC: Urban Institute, pp. 71–141.

Board of Governors of the Federal Reserve System, Flow of Funds data, available at http://www.federalreserve.gov/releases/z1/20001208/z1r-4.pdf

Chirinko, R. S. (1993) "Business Fixed Investment Spending: A Critical Survey of Modeling Strategies, Empirical Results, and Policy Implications," *Journal of Economic Literature* (December): 1875–1911.

Congressional Budget Office. (2000) *Economic and Budget Outlook: Fiscal Years 2001–2010*. Washington, DC: Government Printing Office.

Dornbusch, R. (1985) *Dollars, Debts, and Deficits*. Cambridge, MA: MIT Press.

Dynan, K. and D. Maki. (2001) "Does the Stock Market Matter for Consumption?" Working Paper 2001–23. Washington, DC: Board of Governors of the Federal Reserve System.

Economic Report of the President. (2010) Washington, DC: U.S. Government Printing Office.

(2004) Washington, DC: U.S. Government Printing Office.

(1994) Washington, DC: U.S. Government Printing Office.

Heintz, J. (2010). "The Impact of Public Investment on the U.S. Private Economy," New Evidence and Analysis," *International Review of Applied Economics*.

Holtz-Eakin, D. (1992) "Solow and the States: Capital Accumulation, Productivity, and Economic Growth." NBER Working Paper # W4144.

Kim, S. and N. Roubini. (2008) "Twin Deficit or Twin Divergence? Fiscal Policy, Current Account, and Real Exchange Rate in the U.S.," *Journal of International Economics*, March: 362–383.

Maki, D. and M. Palumbo. (2001) "Disentangling the Wealth Effect: A Cohort Analysis of Household Saving in the 1990s." Working Paper 2001–21. Washington, DC: Board of Governors of the Federal Reserve Board.

Mishel, L., J. Bernstein and H. Boushey. (2002) *The State of Working America, 2002–03*. Ithaca, NY: Cornell University Press.

Munnell, A. (1990) "Why Has Productivity Growth Declined? Productivity and Public Investment," *New England Economic Review*, January: 3–22.

Office of Management and Budget. (2005) Analytical Perspectives, Budget of the United States Government, Fiscal Year 2006. Washington, DC: U.S. Government Printing Office.

Pollin, R. and D. Baker. (2010) "Reindustrializing America: A Proposal for Reviving U.S. Manufacturing and Creating Good Jobs," New Labor Forum, Spring: 17–34.

Sims, C. (1992) "Interpreting the Macroeconomic Time Series Facts: The Effects of Monetary Policy," *European Economic Review*, **36**: 975–1011.

United States Department of Commerce, National Income and Product Accounts data, available at http://www.bea.gov/iTable/iTableHTML.cfm?ReqID=9&step=1

ELEVEN

No Need to Panic about
U.S. Government Deficits

Barry Z. Cynamon and Steven M. Fazzari

The Great Recession and its immediate aftermath has created the largest federal government deficits, by far, that the United States has experienced since the end of World War II.[1] The deficit jumped from slightly more than 1 percent of GDP in 2007 to 10 percent in 2009, 9 percent in 2010, and just under 9 percent in 2011. To put these figures in perspective, the U.S. federal deficit exceeded 5 percent of GDP only twice since World War II (5.9 percent in 1983 and 5.0 percent in 1985). These figures have stimulated loud anti-deficit rhetoric about fiscal irresponsibility from politicians, pundits, and some economists. In addition, serious commentators who seem sincere about their desire to "do the right thing" argue that we must significantly cut spending *and* raise taxes to avoid burdening our children and grandchildren with mountains of public debt.

It is hardly surprising that all this rhetoric has led to a sense of panic about deficits among the U.S. population. In 2011, mainstream political discussion largely converged on the idea that the deficit must be cut *now*. Any thought of further fiscal stimulus to address the perniciously stagnant labor market recovery from the Great Recession seems off the political table. Deficit fears have compromised even the most basic countercyclical fiscal policies, such as extended unemployment insurance. In stark contrast to the broad message of this volume, the political right, and even a share of so-called moderates in the U.S. Democratic Party, claim that the deficit demonstrates the failure of Keynesian policy and they are pushing for lower government spending as a way to boost private investment and

[1] This chapter is an extensively revised version of a keynote address presented at the conference "The World Economy in Crisis – The Return of Keynesianism?" Berlin, October 31, 2009 that appears in the conference volume Dullien et al. (2010).

business confidence by taking "seriously the debt that is threatening our job creators."[2]

In this chapter, we argue that these fiscal fears are largely without merit, and they constrain fiscal policy from doing what it needs to do: continuing to support and even grow demand as the U.S. economy struggles after the recession. Through the lens of basic Keynesian macroeconomics, we present the case for aggressive fiscal policy and associated large deficits as a critical part of the appropriate policy response to the Great Recession. In short, we argue that the government has the power to affect aggregate demand through taxation and spending ("fiscal policy"), and that the constraints on fiscal policy that politicians and talking heads often emphasize stem not from the government's inability to spend, but from a desire to reduce or eliminate government provision of certain public programs. Our argument is that the political debate over *how to spend* money (meaning, ultimately, how the real resources in our economy are allocated) should be determined independently of the important and unique role the government can and must play in regulating aggregate demand. If we restrict the government from adjusting fiscal policy as necessary to boost demand, we are doing it either because we do not believe that the government can be effective in that capacity, or because we are afraid of the consequences of the government determining fiscal policy – especially spending – without limitation. However, it is important to recognize that the only limitation is a political one, one we choose, and that the government has flexibility to regulate demand in ways that can be palatable across political lines and can prevent the waste created by unemployed resources.

An organizing theme of this volume, reflected in every chapter, is that the proximate source of the Great Recession was inadequate demand, the causes of which are discussed throughout this book. Historic declines of both consumer spending and residential construction, magnified by declining business investment, combined to create a massive negative "demand shock" that has idled resources well into the fourth year since the recession began. The increase in the federal deficit, created mostly by automatic stabilizers (falling tax revenues and rising entitlements – primarily unemployment insurance and Medicaid), but assisted by non-trivial discretionary stimulus (most prominently the American Recovery and Reinvestment Act of 2009), played a central role in containing the demand freefall of late 2008 and early 2009. The near consensus among politicians, along with

---

[2] The quotation comes from Texas Republican representative Jeb Hensarling, *New York Times*, "War of Ideas on U.S. Budget Overshadows Job Struggle," June 4, 2011, page B1.

the views of a large segment of the economics profession, however, is that fiscal policy had done what it needed to do by early 2011. This perspective has two components. First, recovery has begun and since recoveries since World War II tend to "gain traction" as they proceed, the time has arrived to dial back policy support. Second, even if the economy could benefit from further demand stimulus, the size of the deficit and the associated rise in outstanding federal debt makes any further fiscal stimulus infeasible, or at least highly undesirable. The latter concern is reflected in commentary peppered with phrases like "we're broke."

We reject both pieces of this conventional wisdom. Much of the discussion in other chapters in this volume explains why recovery of the economic processes that generate growing demand faces a greater challenge than at any time since the 1930s. Mainstream predictions that automatic economic mechanisms will assure adequate demand to purchase full-employment output over a relatively short period of time have theoretical problems discussed elsewhere in this book (see Chapter 1, in particular). As a practical matter, the sluggishness of the two years of recovery following the trough of the Great Recession implies that, theoretical debates aside, demand *is not* growing fast enough. If, as we believe, private demand growth will be inadequate to sustain a robust recovery well into the future, resources will remain inefficiently idle without further demand support from the public sector. As also discussed in Chapter 1, conventional monetary policy is unlikely to do the job. Further fiscal demand stimulus could have an important effect, but any expansionary tax or spending policies will raise the deficit. If deficit fears force fiscal austerity, we believe economic performance will suffer.

We criticize the mainstream view that government budget constraints and the unsustainable size of fiscal deficits severely limit what can be done in the aftermath of the Great Recession. We argue that conventional fears of fiscal stimulus when resources are underutilized arise from a misunderstanding of both the size of the deficit/debt problems and their economic consequences. We also develop ideas about how aggregate fiscal stimulus affects micro distribution and allocation outcomes. These concerns, such as the worry that deficits crowd out private investment or that today's deficits impose unacceptable burdens on future taxpayers, are central to the fear of deficits that pervades both current mainstream economic thinking and the associated public uneasiness with fiscal stimulus. This chapter shows that such fears are largely misguided in situations like the aftermath of the Great Recession.

We conclude with a proposal for a much more active role for national governments in creating demand growth that leads to a different perspective on fiscal deficits than that widely expressed in modern political discussions and most textbook economic analysis. This approach, however, should not be a blank check for any government project that a vote-seeking politician can dream up in the name of demand stimulus. There are also reasonable concerns about long-term fiscal balance should the economy approach full employment of its resources. We propose the need for a set of institutional structures to channel government activity in directions that shore up demand, enhance productivity, and promote a decent society that exploits the opportunity for high material living standards achieved by modern capitalism.

1. Fiscal Stimulus: Where Does the Money Come From?

Even those who appreciate that low demand is the source of stagnation often fear that an aggressive fiscal solution cannot work, especially beyond a year or two, because it requires current borrowing and therefore threatens the welfare of future generations.[3] The usual question is some version of: How can countries *afford* stimulus when their economies are so weak? A careful response to this question provides useful perspective on how increased spending today, by any agent, private or public, impacts the welfare of future generations.

Where does the money come from to finance economic stimulus? The typical answer to this question often draws on simple analogies between government borrowing and a representative household's budget. If a family borrows today to consume beyond current income, implicitly taken as given, then its members must consume less of their income in the future to pay off the loan. So, the argument goes, borrowing today must put a burden on the future. From this perspective, borrowed money for current spending stimulus appears to come from somebody in the future.

The Keynesian response to the misleading household analogy is obvious: for the economy as a whole, current incomes are not given independently of current spending. If there are unemployed resources today, a rise in current spending brings these resources into use. This more intensive use of resources raises incomes today. In the aggregate, where does the money come from to finance stimulus? *Stimulus itself creates income.* Alternatively,

---

[3] Here is typical rhetoric, in this case from Representative John Boehner of Ohio (statement on new federal deficit projections, August 25, 2009): "the Democrats' out-of-control spending binge is burying our children and grandchildren under a mountain of unsustainable debt. ... Democrats ... spent taxpayer dollars with reckless abandon all year ... putting all the sacrifice on future generations."

think about this point in terms of real resources. If stimulus today mobilizes idle labor and productive capacity, then stimulus creates a net gain for society. It is the employment of these resources that is the source of new income, and that new income finances the stimulus.

Although this point contrasts strongly with the typical political discussion of fiscal stimulus, a moment's reflection makes it rather obvious. Effective stimulus today does not borrow real resources from the future in any sense. If a rise in today's spending leads to more economic activity today, that activity does not "steal" labor from the future. Nor does it prevent productive capacity from being used in the future. Rather, stimulus today employs resources that would otherwise sit idle. Although more intensive use of capital today may lead the capital stock to depreciate somewhat more quickly, the least of our worries in the aftermath of the Great Recession is excessive wear and tear on our underutilized capital. In a period of idle resources, more production today has negligible impact on future production opportunities.

One naturally thinks of government stimulus in this context. Nothing in the preceding discussion, however, changes if stimulus arises from fresh acts of private spending. Private spending creates income. Additional private spending today when resources are underutilized does not, in the aggregate, borrow real resources from the future. Nevertheless, private spenders will necessarily have a more narrow perspective on stimulus-creating activity than the government. Private agents cannot avoid the private-opportunity cost of a fresh act of current spending: if they spend today on good X, they have less for good Y, now or at some future date. The fact that my spending today creates an equivalent amount of income and relaxes the budget constraint for someone else today does not enter my current spending choices. Private spenders do not care that they create income for others or mobilize idle resources. Therefore, if the system relies on privately motivated spending to employ its resources, we must confront an inherent problem: the private benefit of spending acts that increase resource use by others are not part of the private spender's calculation about his or her appropriate level of spending. It is this externality problem that creates an opportunity for government action to raise social welfare. We discuss how the government can meet this responsibility later in this chapter, but first we need to consider some indirect effects of demand stimulus that have an intertemporal dimension, and also give rise to conventional fears about the future consequences of policies that raise current demand.

2. What Burden Does Today's Borrowing Impose on Future Citizens?

Suppose new spending is financed with a rise in borrowing. How does the apparent burden of future debt service created by the new borrowing reconcile with the argument that greater spending today, and the production it stimulates, does not borrow real resources from the future? We must address two issues with debt-financed spending, the direct effect of future debt service and possible indirect, or crowding out, effects from widespread concern that more borrowing will increase interest rates.

Conventional wisdom takes as obvious that the future cost of borrowing today is the debt service on the loan, financed in the case of government borrowing by future taxes. Simple accounting demonstrates that these tax liabilities are imposed on future generations, and almost every commentator on these issues starts from this point to criticize government borrowing. What is hardly ever recognized, and is certainly not emphasized, however, is that current borrowing also creates a new *asset* for future generations. The debt service paid from future liability holders to future asset holders constitutes an *intra-* (not *inter-*) generational transfer payment, and it imposes no *net* burden on future generations as the result of stimulus-creating borrowing today. This result reconciles the observation that employing idle resources today does not directly take away resources from future production with the obvious need to service debt created today with future payments. Those debt-service payments are not a net burden on future agents, but rather a redistribution of income among them.

Do the transfer payments arising from debt service make a difference to the agents involved? Do they affect how we should understand the benefits and costs of economic stimulus financed by borrowing? The answer is likely yes, but ignoring the asset side of the generational transfer, as the simple representative household analogy does, is not the right approach. Indeed, a different analogy better illuminates the issue. Consider the standard argument in favor of free international trade. Most economists argue that free trade raises social welfare because it allows each country to specialize in what it is relatively better at producing (the country's comparative advantage). When everyone does what they do best, the combined output of the two countries is higher than it would be if they each produced everything for themselves, so everyone could be better off. Sensible analysts recognize, however, that any practical attempt to realize these net benefits will likely have complicated distributional effects. Even if society as a whole is more productive, there could be some losers. Nonetheless, the comparative advantage argument usually proceeds to recommend that we need, first, to exploit basic gains from trade to maximize aggregate welfare and, second, design institutions to mitigate possible distribution effects for some agents. The story for Keynesian stimulus is analogous. The primary benefit arises from bringing idle resources into use and creating new income, a net social gain at times when many resources are underutilized. Future distribution effects should be considered, and we do so later in this chapter, but they should not divert us from the primary objective.

This perspective shows that the future tax liabilities arising from new government debt creates no direct *aggregate* burden on future generations. This result is fully consistent with the government budget constraint. Much of mainstream economic analysis recognizes this point implicitly because most economists (unlike politicians and the popular press) do not identify the future tax burden of current government borrowing as the primary cost of deficits. Rather, economists worry that current deficits, by increasing the demand for loanable funds, raise interest rates and therefore increase the cost of capital to business, which crowds out private investment.

Keynesian theory provides several responses to this worry. As long as there are unemployed resources, it is logically inconsistent to argue that the demand for and supply of loanable funds determine real interest rates. The problem, known since Keynes wrote chapter 14 of the *General Theory*, is that the supply of saving is not independent of spending. An increase in the demand for funds increases spending. As we discussed previously, additional spending creates additional income when there are unemployed resources, and additional income creates additional saving. The equilibrium condition between borrowing and lending is established by income adjustment, not interest rate adjustment (see Fazzari 1994–95 for further discussion). This condition implies that the deficit, in a sense, *finances itself*. Other things equal, a fresh act of spending – public or private – financed by borrowing will continue to boost income through the multiplier process until new saving rises to exactly equal the injection of borrowing.[4] There is, therefore, no upward pressure

---

[4] Here is a little more detailed intuition. Suppose someone borrows $100 and spends it at a store owned by person A. Then, A's income rises by $100. If A saves the entire $100, the multiplier process ends after one round and saving has risen by the amount of borrowing. Alternatively, suppose A spends half of his new income by purchasing something from B for $50. A's saving then rises by just $50, but now B has an additional $50 of income. Should B save all of this new income, the multiplier process ends and total new saving of A and B offset the additional $100 in fresh borrowing. If B spends part of the new income, however, then the process continues. The multiplier continues to operate until the entire initial injection of $100 leaks into saving by someone.

on interest rates as the result of an excess demand for loans because there is never any effective excess demand for loans. The logic of this argument is not difficult to understand, but it can appear counterintuitive. How can it be that an increase in borrowing does not raise interest rates? The answer is that higher borrowing leads to higher spending, higher income, and higher saving. The increase in saving matches the rise in borrowing (i.e., the supply of loanable funds expands to meet the new, higher demand for these funds) so that interest rates (the *price* of loanable funds) need not increase.

Indeed, in spite of the widespread fear that government deficits affect interest rates, systematic empirical evidence for such an effect is thin at best. Anecdotally, recent major swings in U.S. fiscal policy do not justify any robust link between deficits and interest rates. In the late 1990s, President Clinton trumpeted the first U.S. fiscal surpluses in decades, but interest rates rose. In the first years of George W. Bush's presidency, the federal budget changed quickly from a modest surplus to a large deficit, a very large historical shift when measured relative to GDP. Interest rates fell. As the Great Recession unfolded, the U.S. deficit-GDP ratio increased to levels not seen since World War II. Again, interest rates fell. Interest rates in these periods of major fiscal changes seem to be driven by monetary policy, not government deficits or surpluses. Chapter 10 by Baker in this volume reviews this evidence in detail.[5]

Indeed, it seems that deficits are more likely to *raise* private investment in a recession than to crowd out private spending. Business investment collapsed during the Great Recession and has recovered only modestly. Venture capital funding, an important source of financing for new technology, dried up.[6] These effects of the Great Recession have tangible costs for future generations of workers and consumers, who will likely face a more poorly equipped economy. Effective stimulus to limit such damage and hasten recovery will likely lead to more capital, better technology, and a more productive future.

These observations lead to another question: how much will a given injection of government stimulus actually increase the deficit? The typical intuition is that a dollar of spending or a dollar of tax cuts raises the deficit

---

[5] In addition, see Galbraith (2005) for an accessible review of systematic econometric evidence that casts doubt on the link between deficits and interest rates over longer horizons.

[6] *Business Week* reports that U.S. venture capital funding in the first three quarters of 2009 fell to $12 billion from $22 billion in the same period of 2008. The article also reports on numerous cuts to R&D and engineering spending by global firms ("The GDP Mirage" from "Mandel on Economics" by Michael Mandel and Peter Coy, October 29, 2009).

by a dollar. Yet when stimulus creates income, it also creates income tax revenues. To fix ideas, consider a simple idealized closed economy in which people spend all that they receive in disposable income, but leakages from the spending stream are the result of a proportional income tax. In this case, a dollar of debt-financed stimulus in the form of new spending or a tax cut must generate enough income so that tax revenues rise to *completely offset* the effect on the deficit. This result follows from the previous discussion that deficits are self-financing: a demand injection must raise income until endogenous leakages equal the size of the initial injection. If the saving effects are zero by assumption, tax revenues – the only remaining source of leakages in a closed economy – must rise by the full amount of the initial stimulus once the multiplier process converges to equilibrium. In reality, most people save some of their marginal income, and the economy is not closed so that some consumption spending leaks into imports. It follows that higher government spending holding tax rates constant will raise the conventionally measured deficit. However, the effect is likely to be substantially less than dollar-for-dollar.[7]

Again, this analysis assumes that resources are not fully employed so that demand stimulus can create real income. In Chapter 6 of this book we argue that the proximate constraint on U.S. output for most of the quarter century leading up to the Great Recession was demand, not supply. The collapse in 2008 and 2009 followed by an anemic recovery in output, but a rather surprising rise in labor productivity, makes it even more obvious that the economy had excess resources through 2011, and will have excess resources for years to come. Whereas the practical design of a fiscal stimulus must pay attention to possible bottlenecks and supply constraints (see Tcherneva in the next chapter of this volume), we should not underestimate the flexibility of the labor market to guide flows of unemployed workers into expanding sectors. Stimulus spending on highway construction, for example, most likely could effectively absorb unemployed home builders.

From a conventional perspective, the conclusion of this section is surprising. The typical worries about government deficits, higher interest rates, investment crowding out, and economic burdens imposed on "our children

---

[7] Paul Krugman's *New York Times* blog, September 29, 2009, identifies this effect and proposes that endogenous increases in taxes generate about 40 cents of new government revenue for each dollar of stimulus spending. With a very simple model and rough estimates of how much U.S. tax revenues rose in the recent expansion (including federal, state, and local revenues), we estimate that the effect could be larger, 50 cents to 70 cents for each dollar of stimulus. Import effects would reduce this figure, but induced investment-accelerator effects make it larger.

and grandchildren" are, in general, profoundly misguided. However, as noted earlier, deficit spending can create distribution effects, and we must consider the economics of these effects to completely assess the social impact of fiscal stimulus and higher government deficits.

3. The Distribution Effects of Fiscal Stimulus

Concerns that debt-financed fiscal stimulus imposes a *net* burden on future generations are misplaced. Government debt created today as a by-product of fiscal stimulus transfers a tax liability to the future, but it also transfers an asset. Thus, future debt-service payments go from one group of future agents (taxpayers) to another group of future agents (bondholders). There is no net burden on future agents, but these transfers do affect the *distribution* of claims on future output. These distributional effects may have economic consequences that we explore in this section.

Claims that the U.S. government cannot afford further fiscal stimulus because of current levels of outstanding debt or the current size of federal deficits, if they are to have any basis, must relate to the magnitude of the future transfer payments to bondholders. How large are these potential transfers? The most obvious variable to consider is the real interest rate. In the United States, inflation-adjusted government bond yields have averaged less than 2 percentage points.[8] The 2009 U.S. federal deficit hit 10 percent of GDP. It declined modestly to just below 9 percent in 2010 and is projected by the Congressional Budget Office to decline further to 3.1 percent of GDP by 2016. Suppose that instead of this slow reduction, the federal deficit returned to 10 percent of GDP in 2012 and remained at this elevated level through 2016. Then, as a first approximation, future real debt-service transfers from five more years of historically massive deficits would initially be 10 percent of GDP times five years times a 2 percent real interest rate which equals *just 1 percent of GDP*. Note that this scenario implies massive *additional* fiscal stimulus relative to the baseline projections – well more than 4 *trillion* dollars.[9] Should this policy, along with other factors, put

---

[8] The real yield on ten-year inflation-adjusted U.S. Treasury Securities (TIPS) averaged 1.96% from 2003 through 2009. This figure likely overstates the average real debt service cost because the average maturity of U.S. federal debt is likely to be substantially less than ten years. The average maturity of U.S. debt was about four years according to a Reuters report ("Treasury Plans to Shift to Longer Debt Maturities," November 4, 2009). The same report indicates that the historical average for maturity has been five years.

[9] This figure is calculated as follows. The baseline projections from the CBO, as of January 2011, project budget deficits that sum to 21% of GDP over 2012 to 2016. The counterfactual

the economy back on a robust growth path, this share of GDP devoted to marginal debt service will decline over time. As a kind of premium for the effective income and employment insurance provided by a stimulus policy of this exceptional magnitude, this figure seems small. Remember that it is a *transfer* in the aggregate, not a net social cost.

In addition, the size of this transfer is mitigated by two factors, perhaps significantly. First, as argued previously, effective stimulus will not just return the economy to a predetermined growth path. It will likely affect the long-run path of the economy. It is easy to imagine that effective policy, by raising investment, the development of technology, and enhancing the skills of a more fully employed labor force, could increase potential output by an amount that exceeds the entire transfer figure. Second, as discussed previously, stimulus creates income and tax revenues. Therefore, $4 trillion-plus of stimulus in a weak economy will not raise the national debt by the same amount. This effect alone could easily cut the one percent of GDP debt service figure in half.

These points notwithstanding, even small transfers have distributional effects. Who are the taxpayers and bondholders on both ends of these transfers? We begin by considering transfers resulting from bond sales to domestic citizens. On average, most taxes are paid and most saving is done by high-income individuals. In the United States, the top quintile of income earners paid approximately 82 percent of the income taxes in 2007, and the top quintile accounts for 70 percent or more of saving.[10] To the extent that domestic citizens purchase new government bonds and income tax payments are the primary source of revenue to service this debt, the transfers created by government debt will take place largely among the affluent, at least if these historical patterns continue to hold.[11]

There is another mitigating factor especially relevant to high-income households. Profits and capital gains income are highly procyclical. Effective

---

policy proposed in the text would raise this sum to 50% of GDP. Nominal GDP is roughly $15 trillion. Multiply $15 trillion by 29% (50% less 21%) to obtain $4.35 trillion.

[10] Tax data are from 2007 and the top quintile figure is interpolated from data from taxes for the top 10% and top 25%. Saving data is based on Federal Reserve Flow of Funds and Survey of Consumer Finance. The top quintile accounted for 74% of aggregate saving from 1989:4 to 1998:4. The skewness of saving is even more striking from 1999:1 through 2009:2, a period during which the top 20% accounts for more than 80% of saving. This is because the middle quintiles of U.S. households had negative saving in many of the recent years.

[11] In the 2011 U.S. political environment, however, one could argue that the effect of higher debt service costs could be to raise payroll taxes, or lower safety net entitlement spending.

policy to combat deep recessions and speed recoveries will support profits and asset markets, the benefits of which are highly skewed toward the wealthy. It makes good political theater for well-off households to complain about high taxes, but modestly higher tax rates to service government debt – much of which will be recycled back to the same group as interest payments – is a small price to pay for effective stimulus that enhances economic growth, creates profits, and supports asset prices.

A more politically potent fear of future transfers, and one that animates many criticisms of fiscal deficits in recent years, comes from the possibility that foreigners buy bonds created by the government deficit. If this is the case, then the wealth created by the bonds is owned in part by foreigners, and the future debt-service transfer goes from domestic taxpayers to foreign citizens. In the United States, foreigners own just under half of the federal debt held by the public (2009 data). Of course, the point that debt service is analogous to a transfer payment applies equally whether the recipient is domestic or foreign. One might ask why the presence of an international border makes any more difference than a city or state border. Yet, there is concern about the distribution of political power reflected by foreign holding of domestic assets, foreign transfers may affect exchange rates and trade, and foreigners do not pay domestic taxes on the interest income created by government debt service. (See Blecker's Chapter 8 for more discussion of these issues.)

Consider the case for the United States. The capital surplus from the foreign purchase of U.S. government bonds corresponds to a current account deficit. As such, with foreign financing of deficits the United States can absorb more output, in the form of consumption, investment, and government spending on goods and services, than it produces. The inflow of goods could be viewed as a current benefit, but at the cost of forcing a current account surplus, and corresponding outflow of goods and services in the future. In this sense, foreign debt financing might seem to create a net burden on future U.S. citizens. The future trade surplus, should it ever come to pass, however, also would be a source of future demand that could be beneficial if, as previously argued, insufficient demand is likely to remain a persistent source of underperformance for the aggregate economy (see Galbraith 2005 for further discussion of this point). More broadly, should foreigners become less willing to accumulate assets denominated in the domestic currency (something that seems to inspire fear in the United States), the most obvious result would be depreciation of the domestic currency. The result would be an increase in domestic demand, which would almost certainly be welcome.

This issue must be put in the appropriate quantitative perspective. The recent example suggests that massive deficits for several years create only modest debt-service transfers. Half or more of these transfers remain within domestic borders. If the foreign debt eventually leads to a current account surplus, the extra demand created by higher exports and lower imports is likely to stimulate the domestic economy. It would seem unreasonable to forego the net gains from bringing idle resources into use because of a *possibility* of what is, at most, a small cost to the domestic economy because of foreign debt service, when what costs there are will likely be born in large part by those with the greatest ability to pay who benefit indirectly from stimulus policy in other ways.

In summary, it is difficult to imagine why the transfer payments discussed in this section should be a barrier to effective fiscal stimulus when there is substantial economic slack. Consider the following thought experiment. Suppose that the multiplier is 1.5, a value consistent with empirical evidence on the general effect of government stimulus, that could well be larger in a deep recession. As previously discussed, also assume that each dollar of stimulus generates enough new income so that tax revenues rise by fifty cents. Thus, the deficit from a dollar of stimulus is just fifty cents. If we treat the fifty-cent increase in debt as a "cost," the benefit-cost ratio is 1.5 to 0.5, that is, 300 percent! Yet even this favorable outcome understates the case for stimulus for at least two reasons. First, the fifty-cent increase in debt is not a net social cost, it is a transfer payment. Second, investment, technological development, infrastructure, and human capital will likely rise because the stimulus creates a more productive economy in the future, so the benefit of the deficit-finance stimulus is understated.

4. Fiscal Stimulus after the Great Recession

Several chapters in this volume argue that the Great Recession likely marks the end of an era in which debt-financed consumer spending generates substantial demand growth. There is no obvious source of private demand to replace the consumer engine that powered the economy for nearly a quarter century. The case for government-led demand stimulus going forward is strong. Given the limits on conventional monetary policy discussed in the introduction of this book and Chapter 9 by Epstein, this stimulus needs to include a heavy dose of fiscal expansion. Despite conventional fears, we argue here that such fiscal stimulus is entirely feasible. Typical views of fiscal responsibility discussed in the press and political debates, often motivated by comparing the finances of national governments to budgets of individual households, are misguided in an economy with idle resources. The case for aggressive fiscal policy recognizes that the need for such action is not just a temporary response to a rare event, but likely an ongoing responsibility, a conclusion developed in more detail in Chapter 12 by Tcherneva.

Misunderstanding of these points impedes effective policy making. The ongoing debate in the United States over health care policy provides a useful example. One gets the impression that even supporters of a larger government role in providing health care for U.S. citizens believe that policy options are constrained by rising deficits. People who make this argument seem to be saying that they would support a larger program if the economy were at full employment, but in the current slump the government deficit implies that we "can't afford" the better policy. This approach seems necessary from the perspective of an isolated household that must tighten its belt when faced with the threat or reality of unemployment. However, our perspective implies that, for a national economy, the logic is backwards. The presence of unemployed resources makes the aftermath of the Great Recession a *better* time to pursue a major public program that passes a microeconomic cost/benefit test: the society benefits from the program, and the demand created by the program creates jobs and income by mobilizing idle resources. Worries about the deficit and national debt impose false constraints.

In addition to the need for fiscal stimulus, the analysis here offers some insight into whether demand stimulus should be implemented via higher government spending or tax cuts. It has become close to conventional wisdom that tax cuts are relatively ineffective as demand stimulus because the recipients will spend a relatively small fraction of such cuts, especially when tax cuts are explicitly temporary. In contrast, government spending on goods or services adds directly to demand. We accept this basic logic, but we must also recognize that government spending does not just provide demand stimulus, it also *allocates resources* to specific activities through a bureaucratic process. The allocation of funds distributed by tax cuts, however, is determined by personal choices and market processes.[12]

We propose the following framework as a possible way to address both economic and political considerations in the design of effective fiscal stimulus. Government projects should be justified on cost/benefit grounds, with opportunity costs measured at full employment; that is, costs that assume resources allocated to government activities have a productive alternative use in the private sector. One could reasonably argue that this method

---

[12] Of course, the political process must still determine *who* receives a tax cut.

overstates costs when the economy has idle resources. However, if government projects are pursued as stimulus that would not pass a cost/benefit test with the economy at full employment, the policy structure faces two political problems. First, critics will assert that these projects will not disappear once stimulus is no longer needed, and therefore, they could waste resources eventually. Second, critics who do not understand the logic of demand stimulus, or have other political/ideological motives to defeat the program, will complain that projects waste resources now. Supporters of demand-stimulus policy need the strongest possible cost/benefit rationale for the particular activities they propose to succeed in today's ideologically charged political environment.

In the aftermath of the Great Recession there are, most likely, not enough public projects meeting these criteria to get the economy onto a path approaching full employment.[13] A related problem arises from time lags required to initiate large public works. For these reasons, we believe that tax cuts should remain in the policy toolbox. The analysis in this chapter offers some response to the standard criticism that tax cuts are relatively ineffective because recipients will save a large proportion of them. First, U.S. tax rebate plans in recent years almost always provided a one-time and relatively small payment. If permanent tax cuts would be more effective in boosting demand, why has recent policy tied at least one arm behind its back by repeatedly offering temporary rebates? The obvious answer is concern about the deficit. The discussion here points out, however, that the costs of deficits are typically exaggerated. Furthermore, if tax cuts effectively create spending, they will also create new income and higher tax revenues so that their impact on the fiscal deficit will likely be substantially smaller than it appears in the political discussion of these policies. The perspectives developed in this book also lead to the conclusion that the need for demand stimulus is not likely to be just temporary. With no obvious source of demand growth in coming years to replace the U.S. consumer juggernaut, one can make a strong case for tax cuts with no expiration if both policy makers and the public learn to understand the effectiveness of government deficits in periods of underutilized resources.

Of course, the economy will sustain the most demand-stimulus bang for the tax cut buck if the dollars flow to those who will spend the most.

---

[13] Chapter 12 in this volume by Tcherneva criticizes the idea that generalized demand stimulus can ever effectively generate full employment. We accept the thrust of Tcherneva's analysis. That said, the problem of underutilized resources is so large in the aftermath of the Great Recession that we argue generalized-demand stimulus is an important complement for the more targeted employment programs that Tcherneva proposes.

Republicans managed to cut taxes substantially, and permanently, at various points in the past several decades. However, the distribution of the benefits from these cuts provided inefficient stimulus since so many of the dollars went to the well-to-do. A per-head or per-household reduction in taxes, refundable to those with low taxes, would be much more effective.

Ultimately the decision of how the government allocates *any* spending or tax cut is a political question, a question of how our country will allocate its real resources in the public domain and how the tax burden will be distributed across different parts of the society. This question will be determined by the voters through their elected representatives. We argue that these questions of allocation should be determined without unnecessary concerns about deficits and independently of decisions about the magnitude of a fiscal stimulus necessary to regulate demand and target full employment.

The kind of fiscal stimulus we propose is not a silver bullet. There are deeper structural problems. Most obviously, stagnant real-wage growth in the United States has destroyed a virtuous circle from the post–World War II era in which higher productivity led to higher wages and higher wages created consumer demand as an engine of growth (see Chapters 2 and 7 by Palley and Setterfield in this volume). Policies to restore faster wage growth across the income distribution are likely necessary for a sustainable recovery. In addition, the healthy growth of private demand depends fundamentally on a financial system that distributes credit to households and firms without inflating asset-price bubbles (Kregel, Chapter 4, and Wray, Chapter 3). In this environment, monetary policy can contribute to stabilization and growth more effectively than it did during the consumer era of recent decades (Epstein, Chapter 9). This chapter argues, however, that an aggressive fiscal policy should be a central part of the solution, calibrated to the needs of the economy not just for a few quarters, but for years to come.

When the economy recovers to a reasonable approximation of the full use of resources, it makes sense to have a tax system that funds the level of public spending chosen through a (hopefully) effective political process. Minsky (1986) proposes that the federal budget should be balanced at full employment to avoid inflationary pressure. In many countries, for example, rising health care costs might justify higher taxes at full employment to avoid inflationary deficits. Perhaps the realities of politics force discussions of fiscal austerity even at times like the aftermath of the Great Recession, well before anything approximating anyone's concept of full employment can be reached. However, if some taxes go up to create a credible expectation that the country can "live within its means" once it reaches full employment, then there should be offsetting increases in demand stimulus that persist as long as unemployment continues to plague our society.

It is important to recognize that the U.S. federal government cannot run out of dollars to spend as it sees fit, because it has the unique ability to create dollars. This is not to say that the government has access to limitless resources, but to say that – as demonstrated in war times – it has tremendous access to resources as a result of its unlimited access to dollars. Again, the point is not that the government can commandeer any and all goods and services it wants without social impact, but rather to say that the true constraint on the ability of the government to spend is precisely the political will to absorb the consequences of those impacts and *not* the possibility of running out of money.[14]

The aftermath of the Great Recession is not the time for tight fiscal policy. The fear of government deficits that has already constrained fiscal policy in the United States and has grabbed hold of much of the rest of the world, is greatly exaggerated. This panic and its political reverberations are supported by neither theory nor evidence. The perspectives developed throughout this volume imply that the need for large fiscal deficits will likely be with us for an extended period. False constraints, often based on misunderstanding, should not prevent governments in the United States and elsewhere from taking actions that have great potential to mitigate, if not reverse, the human consequences of the most severe economic disruptions in several generations.

References

Dullien, S., E. Hein, A. Truger, and T, van Treeck, eds. (2010) *The World Economy in Crisis – The Return of Keynesianism*, Marburg, Germany: Metropolis-Verlag, 295–318.

Fazzari, S. M. (1994–95) "Why doubt the effectiveness of Keynesian fiscal policy?" *Journal of Post Keynesian Economics*, **17**(2), 231–248.

Galbraith, J. K. (2005) "Breaking out of the deficit trap: The case against the fiscal hawks," Public Policy Brief, Highlights, No. 81A.

Minsky, H. P. (1986) *Stabilizing an Unstable Economy*, New Haven, Connecticut: Yale University Press.

Wray, L. R. (1998) *Understanding Modern Money: The Key to Full Employment and Price Stability*, Cheltenham and Northampton: Edward Elgar.

---

[14] See Wray (1998) for an introduction to the Modern Money Theory (MMT), a comprehensive theory of the way that money works in sovereign countries.

TWELVE

Fiscal Policy for the Great Recession and Beyond

Pavlina R. Tcherneva

The swift and rather widespread support for fiscal activism during the Great Recession was something of a surprise. After all, since the late 1970s, most mainstream economists have completely abandoned faith in fiscal policy effectiveness, in part because of the empirically and theoretically dubious Ricardian Equivalence Hypothesis (see Barro 1974). Nevertheless, here we are, several years after the global financial meltdown of September 2008, in a position to reconsider the role and place of fiscal policy in stabilizing a devastated economy.

John Maynard Keynes provided the *raison d'être* for countercyclical fiscal policy. He inextricably linked the goal of macroeconomic stabilization to the goal of full employment. He had a rather precise definition for full employment and argued that policy makers had a responsibility to ensure that "everything that could humanly be done has been done by the state … [to produce] a reduction of the unemployed to the sort of level we are experiencing in wartime … that is to say, an unemployed level of less than 1 per cent unemployed" (Keynes 1980:303). This is the definition of full employment that will be used in this chapter and I shall argue that achieving and maintaining this level, while simultaneously stabilizing the business cycle, is possible.

Rather than focusing on full employment, the main goal of fiscal policy in recent years, both in economic analysis and political discourse, has been the stabilization of incomes, consumption, and investment. Employment stabilization is considered to be a *byproduct* of these policies. Keynes, by contrast, believed that the unemployment problem should be solved speedily and directly by one primary method – direct job creation through public works.

This chapter argues that a policy of direct job creation can provide a crucial tool for dealing with the aftermath of the Great Recession and for addressing the unemployment problem at all phases of the business cycle. Conventional aggregate demand-management policies are shown to be inadequate for dealing with the unemployment problem during recessions and incapable of achieving true full employment in expansions. I examine the kinds of fiscal responses that are usually favored by modern economists and policy makers, and consider how the specific policy actions undertaken in the United States to deal with Great Recession reflect the conventional policy wisdom. Next, the chapter briefly summarizes labor market conditions in the United States to underscore the inadequacy of this policy response. Finally, I address the question "what is to be done?" Although there are good reasons to believe that the fiscal push in 2008–09 was too small, this paper will argue that aggregate demand management alone *cannot* restore full employment. Instead, the focus of fiscal policy must be reoriented from the output gap to the labor-demand gap. This approach will not only assist the recovery from the Great Recession but will also, by virtue of its strong regional emphasis, address problems such as urban blight and rural poverty. It is a policy that solves the unemployment problem over the long run by tackling not just its cyclical, structural, and seasonal components, but also the problems of the long-term unemployed, the unemployable, the working poor, and new entrants into the labor market.

1. Modern Fiscal Policy and the Great Recession

The Conventional View

Most contemporary economists (if they accept the stimulative potential of fiscal policy at all) use the "leaky-bucket" analogy to explain how fiscal policy works. Government increases spending or reduces taxes to top off the economic bucket by boosting aggregate demand. Higher aggregate demand raises GDP and production, which in turn reduce unemployment (hopefully) to desired levels. However, because the economic bucket leaks (e.g., some stimulus is lost in transit because of administrative costs and some of it, such as unspent tax cuts and certain investment subsidies, has no direct job creation effect), not all of the money reaches the poor and unemployed. This leaky-bucket analogy comes from the work of Arthur M. Okun (1975), the economist who inspired the economic "law" that motivates this policy approach. Okun's Law (1962) states that a 1 percent increase in unemployment would generate approximately a 3 percent decline in GDP growth. This relationship has been inverted and used as a policy guide that lends support to broad-based demand stimulus policies as an indirect method to fight unemployment. The law indicates that unemployment falls if the government manages to stimulate output growth sufficiently.

Note that 3 percent growth in actual GDP (relative to potential output) brings about only a 1 percent reduction in unemployment – a rather small and unimpressive effect, especially in the face of a large employment gap (Okun [1962] himself cautioned that the GDP-to-unemployment relationship is rather weak). Although economists generally accept the inverse relationship between growth and unemployment, the empirical form of this relationship has received widespread criticism (see, for example, Altig, Fitzgerald, and Rupert 1997; Lee 2000). Furthermore, whereas Okun's law links aggregate demand stimulus to improved labor market conditions, it is an inadequate guide. Its most obvious weakness is the absence of any consideration of the *type* of growth required to produce sizeable reductions in unemployment, much less anything close to genuine full employment.

Fiscal Policy during the Great Recession

Despite the small and untargeted employment effect predicted by Okun's law, the general agreement across the theoretical spectrum is that boosting aggregate demand is the proper objective of fiscal policy. There is some disagreement as to the exact method by which aggregate demand should be expanded, but generally the policy response would include an automatic and a discretionary component. Government spending expands automatically in recessions with the increase in unemployment insurance, welfare benefits, and other transfer payments. In addition, tax revenues decline with economic activity, thus boosting the countercyclical government deficit. Furthermore, a number of discretionary moves can be undertaken to hasten the recovery. These normally include additional tax cuts to households and businesses, as well as direct aid to states and firms in the form of grants, contracts, and loans for the purposes of new investment.

The policy response from the G. W. Bush and Obama presidencies in the aftermath of the September 2008 financial crisis followed the general recipe previously outlined. It also included a few additional government expenditures that are not commonly used as countercyclical stabilization measures. The first large injection of government spending took place under G. W. Bush, and was designed to purchase a large number of nonperforming financial assets from the balance sheets of ailing banks. Although these purchases were executed by the Federal Reserve, they constituted fiscal policy because the Fed cannot purchase private sector liabilities from bank portfolios without congressional authority. Congress provided the Fed with a budget of $700 billion to execute the purchase of asset-backed securities, agency paper, and other assets under the first Troubled Asset Relief Program (TARP). The TARP also facilitated a massive infusion of funds into General Motors and Citigroup and the virtual nationalization of the insurance giant AIG (also see the discussion of these policies in Chapter 4 by Kregel). The objective was to stabilize bank balance sheets so as to get credit flowing again for the purposes of restoring aggregate demand.

The second part of the fiscal stabilization plan consisted of more conventional stimulus activities; that is, the purchase of real goods and services from firms and direct income assistance to households and states. President Obama's American Recovery and Reinvestment Act of February 2009 (ARRA) appropriated an additional $787 billion that included $288 billion in tax cuts and benefits to individuals and firms, $275 billion in contracts, grants and loans, and $224 billion in entitlements. Among the entitlements, the White House enacted the longest-lasting emergency unemployment program in history that included the first benefit increase during a downturn in history (National Economic Council 2010:25). Furthermore, it supplemented the Temporary Assistance to Needy Families (TANF) program with emergency funds, which quietly expired by the end of 2010.

Despite the massive size of both TARP and ARRA, by historical standards, they remained inadequate, as their net effect on GDP and employment was small (Baker 2009). First, as the federal government increased its spending, states, households, and firms continued to slash theirs, offsetting much of the effect. Second, these types of injections did not all boost output; rather, much of the fiscal stimulus (the TARP program in particular) generated demand for non-producible financial assets (or what Hahn called "non-employment inducing demand" Hahn 1977: 39). In addition, some of the tax cut payments received by firms and households were used for deleveraging, that is, they were effectively saved rather than spent, leaking from the economic bucket. Finally, where higher government demand did increase output and production, it did not deliver the employment-creation effect that policy makers aimed for. This was largely owing to the kind of restructuring that takes place in recessions, which results in production with a leaner labor force.

The Unemployment Situation in the U.S.

Upon taking office, president Obama pledged to create or save 3 to 4 million jobs. The ARRA was specifically intended to prevent significant increases in the unemployment rate and launch a strong jobs recovery. However,

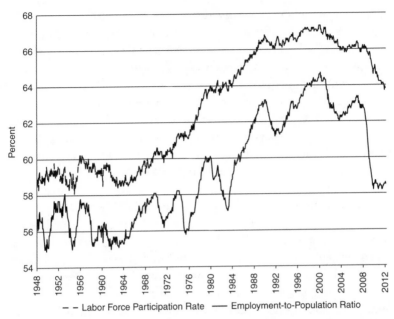

Figure 12.1. Labor force participation rate and employment-to-population ratio.
Source: www.bls.gov

the White House's projections woefully underestimated the severity of
the employment crisis. The Romer-Bernstein report (2009) that lent support to the ARRA program, estimated that without the stimulus package
the unemployment rate would have reached as high as 9 percent, but that
ARRA would prevent unemployment from rising much above 8 percent,
and would then begin to reduce it quickly. In reality, unemployment peaked
above 10 percent even with the ARRA stimulus and has recovered only
modestly since then.

More troublesome is the fact that whatever stabilization we have observed
in the unemployment rate is largely owing to the mass exodus of discouraged workers from the labor market. The labor force participation rate has
been on its longest running and most severe decline in postwar history, and
the employment-to-population ratio has collapsed to 58 percent – a level
not seen in three decades (Figure 12.1), when a much larger share of the
population consisted of "baby boomers" and women who did not take up
paid employment.

Simultaneously, the crisis has destroyed about 10 million full-time jobs,
roughly triple the job destruction of any U.S. recession since the relevant data
series began in 1968, and created record levels of long-term unemployment.

The latter outcome is particularly disconcerting because the long-term unemployment rate has been on a secular uptrend for the last four decades, whereas short-term unemployment has been on a steady decline throughout the entire postwar period. In every expansion since 1968, the long-term unemployment rate has failed to return to the minimum value established during the prior expansion. By contrast, the share of the unemployed who are without a job for just fourteen weeks or less has been trending down during the entire postwar period. This is hardly a picture of an agile U.S. economy with dynamic labor markets that are the envy of the world. Instead, it indicates increasingly sluggish labor market turnover and an inadequate supply of jobs for the long-term unemployed – secular processes that reflect the creation of a greater and greater pool of unemployable labor.

The trouble with the labor market has been brewing since well before the Great Recession, suggesting that the temporary aggregate demand-management policies that are typically employed in recessions have failed to solve the unemployment problem in the past and cannot cope with the significant underlying structural problems that have emerged in the U.S economy. Although the fiscal push during the Great Recession helped put a floor on aggregate demand, it has not generated the vigorous job recovery that was expected and is needed. Some economists have correctly argued that the fiscal response was too small (see, for example, Cynamon and Fazzari, Chapter 11, in this volume), but the historical trends documented here imply that "more of the same" is not the solution to the daunting problem of unemployment. If we are serious about achieving and maintaining anything close to full employment, an entirely new approach is necessary.

2. Rethinking Fiscal Policy

The conventional approach to fiscal policy is backwards: instead of targeting job creation and allowing growth to be a by-product of a high-employment policy, policy makers target growth and hope it will generate the desired employment results. The pro-growth model has continually failed to achieve anything close to true full employment. Indeed, the very concept of true full employment has been abandoned and replaced by the "natural unemployment rate" (Friedman 1968, Phelps 1994).

I argue that there is nothing "natural" about any level of unemployment and advocate a targeted approach for dealing with the unemployment problem that focuses, not on just any kind of government spending, but specifically on direct job creation via public works. Re-examining the role of public works suggests that genuine full employment can be achieved through a permanent "on-the spot" employment program open to all who are ready, willing, and able to work (Tcherneva 2011). The remainder of the paper will make the case that targeting employment directly is the only method for stabilizing an economy that simultaneously generates and sustains full employment over the long run. In sum, the policy approach proposed here is one of labor-demand targeting that would be utilized *during all phases of the business cycle*.

Mis-specification of Fiscal Policy

For Keynes, the intellectual father of fiscal policy, the principal goal of government spending was to secure true full employment and the principle measure for adjudicating among different policy responses was their employment-creation effects (also see Kregel, 2008). Unfortunately, what is widely considered to be Keynesian policy today is largely a misinterpretation of Keynesian prescriptions, which stems from a fundamental misidentification of Keynes's theory of *effective* demand with the theory of *aggregate* demand (Tcherneva 2011). In the *General Theory*, Keynes carefully articulated that employment was determined not simply by the volume of aggregate demand but by the *point of effective demand*, which was very hard to stabilize and fix at full employment.

The conventional textbook theory of aggregate demand deals with the components of GDP and argues that, as consumption and investment decline in recessions, the government sector can boost its expenditures countercyclically to offset reduced private spending. This is because the government is the only sector that can discretionarily change its level of spending. Note that the level of employment does not directly enter into this type of analysis. The main objective is to return the economy to the desirable growth path, as per Okun's Law. However, there is a debate about the specific method by which an economy can be stimulated. Economists who see the downturn as a consequence of the fundamental workings of the economic system that endogenously produce unstable demand, prefer a policy response that directly boosts aggregate demand through government expenditure. Economists who see downturns as a direct consequence of some external or exogenous shocks to the system (such as oil shocks, technology shocks, natural disasters, and financial shocks), prefer to work on the supply side and implement policies that deal with market incentives, which in turn are expected to boost output and employment independently of government spending, thereby providing a 'market solution' to the downturn. Such policy responses include subsidies to firms, cuts in marginal tax rates, and reductions in wages. In both the demand-side and supply-side cases, however, it is hoped that output and employment will recover, either because of the direct government injection of expenditures in the economy or because of the various incentives that reduce costs or increase after-tax incomes from employment and production. As a practical matter, modern fiscal policies adopt both demand-side and supply-side responses (such as direct government spending and cuts in marginal tax rates).

In contrast, I argue that the problem of unemployment is a problem of deficient *effective* demand, not deficient *aggregate* demand (even if the two are interrelated). Put simply, employment in the aggregate is a function of the choices of households and the entrepreneurial decisions of firms, which depend on *expectations*. The expenditures arising from these actions validate firms' decisions to hire a given number of people today. In other words, *future* aggregate demand *and* aggregate supply conditions determine employment decisions today. Employment then would depend on both the *level* and *type* of future total expenditures and the specific cost structure of production today and in the future.

Put simply, aggregate demand management fills the coffers of households and firms, but their expectations of the future may not improve sufficiently to induce them to spend these newly acquired funds on employment-generating activities. In deep recessions in particular, the thirst for liquidity may not be quenched by the supply of more financial assets through tax rebates or government spending. It is thus unclear how large an injection of aggregate demand is needed to induce the private sector to stop hoarding net financial assets and start vigorous consumption and investment. Even when economic activity is relatively buoyant, firms will likely find it unprofitable to hire *all* who are ready, willing, and able to work.

Drawbacks of Aggregate Demand Management

In recessions, aggregate demand management simply fails to stabilize expectations fast enough and make them consistent with strong employment. In expansions it fails to make them consistent with true full employment. This is because of the peculiar, asymmetric nature of aggregate demand. Whereas a sharp decline in *aggregate* demand will produce a decline in *effective* demand and hence employment, once expectations become distressed, a sharp boost to aggregate demand may not improve effective demand swiftly. This is because firms, households, and states set certain processes in motion that exacerbate the economic downturn and further worsen expectations.

During recessions, firms lay off workers, streamline the production process, and implement labor-saving technologies where possible. Households similarly retrench and rapidly curb their spending. States, whose budgets are highly pro-cyclical, raise taxes, and slash social services, investments, and other programs (a phenomenon that continues in the United States well into 2012). In addition, if all of these sectors are highly leveraged, as was the case in the current crisis, the readjustments in spending behavior are even more dramatic. For households, the pain is particularly severe as many individuals not only lose their sole means of support – their job – but also see the value of their assets decline precipitously (e.g., in the form of collapsing retirement portfolios or home values). In the face of such important shifts in behavior, a policy move to increase aggregate demand can help establish a floor on collapsing demand, but demand management policy will be far less effective in adjusting expectations sufficiently to reverse the job losses that quickly develop.

Furthermore, in expansions, boosting aggregate demand alone does not create full employment, even as the economy gathers substantial upward momentum. This is because it will produce an incrementally smaller employment-creation effect as the economy gets closer to full employment. Part of the increase in aggregate demand is captured by price increases and not employment increases.[1] In other words, even when consumption and investment are very high, the structure of the economy produces inflationary pressures in certain overheating sectors that receive a disproportionately higher share of incremental demand, thus producing more unequal income distribution. This is because, as Keynes cautioned in the *General Theory*, when "the increase in demand is directed to products with a relatively low elasticity of employment, a larger proportion of it will go to swell the incomes of entrepreneurs and a smaller proportion to swell the incomes of wage earners" (Keynes, 1964 [1936]: 287).[2] This inflation and distortion to the income distribution prompt policy makers to abandon aggregate demand policies and leave the economy below full employment. Where the economy lands is then called the "natural rate" of unemployment.

Thus, whereas the case for lavish spending to boost GDP is strongest in severe recessions, Keynes was suspicious of the efficacy of this approach. Indeed, although a boost in aggregate demand will improve effective demand, it *cannot fix it at full employment*. To accomplish this, policy must implement a program of direct spending on employing the unemployed, both during recessions and near the peak of the cycle.

---

[1] Some demand may be diverted to foreign producers as local supply bottlenecks develop.
[2] See also Chapter 7 in this volume by M. Setterfield.

Before discussing the advantages of the direct approach to employment creation over aggregate demand management, a final word is needed about modern supply-side and demand-side policies. On the supply side, attempts to deal with the unemployment problem by means of wage reductions are counterproductive, to say the least. Even if employers are able to produce the additional output at a lower cost, they will be unable to sell it in the face of falling demand from reduced incomes. The end result is likely to be more unemployment, not less. Such policy responses are not only disastrous in the process but fundamentally unjust in the result, giving rise to both lower wages and higher unemployment. On the demand side, it is worth noting that decades of postwar aggregate demand-management policies have failed to produce and maintain full employment and create a more equitable income distribution. These policies are nevertheless relatively popular owing to some of the important macroeconomic benefits of government spending.

Macroeconomic Impacts of Government Spending

There are three key impacts of government spending on the macro-economy. These are 1) the income and employment effect, 2) the cash-flow effect, and 3) the balance sheet effect (Minsky 1986). These benefits ensue from any type of government spending, but they have different employment and distributional effects.

Government spending generates income for the private sector. The volume of public spending will affect the aggregate income in the economy and the allocation of spending will determine the distribution of that income. In the contemporary U.S. economy it is clear that, although GDP has turned a corner, it has not yet posted strong growth in the aftermath of the dramatic decline in income that defined the Great Recession. After a 0 percent growth rate in 2008 and a 2.6 percent decline in 2009, the economy recovered at a 2.9 percent annual growth rate in 2010 (marginally improving over the losses from the previous year). The employment effect of these expenditures, as already noted, has been dismal.

Government spending also creates a cash-flow effect. When the federal government spends more on goods and services, transfer payments, subsidies to firms and grants-in-aid to states than it collects in taxes from the non-federal government sector, by accounting necessity, the government sector's deficit produces a surplus of equal size in the non-government sector (including households, firms, and foreigners). The income and cash-flow effects can explain how government deficits, for example, directly contribute to firm sector profits when the government awards contracts to firms at a time when firms are downsizing their labor force.[3]

As the current recession has demonstrated, profits can recover during a recession without employment increasing. During this recession, corporate after-tax profits – which had been declining at a 20 percent annual rate – posted a gain of 4 percent in 2009 and seem poised for an even larger increase in 2010. In the 2001 recession, profits also grew even if at the small 0.5 percent, whereas in the 1990–91 recession, profits grew at an average of 8 percent per year (National Income and Product Account statistics). Such quick recovery of profits is quite typical of previous recessions as well – after a quick dip they manage to reverse trend quickly. By contrast, in every recession without exception, unemployment has increased rapidly and then only sluggishly declined over many years during the subsequent recovery. These trends again attest to the fact that policy has become very effective in stabilizing aggregate income, profits, and cash flows, but not employment.

The final impact of government spending is the portfolio effect. The cash flows, which states, households, and firms receive as a consequence of the federal government's deficit spending, produce new stocks of safe financial assets in their respective balance sheets. The policy actions in the Great Recession have directed cash flows primarily to the business sector (in particular, to the financial sector through the TARP program) and to a lesser extent to states (through grants-in-aid) and households (through unemployment insurance). However, the balance sheets of firms have experienced greater improvements relative to those of states and households.[4] Nevertheless, the uncertain profits outlook coupled with the still highly leveraged balance sheets of the business sector make it unlikely that firms will boost hiring to the level necessary to generate robust labor market recovery. Additionally, although households and states are deleveraging, their balance sheets are still too weak for them to start spending aggressively and so lead the recovery. The onus, then, remains on the federal government sector to continue with its stimulative policies.[5] The challenge is to do this in a way that assures convergence to full employment. The question is: what *types* of fiscal policies are best suited to the job?

---

[3]   This is also clear from Kalecki's equation (1954), which shows that government spending is a source of profits irrespective of the business cycle.

[4]   Especially given the lukewarm efforts to resolve the foreclosure crisis in a manner more favorable to homeowners.

[5]   See also Cynamon and Fazzari, Chapter 6 in this volume.

3. Setting Fiscal Policy Straight: The Case for Labor-Demand Targeting

Because the expectations, liquidity preference, and portfolio decisions that ultimately determine aggregate demand are subjective and beyond the direct control of policy, policy makers should not attempt to generate full employment by targeting these behavioral fundamentals. Instead, the only way to set and fix the point of effective demand at full employment is for the government to target the unemployed directly. Elsewhere I have argued that public policy should provide an unconditional job offer in the public sector to all willing and able to work but unable to find private employment (Tcherneva 2011).[6] This job offer would be available to the jobless both in recessions and in expansions. This would constitute a long-term program for attaining and maintaining true full employment.

Before explaining the reasons why public works are more effective than aggregate demand management in securing full employment, it must be stressed that closing the demand gap – that is, the gap between current and potential output – is an impossible task for a policy maker. First, the way GDP is measured gives little information about the technique of production and the amount of capital and labor necessary to produce a given level of output. Second, a desired "potential" level of output may be achieved by changes in consumption or investment that involve a more capital-intensive technique. Indeed, the shifts in the composition of final demand as it is currently measured, do not reveal the precise shifts in labor demand associated with them. Recall that potential output is *the* only proxy to full employment that the traditional fiscal policy approach *a la* Okun uses. Such a measure of potential output cannot tell us the true full utilization of resources (including labor and capital) over time and may be estimated only for "an instantaneous or brief period of time" (Keynes 1980: 71). As Keynes argued, the only measure of potential output that would make sense would be calculated in terms of man-hours that might be worked (Keynes 1980: 73). Targeting the labor gap however – that is, the gap between the number of people who are working and those who are willing to work in the aggregate – is a policy objective that can only be achieved through a direct job-creation approach.

---

[6]   There are various programs and policy proposals that resemble the policy approach advocated here. These include the employer of last resort (ELR), the buffer stock employment (BSE) model, the job guarantee (JG), and public service employment (PSE) among others. Whereas these programs differ in design and inspiration, they all share one key objective – to provide employment to all unemployed individuals who seek it. See for example Ginsburgh (1983), Harvey (1989), Minsky (1986), Mitchell (1998), and Wray (1998).

There are three main benefits of the direct job-creation approach over alternative fiscal policies. First, it delivers the highest employment-creation impact. Second, it circumvents the problem of fixing the point of effective demand at full employment indirectly by managing the behavioral factors that determine consumption and investment spending, and hires the unemployed directly. Thus, a permanent direct job creation program open to all would maintain full employment throughout all phases of the business cycle. Finally, this approach has a direct method for dealing with structural unemployment, which is generally neglected by traditional aggregate demand-management policies (indeed, many economists consider structural unemployment to be part of the "natural unemployment" rate). Hence, the direct job-creation approach would target its employment efforts to regions that have experienced job losses because of restructuring, and to individuals deemed unemployable by those private firms that are hiring. The direct job-creation program would provide not only on-the-job experience but also would be supplemented by training and education programs that would upgrade the skills of these individuals to help them transition to private-sector work. Additionally, the program would be a safety net, providing employment opportunities when there are no private-sector options for both new entrants into the labor force, and individuals displaced from private-sector jobs who have difficulty reintegrating (such as stay-at-home moms with long gaps in their work experience, at-risk youth who have difficulty completing high school, elderly persons who wish to work but who are being displaced by a younger and/or cheaper labor force, and welfare recipients who need to find work in exchange for the welfare support they receive).

Notable Characteristics of the Direct Job-Creation Approach

There are several other notable aspects of the direct job-creation approach that deserve to be emphasized. First, direct job creation through public works or public service is not a "depression solution." Instead, it is a solution to unemployment at all stages of the business cycle. As already explained, even a strong economy fails to provide jobs for all. Such a program would be a safety net for the jobless in expansions as well as in recessions.

Second, the goal of a direct job-creation program is to provide decent jobs to its participants. These are jobs that use the available idle labor resources to meet some unfilled need in the community and that establish a basic but decent wage-benefit package as a standard for the economy as a whole. These jobs do not compete with private-sector pay, but simply set a universal floor to wages in the public and private sectors. They do not compete with private-sector output either, as they are jobs that provide public goods and services, which the private sector does not supply.

Third, job support to the poor and unemployed is a more effective stabilization method than providing income alone. This is because the policy would maintain and enhance human capital and would increase both purchasing power and the supply of services. By contrast, income support for the unemployed and the poor is a policy that wastes human potential because it leaves idle many individuals who are willing and able to work.

Fourth, this is a policy that does not depend on boosting aggregate demand to generate full employment; instead, it relies on direct hiring irrespective of the stage of the business cycle. Even in severe recessions, when a great fiscal push is needed, the push must nevertheless be targeted to the unemployed themselves. In the aftermath of the Great Recession, for example, we needed both more and better distributed demand; that is, more spending on direct employment opportunities for the jobless. Should such a program become a permanent feature of stabilization policy, maintaining full employment over the long run would depend not on greater overall aggregate demand but on a better distribution of demand. That is, the program would fluctuate countercyclically, expanding in recessions by taking the contract to the workers who are laid off and shrinking in expansions as public sector workers find employment in the private sector.

Fifth, contrary to common myth, the Keynesian approach to macroeconomic policy, which is a unifying theme of this book, does not advocate the creation of useless projects for the sake of job creation. I propose a carefully planned long-term full-employment program – a program that is flexible, spontaneous, and experimental enough to accommodate any new unemployment that might quickly develop, but is also carefully thought-out and designed to address the key strategic objectives of a nation.

Sixth, a direct job-creation program could be executed through public or semipublic bodies. Job creation is done by the community as a whole, including both the private and public sectors, but it really is not the business of the private sector to guarantee full employment "any more than it is their business to provide for the unemployed by private charity" (Keynes 1982: 151). It is the responsibility of the public sector to figure out how to employ those who are left behind, and employing them can be done in cooperation with the private sector – for example, through public-private partnerships.

Seventh, direct job creation will have the same income, cash flow, and balance sheet effects that traditional aggregate demand management has, except that spending by the program will be targeted directly to households. It is a genuine bottom-up approach to economic recovery. It is a program that first stabilizes the incomes and purchasing power of individuals at the bottom of the income distribution, and then "trickles up" to stabilize the rest of the economy. Strong and stable demand means strong and stable profit expectations. A program that provides employment and purchasing power is a program that creates cash flows and earnings. Stable incomes through employment also mean stable repayments of debts and greater overall balance sheet stability.

Finally, Keynes firmly objected to using unemployment to fight inflation. If inflationary pressures develop near full employment, the public sector should retard new projects where possible and redirect job creation efforts to particularly distressed areas in the periphery of economic activity. However, by no means should it discontinue public works, because that is precisely the time when "private enterprise is stopping from overcapacity and is therefore not in a position to expand" (Keynes 1982: 150). Inflation, for Keynes, was to be addressed through various programs that would either defer payments or encourage thrift, but would not slash jobs.

To design a direct job-creation program, a bold and imaginative approach is required, which weds fiscal policy to the goal of full employment. Not only has aggregate demand management failed to achieve this end over the last several decades, but the 2009 ARRA stimulus program (and its successor, the tax policy compromise of December 2010) are particularly weak on imagination, considering the formidable labor market challenges that we face today.

Final Considerations of Some Conventional Objections

The proposed program is not a panacea for all labor market problems. It is a solution to the problem of unemployment over the business cycle that also helps to provide a floor to aggregate demand more effectively than conventional pump-priming policies. Nor is the program a substitute for all other meaningful fiscal policies. It is a voluntary safety net for all of the unemployed who wish to work. There will, nevertheless, remain certain segments of the population who will require income assistance, such as the young, the ill, or the elderly. They can be supported through programs like universal child credits, Medicare, or social security. At the same time, governments will continue to be responsible for setting tax policies in a way to affect the income distribution and promote or discourage certain types of private sector activities that may be advancing or harming the public interest.

Governments can use these tax policies to set investment or consumption on a more sustainable path if they are deemed to be wasteful, speculative, or destabilizing to overall economic activity. Nothing precludes governments from instituting important structural changes that would spur private domestic employment. This may include providing support to specific industries that the government may want to encourage (e.g., tax benefits and investment subsidies for green energy production). These are structural policies that may be warranted on their own merits, but these are not policies for *full* employment. The private sector has its own considerations that may conflict with the objective of hiring all individuals who wish to work. Therefore, wedding policy that aims to spur private-sector activity with the objective of generating *private sector* full employment may neither be possible nor desirable. Instead, there must be a public program that would stand ready to absorb all the remaining unemployed who have not found employment in these new industrial ventures. In other words, there has to be a policy that takes workers as they are and that tailors the jobs to these workers in order to help them enhance their skills, gain the necessary work experience, and start climbing the economic ladder. By contrast, the private sector is in the business of looking for specific people with specific skills to fit specific jobs requirements. It is not in the business of providing jobs for all. Nevertheless, if the private sector faces a shortage of skilled workers, the public sector can work to prepare and upgrade the skills of formerly unemployed public-sector workers for the needs of modern private-sector production. This visible public-sector pool of labor will give firms a very clear idea of the work experience, training, and education these workers have acquired and their suitability for private-sector employment.

Such a policy is not just an alternative to idleness, it is a policy that puts money in households' coffers through employment. It is also a policy that fills the community's needs gap. This brings us to the final common criticisms of public works: namely, that they are administratively difficult to run, prone to corruption, and cannot provide enough projects to usefully employ the targeted population. The response to the first charge is that administrative complexity is pervasive both in the private and public sectors and has hardly stopped firms or governments from undertaking important large-scale initiatives – be they providing global financial services, running military operations, or supporting NASA's scientific research. Neither are problems with fraud and corruption somehow unique to public-sector operations. Pervasive fraud in the private sector, as in the savings and loan crisis of the 1980s, the Enron scandal of the 1990s, or the mortgage origination and securitization of the 2000s, should put those old arguments to rest. Fraud and corruption are a function of poor regulation and enforcement, and every going concern, private or public, must have design features that enhance transparency and accountability.

The question of useful projects is perhaps the most frequently evoked. One way to answer this question is to note that even in the wealthiest and most prosperous nations, one can always find regions plagued by poverty and unemployment. In the case of the United States there are whole cities and states which have suffered from deindustrialization or natural disasters and which have seen little new economic activity to replace long-gone industry (think of Detroit or New Orleans). The revitalization of inner cities alone would take years of strong job creation and dedicated work. The unemployed themselves can deliver that revitalization through a public employment program similar to the New Deal of the 1930s. Wealthier communities also have unfilled needs and unemployed individuals who can fill them. These may include upgrades to infrastructure, the construction of more public spaces, and the provision of public services. In the United States, many public programs and government services have been underfunded and understaffed for decades – at least since Nixon's devolution of federal government programs. A once-strong public education system is on the brink of collapse, environmental standards have been eroded, the public health system is unfit to meet the needs of the U.S. population – these are all challenges that can be met by fully utilizing labor resources. There are jobs to be done at every level of government and there are unemployed individuals with different levels of skills and education to do them. The examples provided here primarily include regular maintenance and operations public service jobs for which the government is already responsible. Other similar examples would include an ongoing program of reforestation, water purification, and soil erosion improvements, which will offer steady but flexible public-sector employment for many semi-skilled and unskilled workers over the long run. The wholesale upgrade of U.S. roads, rails, levies, and bridges can also be accomplished with a bold program of direct job creation. At the same time, child- and elderly-care services are wholly inadequate in this country. Homeless shelters are bursting at the seams and a staggering 12 percent of U.S. citizens rely on food banks for food assistance (Hunger Report 2010). There are many jobs to be done and there are people to do them.

The government can also undertake novel strategic initiatives that can be accomplished expediently only through a big-push policy of public works. The comprehensive weatherization of *all* public buildings, the complete transformation of current energy production grids to ones relying on alternative energy, or the fabled fiber optics project – the IT equivalent of rural electrification – all require the kind of massive infrastructure investment that only government can undertake. Clearly no country is a finished proposition. As countries grow, they face new challenges and develop new kinds of needs.

The public sector can stand ready through a program of direct job creation to provide jobs for all who wish to work in projects that satisfy those needs.

4. Conclusion

The Great Recession and its aftermath provide us with an important teachable moment and an opportunity to uncover the drawbacks of standard policy responses to macroeconomic upheavals. It also provides policy makers with an important moment for action, which may have unfortunately already passed. Four years after the financial crisis, the public has grown weary of massive government expenditures that have delivered so little in terms of job creation. There seems to be little public support for another large round of stimulus spending. What we seem to face, looking ahead, is stagnant growth, high unemployment and income inequality, increasing impoverishment, and a continual squeeze of the middle class. Aggregate demand stimulus may allow the U.S. economy to muddle through the next ten years, but it would be at the cost of great human suffering and worsening labor market conditions. Worse yet, if the calls for significant fiscal austerity in 2012 translate into actual policy, the future may be very grim indeed. We would be wise to remember Hoover's and Roosevelt's early attempts to balance budgets in the midst of a severe economic downturn, which only plunged the economy further into the Depression (also see Chapters 10 and 11 by Baker and Cynamon and Fazzari in this volume). It is thus critically important that economists and policy makers alike reconsider the standard model of macroeconomic stabilization and get to the heart of the crucial problem of unemployment by tackling it directly.

References

Altig, D., T.J. Fitzgerald, and P. Rupert. (1997) "Okun's law revisited: Should we worry about low unemployment?" *Economic Commentary*, Federal Reserve Bank of Cleveland, May 15.

Baker, D. (2009) Testimony before the House Financial Institutions Subcommittee of the Financial Services Committee, March 4, http://www.house.gov/apps/list/hearing/financialsvcs_dem/baker030409.pdf.

Barro, R. J. (1974) "Are government bonds net wealth?" *Journal of Political Economy*, **82**(6), pp. 1095–1117.

Friedman, M. (1968) "The Role of Monetary Policy," *American Economic Review*, **58** (1), March, pp. 1–17.

Ginsburg, Helen. (1983) *Full Employment and Public Policy: The United States and Sweden*, Lexington, MA: Lexington Books.

Hahn, F. H. (1977) "Keynesian Economics and General Equilibrium Theory: Reflections on Current Debates" in G. C. Harcourt (ed.), *The Microeconomic Foundations of Macroeconomics*, London: Macmillan.

Harvey, P. (1989) *Securing the Right to Employment: Social Welfare Policy and the Unemployed in the United States*, Princeton, NJ: Princeton University Press.

Hunger Report. (2010) Hunger in America, National Report prepared for Feeding America, January. http://feedingamerica.issuelab.org/research/listing/hunger_in_america_2010_national_report

Kalecki, M. (1954) *Theory of Economic Dynamics: An essay on cyclical and long- run changes in capitalist economy*, London: George Allen and Unwin.

Keynes, J. M. (1964)[1936] *The General Theory of Employment, Interest, and Money*, New York: Harcourt-Brace & World.

(1980) *Activities 1940–46. Shaping the Post-War World: Employment and Commodities*. Volume XXVII of *Collected Works*, D. Moggridge (ed.). London: Macmillan.

(1981) *Activities 1922–29. The Return to Gold and Industrial Policy: Part II*. Volume XIX of *Collected Works*, D. Moggridge (ed.). London: Macmillan.

(1982) *Activities 1931–39. World Crises and Policies in Britain and America*. Volume XXI of *Collected Works*, D. Moggridge (ed.) London: Macmillan.

Kregel, J. A. (2008) "The Continuing Policy Relevance of Keynes's *General Theory*," in M. Forstater and L. R. Wray (eds.) *Keynes for the 21st Century: The Continuing Relevance of The General Theory*, London: Macmillan.

Lee, J. (2000) "The Robustness of Okun's Law: Evidence from OECD Countries," *Journal of Macroeconomics*, **22**(2), April, pp. 331–356.

Minsky, H. P. (1986) *Stabilizing an Unstable Economy*, New Haven, CT: Yale University Press.

Mitchell, W. F. (1998). "The Buffer Stock Employment Model and the NAIRU: The Path to Full Employment," *Journal of Economic Issues*, **32** (June), pp. 547–556.

National Economic Council. (2010) "Jobs and Economic Security for America's Women," October. http://www.whitehouse.gov/sites/default/files/Jobs-and-Ecomomic-Security-for-Americas-Women.pdf

Okun, A. (1962) "Potential GNP: Its measurement and significance," in American Statistical Association's *Proceedings of the Business and Economics Statistics*, pp. 98–104.

(1975) *Equality and Efficiency, the Big Tradeoff*. Washington, DC: Brookings Institution.

Phelps, E. (1994) "The Origins and Further Development of the Natural Rate of Unemployment," in R. Cross (ed.), *The Natural Rate Twenty-Five Years On*. Cambridge: Cambridge University Press, pp. 15–31.

Romer, C. and J. Bernstein. (2009) "The Job Impact of the American Recovery and Reinvestment Plan," January 10. http://otrans.3cdn.net/45593e8ecbd339d074_l3m6bt1te.pdf

Skidelsky, R. (2001) *John Maynard Keynes, Volume Three: Fighting for Britain 1937–1946*. London: Macmillan.

Tcherneva, P. (2012) "On-the-spot Employment – Keynes's Approach to Full Employment and Economic Transformation," *Review of Social Economy*, **70**(1), pp. 57–80.

Wray, L. R. (1998) *Understanding Modern Money: The key to full employment and price stability*, Cheltenham: Edward Elgar.

PART SIX

THE WAY FORWARD

THIRTEEN

Demand, Finance, and Uncertainty
Beyond the Great Recession

Barry Z. Cynamon, Steven M. Fazzari, and Mark Setterfield

This book consists of a series of chapters written by different authors, with each chapter exploring a different aspect of the causes and consequences of the financial crisis and Great Recession. However, the various perspectives flow from a single, shared vision of how the economy works. This vision emphasizes the pervasive importance of aggregate demand, uncertainty, and finance as the central factors that determine the path of the U.S. economy and employment of its resources. Of course, technology and resource availability are necessary for production, but these supply-side factors usually do not constrain economic activity at the margin, and in the aftermath of the Great Recession, there is no evidence whatsoever that supply constraints are likely to bind in the U.S. economy for years to come. The shared perspective that informs the contributions to this book involves elements of Keynesian thinking that are largely outside the mainstream of macroeconomics. These are, however, essential for understanding the origins of recent events, analyzing the implications of the crisis for economic performance in coming years, and developing policies that have the potential to improve outcomes. Not surprisingly then, and despite the seeming diversity of topics covered in the preceding chapters, a coherent narrative emerges from these chapters regarding the course of events we have witnessed over the last few years, the longer-term developments that preceded them, and their likely future consequences.

In this concluding chapter, we first outline key elements of the shared vision that informs this volume. We then reflect on the various policies proposed in the preceding chapters – recommendations designed to address the failings that gave rise to the crisis, and to put the economy back on a track of shared prosperity, financial stability, and sustainable growth.

1. The Great Recession: What Went Wrong – Where Do We Stand?

The view developed in this volume identifies both real and financial causes of the Great Recession, including the real income stagnation suffered by households across most of the income distribution on one hand, and deregulation and institutional change in the financial sector on the other. The interplay of these factors led to massive debt accumulation, particularly by U.S. households seeking to supplement stagnant incomes in their pursuit of increasing consumption aspirations. Household borrowing was spurred on by a financial sector rendered ever freer of inter- and postwar financial regulations. These regulations came to be seen as unnecessary fetters on an inherently self-regulating "free market," an idealized notion in which financiers and policy makers placed increasing trust and confidence. Ultimately, the self-reinforcing developments in the real and financial sectors proved deadly. They led to the steady accumulation of financial fragility, even as we ostensibly experienced a "Great Moderation" celebrated by mainstream thinking as a permanent reduction in macroeconomic volatility. This is because the pattern of debt-accumulation we witnessed did *not* involve adjustment toward an optimal path for household consumption, facilitated by the removal of regulatory "imperfections" that constituted "sand in the gears" of otherwise perfect financial markets. Instead, it constituted an unsustainable trajectory, but one that was for decades reinforced by steadily increasing confidence in consumption and financial norms that evolved to guide behavior in an environment characterized by uncertainty about the future. As the trajectory progressed, it seemed all the more plausible and reasonable to households and financiers alike, even as it became increasingly precarious.

What all this implied, in the language of the financial instability hypothesis developed by Hyman Minsky, was that by the late 2000s, the growth regime in the U.S. economy was thoroughly dependent not just on the "ordinary workings of the goods and labor markets" (necessary to generate the income flows required to service outstanding debt), but also what came to be perceived as the "ordinary workings of financial markets" – more specifically, their proclivity to roll over existing debt, and keep expanding new credit (Pollin, 1997). These "ordinary workings" were required because of both the increasing dependence of the growth regime on debt accumulation, and the increasingly risky nature of the financial postures adopted by borrowers and lenders. The U.S. economy was, as a consequence, increasingly vulnerable to any bad news in the short run that would give pause for thought to the households and/or financial institutions participating in the run-up of indebtedness that undergirded the seemingly impressive macro-economic performance of the economy. Furthermore, the system came to depend on falling (or at least not rising) interest rates that allowed heavily indebted households and financial units to refinance their fragile positions. In the end – and perhaps not surprisingly given the mixture of real and financial forces that gave rise to the preceding boom – the "trigger" for the Great Recession arose from an untimely (and interrelated) confluence of real and financial events:

- Rising short-term interest rates that the Fed (perhaps naively) assumed were necessary to preempt inflation. It seems clear, however, that the Fed did not realize how precarious financial conditions had become. Higher short rates had devastating consequences on the riskiest segments of the housing market that relied on adjustable-rate mortgages.[1]
- The end of the housing bubble. Housing prices stopped rising, in part because of the rise in short rates and the spillover to the cost and availability of risky, adjustable-rate mortgages. With stagnant home prices, the collateral engine for massive equity extraction that had fueled an ever-increasing consumption-income ratio shifted abruptly into reverse. In addition, the end of the housing bubble suddenly and drastically revised the refinancing options for households vulnerable to default in the event that their introductory "teaser" mortgage repayment terms should expire.
- A historic collapse in new housing construction.
- The subsequent failure of many subprime mortgages, and the consequent writing down or writing off of many mortgage-backed securities. Those securities, issued in abundance as highly rated financial instruments, were suddenly deemed "toxic."

What followed was a sharp lesson in the fundamental Keynesian maxim that money and finance matter for the aggregate demand-generating process and hence for macroeconomic performance. Minsky's "ordinary workings" failed. As wealth was destroyed and, in particular, as credit froze in the initial stages of the financial crisis, so aggregate demand fell – both as the direct result of wealth destruction and the credit freeze, and indirectly,

---

[1] In the middle 2000s, there was much discussion of what Alan Greenspan labeled a "conundrum": the remarkably modest rise in mortgage rates after the Fed began raising the overnight federal funds rate in mid-2004. It is true that thirty-year conventional mortgage rates rose very little between 2004 and 2006. The one-year adjustable rate, however, rose almost 250 basis points from its trough in early 2004 to its peak in mid-2006.

as wealth destruction and the credit freeze suddenly diminished confidence and animal spirits. Even solvent and liquid households and firms began cancelling expenditure plans. The decline in aggregate demand and consequent rising unemployment only worsened conditions in the housing market, making the whole process dangerously self-reinforcing. And so the Great Recession began, with a frighteningly severe economic decline in late 2008 and early 2009.

At this point, raw fear (if not a well-informed understanding of what was happening among policy makers) ignited the most significant Keynesian policy actions that the world has, perhaps, ever seen. Whatever the faults in its design – and there were arguably many – the monetary and fiscal stimulus response to the events of 2008–09 actually engineered something of a "soft landing." Ultimately, we were spared the experience of a second Great Depression and instead experienced "only" the trauma of the Great Recession. There is no doubt that the primary objective of these policies was to stabilize aggregate demand, in large part by shoring up finance and by containing the panic created in the most severe outbreak of economic uncertainty since the early 1930s.

Policy put a floor under the downward trajectory of a structurally flawed growth and financial regime and thus saved us from the worst-case scenario in the short term. However, it now falls to public policy to "pick up the pieces" and to reconstruct the U.S. economy so that it is once again capable of generating widespread and sustainable prosperity going forward. At the time of writing, policy has already faltered in the pursuit of this agenda. The national debate in the United States has been "hijacked" by "austerity buzzards" (to use Epstein's phrase from Chapter 9), whose focus on public deficits and debt conceals their true desire for smaller government at any and all costs. Governments in Europe, meanwhile – many shackled by the institutional constraints that accompany membership of the euro zone – have already gone further along the path to repeating the errors of the late 1930s, when fiscal retrenchment motivated by a perceived need for "sound finance" repeatedly threatened recovery from the Great Depression (until the massive build-up of public spending that accompanied World War II finally eliminated the problem of chronic demand-deficiency).

No one said the path to redemption would be easy. So what have we learned from the experience of the last few years – and more particularly, from the reflections on this experience contained in this volume – that would inform an appropriate policy agenda from this point onward?

2. Where Do We Go from Here?

The first point that deserves to be emphasized is that the "government as the problem" versus "government as the solution" dichotomy that seems to polarize much public debate is false, misleading, and unhelpful. The simple fact is that government is quite capable of playing both roles – that of hindrance and help. Hence, many of the chapters in this book identify sources of error in public policy in the run-up to the financial crisis and Great Recession, even as they advocate policy responses designed to redress the economic circumstances in which we now find ourselves. Clearly, then, informed public policy needs to formulate and promote policies that will aid recovery while remaining wary of and seeking to eliminate those that will obstruct it. This disarmingly simple rule is far more useful in today's economic and financial climate than any broad, ideologically motivated rule expressing either "zero tolerance" for government (beyond certain minimal functions associated with law enforcement and defense), or proclaiming government as the universal solution for problems that emanate only from unruly "free markets." As Nobel Laureate Peter Diamond recently opined, "To the public, the Washington debate is often about more versus less – in both spending and regulation. There is too little public awareness of the real consequences of some of these decisions. In reality, we need more spending on some programs and less spending on others, and we need more good regulations and fewer bad ones" (Diamond, 2011). Diamond's ethos provides a useful starting point, but beyond this general rule, what, specifically, is to be done?

Financial Reform and Monetary Policy

Each of the chapters in this book recognizes the central role played by financial instability in creating the conditions that led to the Great Recession, and in several chapters financial instability is the central theme. It therefore seems clear that rethinking financial regulation is a necessary and appropriate part of any response to what has transpired. As Kregel, Chapter 4, and Wray, Chapter 3, point out, however, we cannot simply put the financial system back into the old Glass-Steagall box. The Depression-era regulatory structure was in large part responsible for the relatively tranquil financial environment of the postwar decades, but it has become anachronistic. Just because the old rules were anachronistic, however, does not mean that all rules must be abandoned (as was commonly argued in the deregulatory march that led to the Great Recession). The first major financial reform package emerging from the financial wreckage of 2008 and 2009, widely known as the Dodd-Frank reforms, have some useful elements, as pointed out by Epstein in Chapter 9. However, Epstein and many of the other authors of this volume (particularly Wray and Kregel, Chapters 3 and 4) find the approach taken so far both too weak and, in certain fundamental respects, misguided.

The economy needs finance to better serve the public purpose, which requires effective structures to serve both of the "two masters" identified by Kregel: a stable payments system and effective channelling of finance to foster the economy's capital development. Wray argues that this means returning banks to their traditional role of "underwriting," that is, assessing risk and project quality as a means of determining the directions that capital development will follow. As Kregel points out, this role was largely lost in the decades prior to the Great Recession as banking shifted from an "originate and hold" model, in which the bank assessed risks that it would then hold on its balance sheet, to an "originate and distribute" model, in which the objective was to maximize the number of loans that could be made and then sold off in secondary markets. Wray asks why banks deserve the public-private partnership implied by institutions such as deposit insurance and discount-window lending if they do not act in the social interest? In Chapter 9, Epstein suggests further direct public intervention in finance, moving in the direction of what he has aptly named "finance without financiers." Crotty, in Chapter 5, meanwhile, highlights the importance of making financial sector remuneration schemes properly compatible with a greater pursuit of social purpose by the financial sector. This is an essential ingredient if the systemic ambitions of Kregel, Wray, and Epstein are not to be "sabotaged from within" by inappropriate managerial behavior that is actively incentivized by the structure of corporate compensation.

Although financial reform is undoubtedly important, both to restart necessary demand growth and to foster capital development, it certainly isn't the be-all and end-all. In particular, financial reform – indeed, *any* policy – that has as its objective simply "getting the private sector borrowing and spending again" isn't what we need. The objective is not to create another unsustainable, debt-fueled growth episode that serves only to leave us wondering when the next crisis will occur (and lamenting its destructiveness when it does).

This perspective diverges somewhat from the mainstream preoccupation with restoring what came to be thought of as "normal" credit market activity prior to the Great Recession. In particular, the Fed seems focused on getting the banks to lend again. Various policy makers seem frustrated by the massive and unprecedented (at least since the 1930s) accumulation of excess reserves in the banking system, which has a parallel in the oft-cited accumulation of cash on corporate balance sheets. Commentators ask a question that seems to follow, at least superficially, from a Keynesian view of the world: why don't they lend and invest, which would then stimulate demand? The answer developed in this volume is that the old way of generating demand through excessive household borrowing is broken. As Wray provocatively asks in Chapter 3: why "should government policy try to get banks to make loans they do not want to make! After all, if banks are our underwriters, and if their assessment is that there are no good loans to be made, then we should trust their judgment. In that case, lending is not the way to stimulate aggregate demand to get the economy to move toward fuller employment."

These observations lead to another important common perspective that emerges from this book: monetary policy as practiced for much of the past two decades has been singularly ineffective in its ability to cure stagnation in the aftermath of the Great Recession. This stands in contrast to the widely held view, perhaps associated most prominently with Ben Bernanke, that monetary policy can effectively restore full employment when demand falters, even if policy rates push up against the "zero bound." These ideas emerged in large part as mainstream economists criticized the Japanese monetary authorities for not responding more aggressively to their "lost decade" problem. However, it now seems clear that such policies as raising inflation expectations so that real interest rates decline even with a constant zero nominal rate are much easier to model and talk about than to implement in a persistently stagnant economy. Moreover, it seems clear in retrospect that when monetary policy did restore demand after macroeconomic hiccups in the decades prior to the Great Recession, it did so, in Palley's words from Chapter 2, "by lowering interest rates and opening the spigot of credit" to facilitate a path of private-sector debt accumulation that was anything but sustainable. It is for these reasons that many of the chapters in this volume propose outside-the-box thinking about monetary policy and financial reform. In addition, we obviously cannot rely *exclusively* on monetary policy to emerge from stagnation. Indeed, Epstein argues that perhaps the most important role for monetary policy going forward is to keep interest rates low as a means to support expansionary fiscal policy, a topic to which we now turn.

The Challenges of Fiscal Policy

In 2011, American politics was consumed with hyperbolic debates surrounding what should have been a routine legislative process to raise the country's legal debt limit. The major parties take different positions in most respects, but almost all of the participants in the fiscal policy debate seem to agree that a primary goal of U.S. economic policy should be to eliminate deficits and even to pay down the national debt. The perspectives presented in this book argue strongly that these goals are fundamentally misguided.

The common vision presented in this volume supports a basic critique of the demand generation process of the two decades leading up to the Great Recession: rising household debt in an environment of increasing income inequality precipitated the collapse. This engine of demand growth will not rev up again, at least for an extended period, which explains the persistent stagnation of the U.S. economy that conventional macroeconomics has failed to anticipate.[2] Aggressive fiscal stimulus is an alternative source of demand that can at least partially offset the spending lost as the household sector retrenches to repair its collective balance sheet. In sharp contrast to the political rhetoric in Washington, large deficits in times like these *are* fiscally responsible. The goal of fiscal policy is not to achieve some artificial and arbitrary target for deficits or debt. Instead, fiscal policy should be functional, that is, designed to serve a particular economic function. In Tcherneva's words from Chapter 12, "a bold and imaginative approach is required, which weds fiscal policy to the goal of full employment."

A first step that may appear bold in the current environment, with austerity buzzards circling everywhere, is to assess what evidence tells us about the size of deficits and debt and the effects they have on actual macroeconomic activity. Most of the authors who contributed to this volume are of an age to remember the widespread criticism of Reagan's supposed fiscal irresponsibility in the 1980s. At that time, the politics of deficit bashing favored the Democrats, but the arguments were similar in direction (if not intensity) to recent Tea Party rumblings: a profligate government living beyond its means would saddle future generations with unsustainable debt service, high interest rates, and low productivity as deficits "crowded out" capital

---

[2] Here is a telling quote from economics reporter David Leonhardt more than two years after the supposed recovery from the Great Recession began. "The past week brought more bad news ... causing economists to downgrade their estimates for economic growth yet again. It's a familiar routine by now. Forecasters in Washington and on Wall Street keep saying the recovery's problems are temporary – and then they redefine temporary" (from "We're Spent," *New York Times,* July 16, 2011).

investment. A full generation has passed since those fears were rampant; what has happened? Interest rates are down, federal debt service is a smaller fraction of GDP, and productivity has risen. On the surface of things, the debt legacy of the Reagan years hasn't hamstrung the current generation. More systematically, Baker in Chapter 10 concludes that smaller government deficits (or larger government surpluses) have not done much, if anything, to improve U.S. economic performance over the past two decades. In Chapter 11, Cynamon and Fazzari take a careful look at the concerns about the burden on future taxpayers arising from current U.S. indebtedness and argue that we could enact massive fiscal stimulus over the next few years, with minimal cost. The sense that federal finances require immediate tightening because "we're broke" (as Republicans like to say) has no basis in fact. What is truly "irresponsible" is the hyperbolic rhetoric of austerity buzzards that scares the citizenry into believing that a catastrophe in public finance is imminent.

Because of the deeply compromised private demand-generation process in the aftermath of the Great Recession, the U.S. economy is likely to need large federal deficits well into the future. A rising federal government debt-to-GDP ratio is likely to result, at least for awhile. Perhaps this outcome, in isolation, is unfortunate (it is certainly viewed that way in political discussion). However, as either higher government spending or lower taxes that stimulate private spending employ otherwise idle resources, the perspectives developed in this volume imply that social benefits will far exceed what are likely minimal costs. The analysis in Chapter 11 implies that debt service would be easily manageable for the United States with a debt-to-GDP ratio of 100 percent or more, nearly double the value of privately held debt to GDP in 2011. Such an increase would support a huge contribution to demand generation, either public or private, in coming years. At a higher debt ratio, the "sustainable" size of the deficit is higher than almost any conventional discussion suggests. A simple example proves the point. Suppose the economy has a nominal long-term growth rate of 5 percent (3 percent from real output and 2 percent from inflation). If the debt-GDP ratio were 100 percent, a federal deficit equal to 5 percent of GDP, much higher than historical values in all but the worst recessions, would leave the debt-GDP ratio unchanged (see Galbraith, 2011, for further discussion).[3]

[3] Government debt critics often point to the long-term future liabilities of entitlement programs, particularly Medicare, for an aging population as the reason that we need current fiscal austerity. We agree that society will have to come to terms with the future resource cost necessary to provide adequate health care. However, destroying jobs today does nothing to make this task easier. Indeed, effective demand stimulus today will lead to a stronger

Although the need for fiscal stimulus emerges rather obviously from the Keynesian perspective on the Great Recession and its aftermath, the most desirable form that such policy should take is less clear. The most obvious class of policies that receives the strongest support from the political left in the United States imagines large public works. Public expenditure projects, in addition to stimulating aggregate demand, can also influence *what* is demanded. That is, expenditures could target infrastructure to get benefits on the supply side as well as generating demand, as discussed in Chapter 10 by Baker. In addition to enhancing the traditional public capital stock, public expenditure can be designed to meet broader social goals, perhaps most obviously to transform the U.S. economy into a more energy-efficient, "greener" economy. The gaping hole in demand, unprecedented since the Great Depression, implies that there are plenty of resources for large projects that could capture the imagination of the country. Indeed, we believe it is important to help both politicians and voters to recognize that the unused resources provide a social opportunity. We need to focus on what can be accomplished, with the twin objectives of mobilizing idle resources *and* transforming important parts of society. This message will serve the interests of society dramatically better than obsessing about public debt or deficit ratios, the costs of which are greatly exaggerated.

We do not presume, however, that useful fiscal policy in these times should take the form of higher government spending only. As argued by Cynamon and Fazzari in Chapter 11, the demand gap is so large that even an aggressive and imaginative program of expanded public projects may not be enough to push us to full employment. The United States has a long tradition of manipulating taxes to meet fiscal goals. As a rough rule of thumb, if the economy still suffers from substantial demand slack even when government spending is, in a sense, optimized given existing political alignments, this is *prima facie* evidence that tax revenues are too high. One way to think about the relative role of tax cuts versus spending increases as appropriate demand stimulus is to recognize that any fiscal action has two dimensions. First, there is the effect on aggregate demand and how that demand relates to the goal of employing idle resources. Second, there is an allocation dimension: any actual fiscal stimulus policy affects the specific way in which unemployed resources will be used. Government spending programs use the political process to determine the second dimension, whereas tax cuts cede the specific allocation process to private decision-making.

future economy that would be better able to handle the challenge of providing health care for the entire population.

Of course, if there are costs to government debt, even if those costs have been exaggerated in recent mainstream analysis, one objective of any fiscal stimulus program is to maximize "bang for the buck." In the case of higher government spending, the initial demand impact is dollar-for-dollar by definition and maximizing impact implies choosing the best projects to enhance social value. In the case of tax cuts, however, their effectiveness as stimulus depends fundamentally on whether or not they will raise spending. This simple principle therefore implies that effective tax cuts should flow to groups that will turn them into aggregate demand. The most obvious implication is that tax cuts should accrue to lower- and middle-income/wealth groups.[4] Furthermore, although distributive justice is not the focus of this book, we would be remiss to not acknowledge the obvious synergy between fiscal policies that most effectively stimulate demand and those that create a more just society.

We also echo Tcherneva's call in Chapter 12 for public policy that does more than just target short-run aggregate demand. Even when the official unemployment rate was low by historical standards, as it was prior to the Great Recession, the U.S. economy suffered substantial problems with long-term joblessness among certain subsets of the population. Those afflicted by this problem are mostly invisible in standard unemployment statistics. Direct job-creation programs have promise in addressing this issue, and we believe they are also an important complement to more conventional stimulus programs that raise aggregate demand in the face of a recession. This point is underlined by the recent tendency of U.S. recoveries to look "jobless," as has been evident again in the aftermath of the Great Recession.

Returning to a theme we presented in Chapter 1, we argue that it is essential to see the policy response to the Great Recession and its aftermath as a problem that the United States (and other countries) must confront for a number of years to come. This isn't the kind of recession we have become familiar with in the postwar period. That is, the Great Recession isn't a merely temporary disruption. It is evident that the stagnation will be protracted. In

---

[4] Political considerations may lead to the conclusion that there is little gained from completely excluding the wealthy. Suppose a tax cut is allocated as a fixed amount per person or per family. The "bang-for-the-buck" argument suggests that the tax cut not be applied to the wealthy. Recognizing that a few percentage points of additional public debt has minimal cost, however, it may be politically expedient to simply give everyone the same amount of tax relief. Problems arise, however, when the wealthy, who spend proportionately less of each additional dollar of income, receive massively *greater* tax cuts than the middle class, or when lower-income people receive little or nothing, as was the unfortunate case with many tax cut programs in recent decades.

that context, the policy response should be both more significant and longer in duration. On the one hand, that makes the challenge more daunting and raises the stakes when we contemplate the consequences of failure. On the other hand, the need to support demand generation over a longer period means that we can and should think more imaginatively. All indications are that the economy will have sufficient unused resources to undertake large, long-term infrastructure projects. Permanent tax changes to boost consumption spending, especially among lower- and middle-income households who have seen their standards of living stagnate in recent decades (see Chapters 2 and 7 by Palley and Setterfield), have the potential to be much more effective than the tax cut policies of recent years, which have been either temporary or largely skewed toward high earners. One somewhat paradoxical aspect of a big crisis is the opportunity, indeed the need, to think big about solutions.

Wages, Productivity, and Global Engagement

Although fiscal policy can and should play a central role in demand generation, larger government alone is not likely to fully replace the pre-Great Recession consumption and housing boom as a source of adequate demand growth indefinitely. Indeed, it is not clear that more government activity on the level we need to once again approach full employment is socially desirable, even if it were politically feasible. This is not to say that there are not significant needs that the government must address. Rather, this perspective recognizes that the demand problem is huge. As such, part of the policy challenge in the aftermath of the Great Recession is to reconstitute the *private* aggregate demand-generating process on a more sustainable basis. As Stiglitz (2011) recently remarked, "[prior to the Great Recession] output growth in the United States was not economically sustainable. With so much of the U.S. national income going to so few, growth could continue only through consumption financed by a mounting pile of debt." Central to the mission of reconstituting the aggregate demand-generating process, then, are policies and institutional changes that reduce the dependence of U.S. households on debt accumulation as a source of rising consumption expenditures and increase the extent to which rising consumption can be funded by income growth.

Picking up on the theme emphasized by Setterfield in Chapter 7, this suggests that, looking forward, a major ambition of public policy should be to revive the income share of working and middle-class households, and to realign wage and productivity growth. Achievement of this ambition would create steady growth in household consumption expenditures that is funded by steady, across-the-board real income growth, and that is therefore financially sustainable indefinitely. On the domestic front, rethinking the changes in labor law that have weakened the bargaining power of workers over the past thirty years could help reach this goal. Reform of laws that have made unionization by workers harder and union busting by firms much easier would at least begin to address the institutional changes in the labor market that have created the disconnect between real wage and productivity growth. Workers have a vested interest in increasing (and then maintaining) the wage share of income. Alleviating existing legal constraints on the exercise of this self-interest would therefore facilitate some reconstruction of the aggregate demand-generating process *within* the private sector *by* the private sector.

However, domestic initiatives alone will likely not suffice on this front. As noted in Chapter 2 by Palley and Chapter 8 by Blecker, the unsustainable, debt-fueled U.S. growth regime that policy must now seek to replace has a distinctly *global* dimension. In the first place – as argued by Blecker – the fabled global trade imbalances that have garnered such attention over the past decade and more are essentially a symptom of an *international* growth regime that emerged as numerous countries responded in different ways to the same phenomenon plaguing their domestic economies: wage stagnation and the concomitant inability of households to fund sufficient consumption expenditure from their real income. Ultimately, then, the reliance of the U.S. economy on household debt accumulation not only provided a temporary salve for its own latent demand deficiency, it also had spillover effects elsewhere. Specifically, it facilitated the reliance on external demand to top off inadequate domestic demand in countries such as Germany and China, as U.S. households became "consumers of the last resort" for the world economy.

Global phenomena have not merely *reflected* but have also *contributed to* the structural flaws in the aggregate demand-generating process that have come to plague the United States and other economies. As emphasized by Palley in Chapter 2, trade agreements (coupled with the steady reduction in shipping costs since the 1960s) have created an anything-but-level global playing field on which footloose corporations can credibly threaten to relocate between national political jurisdictions unless their demands for wage and tax concessions are met. This has contributed – both directly through the resulting pressure on wages, and indirectly through its distortion of the tax system – to wage stagnation. Putting the pieces together, this analysis suggests that fixing the private aggregate demand-generating process requires concerted international action that would see multiple nations attend to the income stagnation afflicting their working and middle-class households. It would also involve commitment to common labor standards to prevent otherwise desirable cross-border trade in goods and services from degenerating into a "race to the bottom" that eviscerates both wage growth and working conditions.

If it is not already obvious, implementing these sort of policy initiatives constitutes an enormous task. It is well to remember, then, that as intimated at the end of the previous subsection, some progress can be made through more modest means. Specifically, fiscal policy can act as a surrogate for labor market and broader institutional reforms by addressing the distribution of after-tax income, and thereby seeking to offset and correct imbalances created by the distribution of pre-tax income. This task is made easier if, as suggested by Crotty in Chapter 5, many of the biggest incomes at the top of the income distribution are composed largely of rents – in which case they can be taxed without impairing productive effort. The revenues raised in this fashion can then be used to either boost the "social wage" (through expenditures on the direct public provision of goods that enhance the consumption of lower- and middle-income households – parks, public transportation, etc.), or through transfer programs designed to enhance the low and stagnant real incomes of the same households.

Finally, it is important to remember that however achieved, restoring robust real income growth to working- and middle-class families will reduce their debt-dependence and enhance their ability to service the debts they *do* carry – developments that are obviously conducive to financial stability. The sorts of policy proposals discussed in this subsection, then, address more than just the problem of fixing structural flaws in the private aggregate demand-generating process. It follows that monetary and financial policy need not bear sole responsibility for the job of restoring the financial sector of the U.S. economy to good health: revitalizing real income growth across the entire income distribution also has an important role to play. This observation only serves to add to the appealingly "bottom up" character of the recovery proposals in this section. Policy targets incomes, and hence purchasing power, from the bottom of the income distribution up through the middle class. The result is more robust and sustainable aggregate demand conditions and better household debt-servicing capabilities. In what might be referred to as a "trickle up" process, strong income growth below the top quintile benefits the rest of the economy, including corporate and financial sector balance sheets, as well as profits and other capital income.

3. Toward a Better Future

The Great Recession and subsequent stagnation has created profound social adversity, some of it represented in statistical measures, and some incalculable. Tens of millions of U.S. citizens have been forced to confront unemployment or significant underemployment directly. Tens of millions more must deal with the stress of unemployment, either because they fear threats to their own jobs or because the incomes of other members of their household have been directly affected. Of course, unemployment is a waste of resources. Society has obvious needs for more production, and idle workers are both willing and able to meet more of those needs. Yet for reasons discussed extensively in the pages of this volume, the economic systems of the most developed countries of the early twenty-first century cannot coordinate their activities to bridge the gap between resources and needs. Outfitted with their statistical measures and quantitative proclivities, this failure is the single most prominent feature of the Great Recession in the minds of most economists, and we certainly agree that the material waste caused by the Great Recession is of first-order importance.

However, material waste may not be the greatest problem that has arisen since late 2007. Unemployment does not just waste resources, it also rips at the identity of those it afflicts and tears apart the fabric of their social life. In the United States, our jobs define to a large extent who we are as individuals. We all know that the question "what is it that you do" refers to our occupations. Consider also how young children are acculturated to an identity largely defined by work by the question asked of them from a very young age: "what do you want to be?" The expected answer is never along the lines of "I want to be a healthy, well-adjusted human being who has meaningful relations with those around me and contributes to the social good." Instead we expect "fireman," "doctor," "teacher," and so forth. In addition, what has come to be known as the American Dream suggests that you can be whatever you want to be if you play by the rules of the idealized economic game – that is, if you take your education seriously, work hard, live within your means, and behave responsibly. Of course, the idea that with good behavior and dedication a person can obtain literally *any* professional outcome is exaggerated. Nonetheless, such ideas permeate deeply into our culture. A natural reaction for people thrown out of work, therefore, is to feel at least partially responsible for their plight and to begin to question their worth. The fact that they are just one of millions of people suffering the same fate probably does not offer much comfort. The objective reality may be that it is the system that has failed unemployed workers and their families, but it is hard to not reflect blame and the associated loss of self-esteem on oneself.

Furthermore, even if people can protect their psychological identity from the ravages of unemployment, there is no firewall for the household budget. The United States has notoriously stingy safety nets, especially when it comes to health insurance. Of course unemployment compromises living standards, but it also adversely affects physical health and family relations.

What is particularly tragic is that there is no physical reason why people must bear these costs. Workers after the Great Recession are neither less motivated nor less skilled than they were in 2006 or 2007. Indeed, labor productivity has *risen* remarkably in recent years. We have not suddenly forgotten how to apply modern technology to produce high living standards. Our capital has not been destroyed by natural disaster. It is our economic system that has failed to coordinate our ability to produce with our ability to purchase. The unstable dynamics of finance and uncertainty leading up to the Great Recession have finally ground the debt-fueled, consumption-led growth engine to a halt, shutting down the aggregate demand-generating process that the United States and world economies came to rely on during the late twentieth century. In the United States, the core problem, as analyzed extensively in this volume, is that a system that distributes its income so unequally cannot generate growing aggregate demand without unsustainable household debt growth and financial excess. We can complain about individually "irresponsible" behavior in taking on too much debt. We can rail against the captains of finance for their greed that led to financial bubbles. The fact is, however, we had come to rely on excessive household borrowing and financial bubbles to maintain the demand growth we needed to even get close to full employment over the past two decades. We can rely on that approach no longer.

The contributions to this book argue that we need a new model to sustain demand growth in coming years. That model requires a greater public role in guiding finance to socially useful activities. It also needs mechanisms to generate more government demand to fill the gap created by the end of the debt-financed consumption boom. This perspective stands in strong contrast to the political ideology that has gripped much of the developed world recently, as it clings to the neoliberal "small government" ideas of the past several decades and promotes government fiscal "austerity" as virtuous. Perhaps most important, the new model must find a way to share more equally the fruits of what could be a highly productive economy. Of course, more balanced distribution will improve social justice. However, faster income growth across the social spectrum is also necessary, we argue, to initiate a new kind of aggregate demand-generating process, one that moves the economy toward – and then maintains – full employment of our resources. It is not just jobs that are at stake. Strong demand growth is also necessary to support the financing and innovation that are necessary for sustained increases in our standards of living.

These problems highlight the fundamental interdependence of individuals in modern society. Economic models that treat the country as a whole as if it were Robinson Crusoe on his own island will neither explain the Great Recession nor offer much help to guide us out of its stagnant aftermath. The Keynesian perspective that underlies this book fundamentally recognizes social interdependence: one person's income is another's spending; we cannot earn income on our own unless others spend. However, interdependence requires coordination. To a remarkable degree, market forces unguided by a centralized authority coordinate social activity. Nevertheless, the inability to fully utilize the economy's productive resources reflects a failure of the market. It seems clear that individual incentives alone are inadequate to assure the social coordination necessary to reach and maintain full employment. As the perspectives developed in this book point out, the solution involves expanding the government's role in coordination. That role may involve the creation of spending and incomes when the private sector will not. It may involve guiding the private sector away from destructive financial behaviors that arise from the unfettered pursuit of private interest in complex and uncertain modern markets. It may involve establishing institutions that raise the prospects for lower- and middle-class income growth in an increasingly globalized world that has concentrated a disproportionate share of the rewards from rising productivity at the top of the income distribution. These actions might appear to threaten private interests, but the reality of social interdependence is that good private outcomes cannot be secured by private action alone. The failure to recognize this point in the ideologies that guided economic policy in recent decades is, in a broad sense, responsible for the crisis we now confront.

The Great Recession marks the end of an era in which neoliberal policies that suppressed or completely ignored the inherent social interdependence illuminated by Keynesian macroeconomics could be plausibly argued to deliver prosperity, stability, and social justice. The results of recent years have been tragic. The immediate prospects for significant improvement are also unfavorable, as it seems that the economic policy establishment has yet to come to terms with the challenges of demand generation without some kind of financial bubble that leads to exploding debt. It is important to remember, however, that although robust and sustainable recovery is not assured, it is not impossible to achieve: it won't come about automatically, but the right policy interventions *can* help resolve the current crisis. We hope that these difficult times give way to a new approach to macroeconomics that is reflected in both theory and policy – an approach that, in the decades to come, allows modern economies to realize their immense potential and to share that potential with all of their citizens.

References

Diamond, P. (2011) "When a Nobel Prize isn't enough," *New York Times*, June 5.

Galbraith, J. K. (2011) "Is the federal debt unsustainable?" Levy Economics Institute of Bard College Policy Note, 2011/2.

Pollin, R. (1997) "The relevance of Hyman Minsky," *Challenge*, March/April, 75–94.

Stiglitz, J. (2011) "The ideological crisis of Western capitalism," Project Syndicate blog, July 6. www.project-syndicate.org/commentary/stiglitz140/English

Author Index

Subject Index

mortgage refinancing ease, 144
social stigma against borrowing, 144–45
tax law changes, 144
uncertainty, 146
Consumer Financial Protection Bureau
(CFPB), 238
consumer of last resort, 174–75
consumers, 136–38
changing attitudes toward debt, 144–45
changing norms affect on consumption,
138, 139–41
consumption standards compared to
reference group, 139
endogenous preferences of, 130–31, 136–41
household behavioral norms, evolution of,
141–42
social norms, behavioral patterns based
on, 131
underlying source of decisions, 130
See also consumption
consumption
changing norms, affect on, 138
consumer credit, change in attitudes toward,
142–46
conventional life-cycle theory of, 130
decline in 2009, 129–30, 151–52
demographic shift toward high-spending
groups, 135, 136
forces shaping in aftermath of Great
Recession, 131–32, 153–54
future income expectation effect on, 134,
135–36
household asset appreciation effect on,
134–35
interest rate effect on, 13
life-cycle model of household behavior to
explain, 132–33, 134–36
macroeconomic implications of behaviors, 131
mortgage refinancing effect on, 144
overview of, 132–34
ratio to disposable income, post-2007, 7
relaxed liquidity constraints effect on, 135,
136
share of disposable income spent on, 132,
133, 149
and social pressures, 141–42
and utility-producing technologies, 138–39
value of current *versus* future consumption
effect on, 135, 136
See also consumers; household debt
consumption expenditures
as diminished growth engine, 174–75

as percentage of GDP, 161, 166
consumption-income ratio, 7, 134–36
consumption norm, 139
control fraud, 68–69
conventionally formed expectations, 116–17, 118
conventional view, on modern fiscal policy
and Great Recession, 282–83, 287
conventional *vs.* adjustable mortgage interest
rate, *305 n. 1*
corporate bonds, *251*
Council of Economic Advisors, 247
countercyclical fiscal policy, 64, 200, 264
Keynes on, 224, 281
creative accounting, 61
credibility, 16, 224
credit
availability of, increasing, 231
ceilings on credit extension, 228
change in attitudes toward, 142–46
contraction of, 9
freeze on, 106, 173, 305–06
See also credit allocation tools; underwriting
credit allocation tools, 225–32
asset-based reserve requirements, 225–32
to contain the U.S. Great Recession, 229–30
in Europe, 228
to provide employment generation, 230–31
for social goals, 226–29
to turn policy into fiscal policy, 231–32
credit cards, 77, 143
credit controls, 227–28. *See also* credit
allocation tools; underwriting
credit default swaps (CDS), 66, 101
pension fund use of, 82
credit rating agencies, 65, 79, 97–98, 238
credit tools. *See* credit allocation tools
currency, ability to print, 245, 248, 280
current account
deficits, 61, 206–07, 275–76
dollar exchange rate, 196
imbalances, 190–93
limits on imbalances, 207
national income identity and, 200
relationship with trade, 198–99
savings and investment and, 199–205
surplus, 275–76
surplus in China, 207
worsening of, 197–98

D
debt
changing attitudes toward, 144–45

conventional objections to, 295–98
  administrative complexity, 296
  fraud and corruption, 296
  private sector employment, 296
  tax policy, 295–96
  usefulness of projects, 297–98
discount-window lending, Minsky on, 75
disinflation, 17, 34, 40–41
disposable income
  consumption ratio to, post-2007, 7
  household debt as share of, 142–43
  share spent on consumption, 132, *133*, 149
distribution effects of fiscal stimulus,
    273–76
distributive justice, 176, 313
District Federal Reserve banks, 88–89
Dodd-Frank Act, 100–01, 232–33, 234–39
  asset bubbles, 235–36
  central bank policy, 234–39
  dangerous and excessive banker
    compensation, 237
  dangerous financial products, 235–36
  excessive leverage, 236
  excessive reliance on short-run borrowing
    from shadow banking, 236–37
  fleecing customers, 238
  fraudulent behavior, 238
  outsourcing regulations to avoid conflicts of
    interest, 238
  shadow balance sheets, 237
  too big to fail financial institutions, 237
dollar
  exchange rate, role in trade deficit, 189–90,
    194–96, 245, 257–58, 262
  flight to, after East Asian crisis, 254
  and multinational corporations, 45, 47
  redistributive effect of, *254 n. 16*
  strong dollar, 34, 43, 45, *46 n. 13*, 254, 255,
    260
dot.com bubble, 51
  versus housing bubble, 42
dynamic-stochastic general equilibrium
    (DSGE) theory, 12

E
East Asian financial crisis
  Chinese exchange rate devaluation, effect
    on, *46 n. 12*
  foreign fund inflows into U.S. as result of,
    203
  response to, 46–48
  trade deficit increase after, 47, 254

East Europe, Minsky on capital development
    in, 74
economic crisis
  warnings of coming, 4, *5 n. 2–6*, 5–6
  See also economic crisis, explanations for
economic crisis, explanations for
  exhausted macroeconomic paradigm, 50–52
  flawed model of global economic
    engagement, 32, 42–50
    China and PNTR, 48–50
    NAFTA, 44–46
    response to East Asian financial crisis,
      46–48
    triple hemorrhage, 43–44, 50
  neoliberal growth model, 32–42
  See also financial crisis
economic inequality, effect on spending, 142
economic recovery, as "temporary," *310 n. 2*
effective demand, 288
electronic credit scoring, 19
Employee Free Choice Act, 177
employer of last resort (ELR), *292 n. 6*
employment, Keynesian goal of full. *See* full
    employment
employment growth, 249
endogenous preferences, 130–31
energy prices, effect of offshoring on, 44
Europe
  austerity in, 221
  central bank policy, current, 224
  central bank policy, post-World War II, 227
  credit allocation techniques in, 228
  institutional constraints, 306
  publicly owned financial institutions in, 233
  unemployment in, 22
European Central Bank (ECB), 224
Eurozone, 154
excessive leverage, 236
exchange rate
  China and devaluation, *46 n. 12*
  current account, 196
  NAFTA effect on, 45
  and purchase of U.S. assets by foreign
    central banks, 203
  realignment of, 210–11
  role in trade deficit, 189–90, 194–96, 245, 262
executive compensation. *See* bonuses;
    rainmakers
expansionary fiscal policy, 28
  and central banks, 223–24, 231–32
  as ineffective, 226
  interest rate effect on, 309